THE
MASTERMIND

THE MASTERMIND

Drugs. Empire. Murder. Betrayal.

Evan Ratliff

RANDOM HOUSE

NEW YORK

Published in the United States by Random House, an imprint
and division of Penguin Random House LLC, New York.

RANDOM HOUSE and the HOUSE colophon are registered
trademarks of Penguin Random House LLC.

Portions of this work were originally published in different
form in *The Atavist Magazine* (magazine.atavist.com).

Library of Congress Cataloging-in-Publication Data

Names: Ratliff, Evan, author.
Title: The mastermind: drugs, empire, murder, betrayal / by Evan Ratliff.
Description: First edition. | New York: Random House, [2019] |
Includes bibliographical references and index.
Identifiers: LCCN 2018035751 | ISBN 9780399590412 |
ISBN 9780399590429 (ebook)
Subjects: LCSH: Le Roux, Paul Calder. | Criminals—Biography. |
Drug traffic.
Classification: LCC HV6248.L343 R37 2019 | DDC 364.1092 [B]—dc23
LC record available at lccn.loc.gov/2018035751

Printed in the United States of America on acid-free paper

randomhousebooks.com

9 8 7 6 5 4 3 2 1

First Edition

Book design by Caroline Cunningham

For Bill Goggins (1963–2006)

It takes very little to govern good people. Very little. And bad people cant be governed at all. Or if they could I never heard of it.

CORMAC MCCARTHY, *No Country for Old Men*

Contents

Cast of Characters

THE MASTERMIND   Paul Calder Le Roux

THE INVESTIGATORS   Kimberly Brill, Steven Holdren, Kent Bailey (DEA)
With: Rizaldy Rivera, Peter Lugay, and Inspector R (Philippines); Thomas Cindric and Eric Stouch (DEA)

THE OPERATORS   Moran Oz, Alon Berkman
With: Boaz and Tomer Taggart, Levi Kugel, Yehuda Ben-Dor, Shai Reuven, Robert McGowan, Asaf Shoshana, Nestor Del Rosario, Omer Bezalel, Babubhai Patel

THE PHARMACIST   Charles Schultz

THE DOCTOR   Prabhakara Tumpati

THE MERCENARIES   Lachlan McConnell, Dave Smith, Felix Klaussen, Joseph Hunter
With: Chris De Meyer, Marcus, Scott Stammers, Tim Vamvakias, Mathew Smith, Patrick Donovan, Andrew and Steve Hahn, Adam Samia, Bruce

Jones, John Nash, Doron Shulman, Philip Shackels, David Stillwell

THE CONNECTORS   Patrick Donovan, Ari Ben-Menashe

THE ATTORNEYS   Joe Friedberg and Robert Richman (Moran Oz defense), Linda Marks (U.S. Department of Justice), Joe Frank Zuñiga (Philippines)

Author's Note

This book is a work of nonfiction. It is based on more than four years of reporting, including hundreds of interviews, hundreds of thousands of pages of law enforcement reports, government databases, court documents, and internal communications from a criminal organization that involved thousands of people and conducted business on six continents. I have worked to corroborate every fact found in these pages, and to speak with as many participants as possible. Unfortunately, I couldn't speak to them all. Some are dead, murdered because of what they knew. Others declined to talk to me, out of a fear that they might meet the same fate. Still others are in prison and desperate to avoid the perception that they have turned on their compatriots. A few are in hiding, running from prosecution or vengeance, real or imagined.

But dozens of the people involved did share their stories with me, at risk of physical danger, legal jeopardy, or professional consequences. In three cases, specified in the source notes, I have altered subjects' names. I did so because they feared for their safety and that of their families, because they were never prosecuted for the crimes described here, and because their names didn't appear in legal proceedings connected to these events. In other instances I have described certain minor players, including some law enforcement officials or family members, only by their job descriptions or connections to more principal figures.

Every individual in this book is real. The events they describe happened.

Prologue

2012 . . . The puzzle

MONROVIA, LIBERIA
September 26, 2012

On a gray afternoon, three men enter a drab hotel room for a business meeting, months in the making. Two are white: a portly South African and his muscled European deputy. The other, with dark hair and a paunch of his own, is Latino—Colombian, or so he says. The hotel is in the Liberian capital, abutting the Atlantic Ocean on the coast of West Africa, but it could be any number of places in the world. The men's business is drugs and weapons, and drugs and weapons are everywhere. They shake hands, nod heads, and begin speaking in the elliptical but familiar way of people who share the vernacular of a trade. They are cautious, but not cautious enough. A video exists to prove it.

"I can see why you picked this place," says the South African, settling his substantial bulk into a maroon leather couch pressed against the wall. "Because it's chaotic. It should be easy to move in and out, from what I've seen." His name is Paul, and to a trained ear his cadence carries a tinge of not just South Africa but his childhood home, Zimbabwe, where he lived until his teens. His large white head is shaved close, and what hair remains has gone gray as he approaches forty. He has the look of a beach vacationer cleaned up for a dinner out, in an oversize blue polo shirt and a pair of khaki cargo shorts. His clothes seem out of keeping with both the scope of his international influence and the deal he is about to complete, with a man he believes to be the head of a South American drug cartel.

"Very easy," replies the Colombian, whom Paul refers to only as Pepe. In the video recording of the meeting, Pepe sits down just offscreen, on a matching couch. His disembodied voice speaks in flawless, if heavily accented, English.

"Very few people, not too many eyes. It looks like the right place."

"Trust me—what's your name again?"

"Paul."

"Paul, trust me, it's the right place. I've been here already for quite a bit of time. And always, me and my organization, we pick places like this. First of all, for corruption. You can buy anything you want here. Anything. You just tell me what you need."

"Yeah, it's safe here," Paul says. "If there's a problem here, you can fix it. I understand this type of place."

"Everything is easy here. Just hand to hand, boom boom boom, you can see," Pepe says, laughing. "Well, thanks to your guy here, now we are meeting." He gestures at the third man in the room, the European employee of Paul's who goes by the name Jack. It was Jack who made the initial connection between Paul and Pepe.

The deal Jack brokered was complex enough that, when I meet him years later, I need him to walk me through it several times. The Colombians, who deal primarily in the cocaine produced in their own country, are looking to expand into methamphetamine, which they want to manufacture in Liberia and distribute to the United States and Europe. Paul, a computer programmer who heads his own kind of cartel based in the Philippines, will provide the materials to build the Colombians' meth labs: precursor chemicals, formulas for cooking them into meth, and a "clean room" in which to synthesize it all. While the labs are being built, Paul has agreed to also sell Pepe his own stash of meth, in exchange for an equivalent amount of cocaine at market rates.

After months of back-and-forth, Jack has urged Paul to travel to Liberia and meet his new associate "boss to boss" to finalize the deal.

"So where do you want to start?" Pepe says. "First of all is the clean room."

Paul tells him that the parts needed to build it are already en route by boat. "If you have any problem, I'll send guys here to assemble it like that." He snaps his fingers.

"We shouldn't have any. I got my guys here, my chemist."

"To compensate you for the delays, we will just, when we do business, we will give you back the money."

"Paul, you don't have to compensate me for nothing."

Paul flicks his hand in the air. "We feel bad it took so long."

"This is just business," Pepe says. "We don't have to compensate, just doing business. This is about money."

Pepe turns to the second part of the deal: the trade of his Colombian cocaine for Paul's methamphetamine, a sample of which Paul has shipped to him from his base in the Philippines. "Let me ask you a question," Pepe says.

"Sure."

"You are not Filipino, why the Philippines?"

"Same reason you are in Liberia. Basically, as far as Asia goes, it's the best shithole we can find, which gives us the ability to ship anywhere. It's the best position in Asia. And it's also a poor place. Not as bad as here, but we can still solve problems."

"You are cooking your shit in the Philippines?" Pepe says.

"Actually, right now we manufacture in the Philippines and we also buy from the Chinese. We're getting it from North Korea. So the quality you saw was very high."

"That's not just very high. That is awesome."

"Yeah."

"I was going to tell you that later on, but now that you talk about it: That stuff is fucking incredible."

"That is manufactured by the North Koreans," Paul says. "We get it from the Chinese, who get it from the North Koreans."

"So my product is going to be the same, the amount that I'm going to buy from you?"

"The same. Exactly the same." Paul nods. "I know you want the high quality for your market."

"Yeah, because the product—you know that one of the best customers, and you probably know that, is the Americans."

"Number one."

"It's the number one. They are fucking—they want everything over there. I don't know what the word is from Spanish. *Consumistas?* Consumists?"

"Consumers," Jack interjects, off-camera.

"Yeah, they buy everything and they never stop," Paul says.

"So everything that I ship is to America," Pepe says. "Trust me, when I brought this, fucking everyone was asking me for it. Everyone."

Paul and Pepe consider different payment possibilities. First they will trade the cocaine for meth. After that, Paul says that he is happy to be paid in gold or diamonds. If they need to conduct bank transfers, he works primarily through China and Hong Kong, although he sounds a note of caution. "We just had, in Hong Kong, twenty million dollars frozen, by bullshit," he says. "You need to be cautious. It becomes worse, because the American, he likes to control everything. And they are there, making a lot of trouble."

"I say fuck Americans," Pepe says. "Americans, like you say, they think that they can control everything, but they cannot. It's not impossible, but they cannot. We have to be very careful."

They discuss shipment methods, and how many kilos of each drug the other could move in a month. Paul owns ships already picking up loads in South America and traveling to Asia, but he much prefers to work in Africa, territory he knows well. His customers are in Australia, Thailand, China. "We are not touching the U.S. right now," he says.

"Why not?"

"Actually we move pills in the U.S.," Paul says. "These American fucks, they have an appetite for everything. They will just spend and spend and spend." Indeed, Paul has gotten rich, fabulously rich, by selling tens of millions of prescription painkillers to Americans over the Internet for nearly a decade. But unlike Pepe's organization, Paul carefully avoids shipping street drugs like meth to the States. "It generates too much heat," he says.

As the meeting winds down, Paul flashes a hint of his technical prowess, offering to send Pepe mobile phones that he has set up with encryption software to allow the two organizations to communicate securely. He tells Pepe he can get him any weapons he needs out of Iran, particularly if a Liberian general can be produced to make the transaction look official. Then he pauses to reflect. "I can tell you, you won't find a better partner," he says. He is a man, he explains, who keeps his organization in line. "One thing I tell all the guys, okay, everyone I deal with: Just don't fucking steal. You know what I'm saying? That's the one thing that pisses me off." Earlier he described an employee who stole five million dollars from him, then began driving a Lamborghini around Manila, buying his girlfriends designer handbags and diamond necklaces. The employee was no longer a problem, he said. "He's moved on, let's put it that way."

Now Paul has more management advice. "Don't steal," he repeats, "and don't fucking run your mouth to the government. You get caught doing anything, remember: You keep your mouth shut. You've got some guys—I'm sure you've had this: They come like this"—he makes a motion as if operating a jabbering puppet—"they get afraid in jail and then they think that the government is going to help them. They think the government is their best friend. I'm sure you've seen this, right?"

"That is only in movies," Pepe says.

"They are running their fucking mouth like this. What's going to happen when you get out, you make the deal? You think we're going to forget about you?" He slaps his hands together. "You have a problem, *we* help you. Your family has a problem, *we* help them. Nobody has a problem. Just follow these rules, we are very straight on that. So I tell you, we do business, you trust me one hundred percent. We will deliver for you. One hundred percent."

"This is a trust deal," Pepe says, before the three men stand up to shake hands. "That's exactly what we are going to do."

In the months before and after Paul and Pepe's meeting, a series of strange events occurred in disparate parts of the globe, events that appeared unrelated. I say "appeared" as if anyone on the outside was observing them at all. At the time no one was, including me. Even if anyone had been, none of these incidents appeared tied to any other as they filtered into public view. Like a handful of random jigsaw-puzzle pieces, each one was incomprehensible without an understanding of the larger picture. It would be a year before I picked up even one of those pieces to examine it, and several more before I began to understand the image that the whole collection of them combined to reveal.

In March 2012, six months before Paul and Pepe's meeting in Liberia, agents from the United States Drug Enforcement Administration walked through the glass doors of a small pharmacy on Main Street in Oshkosh, Wisconsin. They were armed with search warrants targeting its eighty-two-year-old owner, Charles Schultz. A pillar of the local community for four decades, Schultz had been charged with shipping more than 700,000 illegal painkiller prescriptions from the back of his two local pharmacies. In return, the agents calculated, he had received over $27 million in wire transfers from a mysterious Hong Kong bank account.

Roughly a month later, officers from the Organized Crime and Triad Bureau in Hong Kong raided a warehouse in Tsuen Wan, a bayside district north of the city. Inside they discovered twenty tons of ammonium nitrate fertilizer, divided into a thousand bags and falsely labeled as sodium chloride. It was enough to create an explosive ten times more powerful than the one used in the Oklahoma City bombing. On the warehouse lease they found the name of an Israeli Australian citizen, a former member of an elite division of the Israeli Defense Forces. When they raided the man's office and apartment, they turned up deeds for two stash houses, receipts for tens of millions of dollars in gold bars, and handwritten directions to a meeting in Buenaventura, Colombia, with a man named "Don Lucho"—the head of one of the world's biggest cocaine cartels.

Then, in November, a pair of spear fishermen diving off an atoll in Tonga discovered a wrecked forty-four-foot sailboat with a badly decomposed body on board. Lining the walls of the boat's cabin, local authorities found, were 204 bricks of cocaine, neatly wrapped in brown plastic and worth more than $90 million on the street in Australia, where they suspected it was destined.

In early December, three thousand miles to the northeast, a contractor for the National Security Agency named Edward Snowden organized a gathering of cryptography buffs in the back room of a strip mall storefront in Honolulu. After a couple dozen people had assembled, he plugged his laptop into a projector and began an instructional talk about a free program called TrueCrypt. It was, he said, the world's most secure software for encrypting a laptop hard drive, protecting it from the prying eyes of governments. Very little was known about the people behind TrueCrypt, he cautioned; the programmers who created it were anonymous. But Snowden also knew something about TrueCrypt that he was not yet ready to reveal: He had stolen documents from the NSA showing that the agency couldn't break it.

When I began trying to investigate this series of events later, they were tantalizing but baffling to me. As I rewound back through them, each seemed like a kind of message from an adjacent reality that few of us experience directly. In that world, I would learn, a brilliant self-made software programmer from South Africa could single-handedly build a dystopian company to rival today's tech giants. Through his creation, an online startup selling hundreds of millions of dollars' worth of pills to American customers, he would become one of the largest individual contributors to America's burgeoning painkiller epidemic, and the most successful cyber-criminal in history. He would leverage that fortune into a sprawl-ing criminal empire, fulfilling his seemingly insatiable appetite for the clandestine and the illegal. His ambition for wealth and power would slip the bonds of the Internet and enter the realm of flesh and blood. "The scope of his criminal conduct," as one U.S. fed-eral prosecutor later put it, "is simply staggering."

In the adjacent world he came to occupy, everything was for sale if you knew what to offer and to whom. Pure methamphet-amine manufactured in North Korea. Yachts built to outrun any coast guard. Police protection and judges' favor. Crates of military-grade weapons. Private jets full of gold. Missile-guidance systems. Unbreakable encryption. African militias. Explosives. Kidnapping. Torture. Murder. Former soldiers from the United States, United Kingdom, and elsewhere, drifting in the murky realm of global secu-rity contracting, could reinvent themselves as roving assassins for hire. Call center managers in Tel Aviv could wake up and find them-selves arms dealers. Family doctors could turn into conspirators in an international drug cartel at the click of a button.

That world lurks just outside of our everyday perception, in the dark corners of the Internet we never visit, the quiet ports where ships slip in by night, the back room of the clinic down the street. The events of 2012, I discovered, were simply the edges of that world crossing over into our own. And I came to understand how ordinary people could take one morally ambiguous step across that divide, then a second and a third, until suddenly cops or kill-ers were at their door.

There was one puzzle piece I couldn't get out of my head.

At 6:30 A.M. on the morning of February 13, 2012, Jeremy Ji-mena, a garbage collector in the Philippines, had just started his shift. He set out with his driver on their regular route through Taytay, an industrial city an hour east of Manila. It had rained most of the night, and a light drizzle fell as they turned down

Paseo Monte Carlo, a quiet road with no lights. Their first stop was a large vacant lot overrun by low shrubs, a green carpet of vines, and a scattering of banana trees.

The field wasn't an official pickup spot, but local residents often dumped garbage there, and the collectors had informally added it to their route. That morning there was a small pile of trash spilling into the road: two large bags filled with waste and a bulging, rolled-up bedspread. Jimena, a small, wiry man with jet-black hair and a wisp of a mustache, hopped off the truck and approached the pile. When he leaned down and grasped the damp edge of the blanket, he saw a woman's foot sticking out.

Jimena dropped the blanket and ran, shouting to the driver, and the two of them abandoned the truck and sprinted to the municipal headquarters. There they told the local head of security what they had found, and he called the police. Jimena returned to his route in a daze.

He never spoke to the police himself, and never learned who the woman was. When I met him four years later, I didn't tell him what I knew: That her name was Catherine Lee, and she had been an accomplished real estate agent with a husband and a child. That she'd been shot below each eye with a .22-caliber pistol, rolled up in a blanket, and dumped out of a van. That somehow, her death connected back to a pharmacist in Oshkosh, Wisconsin, a warehouse raid in Hong Kong, a wrecked boat in Tonga.

Jimena didn't seem to want to know those details anyway. Mostly he just seemed to want to forget. For years, he told me, he dreamed of her every night. The woman, wrapped in a blanket. Sometimes she would be asking him for help. Other times she would just scream.

So much of reporting, it took me a long time to discover, is waiting. Waiting for people to call back. Waiting for documents to arrive in the mail. Waiting for a plane to take you halfway across the world, only to arrive at the appointed time in a dreary office and sit in a plastic chair, waiting for an official who never shows up. Standing on a doorstep, waiting to see if a victim's family will return. Sending out pleas for information and staring at a phone, waiting for them to boomerang back. All of it, in some sense, amounts to waiting for the same thing: that one sliver of fact that will help make sense of all the ones that came before it.

In December 2015, when I flew to the Philippines to try to untangle the connections behind Catherine Lee's still-unsolved murder, I discovered entirely new magnitudes of waiting. Much of it I did in a rented van, with a Filipina American journalist I'd enlisted to assist me, Aurora Almendral. The two of us were stuck in the grip of Manila's endless traffic, crawling to appointments that would inevitably involve more waiting once we arrived. So it was that one afternoon, a few weeks before Christmas, we pulled up to a neglected cinder-block building on a steep hill in the town of Taytay. We'd been told this was the investigative division of the local police. We walked in, past a woman stapling paper holiday decorations to the wall, through a pair of swinging doors, and into a cramped room with four desks. An air conditioner rattled in the window and three detectives pecked away on ancient-looking computers.

We tried to rouse one of them and explain the reason we were there: to visit the vacant lot where Jeremy Jimena had encountered Catherine Lee's body. The chief of police had promised, over the phone, to take us there, but that morning he'd been called away by a kidnapping. The other cops had no idea when he would return. No one claimed to know much about the body, and in the years since the murder, those people who did know something had tended to disappear. Some murders, perhaps, were better left unsolved.

So Almendral and I settled in to wait, sitting on a bench in front of a framed police "Loyalty Pledge" that hung on the wall. "Remember that an ounce of loyalty is worth a pound of cleverness," it read in English.

If you must growl, condemn and eternally find fault
Why! resign your position.
And when you are outside,
Damn to your hearts content.
But as long as you're a part of the institution,
Do not condemn it.
If you do, the first high wind that comes along will blow you
away
And probably you'll never know why.

It read to me more like the blood oath of a criminal enterprise than the pledge of a law enforcement organization. But this was before I fully grasped how easily, in the right conditions, the two could sometimes come to resemble one another.

After some coaxing by Almendral in Tagalog, an officer named Abigail Del Monte agreed to pull the case file for us. She returned from a back room and proceeded to flip through it idly at her desk, as if trying to discern why I had flown eight thousand miles and then driven three hours to visit a crime scene nearly four years after the fact.

Finally another detective showed up, a friendly guy in a jean jacket. He introduced himself as George Arada. Suddenly everyone shifted into action. "You're here for the Catherine Lee case?" he said. "Okay, let's go." We offered our slightly beat-up van and driver for transportation, and Del Monte decided to join as well. Along the way we picked up the local watchman who had called the cops after Jimena's discovery. Then we drove over to the vacant lot.

At the site, the watchman showed us where the body had been positioned, and how he'd marked off the area back in February 2012. "The body was moved a little bit by the guy who picked up the blanket," he said. "I didn't find out anything about who she was."

We walked over to an older woman selling drinks at a roadside stand. She remembered that day. "I saw the body," she said, "but it was covered up, so we couldn't see who it was. Three streets down, somebody had been missing for a couple of days, so we thought it could be them." Later, word came back from the cops that the body belonged to a real estate agent from another part of the country. When I asked what happened to the missing neighbor, the drink-stand woman said that the family had just moved on.

I wandered around taking photos, looking for signs that Jimena's horrible discovery had somehow transformed this otherwise ordinary place. If the body had left a mark, it wasn't visible.

We piled back into the van, and on the drive to the station I asked the detectives whether they often encountered corpses in Taytay, a city of just over 300,000 people. "Sometimes over five in a month, but not over ten," Arada said cheerfully. "It's kind of a well-known place to dump bodies. Don't tell the chief!" He laughed. The cases were difficult to solve, he said. The bodies were often mutilated or "broken up and stuffed in garbage bags."

I asked if I could look at the case file, and to my surprise Del Monte turned and handed it to me. Photos taken at the crime scene showed Lee's body, unwrapped, dressed in a black jacket and jeans, lying facedown with her feet in the road. A crowd stood at the edge of a police cordon. The facts in the file were spare: A team from the national police's Scene of Crime Operations division had arrived at 7:50 that morning. An autopsy report listed the cause of "instantaneous death": a gunshot wound under each eye.

The investigators had little trouble identifying the victim. She was found with her identification: Catherine Cristina Lee, forty-three, from Las Piñas City, an hour south of Taytay. Also with the body were a cellphone, an Anne Klein wristwatch, a silver bracelet, and a pair of rings, one silver and one gold. She had not been robbed; there was no sign of sexual assault.

Flipping through the file as we drove back to the police station, I came across mention of a 2015 meeting between Filipino officers and a special agent from the DEA's Los Angeles office, along with a copy of his business card. I wasn't the first person, it seemed, to travel to the Philippines and ask questions about the body.

Hoping to make some sense of what happened in Taytay, Almendral and I went to see Rizaldy Rivera, an agent at the Philippine National Bureau of Investigation who we'd learned had been assigned to the Lee murder case. The NBI's Death Investigation Division was housed in a charmless room with tiled floors and the insipid fluorescent lighting that marks bureaucracies worldwide. On the wall was a whiteboard outlining agents' assignments, organized by nickname: "Cardinal," "Undertaker," "Mechanic," "Hitman," "Braveheart," "Snakedoc," "KGB."

A genial cop with a waist-length ponytail and a talent for sharpshooting, Rivera was a natural showman. Almost immediately after we had shaken hands, he urged me to check out his target-shooting videos on YouTube. (Later I did, and had to admit that the clips were impressive—in one he cuts a credit card in half at 20 yards with a handgun, aiming over his shoulder using a compact mirror.) Most people called him Zaldy, but his nickname around the NBI offices was Slayer, bestowed after three shootouts early in his career, one of which left a bullet in his thigh.

Rivera had picked up the Catherine Lee case after her husband contacted the NBI and requested that it look into her murder, the day after the body was discovered. The agency is required by law to take over cases at the request of victims' families, and often those requests stem from concerns that local officers are incompetent, or worse. The ranks of local and national police in the Philippines are rife with corruption, and the NBI had a better, though not spotless, reputation for integrity. In the case of a murder-for-hire, which is what Rivera deduced the Lee case to be, it wasn't unusual to hear whispers that cops themselves were in on the job. Police work pays poorly, with as much as 60 percent of the national police force living below the poverty line. Contract murder was a thriving industry in the Philippines; having someone killed cost as little as 5,000 pesos, or around $100.

"I cannot provide the real names of the witnesses, or their addresses and photos, in order to protect them," Rivera said when we arrived. Otherwise, "I can probably answer any question that you want me to answer." He gestured to a pair of plastic lawn chairs in a cubicle, facing a desk completely devoid of papers or equipment.

We started at the beginning, talking above the sounds of an NBA game—basketball being a Philippine national obsession— from a television somewhere just out of sight. Over the course of an hour, Rivera laid out everything he knew about Lee's murder. He spoke in the world-weary manner of a cop who had seen his share of vicious crimes. But at times, he sounded as mystified as I was about how all the pieces of Lee's killing fit together.

Rivera had reconstructed Lee's movements from interviews with everyone she had encountered the day she disappeared, as well as clues found on her laptop and phone. The day before her body was discovered, Lee had been out showing properties to two foreigners, Canadians named Bill Maxwell and Tony. For some of the showings she had invited along several friends and fellow real estate agents. They'd last seen her climb into a silver Toyota Innova minivan with the Canadians, mid-afternoon, to go look at another property. From the friends and a security guard at one gated community, Rivera gleaned enough detail to generate sketches: two white men, one goateed and the other clean shaven, both wearing baseball caps. But when it came to their identities, he hit a wall. "It was very hard to check with the immigration bureau in the Philippines," Rivera said, "because Bill Maxwell and Tony—the names were fictitious."

As for physical evidence, there was little to go on. The body had been out in the rain long enough that Philippine police technicians were unable to check for trace elements of DNA. The Toyota van lacked license plates, although the security guard had written down the number from a temporary registration sticker. When Rivera tried to trace it, nothing matched. He concluded that the number was probably faked. Without the van, there would be no fingerprints, no hair, no fibers.

One aspect of the crime stood out to Rivera: Lee had been shot under each eye, with what forensics determined was a .22-caliber handgun. "In our experience," he said, "if you shoot a person dead, you don't normally use a low-caliber firearm." Hit men in the Philippines, he said, typically used "Armalite weapons, hand grenades, or a .40-caliber pistol. This is one of the few times that I discovered that the caliber was a .22 magnum." To Rivera, the weapon said something about the crime, namely that it might be a type of "signature killing." He believed that Lee's death was not a crime of passion but a professional murder committed by someone looking to send a message. "That's an arrogant way of killing, putting two bullet holes beneath the eye," he said. "That's not how you normally execute a person."

After a few months, Rivera's leads dried up. Other murders required his attention. But like Jimena, he was haunted by Lee's murder, and his failure to solve it. "I couldn't sleep soundly at night," he said. "I was thinking about that case. But the fact is, I cannot just proceed without solid evidence."

For three years the Lee file languished at the NBI. Then, in April 2015, Rivera got a call from the U.S. embassy in Manila. The Americans had some information regarding the Lee murder: A man the DEA had arrested three and a half years earlier on drug charges had been cooperating with the government, and he had tipped them off to possible suspects.

A few months after that phone call, three DEA agents came to meet with Agent Rivera at the Death Investigations Division. Rivera walked them through what he'd learned about the case, using a PowerPoint presentation to recap the investigation's key points. When he finished, he asked them jokingly, "From one to ten, how would you rate my investigation?" Everyone laughed. The DEA agents confirmed Rivera's hunch: Bill Maxwell and Tony weren't the men's real names. They were not Canadian, nor did they live in the Philippines. They were, the agents suspected, Americans from Roxboro, North Carolina.

Rivera introduced the DEA agents to the witnesses he had interviewed about Lee's last days. The agents showed them photos of the two Americans, Rivera told me, "mingled with seven or eight different photos of seven or eight different individuals." Some of the witnesses identified the two Americans as having met with Lee. Others didn't. But after those sessions, one of the DEA agents faxed a report back to the States. The next day, the two men were arrested in Roxboro.

Rivera was pleased with the arrests, but he also expressed frustration about his own continuing investigation, which he resumed after the DEA meeting. A local accomplice had allegedly helped supply the murder weapon and vehicle to the suspects, but Rivera still didn't have enough information to track him down. He pointed out to me that the NBI hadn't gotten any credit for the arrests, while at the same time suggesting that such credit was unnecessary. "We were not included. We were happy about that, it's no problem with us. We have nothing to gain with being famous."

But something else was bothering him: There was someone, or something, much bigger behind the crime that remained shrouded in mystery. Why would the U.S. government send agents across the world to gather evidence against two Americans for the murder of a Filipino woman? Overseas murders, no matter how tragic, typically don't fall under American jurisdiction. Why not just extradite the pair to the Philippines, where the crime occurred, and hand them off to the NBI?

I had the same questions. Perhaps it was related to something more fundamental about the case that I still didn't understand: Why was Catherine Lee important enough for two men from North Carolina to fly across the world to kill her?

Rivera had an answer, although at first he was reluctant to tell me. The crime, he said, was the work of "the Mastermind." At first, Rivera would only identify this Mastermind as the head of a powerful crime organization based in Manila. But he did tell me the motive behind the murder: The Mastermind had once enlisted Catherine Lee to purchase vacation property for him in Batangas, a coastal region south of Manila. He had given her money, at least 50 million pesos, or around a million dollars. "But the deal never materialized," Rivera said, "because the person who Catherine Lee instructed to do the verification of the land, to arrange the deeds and everything, went off with the money."

That person had also been killed, Rivera said. "The body was never found."

And then the Mastermind had ordered Lee's murder, too. Catherine Lee, it seemed, had stepped across the invisible divide between her world and the underworld, oblivious to the chain of events she had set in motion that would end in her own death.

I asked Rivera if he would tell me the name of the Mastermind, and at first he refused. He had a name but he didn't want to say it. The DEA, he told me, would "neither confirm nor deny it."

But I already knew who it had to be. "If I tell you the name that I think it is, will you tell me if that's the person?" I asked.

"I will confirm," he said.

"Paul Le Roux."

Rivera slammed his fist down on the table, then held my gaze for several seconds in silence. He lowered his voice to a whisper. "This Paul Le Roux," he said, "is a very badass guy."

PART I

OPENINGS

1

The Investigators

2007–2008 . . . Two rookie investigators start pulling on strings . . .
The vastness of RX Limited emerges . . . Going undercover online . . .
Kent Bailey gets drafted . . . A phone call to Somalia

The whole thing started with a spreadsheet. DEA investigator
Kimberly Brill was sitting in her government-issue cubicle in
downtown Minneapolis one afternoon in October 2007 when a
package arrived from FedEx. Not just *via* FedEx, but from the
FedEx corporation itself. On a hunch, Brill and another investigator, Steven Holdren, had sent a subpoena to the shipping company
weeks before, asking for all records on an account used by a pharmacy called Altgeld Garden Drug, on the South Side of Chicago.
Brill and Holdren were what the DEA calls "diversion investigators," who focus on the ways prescription drugs are diverted into
illegal markets. Unlike DEA "agents," diversion investigators
don't carry guns and have no power to arrest anyone. The glamour
busts of cartel bosses and meth distribution rings were typically as
distant from Brill and Holdren's work as a murder case is from a
traffic cop's. Most of their time was spent taking down shady doctors and pharmacy "pill mills," for overprescribing and over-
dispensing addictive or dangerous medications.

Altgeld appeared to be just such a target. Brill and Holdren had come across it by searching the Internet for websites selling a drug called phentermine, a type of amphetamine. Phentermine is a "controlled substance" under U.S. law: illegal to sell without a prescription and heavily regulated because of its potential for abuse, making it a classic candidate for diversion. Brill and Holdren had little problem finding online sellers willing to ship it without a prescription. So they'd bought some using undercover names and credit cards, in what the DEA calls a "controlled buy." When the drugs arrived via FedEx, they had the evidence they needed to go after the pharmacy for illegal distribution. All of this was routine, the kind of low-level buy-and-bust operation that diversion investigators carry out all the time. But Brill and Holdren decided to look one layer deeper: They sent out the subpoena to FedEx requesting data on the shipping account used by Altgeld.

Looking back later, it would seem almost preposterous that such a small decision could lead them into a maze of complexity and criminality, one that connected a small pharmacy in Chicago to a murdered real estate agent in the Philippines. But every chess match has to start with an opening move.

Holdren wasn't at his cubicle when the FedEx package arrived—he had just stepped out for a walk—so Brill opened it at her desk, extracted a small thumb drive, and popped it into her computer. She opened up the spreadsheet file on it and began scrolling through. Then she picked up the phone and called Holdren on his cell.

"Oh my God, Steve," she said. "You've got to see this."

Brill and Holdren were, by most measures, still rookies at the DEA—not necessarily the investigators first on the list for big cases. They had met three years before at the DEA Training Academy in Quantico, Virginia, and were both assigned to the Minnesota office by chance. Brill, a native Minnesotan, had joined the DEA at the age of thirty-three. She'd graduated from the University of North Dakota law school and worked for half a decade as an attorney before deciding to join the government. She was the portrait of a hardworking Midwesterner—friendly and understated, but relentlessly disciplined. "I was a first child, a rule follower," she said. She was attracted to the DEA by the idea of catching doctors and pharmacists who had betrayed their oaths.

Holdren had spent his whole career in law enforcement, also entering the DEA at thirty-three after stints as a Border Patrol agent and an investigator in the U.S. Office of Personnel Management, where he conducted national security background checks. Both investigators were familiar with the basics of tracking Web pharmacies, having undergone an online investigation course as part of their thirteen-week training at Quantico. Called Basic Telecommunications Exploitation, it covered how to use the Internet to build a case using controlled buys.

Long before the national opioid epidemic began making headlines, the DEA had become concerned with the proliferation of prescription drug sales online, and the potential for Web pharmacies to funnel dangerous medication onto American streets. But in their first few years at the DEA, Brill and Holdren both found themselves attacking what they felt was the outer edge of the problem. They would bust one online pharmacy, only to find that another had sprung up in its place. Like a pair of city cops who only picked up corner dealers, they weren't making a dent in the criminal organization supplying the drugs to the street.

Brill and Holdren had been talking for a while about finding a case to work together, fifty-fifty, something that would go beyond local pharmacy raids. "We were trying to get to the head of the beast," as Brill put it. "Somebody had to be paying, and somebody had to be profiting greatly. And they needed help running such a large operation. I don't think we knew. It could be anybody."

Now, buried in the lines of the spreadsheet on Brill's screen were the outlines of a case unlike any that they had ever seen.

There were hundreds of thousands of entries, and they weren't just shipments from one mom-and-pop pharmacy in Chicago. Instead, a single national shipping account, #22328, was being used by more than forty other drugstores. Collectively these pharmacies were shipping thousands of drug orders a week. "You could see that there were these pharmacies all over the country, shipping to customers all over the country," Brill said.

The account had been registered and paid for by a company called RX Limited. There were several emails and two phone numbers attached to the account, along with Florida and Texas addresses that both turned out to be "mail drops," a kind of virtual mailbox bought over the Internet. RX Limited itself was registered as a corporation in Delaware. The organization clearly was trying to act like a legitimate American business, but from what Brill and Holdren could tell, it wasn't any type of pharmaceutical company or wholesale distributor. Other than the mail drops, it seemed to have no real American presence at all.

Whatever RX Limited was, it was engaged in the distribution of a staggering amount of pharmaceuticals. Additional subpoenas produced still more spreadsheets, showing that account #22328 and others connected to it had been used by more than a hundred pharmacies since late 2006. "They were located in different parts of the United States," Brill later testified. "They were smaller, independent pharmacies, so not things like CVS or Walgreens." The investigators discovered that in one three-week period in 2007, these pharmacies had collectively shipped more than 57,000 drug orders. The math was mind-boggling: RX Limited was, at a minimum, responsible for shipping millions of orders of prescription drugs a year through FedEx.

The spreadsheets showed that the customers receiving the pills, like the pharmacies sending them, were scattered around the country. Those customers' orders rarely originated at their local pharmacies. An order placed online in Illinois was just as likely to be shipped from an RX Limited–connected pharmacy in Tennessee as from one down the street.

To understand how all this was possible, Brill and Holdren needed to get inside the pharmacies themselves. Over the next few months, working from opposite ends of the diversion group's small cluster of cubicles in the DEA's concrete tower in Minneapolis, they pulled the names of three RX Limited drugstores off the FedEx account, one each in Minnesota, Texas, and Illinois. With the help of the states' pharmacy boards, they then conducted what looked like routine inspections. On one of the visits, to La Joya Drugs in Chicago, they hit the jackpot: A pharmacy technician happily walked the investigators through the steps they took to fill RX Limited's online orders. RX Limited had provided La Joya Drugs with a free computer, printer, and FedEx supplies, together with a step-by-step manual. The technician would log on to a website, download a document containing drug orders, then open a custom program called PCMS. Inside PCMS, which seemed to be software created by RX Limited solely for this purpose, the technician could check off each order as it was filled, then generate the FedEx label and send out the drugs.

That explained how these small pharmacies were able to ship such a huge volume: RX Limited was supplying both the orders and the technology to fill them. But where were the orders coming from in the first place?

Holdren typed the name "RX Limited," together with the Texas mail-drop address, into a search engine and turned up a site called Acmemeds.com. The site looked like a legitimate online drugstore. Calling itself a "trusted online pharmacy since 2004," it featured a stock photograph of a doctor and a note offering "U.S.-LICENSED PHARMACIES, U.S. LICENSED PHYSICIANS, FEDEX OVER-NIGHT SHIPPING." Visitors to the site could search among dozens of drugs and place an order using a credit card. If they ran into any trouble, they could call a 24/7 toll-free customer service line, or access a live help chat.

By searching the Web using blocks of text and phone numbers they found on Acmemeds.com, Holdren and Brill would eventually discover hundreds of similar websites, with names like Cheaprx meds.net, Allpharmmeds.com, Buymedscheap.com, Your-pills.com, Speedyrxdrugs.com, All-the-best-rx.com, Ibuymedscheap.com, my-online-drugstore.com, Preapprovedrx.com, Matrixmeds.com, and 123onlinepharmacy.com. Not all of the sites were necessarily owned by RX Limited directly. Many of them appeared to be what are called "affiliates": a kind of marketing front that independent contractors on the Internet could set up and use to attract drug-buying customers, who were then funneled into the RX Limited network.

To attract affiliates, RX Limited offered a premade website and the promise of a 60 percent commission on every sale. Those commissions were coordinated through sites like RXPayouts.com, Netbizbucks.com, and Pillengine.com. "Open your own online pharmacy," the banner atop RxPayouts.com proclaimed. "The RxPayouts.com Affiliate Program is the premier pharmacy opportunity on the Internet." The affiliates' marketing strategy seemed largely to involve sending spam email to massive mailing lists, and gaming search engines so that a site like Your-pills.com would appear atop the results when someone searched for a particular drug name on Google.

The websites appeared to offer a wide range of drugs, everything from Propecia, the antibaldness pill, to generic forms of Viagra. But when Brill and Holdren started digging into the pharmacies' records, they discovered that the vast bulk of RX Limited's business derived from three specific drugs. The first, Ultram, was the brand name for a synthetic opioid called tramadol, which—like the better-known opioids OxyContin and fentanyl—was developing a reputation for abuse, although largely outside of the United States. Soma, generic name carisoprodol, was a muscle relaxant often prescribed for back problems. And the third, Fioricet, was also often prescribed to treat tension headaches and migraines. In addition to being powerful painkillers, the three drugs shared another property Brill and Holdren realized was crucial to RX Limited's scope: None were considered "controlled substances" by the U.S. government.

Dictated by an ever-evolving law known as the Controlled Substances Act, drugs that the government views as dangerous are classified according to five "schedules," ranked roughly from most dangerous to least using Roman numerals I through V. Schedule I includes drugs that the U.S. government has deemed lack any medical application and have a high potential for abuse, including heroin and LSD. Schedule II drugs such as OxyContin and fentanyl, by contrast, have medical applications but retain a high potential for abuse and harm. Schedule III drugs are considered slightly less dangerous, and so on.

The RX Limited network of websites did not appear to traffic in scheduled drugs. Indeed, the websites themselves demonstrated a sharp awareness of the lines around U.S. drug law, with prominent disclaimers stating that they did not offer controlled substances. But evidence was growing that Ultram, Soma, and Fioricet weren't, as commonly portrayed, "safe" alternatives to OxyContin. As far as Brill and Holdren were concerned, the drugs were "habit forming" at a minimum. RX Limited's focus on these three painkillers, the investigators concluded, was a deliberate effort to avoid legal scrutiny.

If RX Limited was potentially skirting the law in one way, Brill and Holdren suspected it might be breaking it in others. For starters, Fioricet contained an *ingredient* that was controlled, a schedule III drug called butalbital. In Fioricet, it was mixed with caffeine and acetaminophen, the medication in Tylenol. Whether the combination met the criteria for a controlled substance wasn't entirely clear, but it hardly mattered: As a technical, legal matter, even noncontrolled drugs required a valid prescription to distribute. RX Limited sites like Acmemeds.com seemed to acknowledge this reality as well, with prominent disclaimers: "Our company is committed to meeting and exceeding all Government regulations covering this new form of healthcare provision. Acmemeds.com will only refer your order to certified physicians that are fully licensed."

Even if that were true—though the investigators strongly doubted it was—the volume of prescriptions flowing through the

FedEx account didn't make sense. Over the previous sixteen months, Brill and Holdren estimated, RX Limited had delivered seventy-two *million* doses of painkillers to Americans. Something about RX Limited smelled illegal, and dangerous. They just weren't exactly sure what it was yet.

The best way to figure it out, they decided, was to start making undercover buys. Brill concocted an identity, "Sarah Johnson," arranged for a fake Minnesota ID, and bought prepaid credit cards at the nearby Mall of America. Then, on Acmemeds.com and other sites, she signed up as a customer. For an address, she used a mail drop at a FedEx store near the office. Her first order was for thirty tablets of Soma, the muscle relaxant. On the order page, she was taken to a "medical questionnaire" that the site claimed would be reviewed by a doctor. There she was asked to answer yes or no to questions like, "Is your personal healthcare practitioner aware that you are requesting this medication?" and "Have you had a physical exam in the last 12 months?" The questionnaire had a blank space for symptoms. Brill typed in "back spasms" and submitted her order. A customer service representative from the site followed up with an email, reporting that the order had been "queued" for review.

Over the next year, Brill and Holdren made dozens of such orders, following the same process each time. The symptoms that "Sarah Johnson" offered ranged from "back pain" to "neck" to a made-up condition they called "stratuski." She never heard from a doctor. Each time, her order was eventually approved and shipped out, complete with a tracking number and confirmation email. When the delivery arrived, it came labeled with the name of the doctor who had written the prescription and the pharmacy that had filled it. When Brill and Holdren had the drugs tested at DEA labs, the results were always the same: RX Limited had supplied exactly what Sarah Johnson had ordered.

The investigators were getting a full picture of how RX Limited operated. The network's websites took online orders from customers in the United States, who found the sites through spam emails and ordinary online searches for painkillers. Those orders were then funneled, virtually, to real American doctors who wrote real prescriptions, without ever meeting their patients. Those prescriptions were then sent electronically to real independent pharmacies to be filled and shipped using RX Limited–supplied technology. The doctors and pharmacies themselves were disposable to the organization, Brill realized. Take one out, and another could simply be slotted into place. The network kept humming on.

The scheme was so multilayered that none of the deliveries Brill and Holdren had received made any reference to RX Limited. "The pharmacies don't know the other pharmacies, the doctors don't know the other doctors," Brill said. "None of them ultimately know who they are working for."

Neither, at this point, did Brill or Holdren. There was, however, one unusual name that surfaced several times in the data. It was the thinnest of reeds at first, one they had spotted in the hundreds of thousands of lines in the FedEx spreadsheets. Amid the shipments of pills fanning out across the United States, they found one international order: a package delivered to a hotel in Manila in 2005 to someone named Paul Le Roux.

Kent Bailey was at a bar in Minneapolis when he first heard the name that would come to dominate his life. It was the spring of 2008, and Bailey, a veteran special agent with the DEA—the gun-toting kind—had recently transferred from the Twin Cities to Chantilly, Virginia, to join the agency's Special Operations Division. Located at its own headquarters twenty-five miles east of D.C., SOD was formed in 1994 to coordinate complicated investigations involving multiple agencies and jurisdictions, cases that spanned domestic and international drug trafficking. After a decade and a half chasing dealers on the street, Bailey had been promoted to SOD, as a supervising agent in the Pharmaceutical, Chemical, and Internet division. A weekend visit back to Minnesota coincided with a going-away party for one of the agents on his former team, at a downtown sports bar called Matty B's. At one point during the festivities, a pair of diversion investigators Bailey knew from the office buttonholed him.

"Hey, I want to ask you something," Kimberly Brill said. She and the other investigator, Steven Holdren, had been poking around on a case for several months, something they thought could be big. Between beers, Brill and Holdren outlined the basics of what they'd found on RX Limited, trying to impress upon Bailey that it all amounted to something more than just a typical pill mill. Altgeld and the other pharmacies weren't online businesses; they were merely the frontline fulfillment of a much larger network. "This is national scale," Brill told Bailey. "We think it's illegal. Is there anything you can do to help?"

Bailey, after feigning outrage that they hadn't called him sooner, said he'd take a look. "Send me the email addresses and whatever telephone numbers you have. I'll start running them in our databases to see what's happening."

Le Roux's name had surfaced several more times in the investigation, after Brill and Holdren had initially seen it on the FedEx package delivered in Manila. For one, they'd determined that RX Limited was renting server space at a company called Q9 in Canada, with an account tied to the email plleroux@swprofessionals .com. The email led them to a defunct website for a programming business called Software Professionals, registered in Mauritius but located in South Africa—and owned by one Paul Le Roux. The name had started to rise up their list of important figures in RX Limited.

They also noticed that several of the servers at Q9 were named after chess pieces, they told Bailey. It almost felt like an invitation to join the game. They'd christened the case Operation Checkmate.

A few days after his 2008 encounter with Brill and Holdren, Bailey was back at his desk in Virginia. The East Coast posting wasn't much of a natural habitat for the forty-six-year-old agent. He'd grown up in a tiny town in Minnesota called Thief River Falls, just across the border from Winnipeg. Options out of high school were limited, so he enlisted in the Army at age seventeen to become an airborne radio operator. Believing he was training to manage communications equipment on planes, he quickly discovered that instead he would be carrying a radio and jumping out of them. "My recruiter lied to me," he said. "If I'd known what I was going to end up doing I would have said no frickin' way."

He took to it, though, and eventually he joined the Army's Special Forces 2nd Ranger Battalion in Fort Lewis, Washington. By the early 1990s, back injuries from jumping kept him out of the First Gulf War, and threatened to confine him to a desk job. One day he was assigned to train a group of visiting DEA agents preparing for operations in South America—survival, escape and evasion, booby traps. After a few weeks of hanging out with them, he decided to quit the military and join the agency.

After his training Bailey landed in LA, where the agency was targeting drug-trafficking organizations south of the border. Bailey employed his friendly Midwestern accent to mask a no-bullshit approach to law enforcement, and paid his dues with grueling street work. In an eighteen-month investigation tagged Operation Silent Thunder, he helped crack a methamphetamine ring in which Hells Angels had linked up with Mexican traffickers and white supremacists, resulting in almost three hundred arrests. Over the years, Bailey developed a philosophy about the kingpins on the other side of the law. Even the most successful ones, he concluded, generally weren't the evil geniuses that they appeared from the street. Their every maneuver might *look* perfectly calculated. But when the agents finally had them in custody, they would usually discover that those brilliant evasions were, more often than not, just dumb luck.

After four years in Los Angeles, Bailey's wife pressed him to look for a post closer to their extended family. He found one as a field supervisor in Minneapolis, running a team that did everything from street busts to multistate investigations. In September 2007, when he was offered the promotion to SOD, he viewed it as a step up in title but not necessarily in duties. The Internet division was staffed by diversion investigators, and dealt largely with offshore pharmacies in India and China. He'd worked the Southwest border, and thought he should be chasing Mexican cartels, where the action was. *I have to have agents help me get on the Internet, and I've taken Vicodin once in my life,* he thought. *What the fuck do I know about this?*

But Bailey prided himself on outworking any problem. In Virginia he chose a small desk under an air vent and set up a telephone and three computer screens: one for internal work only, one for classified documents, and one connected to the outside Internet. He viewed the job as a temporary way station. His wife and two kids had stayed back in Minnesota. He'd try to make the best of it.

Now, sitting in front of his monitors in the spring of 2008, he considered Brill and Holdren's pleadings at the bar. He examined the list of email addresses and phone numbers they had managed to gather off the FedEx account and their controlled buys. From the outset, he could see that whatever RX Limited was, it was international, its communications tracing arcs across the globe. The Special Operations Division existed for precisely this kind of case.

Bailey started with a phone number that particularly interested the investigators: a Philippine mobile they'd found registered to Paul Le Roux, the man who had received the package in Manila. Bailey passed the number to an analyst at SOD and got a report back listing its last thirty days' worth of calls. "I see numbers to Ghana," he said. "I see numbers to the Congo. I see numbers to the Philippines, obviously. I see numbers in Brazil."

Then Bailey saw a series of calls that stopped him cold. They were back and forth to Somalia. Suddenly he began to suspect that he was dealing with something larger than just RX Limited. He'd never been to Somalia, but "those are my brothers that went down in *Black Hawk Down;* that's the battalion I served in for twelve years," he said. "People go to those places because they are lawless." He still knew almost nothing about Le Roux, but looking at those calls, he was certain of one thing. "This guy is not setting up a fucking pharmacy in Somalia."

2

The Pharmacist · The Doctor

2006–2008 . . . Charles Schultz grabs a lifeline . . . Prabhakara
Tumpati sees the promise of RX Limited

In the summer of 2006, Charles Schultz was struggling to figure out how to stay afloat. A seventy-four-year-old pharmacist in Oshkosh, Wisconsin, he had been in the drugstore business for his entire adult life. He had opened his first local pharmacy more than forty years earlier, in the early 1960s. Together with his wife, Jeanne, he had built Schultz Pharmacy into an established business, set on a quaint street in downtown Oshkosh, a city hugging the western shore of Lake Winnebago. In the 1980s, he bought a second store, Medicine Mart, 130 miles south in the town of Monroe. For decades, Schultz, who even into his seventies carried himself with an impeccable posture reminiscent of his college ROTC days, was known in the community as a generous boss and devoted family man who cluttered up his house with books.

Over the last few years, however, a plague of misfortune seemed to have set upon him. His business was in steep decline as big-box drugstore chains crowded out independent pharmacies like Schultz and Medicine Mart. A business that had once afforded him enough income to buy a vacation home was now selling items below cost just to keep customers coming in. His family, meanwhile, was beset by health problems. A son suffered from a severe psychiatric disorder that required nearly full-time care. And Schultz himself had been struck by a series of small heart attacks, brought on in part by the stress of running a struggling business and the long hours spent shuttling between Oshkosh and Monroe, well past retirement age.

Then, in the summer of 2006, salvation appeared out of the blue. Schultz received an unsolicited letter, by fax, from a company he'd never heard of called Alphanet-Trading, with an address in Costa Mesa, California. The letter offered him an enticing opportunity: Alphanet could augment Schultz's in-store sales with online prescriptions, without any investment from him. His role couldn't have been simpler: If he signed on as an Alphanet pharmacy, the company would supply him with fully outfitted computers and as many online orders as he could handle. All he would have to do was log in to the company's system, fill valid prescriptions written by American doctors, and ship them using Alphanet's FedEx account. He'd then be reimbursed by bank transfer for the wholesale cost of the prescription, plus $3.50 for each one filled.

At first, Schultz ignored the offer, which sounded suspiciously like a get-rich scam. But when his cash flow tightened the next month, he reconsidered, and conducted some online research to determine if it was real. Alphanet's website looked legitimate enough. Next to a photo of five friendly-looking businesspeople was a pitch similar to the one in his letter.

Alphanet-Trading is your mail order pharmacy partner! We contract with pharmacies in several states to handle order fulfillment for us.

Our mail order program is in essence a prescription refill program in which customers are required to have already received the initial prescription they are seeking beforehand. They must have their primary healthcare provider aware that they are taking this medication.

They are required to have had a complete physical exam by their physician every 6 months.

Schultz was intrigued enough to call the company's recruiter, listed on the fax. He was interested, he told the man, but still harbored doubts about the ethics of the operation. The recruiter quickly dispelled them. Online pharmacies were a booming business, he said, and a cheaper option for patients than constantly returning to doctors for new prescriptions to treat chronic conditions. Alphanet was offering the chance for smaller pharmacies to get a piece of a new market, and help people in the process. The recruiter sent Schultz copies of licenses belonging to the physicians who wrote prescriptions for its network, to prove they were legitimate. He also emphasized that Alphanet didn't sell controlled substances, instead specializing in non-controlled painkillers like Ultram, Soma, and Fioricet. "If an online pharmacy is asking you to ship controlled drugs, you better put your fees away for a lawyer," he added, "because what you are doing is illegal." To further put Schultz's mind at ease, Alphanet's representative gave him the number of a former DEA agent in Florida. Schultz called him up, and the man confirmed that Alphanet's business was above the law.

Schultz felt reassured enough to sign up for the network. The computers arrived by FedEx, with instructions on how to set them up. Before long his pharmacists were filling as many online orders as in-person ones. He hired a new full-time pharmacy technician at each location, just to handle them. "I would come in in the morning. There was a program that I would get into that would have the orders," one technician later said. "I would print the order, the purchase invoice, the shipping statement, the FedEx label." She would then hand the labels off to the pharmacist to fill the order and place the bottle in a FedEx envelope.

As the Alphanet representative had guaranteed, each order came with the name of a licensed physician who had written the prescription. Schultz's technicians noticed that often the doctors were based in Pennsylvania, but otherwise knew little about them, and never spoke to them. "Alphanet gave us copies of the physician licenses on file and we attempted to monitor that patients were not getting more than the physicians approved," Schultz said. The pharmacy rarely interacted with online customers aside from the occasional call about a refill gone missing, referred on to Alphanet customer service.

For Schultz, the business was everything Alphanet had promised, and quickly relieved the pressures that had threatened his livelihood. His bank account began receiving wire transfers from a company called East Asia Escrow Limited in Hong Kong. Tens of thousands of dollars were pouring in monthly, and then weekly.

Someone at the top of all of this was clearly making tremendous amounts of money, Schultz thought. Who that might be, he didn't have the first idea. The Alphanet reps he talked to by phone, with names like "Will Morris," "Mike Gilmore," and "Sam Kent," never said where they were located, or how many people worked for the organization. Nor did they explain why the money came from East Asia Escrow, or mention that Alphanet was another name for RX Limited. Even if they had, to Schultz it would have been just another faceless online company—one that, by 2008, was putting millions of dollars into his bank account. "Alphanet said that its operation was legal and legitimate," Schultz said. "I wanted to believe them."

At the same moment Schultz was finding financial salvation at the end of his career, Dr. Prabhakara Tumpati was seeking some at the beginning of his. In 2008, Tumpati had just finished his residency at Abington Memorial Hospital, in suburban Philadelphia, and was entering the medical field in the middle of a recession. Tumpati's road to becoming a doctor had been nothing short of extraordinary. He was born into a farming family in the remote Indian village of M. Nagulapalli, and his first few years of education had taken place in a local school with a dirt floor and no electricity. Tumpati had a Hindu father and a Christian mother, an unusual combination in that part of India, and they had raised him Christian. His maternal grandmother had converted after his mother suffered a grave childhood illness; the family believed she had been cured after a villager suggested the grandmother pray to Jesus. Faith would lead to providence in Tumpati's own life, too: At the suggestion of a local pastor, Tumpati applied to a children's boarding school, several villages away, run by an Indian American missionary physician from Pennsylvania. From there, Tumpati's intellectual abilities and relentless work ethic carried him to a top-flight Indian medical school, postgraduate work in Norway, and an internal medicine residency at Abington Memorial in the United States. That he landed in the state from which his own missionary childhood teacher hailed only confirmed for Tumpati the power of God's works.

Now, though, he was fully trained, and trying to find his way in the American workforce. His son had been born the year before, and with another baby on the way he and his wife decided she would quit her job as a computer programmer and stay home with the kids. That left it to Tumpati to cover all of their expenses, including the mortgage on a new house. Straight out of residency he took on two part-time medical jobs, one as an associate doctor at an internal medicine clinic started by a friend, the other at a company where he reviewed drug test results from patients around the country.

As soon as he felt he had both jobs under control, he started looking for even more work. Tumpati had always considered himself tech-savvy; back when he had been accepted for residency, an arduous process that was particularly daunting to overseas students, he'd created an online forum called Residentscafe.com where he answered questions for medical school graduates about the residency matching system. The site grew to over six thousand registered users. He'd also created a site called WikiMD.org, a Wikipedia-like medical encyclopedia maintained by volunteers. So when looking for work, he naturally gravitated online. On a forum titled "Physicians Work From Home," he saw a posting for a role with a company called RX Limited.

When Tumpati replied to the posting, a company representative using the name "Aaron Johnson" laid out the job for him: Tumpati would review medical questionnaires from patients who had ordered drugs on a website, and if warranted prescribe them the drugs they were requesting. Tumpati was familiar with the concept of "telemedicine," a burgeoning field in which medical practitioners used the Internet to interact with patients. RX Limited's model struck him as cutting edge, an extension of the remote medicine he was already practicing by reviewing test results. It also paid by the prescription: $2 for each one he issued.

Whatever misgivings Tumpati might have had about the process, representatives of RX Limited worked to assuage them, assuring him that they had "over forty other physicians doing this, and that it is fully valid and legal," he said. "They assured me that they only deal with non–DEA controlled substances, and these patients already have annual physical examinations with their own physicians." He signed up.

RX Limited sent him login credentials for a website where he could access the customer questionnaires and orders. He would examine a patient's responses, click a box to mark the order accepted or rejected, and move on to the next. For a doctor, the work couldn't have been more simple. There were no waiting rooms full of patients to deal with, no insurance forms to fill out. Tumpati assumed that RX Limited's customers already had a diagnosis in hand and were just looking for affordable refills on medications they had been prescribed. "It appeared to me to be a perfect opportunity to not only serve a lot of patients," he said, "but also be able to do so in my free time."

It was also, it turned out, extremely lucrative for a part-time job. Soon he was making enough money not just to cover his expenses, but to save up to start his own practice. And more important, he was able to send some of it back home, to sponsor kids at the same missionary school that had given him a pathway out of his village.

A thousand miles apart, Tumpati and Schultz had no sense that their worlds were now connected. They were merely nodes on a vast network of another man's creation, each unable to see beyond the limits of his own attachment point. Neither paid any special notice to a request transmitted across that network on August 27, 2008. It arrived first to Tumpati: an order from a customer named "Sarah Johnson," placed on a website called cheaprxmeds.net, then bounced through RX Limited's systems to Tumpati's screen. The order was for ninety pills of Fioricet, retail price $170. On the medical questionnaire Tumpati glanced at for no more than a few seconds, Johnson had listed the reason for her purchase as "migraine," the condition for which Fioricet was usually prescribed. Tumpati marked it approved and moved on as it was uploaded back into the digital ether. Hours later, after a virtual trip from Canada to Israel to the Philippines and back, the order arrived on a computer at Charles Schultz's Medicine Mart, in Monroe, Wisconsin. There a technician saw the prescription and queued it for filling. A white-coated pharmacist pulled down a green bottle, smoothed on a label bearing Tumpati's name, slid the exact number of oblong pills inside, and dropped the bottle into a FedEx envelope. The preprinted label was addressed to a FedEx office mailbox in Minneapolis, down the street from the DEA.

3

The Reporter

2013–2015 . . . Rambo gets arrested . . . Murder and North Korean methamphetamine . . . The mysterious Paul Le Roux . . . Lost in the data . . . A lawyer and a deal

"Today we announce the arrest of Joseph Hunter," said Preet Bharara, the United States Attorney for the Southern District of New York, standing at a podium in a dark suit and patterned tie on the morning of September 27, 2013. Photographers snapped away in the front-row briefing room in downtown Manhattan. Television cameras in the back broadcast Bharara's press conference live for the international news. "The bone-chilling allegations in today's indictment read like they were ripped from the pages of a Tom Clancy novel," Bharara said. "The charges tell a tale of an international band of mercenary marksmen who enlisted their elite military training to serve as hired guns for evil ends."

That morning, a federal court had unsealed an indictment outlining precisely what those evil ends were. Hunter, a forty-eight-year-old decorated U.S. Army veteran, stood accused of organizing an international hit squad composed of ex-soldiers from the United States, Poland, and Germany. Their mission: to carry out the murder of a DEA agent and his informant, on behalf of a Colombian drug cartel, for a price of $800,000. "Today's arrests," Bharara said, "are the culmination of a bold and brave global investigation conducted by some of the most extraordinary law enforcement agents in the world—the men and women of the DEA's Special Operations Division." The Thai police had captured Hunter two days before, at a safe house on a golf course in Phuket, Thailand. Two members of Hunter's assassination squad had been picked up at the same time in Liberia, as they prepared to carry out the hit. The fourth and fifth were caught in Estonia, charged with providing security for a drug shipment to the United States. All five would be extradited to New York to stand trial.

The announcement made international headlines, not least because Hunter's actual nickname, according to prosecutors, was "Rambo." When I read about it in the news the next morning, I couldn't disagree with Bharara's flash of showmanship: The whole thing *did* sound as if it were concocted by a novelist. Curious if there was more to the story, I went online and downloaded the indictment. Paging through it, I discovered that if the allegations read like fiction, it was in part because, in some sense, they were. The whole thing—the murder-for-hire of the DEA agent, the drug deal—had been an elaborate setup, a version of what's known as a "reverse sting" operation. The two people that Hunter and his crew were plotting to murder never existed. They were inventions of the DEA, who laid an elaborate trap for Hunter's crew, enticing them into plotting a crime against imaginary victims.

Most of the case had been sealed by a federal judge, but the indictment described a world of amoral mercenaries operating with utter impunity, arranging paid assassinations without a second thought. On recordings made by the DEA using microphones hidden in the Phuket safe house, Hunter was captured preparing his team to carry out jobs for the supposed Colombians, including killings-for-hire that he referred to as "bonus work." "This is real stuff," he told his team. "You see James Bond in the movie and you're saying, 'Oh, I can do that.' Well, you're gonna do it now." He bragged about the kind of bonus work he had done in the past, or paid others to do—including, the indictment noted, "arranging for the murder of two female real estate agents."

The sting operation seemed to have taken a heinous character off the street. But I kept wondering: What had put the DEA on to Hunter in the first place? Was the agency randomly tossing out fishing lines around the world, advertising assassinations hoping that someone would bite? Or had they come across Hunter and targeted him specifically?

Then the story grew even stranger. Two months after the press conference, in November 2013, the Southern District announced another dramatic bust. This time it was of a group of suspects planning to import huge quantities of North Korean–made methamphetamine into the United States. Again the arrests stemmed from a sting operation set up by the DEA, using fake members of a Colombian cartel. Again some of the arrests were made in Phuket. Again much of the case was sealed, shielding it from the public eye, and yet the U.S. Department of Justice again seemed eager to make a big splash. "Methamphetamine is a dangerous, potentially deadly drug, whatever its origin," Bharara said in a press release. "If it ends up in our neighborhoods, the threat it poses to public health is grave whether it is produced in New York, elsewhere in the U.S., or in North Korea."

I was struck by the bizarre set of circumstances shared by the two cases and kept poring over the sketchy information contained in the indictments. Neither made mention of the other, but each referred to an unnamed person involved in the sting, labeled variously as a "narcotics trafficking partner" and "Individual-1"—who appeared to be a cooperating witness. Whether this was the same mysterious figure in the two cases was impossible to tell, but both groups had been arrested on the same day in Thailand, and were being prosecuted by exactly the same U.S. Attorneys. A few days later, *The Washington Post* quoted an unnamed DEA source claiming a link between Hunter and North Korea, but nobody seemed to follow up.

As I dug into the case myself, I started to understand why. I barely got below the surface before I hit what seemed to be a layer of impenetrable rock. I knew from experience that the DEA was rarely interested in talking about open cases, and these two were no exception. "I'm sorry, Evan. There isn't any information we can confirm, deny, or discuss right now, unfortunately," a DEA spokesperson replied when I contacted him. Defense lawyers often leap to proclaim their client's innocence, but most of the attorneys in the two cases were unwilling to comment at all. Others would only meet in person, outside their office, and talk off the record. One lawyer I called just happened to pick up his office phone one afternoon. He'd left that case, he told me, and didn't want to discuss it. I kept him on the line long enough to ask about the mysterious "Individual-1" at the center of the case. He laughed. "Oh, you mean Keyser Söze?" he said, referring to the elusive master criminal at the center of the film *The Usual Suspects*. Then he referred me to the new lawyer on the case and hung up. That lawyer never responded to my inquiries.

And then, suddenly: a name. It came in late 2014, in a leak from an anonymous official at the DEA to a *New York Times* reporter named Alan Feuer, who was covering the federal courthouse where Hunter was to be tried. "Individual-1," the official revealed, was a South African named Paul Calder Le Roux, a computer programmer and some kind of international cartel boss. The DEA official called Le Roux "Viktor Bout on steroids"—a reference to the notorious global arms dealer who had been prosecuted by the Southern District of New York back in 2011. Le Roux, in the anonymous official's telling, was a computer genius who had built an empire selling prescription drugs over the Internet, and then leveraged that fortune into international crimes, from arms trafficking to contract murder. He was also the man who connected Joseph Hunter and his hit team to the crew smuggling meth out of North Korea. All of the figures involved had worked not for Hunter, but for Le Roux. And now it seemed Le Roux had turned against them and was helping the government run them down.

For a brief moment it seemed that the mystery I'd been chasing had been solved. But after a few weeks the headlines disappeared again, obscured by news of a terrorist attack in France, and by the first moves of a presidential race that would end in the election of Donald Trump. Le Roux's existence receded into the shadows with the most important questions unanswered. Namely, where did he come from, and how had a South African computer programmer managed to create his own global cartel? Why had the government refused to release his identity, and then suddenly leaked it? And where was he now?

I became obsessed with finding out.

As I tried to page back through Le Roux's history, his story at first seemed borderless, almost limitless. I spent the better part of a year trying to understand him through the same means by which he'd directed his pharmacy business: the Internet. Late at night, after my wife went to bed and then, as time went on, while my newborn daughter slept, I would open my laptop and plunge into a thicket of data. The first hints of Le Roux were faint, puzzling. Here was his name on a Florida company cited in a 2008 Federal Communications Commission complaint about a marketing call made to someone on the National Do Not Call Registry. There was his email address connected to a gun dealer in Manila called Red White & Blue Arms. Here, lodged in a Hong Kong company database, was Le Roux establishing Net Trading Ltd. in 2006 before changing its name to Ajax Technology in 2008, then transferring the ownership to someone named Robson Tandanayi. There was Le Roux incorporating another Ajax Technology in the United Kingdom in 2006, with a Dutch address, before again gifting the company to Tandanayi.

Each piece of data seemed to lead to a dozen more, until I began to feel like I was engaged in an elaborate version of the children's game Concentration. I would find one clue, stash it away, and hope to turn over another that matched it later on. Unbeknownst to me, I was often flipping many of the same cards that Brill and

Holdren had, a half dozen years before. Like them, I started un-
covering websites related to RX Limited, Le Roux's prescription
pill empire—first a few, then hundreds, then thousands. Their registrations seemed to switch over the years from addresses in the
Philippines to the United States, to other countries and back. Many
of them connected to a single location: Unit 1401 BDO Building,
Paseo De Roxas, Makati City, in Manila's upscale shopping and
business district. A search on that address, in turn, matched the
location of call centers in the Philippines, with names like Call
Xtreme, Dial Magic, and Global I-Net Bridge. Soon my digital files
were stuffed with thousands of these interconnected nodes, spread
across the United States, Panama, the United Kingdom, the Netherlands, Romania, Russia, and the Philippines. I found dozens of
Le Roux–connected companies, with names as inscrutable to me
as Paul Le Roux himself: Southern Ace, La Plata Trading, GX Port,
Everplus, Cycom Tech, Wilex, East Asia Escrow, Martenius Trading, MTCL, Quantcom Commerce, Vischnu Limited, Century Holdings, Amana Holdings, BNPay, Alpha Networks, Diko Limited,
Maximum8. It seemed almost impossible that one person could
have a hand in it all.

One night in October 2015, I was exploring the possible connections to an email address I'd found for Le Roux, pleroux@
swprofessionals.com, from a defunct software company called SW
Professionals. The same address, I discovered, turned up in the
instruction manual for a piece of encryption software called Encryption for the Masses, or E4M. The software was designed to
protect a computer's files from the prying eyes of law enforcement
and the government. I looked up the old website for E4M and discovered that it had been controlled by an Australian company
called World Away Pty. On the corporate registration for World
Away, its owner was listed as a Zimbabwean named Paul Calder
Le Roux. E4M was long since out of use, but its code had formed
the basis of a more famous encryption program—among *the most*
famous file encryption programs—called TrueCrypt. The favored
software of everyone from National Security whistleblower Ed-

ward Snowden to the terrorist group ISIS, TrueCrypt had itself
long been a mystery. Its developers were anonymous. Now it appeared as if Le Roux, at least indirectly, had a hand in it.

The implications were bewildering. Le Roux wasn't just a thug
who'd clawed his way to the top of an organization. Nor was he
simply the clever architect of an online pill network. This was a
man smart enough to create technology that the U.S. government's
elite hackers couldn't crack.

By late 2015, I was awash in information about Paul Le Roux, but
ultimately my lists of names and companies didn't cohere into a
picture of his organization. Fortunately, there was another legal
case connected to Le Roux, targeting his prescription drug network. In Minneapolis, a grand jury had indicted eleven RX Limited employees and associates in 2014, and several of them were
out on bail, awaiting trial. Why Minneapolis, I had no idea. But at
the very least, the case would give me another set of lawyers to
call. As expected, the prosecutors from the Department of Justice
declined to talk.

That October, one defense attorney finally picked up the phone.
His name was Joe Friedberg, and he was perhaps the Twin Cities'
best-known defense lawyer. Friedberg and another heavy-hitting
attorney, Robert Richman, had taken on the case of an Israeli citizen named Moran Oz, one of the eleven defendants in the RX
Limited case. According to his indictment, "MORAN OZ a/k/a
Ron Oz a/k/a Ron Martin was an RX Limited associate who resided in Israel and managed day-to-day operations for, and communications with, RX Limited fulfillment pharmacies." Oz was
facing eighty-three counts of mail fraud, wire fraud, and unlawful
distribution of controlled substances. The indictment described
him as a key player in a massive network delivering millions of
doses of addictive painkillers to American homes.

"I can't give you very much information that would help you,"
Friedberg told me at first. "This is a very strange case." He, like

me, was baffled about the black hole that seemed to surround Paul Le Roux. "The government doesn't want to tell us anything," he said. "They have all these people indicted and they don't have the guy indicted who owned it and started it. We'd at least like to know where he is and where he's been." The government's prosecutor, a D.C.-based attorney named Linda Marks, had proven equally unhelpful. (Why the case was being prosecuted out of D.C., rather than by federal prosecutors in Minneapolis, was another mystery.) Marks had told the defense attorneys, Friedberg said on our call, that she had no idea where Le Roux was. I hung up having learned little more than I already knew.

A week later, Friedberg called back with a proposal. "Typically I would not let a client speak to the press before their trial," he told me. But the defense team was operating so deeply in the dark that they were prepared to take a gamble. They would let me interview Oz on the condition that I not quote him by name before his trial, which was then scheduled for seven months later, in June 2016. Their hope was that I could follow leads Oz might generate for me, then publish information that would inform their case.

A few weeks later, I landed in Minneapolis and checked into a room at a downtown hotel, connected to Friedberg's building by one of the city's Habitrail-like overhead tunnels. When he walked into the conference room the next morning, Friedberg exuded the witty charm that had served him well in some of the most high-profile criminal cases in the city. Richman arrived soon after, seeming quiet and reserved alongside his gregarious partner. But Richman had taken on much of the heavy lifting for the upcoming trial. "This case is extraordinary," he said as we sat down across from each other at a long wooden table. "There are a million documents and probably tens of millions of pages," so many that they'd had to contract with a private company to organize them into a database.

Oz arrived a few minutes later. He was trim and stylish, in his early thirties, with a dark beard and a yarmulke. For a man facing an eighty-plus-count federal indictment, he radiated a natural calmness. Only a small electronic bracelet wrapped around his ankle, half-covered by the cuff of his designer jeans, gave any indication of his situation. He spent a few minutes discussing the logistics of his court-ordered supervision with Richman and Friedberg. Stranded in Minneapolis now for a year and a half, he relied on the generosity of a local Jewish community, which had loaned him an apartment and a car. Then he sat down across from me and told me his story from the beginning.

4

The Operators

2005–2008 . . . Moran Oz and Alon Berkman get to work . . . A new boss appears . . . A trip to Manila . . . The pipeline opens

M oran Oz grew up in Jerusalem, the sort of kid that everyone seems to remember fondly. The smart and curious son of a successful CPA and a dance teacher, he breezed through school: "the guy who could miss class and then waltz in and get an A," as one childhood friend described him. His only flirtations with trouble stemmed from his devotion to Beitar Jerusalem, an Israeli soccer team known for its unruly supporters. In February 2005, Oz had just graduated from high school and completed his compulsory service in the Israeli army. He was visiting an uncle in New York, wondering what to do with his life—go to college? start a business?—when a friend called to say that an acquaintance had launched a startup in Israel and was looking to hire. The only requirements were a good command of English and a basic understanding of computers. Oz flew home and took the job.

The man who hired him was named Boaz Taggart. He'd started the company, a call center called Beit Oridan, with his brother Tomer, who lived in the United States. The term "call center" was a bit of a misnomer, since much of their work happened over email, but such companies typically consisted of banks of cubicles, filled with employees fielding customer service inquiries. In this case, Beit Oridan was part of a larger organization, a network of websites that went by the names RX Limited and Alphanet and sold prescription drugs to American consumers over the Internet.

In 2005, when Oz began working there, the company had eight American pharmacies operating in the network, taking eight thousand orders a week. It was growing quickly, with a recruitment arm that advertised for doctors on online forums like Craigslist, and solicited by fax and phone the kind of independent pharmacies too small to build an online presence themselves. Within a few months of Oz's arrival, the number of employees doubled. Among the new hires was a slight, nervous man named Alon Berkman. Berkman's primary responsibility, at least at first, was to provide support for "affiliate marketers," independent websites that advertised the drugs through email and search engines, and then referred customers back to RX Limited for a 60 percent cut of every order. Beit Oridan's employees were instructed to adopt American-sounding names and say that they were located in Utah. Oz's handle was Ron Martin; Berkman's was Allen Berkman.

Oz's job as operations manager didn't require any knowledge of pharmaceuticals, nor of the technological infrastructure behind RX Limited. He arrived each morning, quickly reviewed the prescriptions uploaded by doctors in the United States, then clicked a few buttons to send them on to one of RX Limited's pharmacies, allocating orders according to each store's daily capacity. The rest of the staff was responsible for recruiting and communicating with doctors and pharmacists, and for customer support: dealing with password problems, lost shipments, expired credit cards, and incomplete questionnaires. New hires were supplied with a "pitch," a standard script that told them how to respond to various customer complaints. "The majority of them were technical issues," one former call center worker said. "There were regulations that we had to be aware of in terms of people using certain drugs." The company also maintained a fraud team, like any legitimate online retailer. If an order was deemed suspicious, "we were immediately instructed to send them up to the fraud team," the former worker said. "And if people had lost packages, we were to refer them to UPS or FedEx."

To the extent that he ever considered the legality of the whole operation, Oz felt that RX Limited was working hard to comply with a confusing tangle of state and federal prescription-drug laws in the United States. For instance, a database held the order history for every customer and tracked the dates and amounts of their last purchases. If a new order showed up more quickly than a drug should have been consumed, the system was supposed to prevent that customer from getting a refill.

The company did at times encounter what Oz and his colleagues thought of as regulatory hitches. If a state changed its rules to ban the shipment of a certain drug, the system had to be adjusted to stop sending orders to pharmacies in that state. Occasionally, Oz would hear about American pharmacies being inspected by their state pharmacy board; they might go offline for a few days, then reappear in the system. But since the company didn't deal in controlled substances, Oz was told that the law was not an issue. When prospective pharmacies complained about their cut of each prescription, $2 or $3, the pharmacy recruiters were prepared with their own script. "The reason we pay so low is that we are doing a legal business," they were told to say. "If you are getting ten dollars you should save it for your bail because that means what you are doing is illegal."

Boaz and Tomer Taggart told their employees that they had a third, silent partner in the business—a programmer Tomer had met after posting an ad in an online forum. But Beit Oridan's staff knew little about him, other than that he handled the technical infrastructure of the company, part of which he outsourced to contractors in Romania. To Oz, the setup didn't seem out of keeping with the call center industry. The Taggart brothers ran the day-to-day operations without drama. That is, until July 2006, when Oz returned from a vacation to discover that Boaz had been ousted from the business with no explanation. Tomer took sole control, running the operation predominantly from the United States.

Boaz's departure did nothing to slow the company's growth. As the staff ballooned, Oz and Berkman recruited friends to work with them, extolling the flexible shifts and salaries generally about 15 percent higher than other call center jobs in Israel.

Then, one afternoon in 2007, a chat message popped up on Moran Oz's computer screen:

I'm your boss now. From now on you report to me.

The message came from one Paul Le Roux, a name Oz had never heard before. He could reasonably infer that Le Roux was the rumored third partner. It was less clear why, without explanation or pleasantries, he had suddenly reached out.

I have to talk to Tomer, Oz responded.

Le Roux told him that Tomer was out.

Oz immediately called Taggart, who confirmed that he was stepping aside for his formerly silent partner, a South African programmer living in the Philippines. When Oz asked him why, he said only that he had been working too hard and wanted to see his kids grow up.

The whole thing was unnerving, but Oz wasn't eager to jump ship. At first the management change did little to alter the atmosphere in Jerusalem, where the company had grown to twenty people. Oz and Berkman were now essentially running the operation, both making good money. What difference did it make who signed the checks?

Le Roux conducted almost all his business over email and the company's chat system, in a gruff style devoid of small talk. He didn't joke, and he never asked questions about the lives of his employees, or offered up any information regarding his own. He was more concerned about security than Boaz or Tomer had been, insisting that Oz and Berkman encrypt their hard drives. But otherwise, as far as Oz was concerned, a boss was a boss.

A few months later, Le Roux announced that he wanted to meet Oz and Berkman in person, in the Philippines. They flew business class via Hong Kong to Manila. A driver fetched them from the airport and deposited them at a luxury condo located next to a synagogue. That night they met Le Roux for the first time at the Hard Rock Cafe in a mall in Makati City, in central Manila.

They had little idea what to expect. They'd been unable to find any photos of—or even references to—their boss online. When he arrived they immediately noted his size; Le Roux was rotund and lumbering, around six feet tall, with an enormous head and the bearing of a man who didn't regret his bulk. More striking than his size was the slovenly dress of their supposedly high-rolling boss. As nearly all employees who met Le Roux face-to-face discovered, he rarely deviated from a uniform of shorts, T-shirt, and flip-flops. His employees often mocked Le Roux's appearance behind his back, not realizing how he played it to his advantage, disarming expectations. "I'm not saying he looks like that on purpose," one employee later said. "But nobody has ever thought the first time they met him that he runs a global criminal empire."

He was in his late thirties but looked younger, his short hair dyed an unnatural blond. To Oz he seemed affable enough in person, in an offensive sort of way. "These Jews can't eat any of this!" Le Roux joked with the waitress. "Just get them some chips."

When it came to business, however, Le Roux projected confidence and control. He explained to Oz and Berkman that he'd originally based the company in the Philippines, in 2004, to avoid taxes. Once there, he'd discovered the country's thriving call center business and started one for RX Limited, called Dial Magic, to cold-call potential customers, enticing them to go online and order prescriptions from RX Limited sites. He groused about his difficulty finding competent managers; the locals were "monkeys" who couldn't handle the responsibility. Now, with his operation expanding, he wanted Oz and Berkman to find job candidates in

Israel who would transfer to Manila. That, it seemed, was the extent of what Le Roux had needed to discuss with the pair in person. Oz and Berkman flew home with recruitment added to their duties.

Finding Israelis willing to move to the Philippines proved easy enough. Many of Beit Oridan's employees were young and single, and keen for an adventure in a country where their salary would go twice as far. The first few transplants didn't take, however. "We sent three managers," Oz said. "One was just to establish the customer service center—renting the location, creating all the infrastructure. After a month he came back. The second one was the same, it didn't work out, I didn't know why." Finally, Oz and Berkman sent Levi Kugel, a blond Israeli American whose first love was playing guitar and who had been hired by Berkman in Jerusalem. Soon after Kugel arrived in Manila, word came back to Oz that they'd found the kind of manager that Le Roux had been seeking. "It was love at first sight," Oz said. "Levi was calling the shots in the Philippines after a short time."

From there, the Israel-to-Philippines pipeline rapidly expanded, fueling Le Roux's exploding call center business. "My understanding was that this was all legal," said Yehuda Ben-Dor, an Israeli American whose experience typified many of the Israelis. "There was nothing fishy about it." Ben-Dor had been living in Tel Aviv when he answered an ad for work in the call center run by Oz and Berkman. He took the job, moved up to manager, and then was asked if he wanted to run a call center in the Philippines. "The thing with Paul's company was that the attrition rate was pretty high, people come and go, and he was always looking for new people. I was the next guy, so to speak. I didn't know anything about the Philippines at that time."

Within a few days of arriving in Manila, Ben-Dor found himself overseeing ten call centers with more than a thousand employees. The epicenter of Le Roux's business was located on the fourteenth floor of the BDO building, a shimmering glass tower in Makati. The open office was an expanse of connected desks, with fifty to sixty Filipino representatives sitting side by side on headsets, hustling to earn a $2 or $3 commission on each drug sale. On the wall was a large map of the United States, individual states labeled with the drugs that could be shipped to and from each.

Most employees rarely saw or heard from Le Roux. Ben-Dor said that in nearly two years working for him, he saw his boss only a handful of times—and remembered the first time clearly. "He called me up and asked me to just come on over to his condo," Ben-Dor said. There he found Le Roux sitting alone at a desk in a massive, largely empty space, flanked by racks of servers. Le Roux dispensed with greetings.

"How's it going?" he asked.

"Good," Ben-Dor told him. He began rattling off numbers, eager to prove that the call centers were performing well.

Le Roux cut him off. "Well, let me know if you need anything," he said.

Ben-Dor's first meeting with the boss who had moved him to the Philippines, housed him, and placed him in charge of a thousand people had lasted five minutes. "You called me all the way over here to tell me that?" he said.

"Yeah," Le Roux told him. "I just wanted to meet you."

Le Roux continued to stay away from Israel, but occasionally requested to speak face-to-face with Oz and Berkman on important topics. In October 2008, he ordered the pair back to Manila for a second meeting. This time he informed them that he would be expanding his operations in Israel. The business was growing faster than his Philippine centers could handle, and he wanted Oz and Berkman to open a new call center in Tel Aviv. "It's time to take responsibility," Le Roux told them, before sending them home to begin hiring immediately. "Money," he said, "is not an issue."

5

The Investigators

*2008 . . . Operation Checkmate slows to a crawl . . . Le Roux all the
way down . . . Tracking a ghost . . . A tip from Hong Kong . . . A river of
money*

O peration Checkmate was proving much more like a chess
match than Kimberly Brill and Steven Holdren had originally anticipated: drawn out, with attacks and counters, and an
opponent thinking several moves ahead. Sitting in their respective
cubicles in the Minneapolis DEA's diversion unit, they combed
through what felt like endless dumps of data—company filings,
shipping records, website registrations—and filled government-
issue five-by-seven notebooks with charts and lines, trying to arrange the scraps of what they found into a narrative. By mid-2008,
RX Limited was essentially their full-time job. "We just went at it
from start of shift till the end," Holdren said. And after the end,
too: At home, the case rattled around in their brains. Brill often
found herself back at her laptop long after she put her two young
children to bed, plotting out strategy and making late-night calls
to time zones around the world. The deeper they immersed themselves into RX Limited's operation, the more elaborate the technical architecture they found, and the more calculating the people—or
person—behind it began to seem.

As months and then years passed, Brill and Holdren kept order-ing drugs. Controlled buys, they knew, would anchor any eventual prosecution. They were struck by how easy it was. RX Limited websites operated like any online store: Customers placed the drugs they wanted into a virtual shopping cart and then "checked out." They filled out the surveys with whatever came to mind, and paid with real credit cards. (Unlike on the more anonymous layers of the Internet that would later become known as the Dark Web, customers didn't require any special software or online currency to buy drugs.) Two days later, the box would arrive.

But there was one quirk to the system: The investigators noticed that when Brill's alter ego Sarah Johnson checked out at an RX Limited site like SpeedyRX.com, her browser suddenly "redirected," or switched locations, to another site called Cartadmin.com. The same thing happened on every other RX Limited–related site. In programming parlance, Cartadmin.com and a second site called SystemsCA.com constituted the "back end" of the RX Limited system, the part that processed transactions. These sites, Brill and Holdren realized, were what linked hundreds of RX Limited af-filiate websites together. If an affiliate used Cartadmin.com or SystemsCA.com as its back end, Brill and Holdren now knew that it belonged to Le Roux.

To understand what this all added up to, the investigators had to travel well past the limits of their DEA training and plunge into the technical thicket of the Internet. Their case against Le Roux would be built in part on an understanding of the Internet's basic ar-chitecture, namely that every computer connected to the network— and every website hosted on it—is assigned a unique number called an Internet Protocol, or IP, address. When Brill typed "Cartadmin .com" into a browser, her request traveled to a domain name server—the Internet equivalent of a telephone directory—which spent a fraction of a second looking up Cartadmin.com and re-turning an IP address for its location. The Internet's directories are managed, in turn, by an international body called ICANN, short for the Internet Corporation for Assigned Names and Numbers.

ICANN controls the distribution of IP addresses, and accredits companies called domain name registrars to sell unique website names like Cartadmin.com and keep records of who owns them.

All these technical minutiae were about to become critical to Brill and Holdren's understanding of Le Roux. Using an open-source service called DomainTools, they conducted background checks on the websites connected to RX Limited, tracing their IP addresses and the histories of who had registered them and where. The back-end sites, Cartadmin.com and SystemsCA.com, traced to a domain registrar operating in the Philippines called ABSystems. That in and of itself wasn't particularly illuminating—ICANN accredits registrars all over the world. But there was something off about ABSystems. For one thing, the company didn't seem to offer a way for the public to actually purchase domains. ABSystems' own web page was empty except for a login page. Wondering what other websites were connected to the company, the investigators flipped around their search, querying DomainTools for every site registered through ABSystems. The list was astonishing:

rx-24-usa.com

rx-2u-usa.com

rx-4discount-usa.com

rx-billing.com

rx-carisoprodol.com

rx-checkout-usa.com

rx-drugstore-meds.com

rx-drugstore-usa.com

rx-fioricet-usa.com

rx-limited.com

rx-listings-usa.com

rx-med-usa.com

rx-meds-usa.com

rx-overnightpharmacy-usa.com

rx-pain-pill.com

rx-pain-pills.com

rx-pharmacy-usa.com

rx-pharmacymeds.com

rx-pill-pharmacy.com

rx-pills-online-usa.com

rx-pillstore-usa.com

rx-prescription-medications-usa.com

rx-results-usa.com

rx-reviews-usa.com

rx-s-usa.com

rx-save-usa.com

rx-store-usa.com

rx-supplier-usa.com

rx-tramadol.com

rx-usa.net

rx-viagra-online-usa.com

rx1-onlinepharmacy.net

rx24seven.com

rx2day-usa.com

rx43-usa.com

rx4cheap-usa.com

rxacc-usa.com

rxactiveusa.com

rxaffiliatenetwork-usa.com

rxarenausa.com

rxbarn-usa.com

rxbestlife-usa.com

rxbiz-usa.com

rxcashcow.com

rxcheapdrugstore-usa.com

rxcheaperdrugs.com

rxclinic.net

rxdealsforyou.com

rxdepot-usa.com

rxdirectdrugs-usa.com

rxdomeusa.com

rxdominicana-usa.com

rxdrugdeals-usa.com

rxdrugplus-usa.com

rxdrugsonline-usa.com

rxdrugstore-meds.com

rxdrugstore-online-usa.com

rxdrugstore-usa.com

rxdrugstore24.com

rxeasybill.com

rxfamily-usa.com

rxfastmeds-usa.com

rxfiller.com

rxfleetusa.com

rxherousa.com

rxhint-usa.com

rxhome247.com

rxinfinity-usa.com

. . . and on and on, an endless variation of drug-related domain names. Almost every website registered to ABSystems was an online pharmacy. And nearly every affiliate Brill and Holdren had connected to RX Limited could be found on the list.

At first they assumed that RX Limited must somehow be collaborating with ABSystems. The agents issued a subpoena to ICANN and received a pile of documents outlining everything the organization knew about it. The company was based at an address in Manila, on the fourteenth floor of the BDO building in Makati City, the same address as RX Limited's main call center. The name on the account was Le Roux's. Staring at the records, they finally understood why that name had kept popping up, and how RX Limited maintained so many prescription drug sites. RX Limited and ABSystems weren't collaborating. They were one and the same, and they were both creations of Paul Le Roux. He wasn't buying website domains, he was minting them himself, by the thousands.

He had built what the corporate world would call a "fully integrated vertical business"—a structure in which he controlled every layer, from top to bottom—and hijacked the very architecture of the Internet to do it. The technical acumen behind it was frightening. "We knew he was a legitimate drug kingpin," Holdren said. "He wasn't a low-level or mid-level guy that we were trying to turn into something bigger. We knew he was the real deal. And he was a genius to put this all together."

To build a case that could be prosecuted, though, Brill and Holdren needed more than just an understanding of Le Roux's brilliance. They needed to establish how the whole thing broke American laws, and then link it to the undercover buys being delivered to their nearby FedEx mail drop. Much of the information the investigators had gathered so far, like the FedEx records requests, required only so-called administrative subpoenas, which the DEA could issue without a court order. Now it was time to go get search warrants.

Poring over the list of domain names controlled by ABSystems, they noticed one nonpharmaceutical website, E4M.net—the home of Le Roux's encryption software in the early 2000s. A search on the site's history turned up another email address for Le Roux: paulca@rocketmail.com. Brill and Holdren, with the help of a federal prosecutor in Minneapolis, convinced a judge to sign off on a warrant for Rocketmail, owned by the Internet giant Yahoo!. The warrant enabled them to capture the previous thirty days' worth of messages from the account. The emails confirmed their suspicion that Le Roux was directing every aspect of the business: making arrangements with credit card processors, manipulating a web of international bank accounts, and using other people's identities to register shell companies around the world. But many of the threads led to yet another email account, pleroux@server73.net. There, the trail went cold. Server73.net, unlike a Gmail or Hotmail account, wasn't a commercial email service to which the investigators could send warrants. Instead it was a private, secure email program that Paul Le Roux appeared to have built himself, much as he had built ABSystems. The investigators had no way to tap into it. "Every time we turned a corner he controlled every aspect of this," Holdren said.

Fortunately, not all of Le Roux's employees were so sophisticated, or so cautious. Many of his correspondents *were* using commercial addresses, and eventually Brill and Holdren obtained warrants on more than twenty separate email accounts. Each produced hundreds and sometimes thousands of messages to sort through.

One particular address, ron_oz11@hotmail.com, seemed to be a hub for communications with many of the pharmacies, and the investigators concluded it belonged to the primary operations manager for RX Limited, a man who went by the names Ron Martin and Ron Oz. The Oz email address and several others— including ones under the names Levi Kugel and Alon Berkman— traced to Israel, where the investigators determined Le Roux was running a customer service center for RX Limited. Most of Oz's email traffic involved problems with shipments, questions about pricing, and other routine correspondence with doctors and pharmacies eager to expand the number of orders they prescribed and shipped.

Oz's responses evinced what appeared to Brill and Holdren to be a detailed knowledge of American law, and he was careful to assert the legality of the operation in writing. "We are happy to know you are interested in joining us in our company," he wrote to a pharmacist in mid-2008. "All products are non-controlled and can only ship to states where our business type is legal. . . . For example we do not work with Florida, Kentucky, Nevada, and Arkansas at all due to local state laws."

"I really love filing these rxs," one pharmacist wrote to Oz, explaining that he had a paralyzed son to support. "If this is going to be a long term thing I need to get the rxs faster off the computer. . . .

I read on your site that this partner filling is 100% legal and we follow all the rules of the fillers state. I hope that is true. IS IT?"

"Of course it is 100% legal, we are in this business for 4 years," Oz replied. "WE ARE NOT FILLING CONTROLLED. Please stop sending so many emails."

While Brill and Holdren were knee deep in IP addresses and domain registrars, Kent Bailey had continued chasing down international leads from SOD headquarters in Virginia. Now, with Brill and Holdren firmly establishing Paul Le Roux as the target atop the organization, he started trying to build a profile of the kingpin they were dealing with. Bailey turned to a DEA analyst based in South America whom he had come to trust on other cases, asking her to assemble a portrait of the mysterious man behind RX Limited.

Despite the breadth of his operation, Le Roux had managed to remain something of a ghost. Not so much as a single photo of him could be easily found on the Internet. But Bailey's analyst discovered that Le Roux *had* surfaced publicly, just over a year before, in the strangest of circumstances: a July 2007 article in the American political newspaper *The Hill*. The story mentioned Le Roux in a brief anecdote illustrating how individuals, not just organizations, were lobbying Congress for their own causes. After describing an American businessman's lobbying to avoid government regulation on his Texas property, the reporters turned to Le Roux: "Another wealthy businessman is close to securing government land," they wrote. "But this real estate is in Zimbabwe, and the case possesses elements of international intrigue." Le Roux had reportedly hired Dickens & Madson, a Montreal-based political consulting and lobbying firm, to pressure the American government into helping him obtain a ninety-nine-year lease on farmland in Zimbabwe. "Le Roux is a wealthy businessman who was born in the nation when it was called Rhodesia," they wrote. "He now holds Australian and South African citizenship but says he wants 'to set down roots' in Zimbabwe."

Le Roux's stated aim, according to the article, was to bring white farmers back to Zimbabwe to work land they had been driven off by the administration of Robert Mugabe. A brief quote from Le Roux framed the effort as a kind of reverse reparations effort for white farmers. "We want recognition that injustice was done in the past and that the land reform program corrects that," Le Roux told the reporters. The lobbyist at Dickens & Madson was a man named Ari Ben-Menashe, described as "a former Israeli intelligence agent with personal ties to Mugabe." He planned to lobby Congress and "possibly the White House" in an effort to bring Le Roux's plans to fruition. What had come of the land effort wasn't clear, but the article at least provided Bailey and his analyst with some basic background on their target.

When Bailey's analyst finally unearthed a photo of Le Roux, they weren't sure what to make of him. He had been captured by a camera while passing through U.S. Customs on the island of Guam, making a flight connection. He didn't exactly look the part of an international criminal mogul: a heavyset man with dyed-blond hair, traveling in a T-shirt and shorts. The DEA analyst eventually turned up a second photo, buried in the newsletter of the exclusive Manila Polo Club, patronized by the city's wealthy and powerful. Pictured with his wife, a Dutch woman of Chinese descent named Lilian, he was identified in the caption as an "online commerce entrepreneur."

Beyond that, Le Roux remained a cipher.

In mid-2008, however, Bailey lucked into a tip. An employee inside a major bank in Hong Kong happened to notice a series of suspicious bank transfers between generic-sounding companies— with names like GX Port, Vischnu Ltd., East Asia Escrow, Southern Ace, Ajax Technology, and Quantcom Commerce—and ten pharmacies inside the United States. The tipster passed the information to the Hong Kong drug enforcement division, which forwarded it to the Hong Kong office of the American DEA. Eventually it found its way onto Bailey's desk in Virginia. Immediately he knew that he was looking at the financial skeleton of Le Roux's organization. "We had identified the vast majority of those pharmacies through the RX Limited shipping account," Bailey said. "Nine of those ten pharmacies were a hit." For the first time, they had a window into the organization's bank accounts.

To open it, the investigators needed legal backup. Most DEA investigations, when they begin to bear fruit, are placed in the hands of a federal prosecutor from the closest U.S. Attorney's office. For Brill and Holdren that office was a few blocks away, in downtown Minneapolis. They had enlisted an attorney there to file for their initial court-ordered search warrants. But when offered a chance to take on the larger case, the prosecutors balked. The office had recently obtained a conviction in a case against an online pharmacy a fraction of the size of RX Limited, and the case had been a huge resource drain. (The pharmacy's owner had been represented by the prominent Minneapolis defense attorney Joseph Friedberg.) "They thought it was too labor intensive, they didn't have the expertise," Bailey said.

Instead, the investigators turned to a relatively obscure section of the Department of Justice in Washington called the Consumer Protection Branch. Largely responsible for ensuring the safety of products purchased by Americans, the branch had a small office dedicated to pharmaceuticals, prosecuting cases of misbranded drugs and pharmaceutical fraud. A senior litigator there named Linda Marks agreed to take on RX Limited.

With a prosecutor on board, the investigators could now file for legal records from foreign governments, requests that had to pass through the Department of Justice. They issued requests for international financial records through the Treasury Department's Financial Crimes Enforcement Network, or FinCEN, which has standing arrangements with certain countries to share information. And they sent subpoenas to the Federal Reserve Bank of New York, which manages the bulk of bank-to-bank wire transfers going to and from the United States, through a program called Fedwire. Their first targets were the banks in Hong Kong that had been wiring money to American pharmacies and doctors.

Even after everything they'd learned, when the data came back they were shocked anew. Bailey estimated that, conservatively, RX Limited was pulling in $250 million a year in revenues—roughly the same as Facebook. In just the Hong Kong bank accounts they'd been able to locate, Le Roux was holding over $50 million in cash in accounts tied to companies like Ajax Technology and Southern Ace. The difference between what Le Roux was making and how much cash he had in the bank meant that a river of money was passing through the accounts and ending up somewhere else. Where, they didn't know yet.

6

The Mercenaries

2007–2009 . . . Lachlan McConnell and the gold . . . Dave Smith and a history of violence . . . Felix Klaussen finds a job . . . The life of a Le Roux mercenary

For Paul Le Roux, Hong Kong's glittering metropolis offered the perfect hub through which to transit—and transform—hundreds of millions of dollars in illicit proceeds. As a global financial nerve center, it was the perfect place to change his virtual cash into something more tangible, obscuring its origins. The quasi-independent Chinese city had a reputation for looking the other way when it came to cleaning money. Under Hong Kong's lax regulations, Le Roux could set up an endless number of corporate shells through which to funnel the money he was extracting from the pockets of American drug consumers.

Lachlan McConnell, a fifty-year-old Canadian with thinning hair and a résumé lined with security jobs, often found himself at the terminus of Le Roux's river of cash. As one of Le Roux's employees on the ground in Hong Kong, he was responsible for what those in his line of work called "asset protection." "It seemed like a constant stream of money coming in from the U.S.," he recalled. "Money turned into gold." Hundreds of bars of gold. Thousands of pounds of gold. Tens of millions of dollars' worth of gold. Money that arrived into accounts for companies Le Roux controlled—Ajax Technology, Southern Ace, East Asia Escrow, and at least two dozen others—was wired to the local subsidiary of Metalor, a Swiss precious metals dealer, to purchase gold bars. That's where McConnell's role began. From his home in Manila, he flew to Hong Kong to supervise runners who picked up the gold, along with an occasional diamond purchase, and transported it to any of several properties Le Roux owned in the city. Each stash house was outfitted with a large safe. From there, the gold would often be packed in military-style black plastic trunks called Pelican cases and moved to the waterfront, to be loaded onto a yacht bound for the Philippines, where Le Roux was based. Sometimes an entire safe might make the trip. On other occasions, the cases were driven to the airport and handed to a pilot to carry, unchecked by customs, on board Le Roux's jet. McConnell didn't inquire about the destination.

Lachlan McConnell was one of the players on a darker side of Paul Le Roux's business, one stocked with modern soldiers of fortune, mercenaries who operated outside the digital realm, in the world of atoms, metal, and flesh. Employees on any one side of Le Roux's multifaceted operation were told little or nothing about those on the other. For people like Moran Oz, who subsisted in the virtual world of RX Limited, whispers of Le Roux's other endeavors amounted to puffed-up rumors and scare stories. For the likes of McConnell, on the gold-and-guns side of the business, RX Limited was just an abstract explanation for how his boss made money. The mercenaries' modus operandi was on the ground, providing the manpower and muscle for a staggering array of projects around the globe.

McConnell joined Le Roux's business in 2008, hired by a friend and British ex-soldier named Dave Smith, who told him only that the client was "a very wealthy individual who had multiple businesses, including but not limited to the world's largest pharmacy." McConnell had lived in the Philippines for a half dozen years, bouncing around in the risk-management industry—a catchall label for everything from guarding industrial sites to personal protection for VIPs to corporate surveillance. He'd gotten his start in his native Canada, working protection details for politicians and diamond dealers, before moving to L.A., where he'd provided security for the likes of Sylvester Stallone and O. J. Simpson. Although he'd never served in the military, McConnell was fluent enough in its lingo—"mission planning," "comms"—that colleagues often assumed he had. He arrived in Manila in the late 1990s, on a contract to oversee protection for a dam project, and stayed. He'd met Dave Smith while both were working for a Manila-based security outfit. Smith left the company under acrimonious circumstances around 2005, and then resurfaced not long after in the employ of Le Roux. How the job came about exactly, McConnell was never sure. But in short order Smith had become Le Roux's de facto head of security and right-hand man, and he offered to bring McConnell on board. Le Roux wasn't just looking for people to help him wash his money. He was looking to expand his criminal horizons.

Smith himself epitomized the kind of untethered international mercenary he would soon hire to fill Le Roux's ranks. He hailed from Northern Ireland and had served in the British military—often he claimed to have been a member of the Special Air Services, an elite special forces unit. "I was in the Regiment," he would say, employing the SAS shorthand. Some Le Roux employees doubted it, but Smith at least carried himself like a well-trained military officer, and his work history seemed to back it up. So, too, did the scars crisscrossing his upper torso, which he said he'd gotten fighting in the Falklands War. He'd spent time in the United States, where he married an American, working as a SWAT team trainer in Boston. "Dave bred loyalty," said Scott Stammers, another contractor Smith brought into Le Roux's organization. "I kicked down doors with Dave. Dave had two sayings: 'Train how you fight' and 'Smooth is fast.'"

In the late nineties, Smith joined the security contracting circuit, working for a series of unusual clients. In 1998, he surfaced in Liberia as a military adviser to Charles Taylor, the country's notorious warlord-president. Smith grew particularly close to Taylor's son, Chucky, mentoring him in combat strategy as the younger Taylor worked to build his own independent military force. After the unit was involved in the slaughter of a rival political group, Smith disappeared from the country. (Charles Taylor was later convicted of crimes against humanity by an international court in The Hague, while Chucky landed in an American prison, convicted of torture.) A few years later, Smith turned up in Iraq as a contractor for Crucible, a United Kingdom–based outfit filling one of the countless security gaps opened by the American invasion. "The difference between a contractor and a military guy is I'm getting paid five times as much," Smith told *Esquire* in a 2004 story on contractors working in Iraq. "And I can tell you to get fucked if I don't want to do it." Along the way, Smith had left his wife and relocated to Manila, where he eventually quit the war zones and started working for Paul Le Roux.

Smith's nominal job was head of security, charged with hiring muscle like McConnell and using it to project his bosses' authority. But the scope of duties sometimes felt limitless. McConnell's first task was to oversee the construction of a shooting range Le Roux was building in Manila, connected to a gun shop he owned called Red White & Blue Arms. A month later, seemingly satisfied with McConnell's work, Smith began dispatching him on international missions. "Dave gave me instructions on what needed to be done," McConnell said. "It was pretty harmless stuff. Good money, working for a rich guy." Le Roux had enlisted what he called "dummies"—family members and associates with clean criminal records he could use as proxies—to register his companies under their own names, or open bank accounts. McConnell's job was to keep an eye on the dummies and make sure they went where they were told. Most were Filipino, but Le Roux also counted among his dummies an out-of-work Zimbabwean named Robson Tandanayi, and an elderly South African man named Edgar van Tonder. "It was just babysitting," McConnell said.

McConnell was soon trusted enough to take orders directly from Le Roux, whom he found to be overbearing but otherwise tolerable. "He was impatient in emails, strict," McConnell said. "He would say, 'This is a fuckup, do what you can do to straighten people out.' Two or three times he sent me an email to say you can't do it this way or that way. Or 'Hurry up.' He wanted things bang bang bang. He micromanaged everything." Occasionally they would meet face-to-face in Manila, and at first McConnell saw little in Le Roux's demeanor to raise alarms. "I found him to be a really nice guy," he said. Le Roux was clearly a wealthy man, but rarely seemed to flaunt it. "He lived in expensive houses in exclusive areas, but he didn't live extravagantly. He would travel in flip-flops and shorts, like a bum."

McConnell's Hong Kong duties eventually expanded to include obtaining and transporting gold around the city, and out of it. Le Roux was bringing in $6 million a week from his U.S. pharmacy operation, Smith told McConnell, and needed to convert it to hard assets. "Initially Paul's thought was to hire a company like Brink's to pick up the gold and move it around," McConnell said. "I said, 'Let's go low profile and move it ourselves.'"

McConnell wasn't oblivious to the fact that he was, at the least, working for someone operating on the edge of the law. The tentacles of Le Roux's empire spread so far that he couldn't see their endpoints, but he knew that they included gold mining and logging projects in Africa, and that his boss owned properties in Asia and Australia. There was talk of darker businesses—that some of the money flowing through Hong Kong was being laundered on behalf of Colombian or Brazilian cartels, or that Le Roux was involved in hardcore drug trafficking himself. "I did know what I was getting into when I started, in terms of the secrecy involved and the precious cargo being moved," McConnell said. "I'm not a stupid person. In some ways there were things that were probably illegal, but I didn't really pay attention. He kept everything so compartmentalized. I heard rumors, but I didn't consider them to be valid without one hundred percent proof."

Some combination of financial necessity and geographical proximity explained why most people drifted into Le Roux's organization, often with little conception of the devil's bargain they were making by signing up. So it was with Felix Klaussen. At the moment he crossed paths with Le Roux in 2007, Klaussen was trying to keep alive a dream life in the Philippines. A former navy diver from Europe, he was living in a condo on Baloy Beach, a glorious stretch of sand in Barrio Barretto, on the west coast of the country's main island. The town had for decades served as an off-duty playground for the sailors at Subic Bay, a U.S. naval base a few miles south. The Americans decommissioned the base in 1992, but the area still maintained a kind of burned-out Fleet Week atmosphere, attracting a clientele of sun- and sin-seeking expats, many of them retired military. The main thoroughfare included the upscale Subic Bay Yacht Club, along with seedier stops like the Wet Spot and Coco Lips, offering cold beer and "bar girls," the Philippine euphemism for government-tolerated prostitution.

Klaussen resided largely on the sun-seeking end of the spectrum. He'd first fallen in love with the Philippines in the late 1990s, when he worked as a wreck diver in Subic, escorting tourists out to see the scuttled USS New York just offshore. In his youth he'd been a champion swimmer, talented enough to have a shot at the Olympic team. But his motivation had come more from a hard-driving father than from any inner desire, and at eighteen Klaussen gave up swimming and joined the Navy, training as a diver whose duties included disabling sea mines. After leaving the military he'd drifted to Baloy, where a friend from his hometown owned a resort.

Klaussen returned home from the Philippines a few years later and took a desk job at a pharmaceutical company, thinking he would settle into a staid, predictable life. Then, in what he later came to view as a bit of twisted fortune, a motorcycle wreck in 2003 left him hospitalized with titanium rods in one arm. Fortunately, his home country had universal healthcare. Coverage included not just the surgery but his salary: fully paid for the first year after the accident, then 80 percent the second, 60 percent the third. Klaussen figured he could make the money last back in the Philippines. So he headed back to Baloy to spend his days lounging on the government's dime.

By late 2006, the end of this arrangement was on the horizon. But this time Klaussen, now in his late twenties, was determined not to slink back home. He'd fallen in love with a Filipina woman he would eventually marry, and would need a local job if he wanted to stay. An old friend who also lived in the Philippines, Chris De Meyer, who had served in the French Foreign Legion, told Klaussen he was working security for a rich man in Manila. The boss was some kind of Internet mogul whom De Meyer knew only as Johan. "Ask him if he could use anyone else," Klaussen told his friend.

A few months later, Klaussen was summoned to meet Dave Smith. He made the three-hour drive to Manila and they convened at Sid's, an expat-friendly pub owned by Johan just outside the city's red-light district. Smith asked Klaussen a few questions about his military and work experience, and seemed particularly intrigued that Klaussen had once run a home renovation business. "Okay, tomorrow let's go see Johan," Smith told him.

The next morning Klaussen arrived at Salcedo Park Twin Towers in Makati City, the high-end business quarter. He took the elevator up to the penthouse, where three guards manning the door searched him for weapons. *What the hell is this guy all about?* Klaussen thought to himself. Inside, Smith introduced him to Johan, a heavyset man with dyed-blond hair, sloppily dressed. In the room there were a table with four chairs, a sofa, a plasma TV. The rest of the condo was largely unfurnished, and appeared uninhabited. "I started to realize that this guy is ready to pack every single moment of the day," Klaussen said. "That's why he lives like that. He's just ready to pack up and go."

Johan sat down and said a few words of greeting, and then immediately switched to business. They spoke briefly about Klaussen's military experience and his knowledge of home construction. "Good," Johan said. "Tomorrow you are flying to Port Moresby, Papua New Guinea. Is that okay?"

Klaussen had never heard of Port Moresby. But he was a man blessed with a preternatural mix of optimism and self-confidence. Besides, he needed the work, and the abruptness of Johan's offer carried with it a sense of adventure. *Why not?* he figured. He agreed to go.

That night, while packing, he did what Internet research he could, discovering that Papua New Guinea was among the most dangerous countries in the world. His duties there, Smith had told him, involved shopping for houses with ocean access in the small town of Madang, on the country's northeastern coast. He flew to Port Moresby, caught a smaller plane out to Madang, and found a dodgy hotel within the budget Smith had given him: 80 U.S. dollars a day. Then he set off in search of a waterfront house to meet Johan's specifications. "I had to report back to him, tell him the price, show him pictures of the property," he said. "Give him the local real estate guy's contact details, and then his lawyer took care of the rest. So basically that was it, very easy, very simple, no nonsense job. But because I was in construction he expected me to check everything properly, that the property was in good condition. Which made sense, in a way."

When Klaussen came back to the Philippines, Johan hired him on a $4,000 monthly salary—enough to afford an upscale lifestyle in Manila. Periodically Smith would call with a job, or Johan himself would request Klaussen's presence at the Salcedo Park penthouse, and he'd be sent off on a new mission. For the first few months his tasks followed the same blueprint as the trip to Papua New Guinea: Catch a flight, shop for waterfront property, report back, fly home. Klaussen picked out a house on a golf course in Phuket, Thailand. He flew to Vietnam to do the same in Da Nang.

Like McConnell, Klaussen quickly realized that Johan was more than just a successful Internet businessman. He was never explicitly told why the organization required so many oceanfront properties. But it wasn't hard to see that the houses were being purchased in the names of shell companies, or by people he never interacted with and wasn't sure were even real. Ostensibly the homes served as a base for employees, who could stay at them if Johan sent them to conduct some business in the country. In some cases, the employees were simply parked in them, ready to be activated when needed. "I knew one Filipino who was staying in a house with a swimming pool by himself in Mombasa for like two or three years, basically doing nothing," Klaussen said. "Getting a salary on standby. 'Go find out this, go to the port, ask the price for a shipment for that small stupid thing.'" But it dawned on Klaussen that the properties served a second purpose, as safe houses to which Johan himself could escape. "You've got all these properties all over the world where you can just drop somebody 500 meters from the coast by boat," Klaussen said. "He's under the radar, nobody is going to find him in that place. Who was going to look for him in Papua New Guinea?"

By late 2008 Lachlan McConnell's own duties expanded to involve a series of missions across Africa. Le Roux had launched a patchwork of logging and gold-buying operations spanning the continent, requiring a constant rotation of security teams overseen by Dave Smith. In search of raw, untraceable gold to buy locally, transport across borders, and then sell at a profit—disguising his own money in the process—Le Roux sent his personnel to procure it on the black market in cities like Accra, in Ghana, and Brazzaville, in the Republic of the Congo. Other times he sent them deep into the jungle to buy from the source, small local mines. McConnell found himself working alongside a shifting cast of ex-military journeymen, hired by Smith and dispatched to lawless regions, carrying in bags of cash and transporting out crates of gold that eventually made their way to Hong Kong.

The stories of how these mercenaries ended up in Le Roux's organization often followed the same pattern. They were former soldiers who had plied the waters of the international private security circuit, flush with gigs during the height of the Iraq and Afghanistan wars. As those conflicts wound down, the men suddenly found their military training a surplus commodity in a flooded labor market, just as a worldwide recession took hold. When they crossed paths with Dave Smith—or heard through their own networks that a rich man was paying decent rates for "gray area" jobs—they jumped at the chance put their skills to work somewhere other than a war zone. "Dave gave me a call and said he had work," recalled a Manila-based former U.S. Navy sailor who, after leaving the service, had worked for the same contractor as Smith in Iraq. "He said there's this South African guy, he's got a shitload of money and he wants to do all sorts of crazy shit. He's got businesses all over the place and he also mines gold. He said what he wanted to do was move some of his gold from a mine in Zimbabwe, and then get it to the Philippines and hopefully to Hong Kong to sell it to some rich buyers. I'm like, okay." The American met with Smith and Le Roux at the Mandarin Oriental hotel in Makati the next evening. "He asked a few questions, my background, did I like traveling," the contractor said. "The next day Dave said, 'You're in. You'll be on retainer and paid this much. You'll be on call with forty-eight hours' lead time, meaning you need to be on a plane forty-eight hours later.'"

Many of these recruits knew little or nothing about Le Roux or his business. Often they never met him at all, receiving instructions through Smith. Some knew the organization they were working for by the name of one of Le Roux's shell companies—Southern Ace or La Plata Trading—while others were hired by Echelon Associates, a security company that served as a front for Smith's teams. Most referred to their employer simply as "The Company." When they did encounter the boss, it was often under another identity. Le Roux had a fake Zimbabwean birth certificate and passport under the name John Bernard Bowlins, and another for a

Johan William Smit. Still another birth certificate listed his identity as William Vaughn. Some people called him Benny, others Johan, John, or just Boss.

"I was forwarded an email from a friend that was working in Iraq," a South African contractor named Marcus said. "They were looking for snipers and close-protection personnel. I sent my CV and was flown to Manila a week later. When I corresponded with him in the beginning, he used the name Alexander. When I met him, he introduced himself as John. I heard Filipinos talk about 'Boss Paul.' But then again, we all used pseudonyms in the Philippines."

Among the handful of Americans sometimes paired with McConnell was a former U.S. Army soldier, Tim Vamvakias. Like many of the recruits, he had spent time in private contracting, in his case as a dog handler in the Helmand province of Afghanistan, embedded with a unit from the U.S. Army's 3rd Special Forces Group. When his diabetes flared up, the company had terminated him. Unemployed and temporarily homeless, he'd joined Le Roux's organization in 2008, connected through his former colleague, an Irish ex-soldier named John O'Donoghue. "He said he had some 'off the grid' and 'covert' security opportunities for me," Vamvakias said. "I was to update my open waters diving license and meet him in the Philippines for further info." After he was settled in, Vamvakias met with Smith in Manila, who told him they were providing security for an Internet mogul. "As far as I knew at the time it was a new security wing that was being formed," Vamvakias said, "comprised mostly of ex–Special Ops guys with combat experience ranging from U.S. Special Forces, British SAS, as well as ex–French Foreign Legion soldiers."

Vamvakias, in turn, recruited his friend Joseph Hunter, a decorated U.S. Army vet with the hulking body of an ultimate fighter. Vamvakias and Hunter had served in the military together for several years in the 1990s. Now, in 2008, they were both working under Dave Smith in the employ of Paul Le Roux.

In Manila, Smith often doled out salaries to the mercenaries in cash from his Infiniti SUV. "Everybody he had to pay had to come to the car, open the trunk," Klaussen said. "Put it in the brown paper bag, there you go. It was mental." The crews crisscrossed continents, from Vietnam to Ghana to Zambia to South Africa. One day they might be protecting a Le Roux employee who had arrived in Kinshasa carrying a duffel bag full of American cash; the next they might be crossing a border in a pickup with millions of dollars in gold hidden in the tailgate, on their way to a remote airstrip. A week later they could be in Malaysia, conducting surveillance on a wealthy executive. Le Roux's businesses seemed at times to be independent arms of some conglomerate larger than them all. He'd purchased timber concessions in Africa and Asia and deployed employees to supervise logging operations: teak logs out of the Democratic Republic of Congo, sold through La Plata Trading; tali logs in the neighboring Republic of the Congo under the banner of Martenius Trading.

Most of the men on the ground had little idea what it all added up to. "You have to understand: things were very compartmentalized," the American former sailor said. "There were times, many times, that one person would not know what the other was doing. To the point that you had no idea how many people are working on this particular contract, let alone that the person you are traveling with might have no idea what his particular mission was." It was a testament to Le Roux's penchant for secrecy in his businesses that Klaussen and McConnell, despite occupying roughly equivalent positions in the operation, never so much as met. There was only one person who maintained a picture of the entire operation in his head, and that was Paul Le Roux.

7

The Mastermind

1972–2005 . . . A young Paul Le Roux . . . Escape to London and Australia . . . Hanging out his shingle . . . Consumed by encryption . . . Divorced and broke . . . A life-changing discovery . . . A new venture

Everyone says that Paul Le Roux was a sweet kid. "Paulie was an utter delight as a baby and child and young man," a relative from his extended family recalled. "He was easygoing, a pure delight, happy, uncomplaining, undemanding, loving, and affectionate. He really was. I never knew what evil lay in him."

He was born on Christmas Eve, 1972, at Lady Rodwell Maternity Home in Bulawayo, in the country then called Rhodesia. His mother, Jill, was seventeen and had already decided to give him up for adoption. "You've disgraced your family, this cannot happen," her mother told her, according to one of Le Roux's half-siblings, born to Jill years later. The family was religious, and had little money. According to Le Roux family lore, the father was a soldier from South Africa who'd traveled to Rhodesia to fight in the Bush War, a fifteen-year conflict between forces of the country's white ruling minority and the black majority seeking liberation from it. Other family members recalled instead that Le Roux's father was Zimbabwean—and married—and had left for South Africa later.

Either way, Le Roux was born in a time when the shadow of violence had unmoored communities. "Life was lived in the moment," the relative said. Laws guarded the privacy of mothers who gave children up for adoption, allowing hospitals to issue short-form birth certificates containing only the adoptive parents' names. The "long certificate," containing the birth parents' information, was filed away and meant to be kept confidential. On Le Roux's long certificate, his first name was listed as "UNKNOWN." A month after the birth, an official addendum was added: "Child to be known in future as: Paul Calder Le Roux."

His adoptive parents, Paul Sr. and Judy Le Roux, had been unable to conceive. They had spent six years on adoption lists, enduring endless rounds of background investigations, requests for character references, visits from the welfare department. When Judy called family members to say that a baby boy had finally arrived for them, she was so overcome with emotion that her grandmother at first thought someone had died. They resolved not to tell the younger Paul that he had been adopted.

Paul Sr. worked as a manager at the Gaths and Shabanie asbestos mines, which at one point churned out 154,000 tons of the stuff a year. ("It's not the bad asbestos," said a childhood friend of Le Roux's. "You have the long fiber and the short fiber. We had the short fiber.") Paul Sr. had moved up the ladder of the mine, and the Le Roux family lived in a safe suburb, along a row of identical three-bedroom brick homes. Social life centered around the pool, bowling, and snooker tables at the Gaths Mine Club, and the young Le Roux was a friendly but quiet kid, uninterested in sports or typical boy antics. "I was in the neighborhood gang," the childhood friend said. "We were thugs, smoking and spray painting the walls and getting into trouble. He was maybe a little bit young, to be fair, but he was absolutely nothing like that." Le Roux lived in a disciplined, meticulous household but not a severe one. He was doted on by parents still grateful to have been given a child at all— much less two, when they were later able to adopt a girl.

The war finally sputtered to an end in 1980, and elections

brought Robert Mugabe to power as prime minister of the new Zimbabwe. The end of minority rule meant a new kind of status anxiety for a white community that had benefited from nearly a century of colonialism. But at least the violence had subsided. Le Roux's parents sent him away to boarding school for sixth and seventh grade, fearing the local education wasn't intensive enough for their precocious son. On weekends he would rotate between family members' homes. "He was fought over, everyone wanted him," the relative said. "Our grandparents worshipped the ground he walked on, honestly. I know this sounds like a fairy tale, but it's true." But Judy and Paul Sr. decided that they hadn't had kids in order never to see them, so they decided to relocate to South Africa in search of better schools. Krugersdorp, their new home forty kilometers outside of Johannesburg, was also a mining town, gold instead of asbestos. Life there was different, though. Paul Sr. was no longer a manager but a newcomer looking to establish his business.

The younger Paul Le Roux had grown tall, trim, and handsome in his teenage years. A decent but unmotivated student, he despised the idea of learning Afrikaans, compulsory in South African schools. He was not without friends, but projected an air of superiority that increased as he grew older. He derided the new countrymen at his high school as "halfwits and morons." In a sports-mad culture where a kid of his size was expected on the rugby pitch, he favored video games played on a console hooked up to the family TV.

According to his cousin Mathew Smith—no relation to Le Roux's later employee Dave Smith*—Le Roux earned his first computer by washing cars. From his initial glimpse at the screen, he was captivated by his ability to create worlds in code. He became "completely antisocial," Mathew remembered. "Every time we went there, he was always holed up in his room. I remember

* To avoid confusion, I will refer to Mathew Smith in most cases by his first name.

going in and seeing lines and lines of numbers." Never a discipline problem at home, Le Roux increasingly seemed to lump his family in with the ignorant people he perceived around him.

When he was sixteen, in an incident he would later recount to employees, the local police raided the Le Roux home and arrested young Paul for selling pornography. The family was scandalized, but managed to keep the story private. "He thought it was the funniest thing," the relative said. "He said quite openly that he'd found a gap to make money. He argued that if he was selling Bibles, curtaining, or study books no one would give a damn. It was a moneymaking business and he didn't care what the commodity was. That's where it all started."

By then, Le Roux had lost interest in any conventional path: graduation, college. He dropped out of high school to follow his interest in computers, and took a programming course at a local college. He completed a year's worth of course material in eight weeks and picked up programming certificates from three separate training courses over a single year.

What eventually propelled an eighteen-year-old Le Roux out of his parents' home, Mathew recalled, was a family trip to the United States—a Disney theme park, the whole works. He was enamored of the everyday technology he saw in the America of 1990: the big TVs, the ATMs, the ubiquitous personal computers. South Africa suddenly felt provincial, stifling. Besides, the nation's white-ruled apartheid system was entering its final death throes. Le Roux faced compulsory military service in a country he cared little about, at a time when large-scale societal violence seemed an increasing possibility. When they landed back at home, he told his family he was leaving.

Eight months later, Le Roux bought a ticket to London. At the airport, Mathew recalled, his bags proved too heavy to check. He ditched his clothes and boarded the plane with a suitcase full of programming books.

Once in England, Le Roux was able to support himself on his technical acumen, answering an ad in a local paper that landed him a job with a small software development company called BEI. "He had very little personality," one of his early employers recalled. "He was against doing anything social. He had no interest in building relationships with anyone, as far as I could see. He just put his head down and got on with the work." He wasn't a brilliant pure coder at first, his boss at BEI said, but someone who could adapt other programmers' code through a mix of cleverness and diligence. "Programming is oftentimes building on someone else's work," said the boss. "It's like Lego bricks: You can put them together and make something new."

Le Roux remained restless, relocating to Seattle to work for BEI remotely for a month, then spending six months in Virginia Beach. In 1994, now twenty-one and back in London, Le Roux met an Australian woman named Michelle and they started dating. A year later, he followed her to Sydney. She was brash and swore like a sailor, according to his relatives, and they married in 1995. Le Roux picked up a variety of contract programming jobs, gigs that gave him a window into the increasingly digital world of corporate banking. At an Australian bank, he was hired to develop "credit process automation," and to implement software to simplify the SWIFT system for international bank transfers. At a travel software company, he built accounting systems. For a Hong Kong brokerage, he created a system to automate the paperwork associated with trading. All of it, intentional or not, was experience that would prove valuable in his more entrepreneurial endeavors down the road.

To his wife, Le Roux seemed obsessed with his work. But he was also living an alternate life online, one in which he expressed naked disdain for his adoptive country. In chat forums about Australia, Le Roux seemed to revel in what would now be recognized as trolling, deploying exaggerated opinions to stir up outrage online. Most of what he posted consisted of juvenile provocation aimed at Australia and its citizens. "This message contains my conclusions after visiting the Australian joke country," he wrote in November 1995, listing his location as Sydney. "The Australian race has not progressed at all."

"All of Australia could disappear into the Pacific and the only difference it would make to the World is the Americans would have one less pussy country to protect."

"People like you should be rounded up, castrated, then shot," he wrote in response to someone who accused him of racism—for asserting that Asians should be "screened out" of Australia "for DNA defects." "Whats more your sperm could be used to create the ultimate germ weapon. Simply impregnate a countries woman, and within 20 years, you will have a race of 'people', which by all accounts, are capable only of collecting the dole." Le Roux seemed to relish his notoriety. His posts so outraged the message boards that one correspondent changed their online handle to simply "fuck@you.paul." "What kind of a dickhead are you?" another asked.

In a coup de grâce, Le Roux penned a thirty-eight-part post on a forum called aus.general in which he laid out the "Advantages" and "Disadvantages" of Australia as a nation. He made it a point to note that "I am ZIMBABWEAN. I left Zimbabwe in 1984, and have since lived in several countries including the U.S & U.K." The "Disadvantages" column included "Internet access is far to expensive, pornography laws in Australia are backward, banks report on everything you do, and movies are about 6 months behind the U.S."

"Drug laws are primitive compared with Europe," he wrote in closing. "The way to combat drugs is in fact to legalise them."

A different Le Roux personality could be found in another set of online forums, with names like alt.security.scramdisk, alt.security .pgp, and sci.crypt—encryption groups where posters engaged in highly technical discussions of the latest software for securing digital files. There, Le Roux described his passion: an encryption program he was writing, initially called Caveo, and later renamed Encryption for the Masses, or E4M. Le Roux's software allowed users to encrypt their entire hard drives—and to conceal the existence of encrypted files, so that prying eyes wouldn't even know they were there. This, he maintained, would be a leap forward in security, since existing encryption methods often inadvertently revealed their presence on a computer, thereby directing authorities to the files that needed to be broken. Worse, they might even expose information about those files—"metadata" such as their name and size—without the code having to be broken at all. Le Roux saw a way to solve both problems, and he released his creation to the world in 1999, after two years of development, with a post to the alt.security.scramdisk board. The software had been written "from scratch," he said, and "thousands of hours went into its development and testing." In the spirit of the burgeoning open-source software movement, he released E4M for free, making the code available for anyone to improve.

On the website E4M.net, Le Roux included a manifesto of sorts, outlining why he believed software like Encryption for the Masses was essential in the digital age. The Internet was exploding amid the dot-com boom, but he noted that little thought was being given to the consequences of digitizing our lives. "If you are worried that someone might have access to your documents, emails, sales projections, contracts, tax returns or receipts, romantic letters, or any other private files, then this product is for you," he wrote.

Privacy is becoming harder to find in the world. Today everyone, everywhere is monitored all the time, by everything from the close circuit recording system at the local store, to digital imaging systems at banks, the subway, and street corners. Governments issue social security numbers, national insurance numbers, medicare numbers, ID numbers, passport numbers, tax numbers, and so on. Some governments even go as far as fingerprinting citizens, as part of the numbering regime. Combine the two and governments have access to large pools of information about you and your lifestyle. The battle for privacy has long since been lost in the real world. As more and more human activity becomes computerised, governments are scrambling to preserve and extend their powers in the era of the information age and beyond. No one is saying that national security is unimportant, that child pornographers should not be stopped, or that crimes should not be punished. It's just that the same tired catch phrases are used time and time again to diminish everyone's rights.

He cited the ECHELON project, a keyword-based intelligence-gathering effort involving agencies in the United States, United Kingdom, and Australia, as an example of global surveillance run amok. Created under the guise of combating " 'rogue nations' and 'terrorists,' " he said, the system had been turned against companies and individuals conducting business that "cannot possibly have National security implications." Encryption, he concluded, "is the mechanism with which to combat these intrusions, preserve your rights, and guarantee your freedoms into the information age and beyond."

On the encryption message boards, Le Roux was helpful and engaging. His grasp of complex technical matters was readily apparent, and occasionally a bit of nerdy humor even shone through. "It's certainly not something you want to try without first telling your wife you will be in your room for a year," he wrote of one particular programming challenge. His own marriage didn't survive the release of E4M, though, and in December 1999 he and Michelle divorced amicably. Court records noted only that "the marriage had broken down irretrievably" and had produced no children.

Le Roux soon abandoned Australia, bound for Hong Kong and then Rotterdam, picking up programming work along the way. His release of E4M as free open-source software left him unpaid for his years-long obsession, so he launched a contract programming company called SW Professionals, nominally based back in

South Africa. Its motto was "Excellence in Offshore Programming"; its website claimed six employees, although it seemed more like a fig leaf for Le Roux's solo contracting efforts. "I worked with him about six months," said Heath Jordaan, a cousin of Le Roux's whose name appeared on the staff page for the site. "I think I saw him for about a week or so that entire time."

One of Le Roux's early clients was a German communications engineer named Wilfried Hafner, with whom he had corresponded online for several years about encryption. Hafner wanted to create a commercial encryption product that would combine some elements of Le Roux's E4M with another piece of software, called Scramdisk. The new company would be called SecurStar, and its product DriveCrypt. Hafner hired Le Roux to help build it.

To Hafner, Le Roux seemed desperate for money. He'd remarried quickly, to a Dutch citizen from Curaçao named Lilian Cheung Yuen Pui, and they'd had a child not long after. He drove a beat-up car and worked out of a Rotterdam apartment so small that, on the phone, Hafner could often hear the baby crying in the background. Hafner himself lived in the south of France at the time, and he said that Le Roux openly coveted his wealthier lifestyle. "He saw that these were rich places, and this was his dream," Hafner said. "He said, 'I am ambitious, I want to have all this.'"

Le Roux's relative, too, knew that the couple was struggling. "Lilian told me that they were dirt poor, both worked long hours, and the child was put into childcare for twelve hours a day," she said. "She told Paul that if any other child was born their circumstances had to change. He had promised her he would do everything in his power to change things."

In his message board postings, Le Roux seemed increasingly bitter that he'd released E4M for free. "The whole point in the beginning of E4M was to publish the code to get peer review and help to enhance the product," he wrote. "In the end people climbed onto my back, did not help one bit, bitched all the time, stole the code for incorporation into their own products, and generally abused the whole situation."

Both Hafner and Shaun Hollingworth, the inventor of Scramdisk, found Le Roux to be a gifted programmer. "He came with some, how do you say, interesting, innovative ideas," Hafner said. "But at the same time, I felt he was a little bit . . . disingenuous." In the middle of the development work for DriveCrypt, Hafner discovered that Le Roux was still tinkering with E4M on the side. Hafner came to believe that Le Roux had incorporated some of his SecurStar code into his personal project. Hafner was furious. Because E4M was an open-source product, the source code that Hafner had personally funded could now be used by anyone to build a rival program. He confronted Le Roux, who apologized and claimed it was all a mix-up. But the damage was done, and Hafner terminated Le Roux's contract.

In 2004 a group of anonymous developers would do exactly what Hafner had feared: They released a powerful free file-encryption program called TrueCrypt, built on Le Roux's E4M. "TrueCrypt is based on (and might be considered a sequel to)" E4M, they announced. The program combined security and convenience, giving users the ability to strongly encrypt files or entire disk drives, including USB sticks. Hafner suspected that Le Roux was part of the TrueCrypt collective, but couldn't prove it. Hafner found an email address for the group and sent a cease-and-desist letter, arguing that the software was based on stolen code. The response of the free-software community could be summed up in an anonymous message board response to Hafner's demand: "FUCK YOU, SecurStar—we've got it already!"

Whether he had a hand in TrueCrypt or not, Le Roux's financial situation was growing more desperate. Not long after he was fired from SecurStar, he could be found openly soliciting work on the alt.security.scramdisk forum. "Hi Guys," he wrote. "I'm looking for crypto/or other contract programming work, anybody out there have anything available? if your reading this group probably I don't need any introduction but I can send my CV as needed."

To make matters worse, Le Roux was about to be confronted with a life-altering secret from his own past. Needing to obtain a new Zimbabwean passport in 2003, he went in search of his birth certificate, contacting a lawyer in Bulawayo to track down his records. The law had changed since his childhood, though, and when the attorney returned with the paperwork it included not just the short form certificate that had been issued to Paul Sr. and Judy but his full birth certificate as well.

The relative recalled receiving a confused phone call from Le Roux, who had made it into adulthood without realizing he was adopted, and was now baffled by what he'd found. "Why is some other person named as my mother?" he asked.

"Things here are always done incorrectly," the relative said, hoping to convince him it was only a clerical error. "You shouldn't be surprised."

Le Roux was incredulous. Finally the relative relented and confirmed the truth. That moment, arriving at age thirty, "shattered his whole world," his cousin Mathew said. It wasn't just the idea that he'd been adopted that traumatized him. He'd had good parents, after all. But something about his name being listed as "unknown" on the certificate seemed to haunt him. "She could have put down any name," he told the relative. "But she put 'unknown.'" Years later, the relative would remember the discovery as the moment when something changed. "I have always felt that was a main driving point in his life. He needed to be someone, be known."

Le Roux, awakened to his alternate past, set out to track down his biological parents. His birth mother, Jill, had followed Le Roux's upbringing in Zimbabwe at a quiet distance, but lost track of him when his adoptive family moved to South Africa. After he contacted her, he then traveled to Zimbabwe to meet her and two of his half-siblings. "He spent the entire day in virtual silence, he was very, very quiet," said his half-sister Sandi, who was struck by the physical similarities between Le Roux and their mother. "My mom just couldn't stop staring at him." But Le Roux seemed affable as they peppered him with questions, eventually opening up about his love of programming and computers—and a new venture he was just getting off the ground.

Since leaving SecurStar, he'd started to formulate an idea that would take advantage of the technical skills he'd built up over the first decade of his career, and make him rich in the process. Accounts would later differ as to how exactly Le Roux had started in the online pharmacy business. The DEA would come to believe it was through partnering up with his biological father, a South African named Darroll Hornbuckle, with whom he had also made contact after discovering his birth certificate. (Hornbuckle was arrested in South Africa that same year for using false prescriptions to sell pills over the Internet.) His cousin Mathew instead recalled that Le Roux had traveled to Costa Rica to open an online casino where a lawyer had turned him on to the online pharmacy business. Moran Oz heard a third account: that Tomer and Boaz Taggart had originally met Le Roux in an online forum, and the three of them started the business together.

Perhaps the truth could be found in a Venn diagram of the three origin stories, but regardless, by early 2003 Le Roux was posting on message boards such as misc.entrepreneurs, looking for help opening a company based in the United States:

WE ARE EUROPEAN BASED PRIVATE INVESTORS LOOK-ING FOR A U.S. CITIZEN OR GREEN CARD HOLDER TO HELP US SETUP A NEW COMPANY BASED OUT OF FLOR-IDA, WE WILL DO ALL THE PAPER WORK WE NEED YOUR HELP TO COMPLY WITH U.S LAW. BUT WE KNOW NOTHING IN THIS WORLD IS FREE, SO WE WILL PAY YOU UP TO $500 TO HELP US. PLEASE ONLY GENUINE PEOPLE. NO TIME WASTERS.

By mid-December, he had registered the domain names RXPayouts.com and BillRx.com under the name George McKennitt, at an address in Weston, Florida, just north of Miami. Six months later, he incorporated RX Limited in Hong Kong.

To his new half-siblings, Le Roux exuded excitement about the prospects for his venture. "I have this online pill business," he told Sandi. "I'm basically finding cheaper alternatives and supplying them to people without them having to go through all this rigama-role." His new family was impressed. "It made sense to me," Sandi said. "I said, 'Paul, that is just genius, because you are serving the people who often don't have the money for medical care.'"

Sandi kept up with Le Roux until he moved his family, which now included a second child, to the Philippines sometime in 2004 or early 2005. Lilian had been unhappy in Europe and Le Roux was eager to escape the winters and the taxes. Soon after, his email responses became sporadic, until eventually he and Sandi lost touch. "It seemed like he literally fell off the earth," she said.

In a way he had, disappearing even from the online message boards he had once frequented. But he was busier than ever. Le Roux opened his first call center in Manila and registered a company in Israel with Tomer and Boaz Taggart. In the incorporation documents, alongside a scanned image of his Australian passport, he still listed his permanent address as the apartment in Rotterdam.

Le Roux's cousin Mathew said that they, too, lost touch in the mid-2000s—perhaps, he speculated, because Le Roux was struggling to come to grips with his family history. Mathew knew that his cousin had become a millionaire in the Philippines, but didn't see him for several years after he learned he was adopted. Then, in 2007, Le Roux called and asked if Mathew and his father could come to Manila. He offered to buy the tickets—all he needed were copies of their passports. His organization was expanding, he said, and he couldn't rely on only hired help. He needed people he could trust.

8

The Reporter

2015–2017 . . . On the ground in Manila . . . Finding Le Roux's people . . . Patrick Donovan's stories . . . Dave Smith lands the job

At times I had trouble explaining—to others and myself—why I invested so much time in understanding Paul Le Roux and what he'd done. In part, it was simply a reporter's curiosity: How did he become what he became? But something felt oddly personal about the search, too. I kept coming across small but eerie parallels between our histories. We were roughly the same age, born three years apart. When he'd lived in Sydney creating E4M, I'd been just a few miles away, studying at an Australian university. In the late 1990s, I'd worked as a software consultant in Amsterdam, vastly less talented than Le Roux but engaged in work not dissimilar to the kind he was doing down the road in Rotterdam. I, too, was enthralled with the early message-board culture that drew in Le Roux, and fascinated by the legal gray areas birthed on the Internet.

There our paths diverged, to put it mildly. My curiosity led me to cover this new universe as a reporter for *Wired,* while Le Roux leveraged his into E4M. But I imagine that we both watched the dot-com gold rush at the turn of the century with some bafflement, me from a poorly paid job at a magazine situated in the heart of the tech industry's extravagance, Le Roux as a technical virtuoso unable to capitalize on the riches flowing from the online world. His story struck me as in many ways similar to that of startup founders I'd covered over the years, whose biographies often paralleled his. The Elon Musks and Mark Zuckerbergs of the world were often, like Le Roux, computer-obsessed teenagers who built companies and fortunes out of their passion, just as software began to rule the world. Le Roux, it seemed to me, may have turned to the dark side of technology in pursuit of the same wealth and influence for which tech entrepreneurs were routinely celebrated on the covers of magazines.

I'd always been intrigued by that dark side myself, seeking out stories about clandestine worlds and assumed identities. Once, for a story in *Wired*, I'd tried to disappear into a new identity for a month while the magazine offered $5,000 to anyone who could find me. (They did, tracking me to New Orleans, where I was living in a dingy apartment rented with a fake ID.) The more I learned about Le Roux, the more I wanted to know how he'd done it, how he had brought so many people along with him, and how it had all gone so wrong.

A few weeks after my trip to Minneapolis to meet Moran Oz, in late 2015, I caught a fifteen-hour flight from New York to Hong Kong, and then another two hours on to Manila. I checked into a simple, whitewashed hotel in Makati City. Le Roux himself was long gone from the Philippines by the time I arrived, having decamped for Brazil and countries beyond. But the vestiges of his dominion remained. My hotel was a few blocks from the BDO building, the glass tower whose fourteenth floor had served as the hub of RX Limited's call center business. Around the corner were the Salcedo Towers, where Le Roux had once occupied both penthouses, and his former pub, Sid's, on the border of the red-light district. It was the first of two trips I would make to the Philippines over the next two years, attempting to sift through the remnants of his operation and track down people who had been inside it.

My contacts cautioned me about approaching Le Roux's former collaborators in Manila, warning that some might not take kindly to my inquiries. I encountered this undercurrent of concern often in my reporting, which over the next few years would take me to Hong Kong, Tel Aviv, Minneapolis, and Rio de Janeiro. It was hard to know how seriously to take it. I tended to assume the warnings were, in their own way, boasts intended to inflate the stature of the teller. Then again, I'd read enough of the Joseph "Rambo" Hunter file to know that there was real menace at the heart of Le Roux's operation.

Between the people who had worked for Le Roux over the years and the authorities who had pursued him, neither were particularly forthcoming. As soon as I said the name Paul Le Roux, doors tended to shut in my face, messages were left unanswered, memories suddenly clouded. Former employees sometimes expressed fears that they would become targets of American law enforcement if their name surfaced in connection with him. But more often they feared vengeance from the man himself. "He is a very dangerous man, a mastermind," one Israeli call center manager told me on the phone before hanging up abruptly.

One afternoon in Manila I walked a few blocks from my hotel to the high-rise offices of Blu, an energy drink company owned by Shai Reuven, an Israeli I'd heard had once been one of Le Roux's top lieutenants. A receptionist viewed my business card skeptically and said that Reuven was out of the country. She'd be sure to pass along the message that I wanted to meet him. I got the same response at the consulting business of another Israeli whose name I'd seen connected with Le Roux's early call centers. Staff members insisted that he was out. But an hour later he emailed, suggesting we meet at a crowded coffee shop. When he arrived, he immediately asked that I keep him anonymous. "I was already detained the last time I entered the U.S. and interrogated about Le Roux," he said.

He'd joined Le Roux's operation in 2006, he told me, recruited from a job at a call center in Israel. "Paul liked to hire Israelis," he said. "I don't think he particularly liked Jews, but he thought we were the most honest, cheapest, hardworking labor he could find." Arriving in Manila, the manager discovered that Le Roux's call center was already employing around twelve hundred people. The business, as he understood it, conducted telephone and email sales for pharmaceuticals in the United States on behalf of RX Limited, an independent company. "I later learned that it was just working for him, a captured client," he said. The business was a mess. "Very poor organizational structure and management," he said. "I laid off two-thirds of the staff."

Le Roux was "not a pleasant person," he said. "He was a really big racist, an asshole. For Paul, everyone was a 'nigger.' I was a 'white nigger.' Or a 'floppy,' which is a South African term for 'nigger.'" He was especially offensive, the manager said, in dealing with his local employees, "calling Filipinos monkeys, to their faces."

Le Roux, he knew, owned dozens of properties around Manila, although the manager had little idea what he did with them. Only once did he recall even interacting with Le Roux outside of work, when the boss invited him down to his beach house in Batangas, a coastal region south of Manila. He met Le Roux's wife, Lilian, who seemed friendly and largely minded their two children. He and his boss rode jet skis—one of the only episodes of intentional fun I ever heard of Le Roux engaging in. "Even that was more of an activity than a social venture," the manager said. "Driving down and back, he was working at a laptop. I don't believe that he had a social life. He was a workaholic, from what I understood, eighteen, nineteen hours a day. At no point did I ever meet anybody that was introduced as his friend, nor did he mention or talk about one."

The work was challenging, though, and the pay was good—particularly for Manila. As far as the manager understood it, it was also perfectly legal. But over time, he began to feel uneasy, sensing that there was more to Le Roux's world than he could see. "I had heard which direction he was going with his life choices," he said. "There's a difference between doing a gray business and just being interested in illegal business. I could see that he was more interested in that." After a year in charge of RX Limited's call centers, he told Le Roux he wanted out, and his boss didn't object. There were always more call center managers he could ship in from Israel.

After he left, the manager started hearing rumors around Manila that Le Roux's businesses had expanded to include gold and weapons ventures, and that he'd surrounded himself with armed guards and begun threatening difficult employees with violence. "I got out at a perfect time," he said.

That shift in Le Roux's business—from successful but shady online entrepreneur to brutal cartel boss—was the aspect of his story I found most difficult to understand. Here was a man making tens of millions of dollars a year on the Internet by the mid-2000s—skirting the law, sure, but without much apparent risk—who then decided to expand into realms manifestly more dangerous. From the perspective of the straight business world, it made no sense. Why diversify into more difficult businesses than the one in which you're minting money? Mostly, my questions were logistical: How does a computer programmer operating in the gray world of call centers even make contact with the world of mercenaries, arms dealers, and contract killers? Did he meet them at the bar? Find them online? "I don't even know how he got his connections later," the call center manager told me.

The answer arrived in the form of Patrick Donovan, a well-known figure in Manila's security contracting community. I'd first come across his name on the staff page of a defunct website for a security company that also listed Dave Smith and Lachlan McConnell as employees. It had all seemed too much of a coincidence, so I sent an email to Donovan asking for an interview. "I'm not real game for talking on phone, especially given what you want to discuss," he wrote back. "Myself and my colleagues have discussed this some time ago, sooner or later someone will be knocking on our door, mine in particular. I am not sure of your agenda." I tried to reassure him that I was simply gathering as many perspectives on Le Roux as possible. "The 'Fatman' caused a lot of issues here which are very sensitive," he replied, "therefore my colleagues and I will have to discuss this first." A day later he wrote again and said he was willing to talk, but only face-to-face. "I wish to make it clear I at no time worked for the Fatman," he added.

On my next trip to the Philippines, we arranged to meet at a bar he owned on P Burgos Street, the expat-heavy central artery of Manila's red-light district. It was a weekday afternoon with only a scattering of lunchtime customers. Amid the framed English soccer jerseys on the wall was a poster from the TV show *Breaking Bad,* captioned, I'M THE ONE WHO KNOCKS. Donovan wasn't hard to pick out: a hulk of a man, probably six-foot-four with a head shaved to the point of polish and the swollen torso of a body-builder, his arms tattooed along their length. He was easily the most intimidating physical presence I'd ever encountered. He'd just come from training a promising mixed martial arts fighter, he told me as his hand swallowed mine. Then he lit a cigarette. Not knowing how to start, I told him the bar seemed like a homey place. "I was shot right out front there," he said, in a thick Irish brogue, launching into a story about the failed assassination. As a kind of unconventional stating of credentials, it was hard to know what to make of it. "I assume you want privacy," he finally said, "so we'll go upstairs to the office."

We took an elevator up two floors to a dimly lit hallway, where Donovan unlocked the door to a small office strewn with stacks of papers. He took an energy drink from a minifridge and sat down at a wooden desk. I pulled out a tape recorder. He told me I could ask him anything I wanted about Le Roux. "I didn't work for the guy, so I've got nothing to hide," he said. "If I did, I would have known the minute you landed. I would have put surveillance on you to see who you go speak to first, before you speak to me, just to see what your game is.

"Your life, in this country, right now—I could go up to Tondo, give them a bag of shabu for about thirty dollars," he continued, using the local shorthand for methamphetamine. "That's what your life is worth. 'Go kill him.' And they'll do it."

"Well, don't do that," was all I could think to say.

He laughed. "You're okay, don't worry about it. But you made a lot of people nervous coming here."

Alternating between energy drinks and cigarettes, Donovan proceeded to tell me his account of how he'd come to intersect with Paul Le Roux. Some of it I would later confirm, while other portions—like many of the tales people in Le Roux's world told me—I could only triangulate against whispers and rumors. Donovan's antipathy for Le Roux, at least, seemed real. When Le Roux had started killing people in the Philippines, he said, "there was a lot of heat that came down. He caused a lot of problems. So he would have got it one way or another."

A former British military officer, Donovan had landed in the Philippines in the mid-1990s, a decade before Le Roux. He and an American had been running a business in the United States, finding and forcibly returning kids who had been spirited out of the country by one of their parents. After some bad publicity from a botched job, Donovan and his partner had come to Manila to hunker down until the bad press blew over. "We got to know some people, and we got to realize they did not have a clue what security was here," Donovan said. So they'd stayed and started their own firm, training security guards to protect dignitaries and conducting "risk assessment surveys" for businesses. After a few years, Donovan's partner got caught up in the hunt for Yamashita's gold, a long-rumored stash of treasure supposedly hidden somewhere in the Philippines by a Japanese general during World War II. "That seems to destroy people here," Donovan said. "I said nah, I'm going my own way." He started his own security company.

Over the years, Donovan said, he fell almost accidentally into the Philippine underworld of graft and corruption, a natural prod-

uct of a thriving security business. He had often provided free firearms and SWAT team training for the Philippine police and
military, and soon discovered that he had a growing Rolodex of
powerful figures willing to return the favor. "We're talking about
people who need help, and I know people who know people," he
said. "A container full of wine gets stuck in customs, could I help
someone out. I make a call, boom, it's out, he owes us."

Expats operating in the Philippines' thriving call center industry often availed themselves of Donovan's services, he told me. At
the industry's fringes were "boiler rooms"—call centers hawking
questionable investments or full-on scams to customers in the United
States and elsewhere. Such outfits were happy to pay a little protection money to avoid raids by the Philippine police, who selec-
tively enforced what few regulations were on the books. "It's the
kind of country where you've got to pay to play," Donovan said.
"It's their country, you're here. That's how they make their money,
when they come and raid you."

It all paid off well enough for Donovan, who also invested in
several bars in the red-light district. One evening he met a fellow
Irishman named Dave Smith in one of them. "I could tell by the
way he stood that he was military. I could tell by his accent he was
Northern Ireland," Donovan said. They became friendly, and
when Smith got into a jam—the wealthy man he was protecting
turned out to be a scam artist and fled the country—Donovan
hired him. "I said I can't pay you much, but you know, as we grow,
I'll take care of you."

Sometime in the mid-2000s, Donovan said—he couldn't remember precisely when—an Israeli acquaintance from the boiler
room business told him that a South African online businessman
named Paul Le Roux had just relocated to the Philippines. He was
looking for the kind of protection Donovan could provide. They
arranged to meet at the Makati Shangri-La hotel, where Le Roux
was staying. "The first day he was supposed to meet me, he put it
off because he was looking at condominiums," Donovan said.

"The second time he was supposed to meet me he left me waiting. The third time I said, 'Go fuck yourself, I'm not interested.'" The Israeli acquaintance begged Donovan to try again. He agreed to one more meeting.

On the appointed day, the Israeli acquaintance called to back out. "I was already set to go, so I said, okay, I'll go," Donovan said. "I took out my .45, loaded it, and I stuck it right here in my waistband." By now Le Roux was occupying a penthouse condo in one of Manila's most exclusive buildings. "I was escorted in the building up to his door, and these two big guys were beside me," Donovan said. "But they were standing back from me, and when they are doing that, warnings are going off everywhere. I open the door, there was nothing in there. No furniture, nothing. So now I'm kind of moving back so I can keep in line with them, I could see what they are doing. The next door they opened, there was plastic all over the fucking floor. Plastic, and a step ladder, like somebody was going to paint." Donovan put a hand on his gun.

"Then they pushed open the third door, it was a tiny little room, and there was Le Roux, sitting behind a little desk. Wall-to-wall servers. I was like, what the fuck?

"Now he's sitting there, belly like this, he's got bleach-blond hair. He looked like a pikey. You know what a pikey is? You know, people who live in caravans, Irish guys. That's what he looked like."

In Donovan's telling, the conversation was a short one.

"Can you tell them to fuck off?" Donovan said, gesturing to the bodyguards. "I don't like people standing behind me."

"Wait outside," Le Roux said to the guards. He gestured to a chair in front of the desk. "Sit down."

"No, I don't want to sit down. What do you want?"

"I know you've got connections," Le Roux said. "I know that you can tell generals what to do and they'll do it."

"Where are you going with this?"

"I have a business that I need protected, and I'm willing to pay you to come work for me. I'll pay you a lot more than what your company makes right now."

"Dude, I don't work for anyone, I work for myself. And as a matter of fact, if you don't stop fucking researching me"—at this point, Donovan said, he had pulled out his gun—"I will put a stop to it."

"There's no need for that," Le Roux said.

"I don't like you, I'm not going to work for you, stay the fuck away from me, you hear me?"

"Okay, I was just trying to give you a job."

"I don't want your fucking job," Donovan said. Then, he told me, he walked out.

A few months later, Donovan said, he noticed his friend and employee Dave Smith driving a nicer car and sporting a new wardrobe. Suspicious, he made some calls and discovered that after Donovan had rejected Le Roux, he'd met Smith and hired him instead, at $15,000 a month. "When I found out I said, 'Dude, just man up. If you are working for him, I don't own you, you are free to work for him. Good for you, get the fuck out of my office, and if I ever see you again I'll fucking kill you myself.'"

Smith, by Donovan's account, brought Le Roux Donovan's contacts, along with Smith's own international network of military contractors from his time in the United States, Iraq, Liberia, and beyond. With Smith as his right-hand man, hiring teams of mercenaries to do his bidding, Le Roux could now operate freely in the Philippines with little concern for legal repercussions. There was no problem that he couldn't buy his way out of, no law enforcement agency that couldn't be captured, no intelligence that was out of reach.

By the time Smith joined, RX Limited was earning Le Roux tens of millions of dollars from prescription drug sales in the United States. But the kid who had once locked himself in his bedroom, losing himself in code, had gone as far as his technical skills could take him. He wanted to be a different kind of businessman, a lord of the real underworld, not just the virtual one. "He made money on the pharmacies, and then he decided that he wanted to make more money, fast," the Israeli call manager I met in Manila told me. Le Roux wanted to diversify, to be bigger. "The only way to do that was illegal."

9

The Operators

*2008–2009 . . . Oz and Berkman expand in Israel . . . Ari Ben-
Menashe and the Zimbabwean gambit . . . Swimming with sharks*

"**M**oney is not an issue," Le Roux had told Moran Oz and
Alon Berkman on their second trip to Manila in 2008.
They had now risen from employees to de facto supervisors, in
charge of all aspects of the Israeli operation. As soon as they returned from the Philippines, they began building out the company's call center operations in Tel Aviv. Le Roux sent an advance
man, a Zimbabwean named Robert McGowan, to Israel to register a new company called Customer Service Worldwide, or CSWW.
McGowan stayed in a hotel for a few days while Oz drove him to
lawyers and banks to sign paperwork, then left and never returned.
CSWW officially opened in 2009, housed in an eleven-floor tower
not far from the government center of Tel Aviv. The Israeli national government's Money Laundering and Terror Financing Pro-
hibition Authority was located on another floor of the same
building. Now that Le Roux was shifting some of his call center
operations to Israel, CSWW would handle customer service in Tel
Aviv, while another new company would manage the accounting

and back office work. To cover the two companies' expenses, Le Roux began wiring $300,000 a month from a bank in Hong Kong.

Oz brought in Dov Weinstein, an experienced CPA and a family friend, to make sure the company's books were clean. "They mentioned all the time that there was a South African guy that hired them," Weinstein said. "He was working in the States, he asked them to be the back office, the telephone center." Weinstein got the sense that Oz and Berkman were uneasy about Le Roux. "If you ask me, I think that maybe they did not trust him," he said. Still, Oz and Berkman gave no indication that they were worried about running afoul of the law, much less about becoming a target of American authorities. They liked America. Oz had gone there on his honeymoon in 2008, a baffling choice for anyone who thought they might be breaking American laws.

The business was starting to look like a juggernaut. RX Limited's profits were climbing, and the company's growing volume of orders in the United States—fueled by the company's increasingly aggressive spam email marketing—created a need for more doctors and pharmacies, along with an endless stream of customer service requests. In the Israeli offices, there was talk that Le Roux might be planning an initial public offering, the ultimate coming-out party for any tech startup.

Oz and Berkman continued recruiting Israelis to fill jobs in the Philippines, but over time they discovered that Le Roux was often giving the transplants entirely new duties once they arrived, employing them in parts of the business for which they had zero experience. A childhood friend of Oz's named Asaf Shoshana transferred to the call center in Manila, then reported back to Oz that he had been put in charge of logging businesses in Vanuatu, Mozambique, and the Democratic Republic of the Congo. Shoshana, who had served in an elite unit of the Israeli Defense Forces called the Duvdevan, told Oz the work all appeared legal and legitimate. Another transplant, Shai Reuven—who fellow employees whispered had Mafia connections in Israel—told colleagues that he had been assigned to run an operation procuring gold directly from African mines. Still others—some of whom had served in the Duvdevan alongside Shoshana—were sent to guard stash houses that Le Roux owned in Hong Kong.

Levi Kugel, the blond musician friend of Berkman's who had also transferred to the Philippines, similarly moved beyond the call centers to other duties for Le Roux. Periodically Kugel would return to Israel, and he and Oz began casually discussing the idea of going into business themselves, starting their own wholesale pharmacy in the United States. RX Limited had grown so quickly that it often had trouble finding enough pharmacies to fill its orders. By opening their own, they reasoned, they could making money selling to RX Limited and save Le Roux some in the process.

They hadn't yet broached the idea with Le Roux. But Oz knew that Kugel had earned the trust of the boss. After briefly running a call center in the Philippines, Kugel had moved on to acquiring real estate in Manila for Le Roux, and now bragged that he was traveling the world on mysterious new business under the alias Steve LeBaron.

Ari Ben-Menashe didn't find it terribly surprising when a Steve LeBaron showed up on his doorstep in 2007, asking him to lobby a foreign government on behalf of a wealthy man in the Philippines. Ben-Menashe was, after all, the kind of man you seek out if you need a certain type of geopolitical favor. An Iranian-born Israeli who had been an officer in the Israeli Military Intelligence Directorate in the late 1970s, Ben-Menashe first came to international prominence—or notoriety, depending on your perspective—as the source of an Israeli government leak that the United States was selling arms to Iran. The information helped spawn the investigation into the Iran-Contra affair. He was later accused, and then acquitted, of selling military planes to Iran himself, and wrote a book claiming Ronald Reagan arranged for Iran's American hostages to be held until after his 1980 election to the presidency.

All of which earned Ben-Menashe a reputation as a dubious

chronicler of his own story. "Ari has put five or six dozen journalists from all over the world through roughly the same paces," the investigative reporter Craig Unger once wrote. "Listen to him, trust him, print his story verbatim—then sit round and watch your career go up in flames."

By the 2000s, Ben-Menashe had settled in Montreal and nominally ran an international consultancy called Dickens & Madson, profiting off the international connections he'd forged around the world. In Zimbabwe, he was widely known to have developed a close relationship with President Mugabe, related to a bizarre 2002 incident in which Ben-Menashe claimed that an opposition party leader had sought his help "eliminating" Mugabe. (A judge later concluded that the party leader had meant only that he would win an election.) And it was Zimbabwe that Steve LeBaron had arrived to discuss. "He came to Montreal initially, not knowing whether he was going to find me or not," Ben-Menashe said. "Funny enough he found out that my home number was listed. All this international intrigue, and my phone number is in the white pages."

LeBaron told Ben-Menashe that his boss, a white Zimbabwean named Paul Le Roux, was interested in talking to high-level officials in Zimbabwe's government. Ben-Menashe agreed to meet with Le Roux, who traveled to Montreal not long after, flying from the Philippines with a stopover in the United States. "He was an interesting guy," Ben-Menashe said. "Not that well educated, you can't call him an intellectual. I would define him as street smart. He didn't look like the criminal type." As Ben-Menashe came to understand, Le Roux "was a bit of a computer-type wiz" who had gotten rich selling prescription drugs online. Now, Le Roux told Ben-Menashe, he was willing to pay millions to persuade Mugabe's government to lease him a large amount of farmland. Le Roux, in turn, would sublease it to white farmers who'd been driven off their land.

Le Roux also told Ben-Menashe he hoped to obtain a diplo-

matic passport from the Zimbabwean government, which he believed would grant him the ability to travel to many countries
without being searched, and potentially provide immunity from
criminal prosecution. "We understand you have a lot of influence
there," Le Roux told him. Ben-Menashe later claimed that he
quickly informed Le Roux that a diplomatic passport was out of
the question. The land—three hundred square miles of it—could
be arranged.

Le Roux's passport request raised some suspicions, Ben-Menashe
said, so he asked friends in Zimbabwean intelligence to look a little deeper into Paul Calder Le Roux. They reported back that he
was born out of wedlock to a mother in Bulawayo, then adopted
by another family. After Mugabe's takeover instituted majority
black rule, when Le Roux was a child, his family left for South
Africa. He was now married to a woman of Chinese origin from
Curaçao who carried a Dutch passport. Le Roux also "had some
connections with the U.S. government," Ben-Menashe claimed his
Zimbabwean contacts informed him, without specifics.

According to disclosure forms Ben-Menashe filed with the U.S.
Department of Justice under the Foreign Agents Registration Act,
Le Roux paid Dickens & Madson $6 million for their services. Le
Roux "deals in Internet commerce and in the installation of call
centers in Southeast Asia, Costa Rica, and Israel," the forms stated.
"He intends to become involved in leasing of real estate for farming and other purposes in Zimbabwe." Dickens & Madson would,
in addition to lobbying Mugabe's government directly, "attempt
to arrange meetings with representatives of the executive and leg-
islative branches of the U.S. government" to lobby for policies favorable to the land purchases. Ben-Menashe then introduced Le
Roux to a Zimbabwean government minister in charge of land
reform. "They kissed and hugged, I'll never forget it, white Paul
Le Roux and this minister," Ben-Menashe said. "And the minister
told Le Roux, 'Welcome back home.'" As far as Ben-Menashe understood, the land leases were a done deal.

Le Roux had ambitions beyond acquiring Zimbabwean land. He mentioned to Ben-Menashe that he was looking to expand his logging business. Ben-Menashe, always ready to turn a deal, offered to approach his contacts in the government of Vanuatu, a small island nation in the South Pacific, who could provide Le Roux with permits in the country for rare hardwoods.

Over their several-year business relationship, Ben-Menashe said he felt like he had gotten to know Le Roux, visiting a house Le Roux had purchased in the ritzy Manila gated community of Dasmariñas Village, home to Philippine celebrities and business titans. He recalled Le Roux mentioning several times that he was adopted, and that he'd tried to build a life that would overcome his upbringing.

One incident in particular stuck out in Ben-Menashe's mind: While vacationing in Mexico, Ben-Menashe had once received a call from Le Roux wanting to discuss accelerating the Vanuatu project. "I said, Well, we're in Mexico. He said, I want to come and see you." A few days later, he suddenly showed up. The whole thing, Ben-Menashe said, was "curious. We could have discussed it on the phone."

Ben-Menashe made introductions in Vanuatu, he said, and Le Roux arrived with a crew of Israelis to begin the timber project. "I'm not sure what happened later," Ben-Menashe said. "He spent a lot of money for things that he may or may not have done." That, according to Ari Ben-Menashe, was the last he ever saw of Paul Le Roux. "Suddenly everything went funny," he said, "and then he disappeared."

In early 2009, Moran Oz got a call from Le Roux, demanding that Oz and Berkman return to Manila. He had plans to open up a new call center in the Philippines and wanted them to come take a look at the site, on an island called Cebu. So Oz and Berkman flew to Manila and checked into a hotel in Makati. That evening, Le Roux told Oz that Berkman would stay behind while Oz met with some

Brazilian partners to evaluate the location. They'd travel to Cebu overnight on one of Le Roux's yachts.

The next morning Le Roux picked up Oz at the hotel in his BMW. They stopped for breakfast at McDonald's, then headed west toward the coast, to the town of Subic, where Le Roux kept several boats. Le Roux pulled into the Subic Bay Yacht Club, where he put Oz up in a hotel for the night, paying the bill in advance. The Brazilians would meet him at the marina the next morning, he said.

The whole thing felt off to Oz—the Brazilians, the boat, and especially the way that Le Roux had driven him personally, separating him from Berkman. He messaged a friend from his hotel room that night, "I don't know what is happening, but something is weird." His friend told him to check out and leave. But Oz had trouble comprehending what could be wrong. "Everything is going great with the company," he thought. And anyway, what real choice did he have at this point?

When Oz arrived at the dock the next morning, three men were waiting to meet him: a friendly gray-haired Brit named Dave and two quiet, muscled men with shaved heads—Joe and Chris—who Oz assumed must be the Brazilians. They looked to him more like bodyguards than partners in a call center. But Dave said he was eager to talk business, and invited Oz aboard a small yacht with three bedrooms. Dave said he'd take one, Oz another, and the Brazilians would share the third. The sun was shining as they cruised out to sea. Oz sat on the back deck, taking in the view.

A half hour into the trip, with the shoreline receding out of sight, one of the two Brazilians came to the back of the boat and asked Oz to stand up for a moment so he could retrieve something from a storage compartment. Before he could consider why the man seemed to lack a Brazilian accent, Oz was already overboard.

He assumed at first that he had tripped, and quickly regretted that he'd slid his cellphone into his sock. When he looked up, he was relieved to see the boat circling back around to pull alongside him. He expected the men to throw a ladder over and haul him aboard. Instead, one of them was holding a rifle. Seconds later, bullets were piercing the surface of the water around him. When the shooting finally stopped, Oz was unhurt.

"That was to frighten off the sharks," the armed man said. "Don't think I missed. The next time will be for you."

Oz could see that Dave was now holding a satellite phone. "You are stealing from Paul," he said. "You need to tell us where you put the money."

Oz, fighting off panic as he treaded water behind the boat, tried to focus his mind and understand what Dave could mean. Whatever they had heard, he told him, it was all a mistake.

"This is the deal," Dave said. "Confess, and we'll kill you now. Keep denying it, and we'll wound you and leave you to the sharks. Your choice. Just admit it. We know you are talking to Levi."

Now Oz understood. Somehow the business he and Kugel had discussed—the plan to open a pharmacy in the States—had gotten back to Le Roux. Why they were accusing him of stealing he didn't know, but bobbing in the water Oz frantically explained that he and Kugel were just talking, that the idea was meant to help Le Roux, not steal his business. "I would have told Paul if we had done it," Oz pleaded. "I would never do something behind his back."

"He keeps denying it," Dave said into the receiver, listening for instructions from someone that Oz now surmised could only be Le Roux.

Perhaps Oz's boss had never intended to kill him, only to terrify him. Or perhaps Oz talked his way out of his own execution. Whatever the reason, one of the men finally pulled him back on board. They motored to a small, isolated island, where they anchored for the night. Dave went ashore and brought a prostitute back to the boat. Oz spent the night on deck, pretending to be too seasick to stay in his bunk, but with no way to get off the boat.

Thirty-six hours later, they headed back to the marina. "We are like an octopus," Dave told Oz. "We have tentacles all over the world. You need to understand that we can reach you everywhere, even in Israel." He warned that if Oz was ever disloyal to Le Roux again, they would kill him and his family. "You are not safe anywhere," he said.

The next day at the yacht club, Le Roux picked Oz up for the drive back to Manila, acting at first as if nothing had happened. When Oz confronted him about what he had just endured, Le Roux denied knowing anything about the incident. "I'm sorry about my partners," he said. But before he dropped Oz back at his hotel, Le Roux left him with a warning of his own. "You may be thinking about quitting when you get back to Israel," he said. "You're very important to me because this pharmaceutical business is my bread and butter. I would suggest that you don't want to deal with these guys. They will find you. Do whatever they say. Don't go back and panic."

PART II

PAWNS AND KINGS

10

The Investigators

2008–2009 . . . The wrong kind of evidence . . . Two guys from Kentucky . . . Bailey hits the road . . . A disappearing target

By the time bullets were raining down around Moran Oz off the Philippine coast, the DEA investigation into RX Limited and Paul Le Roux was approaching its two-year anniversary without a single arrest. "I think the longest I'd ever worked a case, from opening to final takedown, was eighteen months," said Kent Bailey. It wasn't that the investigators lacked evidence. If anything, they were drowning in it. By now Kimberly Brill and Steven Holdren, working from Minneapolis, had catalogued millions of drug orders attached to RX Limited's shipping accounts. They'd mapped the full length of the company's supply chain, from doctors like Prabhakara Tumpati in Pennsylvania and pharmacies like Charles Schultz's in Wisconsin, to shell companies like Ajax Technology in Hong Kong, and to the domain registrar ABSystems in Manila. Their controlled buys showed exactly how easy it was for American customers, without ever seeing a doctor, to order RX Limited's pills. Through their email search warrants, they had homed in on figures whom they believed to be crucial to Le Roux's operation, including Moran Oz and Alon Berkman. All told, RX Limited appeared to constitute the largest Internet drug ring the DEA had ever uncovered.

The problem wasn't the amount of evidence, but the type. The virtual fingerprints of Le Roux and his operators were all over RX Limited, but they were just that: virtual. The federal prosecutors who had taken on the case, Linda Marks and her team at the DOJ's Consumer Protection Branch, needed more. Without a source inside the organization—someone they could flip and put on the stand to testify to what they had seen firsthand—the prosecutors lacked the ultimate proof. "We didn't have evidence saying that was *him* behind the keyboard, writing those emails," said Bailey. They needed informants, or another way to catch Le Roux working in real time.

The investigators had started to sense that Le Roux was involved in larger and more sinister endeavors than just the online drug business. There had been signs since the beginning: the mysterious calls to Somalia on Le Roux's cellphone, the story in *The Hill* outlining Le Roux's millions in payments to Ari Ben-Menashe. The warrant on Le Roux's email turned up cryptic references to exotic-sounding projects and Le Roux–funded mercenaries that seemed to have no relationship to RX Limited.

Among their most perplexing discoveries was a pair of Le Roux employees in Kentucky. Joseph Hunter, from the small city of Owensboro, a hundred miles southwest of Louisville, had turned up on a list of calls to and from Le Roux's Philippine cellphone. When the investigators ran a background check, they discovered he was a former U.S. Army soldier with a cabinet full of awards who had left the service in 2004. Bailey had Hunter flagged in the federal government's flight passenger tracking system, and discovered he was traveling regularly back and forth between the United States and the Philippines. "What the frick are *you* doing with Le Roux?" Bailey wondered.

The other Kentuckian was an Israeli American named Jon Wall, who had worked as a call center manager for RX Limited in the Philippines, then returned to his native Louisville in 2008. After

Brill and Holdren found his email address in an account they were monitoring, they wrote up a warrant for Wall's email. The messages revealed his main job to be purchasing goods in the United States and shipping them to Le Roux and his employees across the globe, using a shell company he'd registered in Kentucky called Phalanx Trading. "The supply officer," Brill and Holdren took to calling him. Some of the purchases, like computers and servers, made sense for an operation with the technical infrastructure of RX Limited. Others, like cars, a yacht, artwork, jewelry, and a Westwind jet, could be chalked up to a wealthy businessman's whims. But shipments of vacuum hoods, mining gear, logging equipment, and drone parts pointed to something else. What, exactly, the investigators had no idea. In one email exchange, Le Roux's employees discussed purchasing helicopters to ferry employees out to logging sites in the Congo. "None of it made sense," Bailey said. "Why are you looking to set up a timber company in the Congo?"

At least one of the shipments, of military-grade scuba-diving gear Wall had purchased, was suspicious enough that the FBI independently flagged it as a prohibited export. They brought Wall in for questioning, but accepted his explanations and let him go.

Bailey, Brill, and Holdren tried tracking the shipments to their ultimate destination, in the hopes of learning more about Le Roux's aims. They had an agent in Chicago intercept two boxes of engine parts bound for the Congo and add a tracking device. The device died before the shipment left the States. They tried again with cars, arranging to attach trackers to a Ford Explorer leaving South Carolina and a BMW that Wall shipped through Long Beach, California. After the laborious process of convincing federal judges in both districts to grant warrants, they watched hopefully as the cars crept across the ocean to Hong Kong, on to Manila, and finally to Le Roux's house in Dasmariñas Village. And then they barely moved. "We found out that he didn't leave the house that often," Bailey said. "He clearly wasn't going to work every day."

At times it seemed almost laughable. Here were Brill and Holdren in Minneapolis, equipped with a couple of desktop computers, some notebooks, and a mail drop at FedEx, taking on a global network worth hundreds of millions of dollars, operated by an encryption expert with an unending supply of shell companies, thousands of employees, and impenetrable email servers.

To make any progress, they were going to have to put boots on the ground overseas. For over a year, Bailey had tried to impress upon his higher-ups at the Special Operations Division in Virginia that they were onto more than a typical online pill-mill jockey. Le Roux was selling millions of doses of prescription drugs, yes, but the investigators had a hunch that he was a much more significant international criminal. The response to Bailey's briefings had been the bureaucratic equivalent of a pat on the head. The case was too complicated and too technical, he was told. SOD was built to take down cartels, not programmers. Finally, Bailey approached his boss at SOD, Derek Maltz. "I gotta go to the Philippines on this," he told him. If he could get the Philippine authorities to conduct surveillance on Le Roux, he was convinced the DEA could find a way inside the organization.

Maltz agreed, and in the summer of 2009 Bailey flew with his analyst to Hong Kong and Bangkok to brief law enforcement officials, before heading on to Manila. The U.S. embassy liaison warned that it was too risky to meet with the Philippine National Police or the National Bureau of Investigation, and instead arranged a meeting with the commander of the Philippine Drug Enforcement Agency, which they viewed as less corrupt. When Bailey and his analyst arrived bearing gifts from SOD, the commander seemed friendly enough. The United States and the Philippines maintained an important alliance, he said, and the agency would do anything it could to help. Le Roux, however, was not on their radar. Bailey tried to prevail upon PDEA to set up surveillance on Le Roux, laying out the case as an easy win. The U.S. DEA had already pinned down Le Roux's locations, he told his Philippine counterparts: the house in Dasmariñas Village, the fourteenth-floor call center in the BDO building in Makati, a warehouse outside of town where shipments from Jon Wall had ended up. They had information on his cars, boats, planes, and shell companies. They had tied him to a gun store, Red White & Blue Arms, operated by a man named Michael Lontoc—who also happened to be a member of the Philippine national target shooting team. It was the kind of intelligence law enforcement agents typically salivate over. But the PDEA commander offered only vague assurances that they would follow up.

A couple of weeks later, after Bailey was back in the States, a PDEA liaison called to report that they'd obtained a search warrant and raided one of Le Roux's call centers, confiscating computers and detaining several Israelis. Bailey was elated, ready to hop back on a plane to the Philippines and help comb through the evidence. But the liaison told him that they hadn't found any wrongdoing, so they had returned the computers and released the men. Bailey was incredulous. "They were like, 'Okay, yeah yeah, we're close friends, we're allies,'" he said. "So it comes time to get down to the search and they say, 'Oh, we gave all that stuff back.' Really?"

Undaunted, Bailey redoubled his efforts, hopping from country to country to ferret out information or lean on local authorities. Eventually his world tour would come to include destinations as disparate as Ottawa, The Hague, Dubai, Accra, and London.

Le Roux's tentacles seemed to extend to every corner of the world, often in mystifying ways. Six months before Bailey's trip to Manila, British authorities had arrested a former British soldier turned military contractor—who'd fought in Chechnya after leaving the service—on suspicion of money laundering. He had been wired £150,000 from an account in Hong Kong belonging to Le Roux. After determining that Le Roux had Australian citizenship, the Brits contacted Australian authorities, who sent them to Bailey.

The mercenary told the British police that he'd met Le Roux through Robert McGowan, the Zimbabwean, and that Le Roux had expressed interest in funding a hunting lodge. Both Bailey and the U.K. authorities believed the story was bogus: The money had been transferred to him in small increments over several days, a practice known in the money-laundering world as "structuring." The British authorities froze the money with an aim toward prosecuting the mercenary. But Bailey feared it would spook Le Roux, and he pushed them to let the mercenary go. As it turned out, Le Roux didn't spook easily—he personally called the Metropolitan Police and demanded his money be returned. Bailey couldn't understand why a man of Le Roux's means even bothered over a few hundred thousand dollars. "He's lost more money than that without even noticing," he said.

Over time, the investigators started to get the unnerving feeling that Le Roux sensed where and how authorities were tracking him. His name progressively disappeared from the FedEx accounts and website registrations they'd used to establish his role in the first place. Ownership of companies they had identified as Le Roux's, like Southern Ace and Ajax Technology, was gradually transferred to Zimbabweans like Robert McGowan and Robson Tandanayi, and a South African named Edgar van Tonder. Le Roux had built yet another impenetrable email server, "fast-free-email.com," and seemed to be moving his employees off of commercial services and onto it. It was as if he had realized his early errors and was now in the process of undoing them.

As Brill, Holdren, and Bailey struggled to get any foothold inside his organization, Le Roux was descending deeper into his own systems. "He wasn't careful enough at the beginning to keep himself out of it," a former official at the Department of Justice said later. "He was clearly the mastermind of the operation. If he had gone the anonymous route a little bit earlier in the enterprise, we would have had no chance of figuring out who was really behind this. It would have just taken too long to get past that first layer."

11

The Mercenaries

2008–2009 . . . Inside The Company . . . The Bulawayo connection . . . McConnell gets a new assignment . . . Klaussen settles in . . . Joseph Hunter and the enforcers . . . Dispatched to Somalia . . . First days in Galkayo

For the likes of Lachlan McConnell and Felix Klaussen, the world of The Company—as Le Roux's mercenaries sometimes called it—was a potent combination of a rich man's fantasy, a military operation, and an anything-goes underworld. To thrive—and even, at times, to survive—often required a calm resourcefulness and reserves of courage. At other times, their jobs could feel like a paid adventure. There were scouting missions to be conducted in the forests of Vanuatu, gold dealers to negotiate with in the back alleys of Accra, military-style rafts to pilot under the cover of darkness in the South China Sea. "I'd sit there and think: 'Did that really just happen? Did I really just survive that?'" said Tim Vamvakias, the former U.S. Army K9 handler, of his years working for Le Roux. "The whole lifestyle was surreal. You never knew what was coming next."

Surviving in Le Roux's organization also meant tolerating his mercurial micromanagement. He seemed to keep every detail of the sprawling organization in his head—"his hard drive," Felix

Klaussen called it—with complete command of even the most trivial minutiae. He was driven by a single-minded devotion to growing his business. "You rarely saw him or heard that he was going out," said Klaussen. "He wasn't interested in life at all."

Le Roux's attention roved like an all-seeing eye across his disparate projects. No matter the country or time of day, employees knew to answer the phone if one of Le Roux's numbers came up. "It was almost like the guy never slept, and you never knew which personality you'd get on the other end," said Vamvakias. "His insane behavior at random times is what really threw me. When he called he never said who he was, but you knew it was him. And right from the moment that you answered his call, he would start. Sometimes calm and other times irate, and most of the time you never even knew why. I remember one time he called me in the middle of the night and just started shouting and didn't make any sense whatsoever. He kept referring to me by another name and when I finally was able to cut in and tell him who he was speaking with, it suddenly got quiet and then he calmly apologized and hung up."

As in any sizable corporation, employees spent an inordinate amount of time creating and filing reports, demanded by Le Roux in order to track the progress of even the smallest missions. If he wanted a rival timber operation burned to the ground in Papua New Guinea, he expected a memo outlining how the mission had played out. Often his expectations were at odds with the contractors' technical competency. " 'Make a spreadsheet and a master plan in Excel,' " Klaussen remembered Le Roux demanding of his security teams. "They didn't get it. It was a simple thing—at least for him it was. But for somebody who never had a computer, it was Latin." Le Roux issued trusted employees addresses on The Company's private email server, fast-free-email.com, and laptops preloaded with TrueCrypt. If they were ever approached by law enforcement, they were told to close the computer immediately. The TrueCrypt software would be activated as soon as the laptop lid was shut. (Le Roux himself worked on a well-worn and cumbersome old laptop, outfitted with decade-old Microsoft software that he had used his programming skills to fully secure.) But many of his employees struggled to understand and implement the security measures. "I cannot open this thing!" Klaussen recalled an exasperated Le Roux responding to employees' improperly encrypted emails. "I cannot see what you're writing. What the hell did you do?"

Lachlan McConnell, the Canadian who moved Le Roux's gold in Hong Kong, learned to take whatever orders came and not ask too many questions. Company missions often began with an email from Le Roux's second in command, Dave Smith, conveying only a set of geographical coordinates: Arrive at point X within 48 hours and await further information. McConnell recalled once being ordered to Subic Bay to meet up with a British boat captain named Bruce Jones, who regularly piloted Le Roux's yachts back and forth to Hong Kong. Captain Bruce, as he was known around Subic Bay's raunchy bars, was a tanned, long-haired former ferry captain from Bristol. Le Roux had recently purchased a Chinese fishing boat, called the *Mou Man Tai,* and modified it into a low-rent yacht, its high bow built to travel the difficult waters of the South China Sea. McConnell's task, he found out upon arriving, involved accompanying Jones and his wife on a maiden sail to ensure the boat was seaworthy. On the route south to Indonesia, a storm blew in. "We lost both lifeboats, developed a hole in the boat, and almost sank," McConnell said. Jones managed to maneuver the damaged boat to the closest coastline, only to be greeted by a group of men with guns, demanding to know why they'd landed in an unauthorized area. They talked their way out of trouble, and the boat was repaired and returned to Le Roux's rotation, leaving McConnell with another you-had-to-be-there tale of working for The Company. "Considering I thought it was legitimate, it was fun," McConnell said. "When he told me to do something, I did it."

In Le Roux's employ, though, "legitimate" work quickly became an elastic concept. It wasn't difficult to see that an organization washing millions of dollars in cash and gold across Africa came with an undertow of violence. Le Roux had interests to protect, after all, and they didn't always involve keeping boat captains company or arranging gold transfers in Hong Kong.

On one occasion, Le Roux dispatched McConnell and an American contractor into the jungles of the Democratic Republic of the Congo. Their assignment: to locate some logging equipment Le Roux believed had been stolen, and the manager of the company he believed was behind the theft. They spent several days sleeping in a mud hut, snooping around logging camps, taking photographs of Le Roux's gear being used by a Malaysian company. "We made the trip back, turned the report in, and that was that," the American contractor said. Whatever happened after that wasn't their business. "Common sense will tell you why they want somone surveilled," he said. Another time, McConnell was ordered to Canada, where he was given photographs and asked to verify the location of an ex–business partner of Le Roux's. He did, dutifully writing up and submitting his report. Perhaps, he told himself, the intelligence was for a lawsuit.

When Le Roux asked McConnell to surveil Le Roux's own family, however, the brutal realities of his boss's venture became harder to ignore.

Much of Le Roux's business in Africa, from gold buying to timber extraction, passed through a Zimbabwean cousin, Mathew Smith, who lived in Le Roux's hometown of Bulawayo. The city had been devastated, along with the Zimbabwean economy, by a decade of hyperinflation that peaked in early 2009, so bad the government briefly printed $100 trillion notes. It was a place that had always maintained a kind of frontier mentality, a town where gray-market moneymaking schemes were often a part of life, especially in hard times. Mathew had spread Le Roux's work to friends and associates in town, including Andrew and Steve Hahn, a pair of experienced gold dealers; an out-of-work local named Robson Tandanayi, whom Le Roux paid to act as a "dummy" on company registrations; and Robert McGowan, a thirty-year-old Zimbabwean engineer assigned to import logging equipment from the United States.

For a time, with Bulawayo as the hub, the spokes of Le Roux's African ventures seemed to be spinning smoothly. In a typical operation, Le Roux would first dispatch employees on blind missions to countries as disparate as Ghana, the Congo, Mali, and Zambia to find black-market gold dealers he could buy from directly. The Hahn brothers would then be flown in to assay samples of the product, testing it for purity. If the gold checked out, McConnell and other members of the security team would arrive with bags of cash, complete the transaction, and shepherd the gold out of the country. As Le Roux grew more confident in his Bulawayo charges, Steve Hahn even convinced Le Roux to invest in a gold mining project of his own. Everyone was making money.

Then, in July 2008, the Hahn brothers told Le Roux that they had traveled to Zambia to purchase seventy kilos of gold from a local dealer, at a price of $1.5 million. When they returned to Bulawayo and opened their haul, however, they claimed to have discovered the gold was fake. Someone must have swapped out the samples they had tested, they told Le Roux. Suspecting that the brothers had instead pocketed some or all of the money, Le Roux deployed McConnell and the American contractor to Bulawayo and Zambia to investigate, and ordered the Hahn brothers to Manila. He also called in the outstanding funds he'd sent Mathew for other missions. When his cousin came up $52,000 short, Le Roux concluded that his own family was stealing from him.

McConnell and the American contractor were supplied with dossiers on Smith and his father and ordered to pin down their locations. For the American contractor, the assignment was a red flag that it was time to get out. If Le Roux was paranoid enough to suspect that his family had betrayed him, he told McConnell, "You have to be very careful."

"Why's that?" McConnell asked.

"It's like the domino principle: When the man at the top starts getting nervous, thinks people are cheating him, the dominos start to fall."

Felix Klaussen, who'd joined the organization largely to extend his beachfront life in the Philippines, found himself drawn deeper into The Company's world with each passing month. His employer, whom he still knew only as Johan, or sometimes John, told him to come up with his own cover name. "He couldn't repeat that enough to everybody: Don't use your real name," said Klaussen, who only discovered Le Roux's real name months later. Klaussen selected "Jack Anderson."

He had relocated permanently to Manila, moving into a shared house in Dasmariñas Village with Chris De Meyer, the friend who had gotten him the job. A third bedroom was occupied by a former American soldier, Joseph Hunter—or "Rambo," as some called him. In his late forties, Hunter looked the part of a soldier of fortune: barrel-chested, with a shaved head, a bodybuilder's neck, and a resting expression of menace. "He had this dark, ominous presence," one of Le Roux's former employees said. "You definitely knew what he was all about."

Hunter was one of a handful of Americans—along with Tim Vamvakias, from California, and a North Carolina resident named Adam Samia—in a security operation that consisted largely of Israelis, South Africans, and Europeans. He had grown up in extreme poverty in Kentucky, without a father, raised by his mother and grandmother. He'd enlisted in the Army in 1983 and joined the Rangers two years later. But eight months into his career in special operations, a friend in his unit was killed during a training exercise, and Hunter, deeply traumatized by the death, took a medical discharge from the Rangers. He spent the rest of his twenty-one-year military career as a drill sergeant, military police trainer, and sniper instructor, rising to the rank of sergeant first class. He'd earned both a National Defense Service Medal and a Global War on Terrorism Medal, and his home state named him a

Kentucky Colonel, an honorific reserved for Kentuckians "unwavering in devotion to faith, family, fellowman, and country."

Hunter's path into Le Roux's employ echoed those of other ex-military guys. Discharged in 2004, he'd returned to his hometown of Owensboro to settle into life with his wife, her two teenage boys, and a pair of dogs. But home life was dull compared to overseas deployments, and the wars in Iraq and Afghanistan beckoned, with private security firms promising large paychecks and the chance to see real action. After getting hired and then quickly fired by Blackwater Security Consulting, he caught on with DynCorp, a contractor with close ties to the U.S. military. In 2006, Hunter headed to Iraq, where his job was collecting DNA samples from Iraqis and investigating bombings. He worked under constant threat of sniper fire and mortar rounds, and assisted the wounded after mass-casualty suicide attacks. He returned home after two years a changed man, increasingly short-tempered and moody. He had trouble sleeping and startled easily. "I spent a lot of time in my garage," he wrote later. "I avoided being in public. I just wanted time alone. I didn't want to go out or do anything. My wife said I needed help, but I couldn't do contract work if I got help." Instead, he signed up again with a similar outfit, Triple Canopy, and returned to Baghdad. After a year, his friend Tim Vamvakias told him that he'd lucked into a cushier gig, working for a rich man in Manila.

In the Dasmariñas Village house, Klaussen at first found Hunter a sullen presence. But slowly he opened up, and both Hunter and De Meyer let on that they were serving as a roving enforcement team for Le Roux. Their work could constitute everything from intimidation of debtors who had missed a payment to shocking violence against those Le Roux suspected were stealing from him. "Most of the time, I think they didn't use guns," Klaussen said. "Joe was very capable of eliminating somebody without a gun." Assassinations were called "bonus work" or "wet work." The assignments were doled out by Dave Smith, and Le Roux required photographic evidence that a job had been completed. "Sometimes, after, they spoke about what they did: 'I snapped that guy's finger and heard that crack,'" Klaussen said. "They were boasting about it. They enjoyed it."

Klaussen was disturbed by their stories, even if he was uncertain how much to believe. Chris, after all, was an old friend. "I told him many times: 'What the fuck is wrong with you?'"

The money is good, De Meyer would respond.

"It's not about the money. You never think that that guy may have actually done nothing wrong? Why would you do that?"

It's fun, De Meyer would say.

Klaussen figured that as long as he wasn't ordered to commit violence himself, he could live with working for an organization that perpetuated it. His own duties often struck him as a pointless waste of his skills, like when Le Roux ordered him to the Comoros Islands, off the coast of Mozambique, to register one of his yachts, the *Mou Man Tai*. Klaussen was instructed to talk to a local lawyer, who took him to a government minister. Unable to locate a hotel on the island within Le Roux's standard $80-a-night budget, he booked one for $250. For a week, he waited for Smith to approve the hotel and send funds by Western Union. Eventually they arrived, but in the meantime Le Roux had decided to register the boat in the Philippines. Klaussen returned home.

"Many, many times we did things, we were like what the *hell* are we doing here? We didn't see the point of it," he said. "You ask yourself why. But it's just something that comes up in his mind and only he knows the exact reason why. He just sends you."

Many days, De Meyer played video games on the large-screen TV in the house, waiting for Smith to send down a new job from Le Roux. "He tried to keep you busy, because he was paying you no matter if you worked or not. But sometimes you had a week or two weeks where you had nothing to do," Klaussen said.

The three housemates had little idea what the rest of The Company was up to. They would see what they assumed were Le Roux employees hanging around Sid's, his bar, but kept their distance. They knew the boss liked his underlings siloed from each other.

"Everybody was scared of Le Roux, they all knew what he was capable of," Klaussen said. "And he wasn't shy to turn on you." Klaussen, Hunter, and De Meyer made a pact: If any of them found out one of the others was on Le Roux's target list, they would let him know. Then they'd set up an imaginary hit, fake the pictures, whatever it took to assuage Le Roux and give the would-be victim a chance to escape.

Klaussen soon got a firsthand look at what happened when Le Roux thought he'd been betrayed. In late 2008 he was handed a new job in Manila: keeping watch over Steve Hahn, one of the Zimbabwean brothers who had lost over a million dollars of Le Roux's money. As Klaussen understood it, Le Roux had offered a straightforward answer to the problem of the Hahn brothers. "Many times he told Dave Smith, 'Just fucking kill them. I don't want to hear about it anymore,'" Klaussen said. Smith came up with an alternative plan: lure the brothers to Manila on the promise of more money and then set them up. They bought the ruse, and when they arrived in the Philippines Le Roux instructed them to pick up a briefcase full of cash at a lawyer's office. As they left the office, their taxi was pulled over by police, who had been conveniently tipped off by Smith. Inside the briefcase they found not money but five kilograms of cocaine. The cops arrested Andrew, while Steve remained free, held in a Manila townhouse under the supervision of Klaussen until he could come up with the money. "Smith kept them alive," Klaussen said. "Smith kept it floating because I think he smelled money." Le Roux, on the other hand, "didn't have the patience to wait. 'Fuck them, they don't have the money. They lost it? They lose their life.' That was Le Roux."

Guarding a target of extortion while his brother languished in a Philippine prison was the kind of task that would feel like madness in the outside world—"mental," as Klaussen liked to put it. But it somehow seemed perfectly logical within the morally scrambled confines of The Company. Soon, Smith was dangling more money in front of Klaussen to take on "wet work" with De Meyer and Hunter.

"I've got something," Smith would tell him. "You've got to go and break a few fingers, and you've got to cut one off. You okay with that?"

What the fuck is wrong with these people? Klaussen thought.

Then, in early 2009, Le Roux himself called Klaussen to a meeting with a proposal. He had a different kind of job, a critical project for The Company that he needed someone responsible and ambitious to oversee. The goal, as Klaussen understood it, would later seem comical, unbelievable: Le Roux wanted to start a tuna-fishing business in Somalia.

It sounded mental. But once Le Roux explained the logic, Klaussen grasped the power of the idea. For the previous few years the international media had been riveted by stories of Somali pirates, who ventured out into the Indian Ocean on rickety boats, armed with AK-47s, and stormed passing ships. Their business model was simple: Demand a ransom for the release of crews and cargo, and wait for Western governments and shipping companies to pay up. Less known was the origin of the piracy industry, which had emerged as an effort to drive away foreign fishing boats that were illegally trolling Somalia's well-stocked waters in search of tuna, sharks, and other valuable catch. The pirates had since moved on to hijacking more lucrative prey—oil tankers and cargo ships—although to Western media they still spun their mission as a kind of unofficial "Somali coast guard," one the broken state couldn't supply. But they had also largely succeeded in their original goal of scaring off the foreign fishing boats that had been depleting fish stocks. Now the fish were thriving, with no one to harvest them. Le Roux showed Klaussen satellite photos of massive schools of tuna, just offshore, waiting to be scooped up. He reasoned that a locally based company, operating with the approval of the pirates but shipping their catch internationally, could make a killing.

Notwithstanding the fact that Somalia was considered one of

the world's most lawless and volatile countries, the idea had a certain absurd elegance. In some ways, it echoed the development projects that organizations like the World Bank and United Nations fund all the time. Typical of Le Roux, the plan was a kind of hack. Just as he had exploited a hole in the American healthcare system to sell painkillers, he planned to take advantage of a dysfunctional government to exploit the resources it couldn't harvest.

Le Roux had even figured out the logistics and sent advance men to begin scouting locations for the operation. Now he wanted Klaussen to take the reins. Using a shell company called Southern Ace, he would set up a base camp several hours inland in Galkayo, a city of 500,000 that straddles two regions of central Somalia, Puntland and Galmudug. Once he'd established a secure facility there, he would expand to the coast, where Southern Ace would provide boats and equipment for local fishermen, build a plant to process and freeze the tuna, and pave an airstrip to ship it out to lucrative markets. "He had it all nicely planned out," Klaussen said. "So why not? There's nothing illegal about that. It's a bit dangerous, but that's okay."

A few weeks later Klaussen found himself in Nairobi, laying the groundwork for the project. There wasn't much in the way of blueprints for building an international company in Somalia, which lacked a functioning central government and was controlled instead by an assortment of competing clans. Al-Shabaab, the militant Islamic group designated by Western countries as an international terrorist organization, was on the rise, having gained control of large swaths of territory in 2006 after a U.S.-backed invasion by Ethiopia. Galmudug state, where Klaussen was meant to set up, was considered so volatile that the U.N. itself rarely ventured there; international NGOs limited their presence to local Somali staff. The president of Galmudug himself, a former Somali ambassador to the United States named Mohamed Warsame Ali, sometimes conducted state business from Nairobi, a thousand miles away.

Klaussen tracked the president down and negotiated a deal for Southern Ace to operate freely from Galkayo out to the coast, building water pipelines, factories, and airstrips for "local harvesting of various fish products for export to Middle and Far Eastern markets." Southern Ace's fleet would include up to fifty vessels, the agreement stated, "7–8 meter boats supplied by a builder in Mogadishu, outboard engines we will import from Hong Kong. These boats and engines will be provided to fishermen in return for an agreed percentage of the catch." In return, the state would receive a 10 percent share in the business.

Klaussen also hired a well-connected local from Galmudug named Liban Mohamed Ahmed to help make arrangements on the ground, dole out local payoffs, and navigate the delicate politics of the area's clans. With his help, Klaussen leased a three-story block house in Galkayo, white with fringes of sky blue. It was set back on its own property, with room to create a kind of compound that could serve as the Southern Ace base of operations. The property was surrounded by an eight-foot wall that Klaussen ordered topped with barbed wire. Liban also recruited a security force, composed of local fighters who would be paid to guard the compound, its employees, and Klaussen himself. From the roof, Klaussen and his men had an unimpeded view of the surrounding city, and out to the desert on the horizon. They installed a pair of satellite dishes to maintain constant Internet access.

After two months, everything was set up. When Le Roux called to check in on progress, Klaussen reported that he was ready to move full-time to Galkayo and ramp up the project.

"I need to talk," Le Roux said.

"Okay, no problem," Klaussen said.

"No, no, not like this, I need you to get the first plane out to Hong Kong. I need to talk to you in person."

The flight from Nairobi to Hong Kong was fourteen hours. "How long should I stay?" Klaussen asked.

There would be no "stay," Le Roux told him. Klaussen was to fly to Hong Kong for the meeting, then turn around and fly back immediately after. Klaussen hung up and called a travel agent, who booked him a ticket.

Arriving on the red-eye from Nairobi a few mornings later, Klaussen met Le Roux in a hotel restaurant that hadn't yet opened. The boss wasn't interested in breakfast. "Fuck off, we're talking," he said to a waiter who approached the table. He had ordered Klaussen there to convey a single message: Before the fishery was even up and running, the project was already burning money—on bribes, on security forces, on property. They were going to need to bring in some cash to defray the costs, and quickly. Le Roux would be developing additional plans for the project beyond fishing, he said, starting with establishing Somalia as a transit point for pharmaceuticals. "We need to get self-sufficient," he said.

For Klaussen, the vague directive was concerning—a business as elaborate as tuna fishing would take years to break even, much less turn profitable. And whatever schemes Le Roux had in mind for faster money were likely to be even more risky. But the project was just getting started. If Klaussen could show progress on the ground and the potential for long-term profits, he thought, Le Roux would come around. He caught a flight back to Nairobi and headed into Somalia.

On the ground in the dusty streets of Galkayo, he connected with two employees Le Roux had sent previously to help get the project started. One, a South African who rarely ventured outside and loudly disdained the Somalis, Klaussen arranged to have sent home after he drunkenly fired weapons from the roof of the compound. The other, a corpulent Zimbabwean named Mischeck who had once served in the notorious Zimbabwean secret police, Klaussen designated head of security. Mischeck in turn recruited a handful of other Zimbabwean security personnel, all of whom seemed to fear him, listening with respect as he recounted tales of torturing and murdering suspects back home. "To me he was just a big teddy bear," Klaussen said. "I actually got him on the roof and made him work out. Lucky I didn't kill him." They were soon joined by a pair of colleagues from Le Roux's security team, a doughy Brit and an Australian, the latter of whom spent much of his time blitzed on a mix of illegally imported booze and orange Valium tablets bought at a local market. He liked to call himself "Agent Orange."

It was a motley team, but Klaussen had little choice but to attempt to mold it into a competent organization. His days were spent navigating a culture that was utterly foreign to him. "I had daily meetings with elders, people from the area, neighbors, everything. You've got to keep everybody happy," he said. "It's not, 'I'm here and I've got money, you are going to do what I say.' It doesn't work like that." Liban, his local point man, had organized an initial security force of several dozen fighters, answering only to Klaussen. But given the environment, he was going to need more. As the months wore on, the payroll would come to include hundreds of Somalis. The larger the operation, the more they feared catching the attention of al-Shabaab, the Islamic militant group, or other hostile forces. "The word started getting out that there was a foreign company in that area of Somalia spending a lot of money, giving a lot of people jobs," Klaussen said. "Everybody needed something, everybody needed a piece of the cake. And the extremists start thinking about it, and we became a target."

Klaussen's team, with the help of Liban, purchased guns in the local market for their expanding defense force—cheap Chinese knockoff AK-47s flowing in from Ethiopia. In May 2009, just a few months after telling Klaussen he needed to make the operation self-sufficient, Le Roux emailed detailed instructions on how to manage its security:

1. You should setup a small workshop in the house and buy a welding machine and "up armour" the vehicles with steel plates in the doors of the cab

2. I suggest you get sandbags and deploy them on the balcony and roof and create firing positions

3. Even with the upgrades u requested below, u are still lightly

armed, in addition to the other stuff u request: I suggest you should get 4x LMG (7.62) and 2 x HMG (12.7mm 50 cal units) +spare barrels, I would suggest 3–4 units deployable on the roof

4. On the two vehicles you should weld a detachable weapons mount and ammo can on the back for the 2 x HMG (but don't actually mount them unless u need it in an emergency for the reasons we discussed before)

5. As a precaution I suggest u look to get a second house to act as a safe house that a minimum number of people know about should u need to evac (and u should stock it with food/water/, med kits, and comms gear)

He also hinted that he had even bigger plans for arming the operation. He'd developed contacts in the former Soviet republics who could fly in heavier weapons from Ukraine. To Klaussen, it sounded like Le Roux was planning to break an arms embargo that had been internationally imposed on Somalia. "But at the end of the day we needed those guns," he said.

All of this was just the preliminary security required before the real work of tuna fishing began. They were still importing the basics: engines for the boats, construction equipment for the factory, graders to build an airstrip on the coast to fly out the fish. A working operation was a long way off, but Klaussen felt like he had arrived, at the helm of an international development project in the most dangerous country on earth. "I had nothing, basically. No backup. Nothing whatsoever," he said. "I just had to count on the guys that were working for me." He knew the situation was absurdly precarious: a white man navigating a Somalia that existed in a perpetual state of political chaos, with memories of foreign meddling still fresh in the minds of a heavily armed population rightly prone to conspiracy theories. "You've got to give them the feeling that you trust them—and then you have to be able to make them trust you," he said. "Because for them every white guy is an American. Every American is CIA."

One hot evening that summer of 2009, Klaussen and his men

hauled an old TV from the upper floor of the house down to the courtyard inside the first perimeter. The compound had a defensive force of fifty, and Klaussen had an idea of how to cement their trust. He gathered the fighters and set out chairs in a semicircle around the TV. Then he connected his laptop to it, pulled up a movie, and hit play. The opening scenes of *Black Hawk Down* flickered onto the screen.

Klaussen had learned that the paramilitary group his fighters were affiliated with, Ahlu Sunna Waljama'a, had in the past been aligned with General Mohamed Aidid—the man who led the attack on U.N. and U.S. forces in Mogadishu back in 1993, in the battle that gave the film its name. "It was my way of saying 'I'm on your side,'" Klaussen said. "'We're here to do a job. Let's work together.'"

When the film arrived at the eponymous scene in which the Somalis shoot down the American helicopter, the guards stood up and cheered wildly.

"Oh God, what have I done?" Klaussen thought, laughing to himself. "If a drone catches this moment, I'm gone forever. They're just going to drop a bomb on it." But the scheme seemed to work. "From that day on I had all the respect I needed," he said. The security force, which would eventually balloon to over three hundred fighters, had never heard of Johan, or Paul Le Roux, or Southern Ace. As far as they knew, Klaussen was the man they were hired to protect.

12

The Doctor · The Pharmacist

2008–2010 . . . Tumpati brings in recruits . . . A booming pharmacy business . . . RX Limited attracts attention

For Dr. Prabhakara Tumpati, the Pennsylvania physician writing prescriptions for RX Limited, the network was proving more lucrative than he could have hoped. He used his own bank accounts to collect his fees for writing prescriptions, and paid taxes on the income, despite the fact that every year RX Limited neglected to send him any official tax forms. "I reported every penny," he said. He had begun training on the side to practice sleep medicine, and was saving money from RX Limited with an eye toward opening his own clinic.

He was now reviewing hundreds of patient questionnaires a day—an insane number of patients in the context of an ordinary doctor's office. "I wasn't worried because I actually reviewed each and every patient's history and had some set criteria," he said. If a patient mentioned they were taking other painkillers but were now requesting Ultram, for instance, he would flag the order as problematic. He came to see the model of RX Limited itself as a form of what is called "asynchronous telemedicine," in which doctors have the ability to evaluate patients remotely, pattern-matching their symptoms, without having to meet them in person. "You don't investigate a headache every time," he said. "If you go to the emergency room that is exactly what they will do. They will give you an MRI or a CAT scan, a two-week prescription for Fioricet, and a five-thousand-dollar bill." With RX Limited, he was doing the same for a fee of $2 a prescription. Adopted on a wide scale, he believed it could revolutionize the country's healthcare system.

Tumpati was captivated enough by the idea that he leaned on RX Limited to let him improve the business. He attended meetings of the American Telemedicine Association, networking with companies innovating in the field, and tried to connect them with his RX Limited contacts. (One RX Limited representative had told Tumpati he was based in Detroit, and once supplied an address there.) Tumpati proposed they look into adding video conferencing, so that the patients could be viewed remotely by RX Limited's doctors, rather than relying on questionnaires. He suggested they find a way for patients to upload their medical histories to the system.

The reps at RX Limited were noncommittal, and Tumpati began to sense that they dreaded his calls. "They acted like they were going to talk to their manager, or board, or whoever the person is, and get back to me," he said. "I never gave up hope, I thought they would come back, that they would improve the system."

Meanwhile, he told himself he was following in the footsteps of his heroes. Growing up in India, he'd read about a famous doctor who performed more than a hundred thousand eye surgeries to restore children's sight. "That was something that stuck to me, saying, 'If one doctor can reach out to that many people, one day maybe I will be able to.' When I saw this opportunity, I was like, Wow, look at this, I am helping a lot of people." Sure, he was getting paid handsomely for those prescriptions. But he was saving a poor person with no insurance hundreds of dollars on medications to treat their pain.

Tumpati soon proved eager to spread the beneficence, and the wealth, by recruiting colleagues into the network. "Hi Aaron, I spoke to another physician who is licensed in New York that is very interested in telemedicine," he wrote in one email to his main RX Limited contact, "Aaron Johnson." "Please mention my name and tell him that I gave you his number." Among the doctors he recommended was the friend who had given him a part-time job out of med school, a fellow Indian American named Anu Konakanchi. The two had met while Tumpati was a resident and grown close enough that Tumpati sometimes referred to her as "Akka," a term meaning "older sister" in his native language of Telugu. She was reluctant to sign on at first, but Tumpati assured her that the network was legitimate, and she agreed that he could pass her information on to Johnson. When Johnson called her, he further reassured her that the company was on the up-and-up. Konakanchi, convinced, signed up and started filling out prescriptions. Soon she, too, was approving hundreds a day. She'd been struggling to make money in her solo practice, she said later. Now, she was suddenly receiving tens of thousands of dollars a month in wire transfers from the Hong Kong bank of a company called Southern Ace. "It helped with paying off my practice debts, my overhead, my malpractice, my expenses for having an office, staff," she said. "For the first time, I was able to take some income for myself."

Tumpati went on to recruit eight other physicians into the network. Through his connections in the Indian physician community, he knew doctors from all over the country. "The volumes were getting bigger and bigger," he said. Tumpati didn't oversee their work with RX Limited, for which they received $2 per prescription and he received a $1 referral fee. The setup was essentially what's known as a multilevel marketing scheme. But instead of selling cosmetics or herbal supplements, the participants were prescribing painkillers by the thousands.

Unlike Tumpati, Charles Schultz wasn't interested in suggesting improvements to the system he knew as AlphaNet. As far as the pharmacist in Oshkosh could tell, the whole thing was running smoothly. He was now making $4 a prescription filling online orders, and the two technicians he had hired at his stores, Schultz Pharmacy and Medicine Mart, were each filling as many as a thousand to fifteen hundred a day, enough to keep both pharmacies in the black. Schultz himself, who had been diagnosed with severe heart disease in 2007, had become a less frequent presence at the stores.

Employees at the two pharmacies would later say that the system seemed ripe for abuse. "I would see a husband-wife ordering, going to the same address," one recalled. Sometimes they would reject prescriptions "if there wasn't a diagnosis that made sense for the drug they were asking for, if they had received that medication recently, more recently than what they should be needing a refill for," one pharmacist who worked for Schultz said. "If somebody was trying to secure medications with multiple names, we could figure that out. If somebody would have ordered drugs under John Smith and then J. A. Smith or Joe Smith, and they were all at the same address or same date of birth." They would report abnormalities back to Ron Oz or other AlphaNet representatives, and move on.

If any of them had typed some of the AlphaNet websites that came attached to the orders into a search engine, they might have been doubly suspicious. AlphaNet, otherwise known as RX Limited, had been tracked for years by online organizations dedicated to stopping illegal spammers and shady pharmacies from operating on the Internet. A Portland, Oregon, company called LegitScript regularly included AlphaNet on its published lists of "rogue pharmacies"—operations that offered drugs without valid prescriptions. At one point, LegitScript determined that the thousands of websites affiliated with AlphaNet and RX Limited constituted half of all the rogue online pharmacies in the world.

But Schultz's employees trusted that their boss knew what he was doing. "Occasionally we would get a call saying 'I found this medicine in my son's possession and it's not from his doctor, can you explain that?'" one pharmacist said. "Most of the time I would say, 'Well, ask your son, but we have privacy issues that we need to consider. We can give you the name of the company and the prescribing physician who ordered it.'" They'd pass on a phone number for AlphaNet. They never heard anything more about what happened to the patients.

13

The Operators

2009–2010 . . . Living in fear . . . Nestor Del Rosario rises . . . Warning signs . . . Summoned to Kenya

Back in Manila the morning after his harrowing boat trip, Moran Oz rushed to find Alon Berkman, his Israeli colleague. By this point, Berkman knew something was amiss. He'd been unable to reach Oz or Le Roux for thirty-six hours. Now Oz turned up back at their hotel, looking ashen. The two of them immediately switched locations, hoping Le Roux would be unable to track them. They bought tickets for the next flight out of Manila to Hong Kong, and then back home.

After Oz returned to Israel, friends noticed that his demeanor had changed. One childhood friend said that Oz wouldn't tell him what happened on his trip, making only cryptic statements about his boss. "I don't think I should be working with this guy," he told the friend. Oz installed security cameras in his home, bought a gun, and varied his routes to work. "He was different, like he was shut down," the friend said. "He was suspicious. We didn't know of what."

Still, he went back to work managing the call centers in Tel Aviv and Jerusalem alongside Berkman, who had taken on accounting duties for the larger company, working even more closely with Le Roux. The boss had always been direct in his communications; he knew what he wanted and didn't solicit his employees' opinions. Now Oz found him increasingly controlling and easily enraged. Le Roux began asking for daily "task emails" from employees. "An employee must apply to the company's rules or actions will be taken against him," Le Roux wrote. "This is Manager's request and he will stand to his word. (You know.) Please take responsibility for this so we won't need to go there." Over time Le Roux became more and more threatening, berating employees when something wasn't done in the way he'd asked, and explicitly suggesting what might happen to them if they didn't rectify it. "Alon better answer the phone or he won't have a hand to do it with or a tongue to speak," he told one of Berkman's coworkers. Occasionally, when he was angry with Oz, Le Roux would bring up the boat incident as a threat, asking him whether he wanted to "go back in the water."

Oz and Berkman had once held on to their boss's veneer of being an Internet mogul with some unusual tastes. They assumed that he ultimately aspired to mainstream business success, even respectability. "Paul had, at some point, a plan to build two towers [in Manila] and call them the Le Roux Towers," one call center manager said. "He wanted to create an investment company in Dubai to invest in startups. Those were his plans in 2008 when I got to the Philippines." Le Roux was even rumored to have brought in an architect from Zimbabwe to design the "Le Roux Towers" and scout for locations. But a year later he'd abandoned the plans, and the employees' talk of an initial public offering was a distant memory. "Something happened that flipped him completely," the manager said. "He always had tendencies to the dark side. I guess he said, Fuck it, I'm in the Philippines, I'm already bribing the police, the NBI, judges, whatever. I can just use that to make some real money. He wanted something that made a 5000 percent return on his investment, not something that made 10 percent a year."

In Manila, the man Le Roux increasingly relied upon to execute that vision was a Filipino deputy named Nestor Del Rosario, who had managed legitimate call centers for Accenture before joining RX Limited. Despite his denigration of Filipinos, Le Roux had come to trust Del Rosario, who had a knack for accomplishing the most outlandish tasks that sprang out of his mind. "Nestor was his go-to guy," Felix Klaussen said. "You didn't fuck around with Nestor. He hired every Filipino that worked for Le Roux. They all came through him, had to answer to him. If a Filipino screwed up Le Roux called Nestor, and Nestor would sort it out. He wasn't a scary guy. Straight guy, protecting his boss and his boss's interests. Very loyal."

Del Rosario confided in the Israeli call center manager that Le Roux had ratcheted up his duties over time, pushing him into increasingly illicit endeavors. First he was managing the gun store that Le Roux owned in Manila, Red White & Blue Arms. Then, he said, he'd been involved in framing one of Le Roux's Zimbabwean employees, Andrew Hahn, arranging for drugs to be planted on him and tipping off the police. Even more extraordinary, the call center manager said, Del Rosario was increasingly being sent abroad—along with a guy from HR named Ogie—on weapons-buying missions to Iran and Pakistan.

Del Rosario's claims were of a piece with the constant swirl of whispers about Le Roux. "I heard he was doing human trafficking, he was doing arms trades, he was having people killed," one Israeli call center manager said. "It sounded like a comic book, and I didn't know what to believe and not to believe. I heard that he had an airplane business where he was making airplane engines and hiring people to fly to other countries to smuggle drugs. It was too surreal to believe that this guy was actually getting away with stuff like this. I didn't know what of it was credible information. I could only confirm what I knew."

Occasionally, Le Roux himself would muse cryptically to call center employees about grandiose ambitions that were hard to take seriously. "He never told me his exact plans," another call center manager said, "except to have 'his own little kingdom.' 'We'll have a kingdom in Africa.' 'People will refer to me as the great leader.' I heard that so many times."

As his early success in the pharmaceutical world metastasized into larger criminal pursuits, Le Roux struck his employees as increasingly paranoid. "His visibility was decreasing; from 2008 moving forward you would see him physically less and less," the call center manager said. "That's when he started changing his email address." Le Roux began using email servers he had created and encrypted himself—the first was called server73.net, then my-free-email.com. He provided custom email addresses to trusted employees, creating an entirely self-contained communication system, walled off from potential government snooping. He also ramped up his use of dummies, ensuring that his name was removed from companies that conducted the organization's business in Hong Kong, the United Kingdom, and beyond. He seemed to constantly test and question the loyalty of employees, sometimes slipping extra money into their salaries to see if they would return it.

Le Roux ordered Del Rosario to sell off any Manila properties that could be connected to his name, and to scout for an island off the Philippine coast for Le Roux to purchase. He wanted somewhere with cellphone reception and space for a landing strip that could accommodate private planes, along with boat slips so he could move cargo in and out by yacht.

As the true nature of Le Roux's business became clearer, RX Limited employees were left to ponder the moral implications—and the danger—of staying on board. Eliel Benaroch, one of Le Roux's more trusted call center managers, recalled an afternoon when Le Roux summoned him to the Manila Polo Club. "Meetings with Paul were not something that was planned," Benaroch said. "He would call you that morning or in the night, because he never slept, and say we need to have a 'sit-down.' Usually you'd go right away. He'd say, 'Come to my house,' or he loved the Hard Rock Cafe, he loved the nachos. He'd never order you anything, that's how cheap that guy was. It was a message of power, I am paying you but I'm not buying you anything. I met him at Hard Rock a few times, at the polo club, or in the car. He'd call you and say 'I need to meet,' pick you up, and drive around for twenty minutes. You'd talk about what he needed to talk about, then he'd drop you off." On this day, Le Roux proved to be in an expansive mood. "The real money is in the controlled drugs," he told Benaroch. "You are only seeing a fraction of what The Company is doing. You could be doing so much more."

"He made it seem," Benaroch said, "like there was a whole other business running in the background."

In Israel, for Oz and Berkman, things felt like they were starting to return to normal. Then, in early 2010, Oz got a call from Le Roux proposing that the two of them meet him in Kenya. It seemed like a setup: The Israeli operation had no business there, and Le Roux was typically unforthcoming about the reason for their meeting. At first Oz tried refusing to go.

"Don't be afraid," Le Roux said.

"How can I not be afraid?" Oz replied.

Le Roux then took a direct tack: They had no choice. Oz knew what defying him would mean. They agreed to fly to Nairobi.

A colleague in Israel questioned their decision, given Oz's near-death experience the last time he saw Le Roux. "I remember asking them, 'What the fuck, why are you going after what happened last time?'" he said. But Oz told him that Le Roux had little incentive to hurt them. Before, he had suspected Oz of stealing. Now, he believed he'd frightened them into absolute loyalty. Besides, he needed Oz and Berkman to keep RX Limited's massive operation running smoothly.

The two Israelis landed in Nairobi on a night flight and took a taxi to a hotel Le Roux had selected. The next morning, he arrived in the lobby flanked by two security guards, who sat down at a nearby table. "We didn't know what to think because we didn't do anything wrong. Everything was okay," Oz said. More than the risk to their personal safety, he said, "we thought he chose Kenya because he was going to ask us to do something illegal."

It turned out that Le Roux just wanted to discuss some changes in the business. He instructed Oz and Berkman to expand the Tel Aviv operation and open a new call center in India, which would start marketing directly to customers through cold calls and spam. He was cutting out the online affiliates who solicited Americans for orders and took a 60 percent cut on each one. Instead, Le Roux said, he had a database with millions of customer leads that RX Limited could solicit. (Only later would Oz discover that Le Roux had stolen the data from the marketing affiliates themselves.) They would find their own customers, Le Roux told them. And then he said the two were free to go.

14

The Reporter

2016–2017 . . . Social media mercenaries . . . Finding Robert McGowan . . . The files of Mathew Smith . . . Sex for fun and profit . . . Patrick Donovan's last encounter

It was strange, at times, how easy it was to find many of Le Roux's former employees. I'd expected that, as a criminal diaspora spread around the globe, they would be hunkered down, off the grid. But all I needed was a starting place—a few names from an indictment, an address on a website registration. Thanks to social networking, one source would quickly turn into three, and then five. Often their Facebook pages were left unprotected, open to the public, and I perused their list of friends for new contacts, or connected them back with old names. They'd posted photos of their adventures working for Le Roux, posing in front of sparkling cityscapes in Hong Kong or draped in bandoliers in a Somali compound. Sometimes I found fake Facebook profiles they had created using their aliases, easily discoverable because they'd then made the mistake of friending their own real identity, collapsing the ruse. Le Roux, despite being an influential cryptographer and noted paranoid, himself appeared to have once set up a Facebook profile under one of his false identities, Bernard Bowlins. He'd posted nothing, but connected with exactly one person: his own cousin.

Dozens of call center employees included RX Limited's call centers and corporate shells on their public-facing social media profiles. When I contacted them, they often had no idea whom they had once worked for, or that there had been anything dubious about it at all. "We thought it was an outsourcing company for something in the States," said one Israeli American who had worked at RX Limited's Tel Aviv call center. "We took it as a customer service job. Both me and my roommate worked there, we kept laughing at how hilarious this company was. Maybe looking back there were some red flags we should have noticed, but I was an eighteen-year-old kid."

Stranger still were the employees from the mercenary side of Le Roux's business who proudly listed shell companies like La Plata Trading or Southern Ace as their former employers. One former team member advertised his work for Le Roux as "protective security operations for Clients in Papua New Guinea, Indonesia, Sri Lanka, Tanzania, Mozambique, Ecuador and Peru." I discovered later that his work in Papua New Guinea included setting fire to a rival timber operation. "You're the second journalist to contact me," replied another contractor, a former South African policeman named Marcus, when I emailed him to ask about Le Roux after finding Southern Ace on his online résumé. "Maybe I should change my LinkedIn profile." His duties, it turned out, consisted primarily of assassinating employees and business associates who Le Roux believed were cheating him.

For years I pinged these people with messages, and the ones who were willing to talk often insisted on moving to secure email services and encrypted chats. Some initially voiced suspicion that I was working for the U.S. government, part of a sting operation designed to trick them into admitting wrongdoing. Others assumed I was one of Le Roux's minions, arriving to intimidate them or seek vengeance. "What's your real name?" one Filipina former employee responded when I contacted her on Facebook. "And how did you get my name? If you see him can you tell him there's a special place in hell for murderers like him? If you work for him, please know I'm no longer scared."

For a few who had made it through their time with Le Roux unscathed and unbothered by law enforcement, it was just an amusing footnote to their lives. "I knew the boss was some kind of Internet guru," one American security contractor told me when I found him in the Philippines. He'd done a brief stint with The Company, buying black-market gold in Ghana. "He had multiple revenue streams, he's buying some gold, buying some fucking weapons, doing different shit. It was all compartmentalized. I didn't mind doing some stuff in the gray area. It was nothing compared to Iraq and Afghanistan."

The most maddening part of trying to unravel Le Roux's organization, it turned out, was not finding these people but making sense of their experiences, many of which overlapped and contradicted each other. As I mapped Le Roux's sprawling network—physically, on my bedroom wall, in a collection of multicolored Post-it notes as if from some demented corporate ideas meeting—lines began to intersect. Israelis associated with call centers in Tel Aviv turned up in Vanuatu running international logging operations. Zimbabweans I found on company registrations in Hong Kong showed up on property records in Australia.

I'd like to claim that this was some kind of linear process, a journalist-turned-detective expertly following a trail of breadcrumbs down the path to the secret lair. But, in truth, people and stories came to me scattershot, and I found myself constantly circling back to reevaluate some fact that I'd been told before. I piled up puzzle pieces and then sifted through them, seeking connections, and then set out to pile up some more. It was discovery by accrual, and as I stumbled my way through, a picture of the empire that Le Roux had built slowly began to come into focus.

Often, the people I thought would open the doors of Le Roux's history only led me to more locked ones. One character who had long confounded me, amid the collection of Le Roux employees' names stuck to my wall, was the Zimbabwean engineer, Robert McGowan. I'd seen his name first on a patchwork of corporate registrations tied to the heart of Le Roux's business. In the United Kingdom he was listed as the director of Southern Ace, a company used by Le Roux's mercenary arm. In documents from ICANN, the international organization that accredits website registrars, he was listed as the former head of ABSystems, Le Roux's registrar in the Philippines. There were dozens of RX Limited websites in McGowan's name, from rxfleetusa.com to pills24-7.com to pharmacybuycheapusa.com. He was attached to Florida-based companies with names like Armada Commerce and Quality Fountain, and tied to a Miami address used by RX Limited's operations in the United States. Adding it all up, McGowan seemed to be as significant as Le Roux himself, but he'd never turned up in any of the court cases in the United States.

In early 2016, I flew to Tel Aviv to trace the Israeli end of the network and discovered McGowan's name yet again, on documents establishing the first iteration of CSWW, Le Roux's Israeli call center company. Included was a copy of McGowan's passport, along with Le Roux's. It all seemed to point to the conclusion drawn by an Israeli magazine, in a 2011 article about the mysterious call centers selling pharmaceuticals from Tel Aviv and Jerusalem: McGowan must be a major figure in RX Limited.

With his passport information in hand, I was able to track him down on Facebook from my Tel Aviv hotel room. We traded messages and he sent me his number. When I finally spoke to him, he freely admitted working for Le Roux, but seemed perplexed by the scope of operations attributed to him. He'd been recruited into the business by Le Roux's cousin Mathew, in Bulawayo, and told that Le Roux was a wealthy South African who needed help with logging projects. Le Roux flew McGowan to Manila and explained that for his African endeavors he required heavy machinery and lubrication oils, which would be purchased in the United States using corporate entities set up in Hong Kong. "I had a list of questions: What are the companies going to be used for and things like that," McGowan told me. "Everything I did, I tried to keep straight and aboveboard." McGowan flew to Hong Kong and opened a company called Diko Limited. Then he shopped for Le Roux's list of logging and mining machinery at the best prices. When he found earth-moving equipment in Texas, Le Roux paid him to travel to the United States and create a pair of companies to handle the export: Armada Commerce and Quality Fountain.

McGowan also recalled taking a single trip to Israel to complete the paperwork for CSWW, where he briefly met Moran Oz and Alon Berkman. But he claimed to know nothing about the underlying businesses. When I pressed him about his role at ABSystems, he seemed even more baffled. "I've just Googled that right now," he said. "I've never heard of it until you sent me an email this evening. I don't even know what that is. What is it?"

I explained that he appeared to be in charge of the domain registry behind much of Paul Le Roux's fortune. "Have you got copies of this, can you send it to me?" he said.

He told me that for years he'd been fighting the perception that he was somehow influential in Le Roux's business—or indeed, that he *was* Le Roux. In fact, he said, Le Roux had stolen his identity and used it around the world. "They got copies of my documents, my passports, and used it to set up these fictitious companies," he said.

In 2009, Le Roux had suddenly abandoned his logging operations in Africa and cut off communications with McGowan, who was left holding debts for the equipment he had purchased. He told me that he'd traveled to Manila to get some answers. Other people in Le Roux's orbit, including Mathew Smith, warned him it could be dangerous. "I said, 'Why should I not go? I've got nothing to hide,'" McGowan said. When he arrived in the Philippines, "It was like a wild goose chase: go here, go there. I don't know if he had someone following me."

McGowan eventually confronted Le Roux, who told him that it was all a misunderstanding. He wanted to keep working together. "That was the last time I saw him," McGowan said.

McGowan passed me an email address for Mathew Smith. A few weeks after I sent him a note, Mathew wrote me cryptically from a Gmail address in the name of his dog, Lulu—subject line: "PLR." "He is an interesting character," he wrote of his cousin. Le Roux, he noted, "had a legitimate Congolese diplomatic passport in his own name and a Bulgarian passport in another name." From there we struck up a correspondence over email, phone, and online chat. At first he asked me to refer to him in my published reporting only as "Lulu." But two years into our conversations, he changed his mind and agreed to go on the record.

After growing up close with his cousin, Mathew told me he'd lost touch with Le Roux in the early 2000s, when he moved to the Philippines. But in 2007 Le Roux had suddenly reconnected, saying that his business was expanding and that he needed trusted friends to help him grow his operations in Africa. He bought Mathew and his father tickets to Manila to discuss the possibilities, and before long Mathew had signed on to help Le Roux from Bulawayo.

Mathew set about recruiting additional family and other locals like the Hahn brothers and McGowan. An in-law of Mathew's told me he at first thought Le Roux was a rich businessman looking to reinvest in Zimbabwe. Le Roux's first mission for the in-law, in 2007, involved traveling to Montreal to meet an Israeli named Ari Ben-Menashe and sign some documents he didn't understand related to farmland back in Zimbabwe. Then the jobs multiplied. Le Roux sent the in-law to the Democratic Republic of the Congo to shop for timber concessions with an Israeli named Asaf Shoshana. Back in Bulawayo, he helped two guys from Le Roux's security team, Lachlan McConnell and Joseph Hunter, find stash houses for gold. He and another local then arranged the acquisition of Le

Roux's diplomatic passport in the Congo, strapping $100,000 in cash to their bodies to cross the border and pay for it. "Thinking back now, that was quite a risk," he said. Le Roux paid well, $5,000 or more per mission plus all expenses paid. It was, one Bulawayo employee said, "like a cash cow walked into town."

Over two years, Mathew watched his cousin's business morph from a seemingly masterful hustle to something much more sinister. He forwarded me transcripts of chats he'd had with Le Roux in 2008 and 2009, a virtual encyclopedia of his schemes and a record of his slow drift into violence. I paged through thousands of words about paid-off customs agents in the Congo, copper prices on the London Metal Exchange, and specific brands of logging winches. There were endless negotiations over gold ("how are they providing it, as metal or as dust? . . . one ton will not be enough"), diamonds ("we have the buyers, but they want quality, the[y] have huge money but need good quality 10ct and up"), and weapons he needed for Philippine generals ("RPG-7 two units needed with 20 rounds, 10 grenades, plastic explosives, 4 MP5's with 2 15 clips ammo each, it is just a sample order to check if i can supply, i need it delivered in mozambique, i will take it from there to asia myself").

Through it all Le Roux gave off a sense of constant, manic urgency. "Coming under serious pressure here to get moving in congo from the government there," he wrote. At another point, he discussed how to transfer a million dollars in cash into the Congo to purchase gold. "U need the full 1 million?" Le Roux asked impatiently. "Problem is for such huge amount i will need to send one of my own people to accompany the money . . . Security people with weapons and training." Le Roux's adoptive family, seeing him more often again, noticed that he spoke in a strange accent, sometimes sounding American or British. Le Roux told a relative he had affected it so that no one could pin him down to a specific country. In one chat, he asked his cousin Mathew to create an escape hatch that would allow him to disappear and never be found.

LE ROUX: i need a dead body certified as me and a death certificate

LE ROUX: i talked to you about it in HK

MATHEW: yes

LE ROUX: then i will need a way out to Mozambique without going through a border

LE ROUX: and my guys will collect me there and get me out the country

LE ROUX: at the same time i will need a new identity

LE ROUX: RSA [Republic of South Africa] is ok but it needs to check out 100%

LE ROUX: ie: birth certificate in the records etc.

LE ROUX: not just a pp [passport]

LE ROUX: the body should have a certificate saying died from multiple gun shot wounds

LE ROUX: and then be cremated, although when i am there they can take dna from me etc if it is needed,

LE ROUX: i dont know the system there

MATHEW: understood

Mathew urged him to quit, retire to a quiet part of Africa, and live on his riches for the rest of his life. "But he said he loved what he did and wouldn't give it up," Mathew told me. "He was always after the next big deal." To Mathew, his cousin was still the clever, computer-obsessed kid made good, a near-billionaire who had beaten the system and done them all proud. He told me he'd once seen what he estimated was tens of millions of dollars in Le Roux's office. "Cash," he said. "It was fucking ridiculous. It was in wicker baskets lined up on the side of the wall."

Le Roux in turn seemed to treasure his family's pride. "I remember meeting him at the Hong Kong airport once; he told me he was flying to Lithuania, but it could have been anywhere," Mathew told me. "He had this nice suit on and wanted me to take his picture to show all the family. For some strange reason I felt really sorry for him." At times there were glimpses that Le Roux longed to get out of the business. Once, sitting on a plane next to a relative, he pulled out his tablet to show off something. "He got all flustered and shy, and wanted me to see his 'greatest achievement,'" the relative said. "It was an article written by him for some travel magazine. I read it and was astounded, it was really good." Le Roux told them he'd been submitting stories under pseudonyms for years without success. "He wanted to be a writer. It was his greatest ambition."

But something seemed to amplify Le Roux's worst impulses— greed, impatience, a sense of superiority—and in conversations with his cousin he displayed an increasingly cavalier attitude toward violence. He often claimed to be laundering money on behalf of mysterious "Brazilians," and in late 2008, when the Hahn brothers lost more than a million dollars in a gold deal, Le Roux said it was the Brazilians who would make sure it was paid back. "The gloves will come off soon on all the people there who owe them money," he wrote. The Brazilians were, he said, "pulling in people from South America who solve these problems. Many times I said MAKE SURE THAT WE DO NOT LOSE MONEY."

MATHEW: its in his interest to pay you out asap

LE ROUX: does he have kids?

MATHEW: bud . . . you make me nervous when you ask questions like that

MATHEW: he is paying you out

MATHEW: and quickly

LE ROUX: the people who owe the money will pay it

LE ROUX: all they will do is grab the guys kids until he pays

LE ROUX: simple as that

Mathew told me that he'd flown to Manila alongside the Hahns back in late 2008, all of them hoping to straighten out their debts to Le Roux. The first night after he arrived, Le Roux failed to show up at a dinner meeting. Then Mathew got a call warning him that Andrew Hahn had been set up with a briefcase full of drugs and arrested. Mathew immediately went to the airport and caught the next flight to Hong Kong.

He checked into a hotel, assuming he was safe. Then the landline rang. It was Le Roux, asking why he'd run away. "I put the phone down, checked out, and rushed to the airport," Mathew said. He then hid at a friend's apartment in Singapore while he tried to figure out Le Roux's intentions. In an online chat, he accused Le Roux of trying to take him out. "I thought you were hunting me," he said.

Le Roux responded with a smiley face. "Buddy if I was hunting you," he wrote, "you would be dead."

Mathew returned to Bulawayo, and over the ensuing months things seemed to return to normal. Steve Hahn had been allowed to return home—with his brother still in a Philippine prison—to try to raise the money to repay Le Roux. Apparently, he didn't work fast enough: One day Joseph Hunter turned up, ordered him into a car, and shot him in the hand before making Hahn drive him to the airport.

Chatting online not long after the shooting, Le Roux began to hint to Mathew that a similar fate awaited him, for $52,000 he had taken from the organization and never paid back. The money was of course "chump change," Le Roux said. He was worth hundreds of millions of dollars. "BUT it is a matter of honor. . . . It is the principle here, it is a shame you can't see that."

"Dude I very clearly understand," Mathew said. The gun that had been used on Steve Hahn, he noted, had been bought at Le Roux's request by Mathew himself.

"Yes but he is alive," Le Roux said. "Nobody wanted him dead. Dead people don't repay their debts."

A few weeks later, in May 2009, Mathew was asleep at home in Bulawayo when he was awoken by an explosion. Someone had thrown a petrol bomb through his bedroom window, lighting the curtains on fire. When he rushed to look out, four shots shattered the glass, one passing through a door, centimeters from his head.

Now, finally, Mathew knew what his cousin had become, and what he was capable of. It was no longer the mysterious "Brazilians" who were threatening to mete out violence, if they indeed existed in the first place. It was Le Roux himself. "I spent the next five years in absolute fear," Mathew said.

Violence wasn't the only form of depravity coursing through Le Roux's world. As I delved further into it, I discovered an underground river of sexual depredation. Le Roux himself often bragged of his sexual adventures—"15–20 a week," he once wrote to his cousin, "sometimes 3 per night. Depends on my cock." Le Roux had a habit of sending photographs of his conquests, like a teenager seeking approval. "I take these pics to remind myself why I bother to make money," he wrote. In Manila, where prostitution was tacitly permitted, participation in the trade was woven into the lifestyle of Le Roux's employees, from call center managers to mercenaries.

None seemed to relish the bar-girl culture in the Philippines more than Le Roux himself. "Bitches," he called them, in chats with his cousin.

LE ROUX: going to setup some orgies here with these bitches

LE ROUX: btw one of my guys has put brands on his bitches

LE ROUX: did i tell u this? he puts his initials on the back of their necks. . . . . . .

LE ROUX: in tatoos

LE ROUX: basically he is branding them like cattle here

At times, Le Roux's business seemed to consist of a toxic blend of money, corruption, and sex. "I need a white hooker for PNG," he wrote to his cousin at one point.

"PNG?" Mathew wrote.

"Papua New Guinea," Le Roux responded. "Promised it to a government minister there, vital to my business."

"Out of curiosity did the gov minister just come out and ask you?"

"No, we provided him hookers in Philippines when he was here," Le Roux said. "My man promised him a white one next time."

That a man who was making as much money as Le Roux would bother to arrange the transport of prostitutes across the ocean was itself mind-boggling. But there was something much darker I had heard about Le Roux's exploitation of women. In the chats, I was surprised to find a passing mention of it. "Getting more bitches here from around the region," Le Roux wrote.

Two sources told me that in the late 2000s, Le Roux's appetite for sex became so voracious that he sent emissaries out to remote parts of the Philippines, directing them to pay women to travel to Manila, move into his condos, and remain at the beck and call of Le Roux's desires. I'd first heard it from Moran Oz, who said that he knew an employee who had been assigned to the task. "He went to far-away villages where they have no money," Oz said. "He used to send him pictures, to choose, 'Here: one, two, three, four.'" Le Roux's aims, Oz had been told, were more than just carnal: He intended to produce as many children as possible, to eventually create a trusted brigade of his own offspring.

After months of searching, I finally found the employee in question. I told him what I'd heard and that it seemed hard to believe. "First of all," he said, "when you talk about Paul Le Roux, everything you hear is probably true." He had been working in the call center, he said, when Le Roux came to him with a new assignment. "He proposed it to me in a way I couldn't really say no," he said.

At first he thought he was collecting women for Le Roux to open a bar. "It's a very common thing to do in the Philippines. You have a girly bar, you bring politicians to the girly bar." That was not the reason. "What you heard is what he told me," the employee said. " 'I'm going to impregnate them, and build an army of kids.' I really thought he was kidding. Yeah, what the fuck are you on about, man?" Le Roux asked him to make a spreadsheet to track the women: their names, dress size, age, medical checkups. The operation was given top priority by Le Roux, who sent his emissary to China to try to find women there. "He talked about it like that: 'this operation'; it's not human beings, it's a task. It was just insane. That's when I left." In 2009, the employee went to see Le Roux at one of his condos and told him that his parents were getting divorced. He needed to return to Tel Aviv.

"Okay, you go for a few months," Le Roux replied. "I understand, that's family. That's something I never had. My mother was a whore, and I had to kill my father because he stole money."

The employee laughed nervously, as the statement hung in the air for a moment.

"I didn't actually kill him," Le Roux said. "I let him live."

The employee left for Israel and never returned to the Philippines. The last he heard, he told me, someone else had taken over the spreadsheet. "I managed to somehow morally justify" the work at the time, he said, driven in equal parts by greed, youthful ignorance, and Paul Le Roux's menace. "It seems like complete madness today. You can twist reality if you work for Paul. I was there. I take responsibility. Why did I stay? It was fear, yes. But it was something else. It was like a fly to the light. You are attracted, but you are blinded."

The more I learned, the harder it became to tease apart the myth and reality of Paul Le Roux. His life was so confounding that it had a way of throwing off a person's radar for bullshit.

Patrick Donovan, the jacked-up Irishman who had employed Dave Smith before Smith left to run Le Roux's security, told me several seemingly outlandish and difficult-to-confirm stories of his own. Sitting in the cramped office upstairs from his bar in Manila one afternoon, Donovan recounted, for example, how he and Smith had once been asked to develop a plan to invade and occupy the Seychelles, a country made up of small islands in the Indian Ocean, eight hundred miles off the coast of Somalia.

Sometime in the period before Smith went to work for Le Roux, the story went, a high-level political operative with connections to the Seychelles had summoned Donovan and Smith to a meeting at the Makati Shangri-La in Manila, looking for mercenaries who could carry out a coup. "They wanted to know would I be willing to train an army," Donovan told me. "So I said, 'Are you out of your fucking minds?' They said what's the problem, couldn't you do it? I said yes, it could be done. But you want to overthrow a fucking government. I'm not that guy." Nonetheless, he claimed, he and Smith decided to game out the idea, just to contemplate whether it was possible. "I drew up a plan for them, to show them how it could be done," Donovan told me. "At one time of the year, in a sports stadium, every single politician and police head is in that fucking stadium, for one particular event." If you targeted that event, Donovan surmised, you might collapse the government. "I said this is the best I can do to help you. That's the way you can do it. I'm out." He hadn't thought much about it, he told me, until Smith had left his firm. Smith, he said, had taken the coup plan and the contacts to Le Roux.

Donovan could have been lying to impress me. Only he and Dave Smith really knew what, if anything, transpired at the Shangri-La. It was all very elaborate for a man who hadn't wanted to talk to me in the first place. All the same, it was pretty easy to dismiss it as the kind of tale that gets circulated among mercenary types over too many drinks.

Except that I knew that in the U.S. government's case against Joseph Hunter, there were transcripts of Hunter describing a plan to invade a set of islands he remembered as the Maldives. "We have guys in Somalia buying weapons that are making an army," Hunter said on one of the videotapes. "They was making an army in Somalia because we were gonna invade an island, Maldives, you can't make it up. Not even in a movie. This is real stuff." And I knew that in my own interview with another of Le Roux's former security men, he'd made an offhand comment about how he and Dave Smith had once sailed a boat into the Indian Ocean, as a trial run for the operation. "As Dave Smith said it, Paul Le Roux would finance a takeover by the former president," the mercenary said. "Obviously it didn't come to fruition. I didn't put much to it, because it sounded kind of fantastic. When we were there we didn't do anything for two days except sit in the hotel."

Another story Donovan told me was about the last time he ever saw Le Roux. Donovan was sitting outside a Starbucks on Ayala Avenue, a busy thoroughfare in Manila, on a weekday afternoon. "He was coming by in an SUV, and a follow car, for his bodyguards. He stopped and got out, and the bodyguards got out. He came right up to me," Donovan said. "He didn't even say my name. He just leans over and he goes, 'Know where to get ten thousand AKs?' Randomly out of the fucking blue just like that."

As it happened, Donovan *did* have an arms contact, someone who knew precisely where to get a lot of assault weapons. Smith, he assumed, must have passed this information on to Le Roux, prompting the question.

"I told you to fuck off," Donovan said to Le Roux. "I don't want to deal with you."

Le Roux seemed unfazed. He just looked at Donovan and said, "Come see me in my office."

Donovan never did. But he heard, months later, that Le Roux had a cargo ship full of guns coming into the country. So he decided to make sure it got stopped. "I gave the information to somebody who I knew would give it to the right people, to get it tagged," he said.

15

The Ship

*2009 . . . A crucial interdiction . . . Weapons go missing . . . Captain
Bruce seeks a way out . . . A reporter under threat*

On August 19, 2009, customs officials in the port city of
Bataan, three hours west of Manila, received a tip: A large
ship was anchored off the coast, carrying suspicious cargo. When
three Philippine port officers motored out to the vessel, they noted
that it lacked a national flag, although the word *Panama* was
painted on its hull. They boarded the ship, called the *M/V Captain
Ufuk*, and questioned the skipper, a South African named Lawrence John Burne. The rest of the thirteen-member crew were from
the Republic of Georgia and spoke no English.

One officer noticed twenty large unmarked wooden crates on
deck. When Burne was unable to produce a cargo manifest for the
boxes, the port officer called his superiors. Soon, a team of customs agents arrived with reinforcements from the Philippine National Police and Coast Guard. In three of the crates, they found
fifty-four Indonesian-made assault rifles. A fourth contained forty-
five bayonets and 120 empty gun magazines. The arms appeared
to be only the remainders of a much larger shipment.

During Burne's interrogation, he revealed that he had very recently taken over for another captain, Bruce Jones, a British sailor well known around the pubs of Subic Bay. By the time the port officers had pulled alongside the *Ufuk*, Jones was long gone, as were sixteen crates full of weapons. The evening before the ship was intercepted, they would discover, a small yacht called the *Mou Man Tai* had motored out from the Subic Bay Yacht Club, taken the weapons and Jones onboard, and sped off into the night. The guns were bound for a Manila gun dealer called Red White & Blue Arms. The *Mou Man Tai* was found a few days later, anchored off a remote fishing village, and traced back to Dave Smith. But neither Jones nor the guns were on it. Jones, labeled in the press as the brains behind the shipment, became the subject of a manhunt.

It was an election season in the Philippines, and officials feared that the influx of guns might portend a rash of political terrorism. Some believed the weapons were destined for rebel groups operating in the southern part of the country, including militants from Abu Sayyaf, a terrorist group linked at the time to al-Qaeda. Mar Supnad, the local reporter who broke the story, said the news of the shipment "exploded like a bomb."

Five days after the seizure of the *M/V Ufuk*, Supnad got a call from a family friend named Joe Frank Zuñiga. A prominent local lawyer, Zuñiga told the reporter that he was representing Bruce Jones, who was hiding in the mountains above the coast. Jones wanted to meet with Supnad for an interview, to "tell to the world that he has nothing to do with the illegal shipment of guns."

The next day, Supnad drove to the address he'd been given by Zuñiga. It was dark when he arrived at a small house, where Jones and Zuñiga awaited him. The three drove to a nearby restaurant, emptied of customers, and talked over a red-and-white-checked tablecloth. Supnad recalled that Jones seemed distressed to the point of tears. "I am not a terrorist," he said.

Jones told Supnad his life story: He was forty-nine years old and had come to the Philippines in 1993 from Bristol, England, after an itinerant life at sea. He was married to a twenty-five-year-old local Filipina named Maricel and lived just outside Subic. Jones had already been working for Paul Le Roux's organization, captaining boats to Hong Kong and back with gold aboard, when Dave Smith approached him about sailing a ship from Turkey to Indonesia to the Philippines. La Plata Trading, one of Le Roux's Philippine companies, would pay for the journey and supply the crew. Smith arranged for Jones to fly to Turkey and purchase the *M/V Ufuk,* a rusty but seaworthy twenty-four-hundred-ton vessel. Along with the Georgian crew, Jones sailed down the coast of Africa, stopping in Ghana before rounding the Cape of Good Hope and heading for Indonesia.

At a dock in Jakarta, he picked up the cargo, a shipment of weapons from a company called PT Pindad. Then, along with Joseph Hunter, who came on board in Jakarta for protection, he set out for the Philippines. Jones told Supnad he believed the shipment was legitimate: He had been supplied with an end-user certificate—a document in the arms trade establishing the legitimate government purchaser—indicating that the guns were meant for a buyer in Mali. Some fifty Indonesian police and soldiers had supervised the pickup.

As Jones piloted the ship toward the Philippines, he got a call from Smith telling him to delay bringing it into port. When the *Ufuk* had been in a holding pattern for several days, Jones began to worry. His wife was pregnant, due any day. Jones told Smith he wanted to get off.

That night, Smith and another mercenary, Chris De Meyer, brought high-speed rubber rafts alongside the *Ufuk*. Jones was replaced on board by Burne, the South African captain, and the sixteen crates of guns were transferred onto the rafts and then to the *Mou Man Tai*. The smaller boat took Jones and Hunter back to Subic.

Jones was telling Supnad all this to signal to the authorities that he was willing to spill what he knew about the people who had hired him—a well-financed syndicate, he called it, whose owner held passports from three countries. In return, he wanted the government to keep the syndicate from exacting vengeance on him.

Supnad published his story about Jones on August 26, 2009, under the headline "British Captain of Arms Ship Seeks Gov't Protection." Two weeks later, Jones surrendered to the Bureau of Customs. According to a report from the Philippine Office of the Special Envoy on Transnational Crime, "Jones told investigators that he was hired by La Plata Trading Inc. through the help of Smith last August, to buy the vessel worth $800,000 in Turkey and the Indonesia-made assault rifles and pistols for $86,000."

The Philippine government charged thirty-seven people with illegally importing guns—Burne and the entire Georgian crew, plus Jones and a dozen names associated with Le Roux's organization, some of them aliases. The indictment covered the supposed owners of La Plata Trading and Red White & Blue Arms, including "David Smith a.k.a. Dave Smith," "Michael T. Archangel," and one "Johan a.k.a. John Paul Leraux."

Mar Supnad's account of his meeting with Jones was a scoop, but soon Supnad himself began receiving threats. The first one was "friendly," he said: A journalist colleague invited him to meet for coffee in Subic Bay and offered him 500,000 pesos (around $10,000) to stop writing about the *Ufuk*. He turned down the bribe and published an article about it instead. "The emissary," he wrote, "told this writer that top PNP and DOJ officials will handle the gun smuggling case provided there will be no more exposé in the newspapers."

Not long after came a second veiled threat: Someone from the syndicate approached Supnad's editor and suggested Supnad take a three-month trip to Hong Kong or Macau, fully paid for, rather than write any more stories about the *Ufuk*. Again Supnad said no, and his editor agreed. "Just continue writing what you know about the smuggling," the editor told him.

Supnad started varying his route to work and avoiding the Subic area entirely. He changed the plates on his car regularly and sometimes wore a wig. He heard rumors that he was on a hit list, that the syndicate had paid off a police official to make the *Ufuk* case—and the charges against "Johan," the man behind it—go away.

Zuñiga, Bruce Jones's lawyer, pleaded publicly for the Philippine Department of Justice to place Jones under witness protection. "Mr. Jones is afraid for his life," Zuñiga told a reporter. "He is a victim and not a suspect."

16

The Mercenaries

2008–2010 . . . The M/V Ufuk blows a cover . . . A gateway to Iran . . . Expanding in Somalia . . . Shifting priorities in Galkayo . . . Klaussen wants out . . . A threat and a promise

In Manila, the confiscation of the *M/V Ufuk* and its captain had thrown the security side of Le Roux's operation into disarray. Philippine customs was supposed to have been paid off. Now Le Roux wanted to know why they hadn't been. He began doling out new bribes to try to make the court case disappear, but the incident was more than just a legal problem. Two of Le Roux's companies, La Plata Trading and Red White & Blue Arms, had been exposed. The captain of the ship, Bruce Jones, was in the press, telling the world that he planned to snitch on the organization. Even if Le Roux's own name had barely surfaced in the court documents, as "Johan a.k.a. John Paul Leraux," others had. The names of two of his important deputies, Dave Smith and Nestor Del Rosario, were all over the case. Le Roux left the country for Hong Kong and then Mexico, and told the members of his security operation to keep their heads down.

Also found among the accused in the *Ufuk* case was an alias of an Israeli employee named Shai Reuven—aka "Michael Ross,"

"Michael Archangel," or "Michael Vaughn"—who had risen to prominence in Le Roux's organization as a jack-of-all-trades. Reuven was the flashiest of Le Roux's men, "always dressed to the nines in Gucci," as Lachlan McConnell put it, and was rumored among The Company's employees to have ties to organized crime back in Jerusalem. From Manila, he had managed some of The Company's gold and timber ventures. He was also among the most disliked by the mercenaries, known for an unpleasant cocktail of arrogance and incompetence. "Most of the people I knew there hated [him]," Tim Vamvakias, the American soldier, recalled. "But the boss had a special interest and protection over him, so it was what it was."

The *Ufuk* was a kind of unintended coming-out party for Le Roux's criminal expansion, from online pharmaceuticals into large-scale illegal drug and arms trafficking. Among his employees, that transformation was increasingly an open secret. His entry into the drug trade was partly a product of happenstance. In late 2009, a fishing vessel called the *King Yue I,* bound for Hong Kong—and unrelated to Le Roux—was intercepted in the Pacific and pursued for seventeen days by a U.S. Coast Guard cutter out of Guam. As the chase approached the Philippines, the *King Yue*'s crew tossed two tons of cocaine overboard, a bounty that proceeded to wash ashore over the next year in shrinkwrapped bricks. Sensing a business opportunity for Le Roux, Dave Smith scoured the country, buying the found coke for pennies from Philippine fishermen and generating an enormous stash that Le Roux could now sell on the streets at outlandish profits. "That was by complete fluke," a former employee who helped distribute the drugs told me. "He got some of it free, and he bought some of it very very very cheap. Dave scooped a lot of the stuff up, and different parts were packaged and sent to different countries."

The lucky haul whetted Le Roux's appetite for the drug trade, and Smith became the point man for a new narcotics arm of the business. To more easily move contraband in and out of the Philippines, Le Roux ordered an airstrip constructed on a piece of property in Batangas, facing the South China Sea. On the east coast, he bought an island to facilitate shipments from the Pacific.

Soon, Shai Reuven was telling his fellow employees that he had been sent to Colombia make contacts with cocaine producers, and another Israeli was rumored to have been ordered to Mexico to try to find a cartel connection for Le Roux. (He was instead taken captive and beaten, the story went, lucky to escape with his life.) The details sometimes changed in the telling, but the whispers captured the weird truth of Le Roux's philosophy for expanding his empire: throw money or employees at the wall and see what sticks. Any particular assignment could seem inane, even naïve, but in the aggregate the approach got results. "He just sent his people," said Felix Klaussen. "Sometimes they come back with nothing. Sometimes they come back with information. And then when some guys finally get in contact with a serious source or with a serious supplier, if necessary he gives them a call and wires them a couple million dollars. Then, okay, this guy is serious. Everything was a tryout for him. He could send ten people to the same city until he got the result he wanted."

The same philosophy held for arms deals. Nestor Del Rosario had risen from call center administrator to the manager of Red White & Blue Arms to the overseer of Le Roux's efforts to buy and sell weapons in Iran. For this latter mission, Del Rosario was ordered to fly to Tehran and find contacts in the Iranian government to transact with. Le Roux was hoping to sell them an explosives formula he had perfected—his own variation on erythritol tetranitrate, or ETN, a cousin of plastic explosives that was powerful and simple to produce. Somewhat miraculously, Le Roux's faith in Del Rosario paid off, and he made contact with a government official who eventually agreed to buy the formula for $5 million. But Le Roux had a more lucrative project for the Iranians: missile-guidance-system software, similar to that used in U.S. Tomahawk missiles, that could potentially help the country extend the reach of the nuclear capabilities it had been trying to develop for decades. He'd hired a team of more than twenty engineers to work on the project at a warehouse in the Philippines. Most had been recruited from Romania—including several through Craigslist—having been told they were working on "spectral analysis" software for underground mining.

So eager was Le Roux to find his way into more and bigger illicit deals that he was often willing to take a chance on highly speculative ventures, based on little more than a trusted employee's assertions. "If you had an idea and you came to him with the figures, and if he liked the money, he would give you three million, five million, twenty million just like that," one former employee said. "He would give me 10 million in a Pelican box if I asked for it, in an hour, in cash, in perfect notes."

The *M/V Ufuk*, in other words, represented only the visible outer edge of the dark universe that Le Roux now inhabited. Lachlan McConnell felt the gravitational pull of Le Roux's schemes. "At one point they wanted me to go somewhere in Eastern Europe to buy weapons," he said. "I said, 'Sorry, that's illegal, I'm not going to do it.' I'm not stupid. You have to not cross a line, and I said from the beginning there were certain things I wouldn't do."

McConnell instead shepherded gold in Hong Kong and helped arrange international shipments of equipment to Le Roux's various projects, including Somalia. He had little idea what was happening in the Somali outpost, only that it required an array of gear: military uniforms, shipped through Hong Kong; outboard motors, sent to Dubai. Le Roux had offered the fanciful explanation that he was starting a lobster farm. It sounded odd, but it wasn't even the oddest thing McConnell had heard from Smith about Le Roux's various schemes. "I didn't put much into it," McConnell said. "Dave tended to brag a lot."

Over the course of 2010, Dave Smith's behavior had become increasingly erratic. He confided in McConnell that he had been "borrowing" gold bars from under a hot tub behind a house in the Philippines—where he'd stashed them for Le Roux—and selling them to cover his own debts. He was planning to pay it all back, he said, and Le Roux would be none the wiser. He prevailed on McConnell to hold $150,000 of the "borrowed" money for him, in a Hong Kong account that McConnell controlled. McConnell reluctantly agreed.

Smith also confided that he had been paying contacts in the Philippine police force to manufacture cases against Le Roux—tipping them off to his drug shipments coming into the country—then having Le Roux pay to make them go away. It was a dangerous two-sided game that allowed him to skim off the difference. "I think he started taking drugs, and that's probably why he started being loose and spending the stuff," McConnell said. "He was pissed off because he wasn't really making much money, and he was doing so much."

For Felix Klaussen in Somalia, the confiscation of the *M/V Ufuk* in August 2009 was only a distant curiosity in the face of more pressing concern: pirates. Over the previous six months, Klaussen had laid the groundwork for the tuna-fishing operation. He'd known before arriving that he would need the cooperation of pirates operating along the coast. And to Le Roux, collaborating with pirates was part and parcel of his approach. "For him it was very convenient," Klaussen said. "Pirates, they're businessmen, you can do business with them. You can ask for their protection, and in return he gives them protection."

Now, with the inland compound established and secured in Galkayo, it was time to go and get that cooperation. Liban, his local point man, had made arrangements for the head of a pirate syndicate to travel to the compound for a meeting in the summer of 2009. Le Roux, ever the micromanager, sent detailed notes on exactly how he expected Klaussen to conduct business:

It is good you have an opening with them, as u know (i understand u already discussed the matter with dave) we are not there just for fishing, u need to become self-sufficient (in terms of money) while we ramp up the fishing and the other areas of business we interested in, that means oil, it means fishing, it means other businesses i will discuss with u in person. What we are doing now is setting the ground work for co-opperation with all our friends in many profitable areas where we can help each other.

Bottom line: you should meet with them, listen to what they have to say (the real reason they want to see u is probably different as nobody is fishing anymore in somali waters other than locals, talking about 'illegal fishing vessels' is their code, it just means commercial ships passing their waters..)

In any case after u talk with them tell them u need to go back to Asia to talk with the company owners about it and we will need another follow up meeting when u return.

On the day of the meeting, the pirate and his crew arrived in a gold-colored Toyota Land Cruiser. The transaction was a simple one, and Klaussen easily secured approval for his boats to fish in the pirate's territory. But the pirate had a more pressing issue: Would Klaussen be interested in buying the Land Cruiser? It was too conspicuous for him, he'd discovered. "The drones are spotting me, they can pick me out of anything with the golden car," he told Klaussen. "Why don't you just buy it? You have a registered company, you are not doing what I do." Klaussen acquired it on the spot.

The pirates may have been on board, but the rest of the Somalia operation was creeping along. Le Roux was wiring millions into the country from accounts at Wilex and La Plata Trading, and buying equipment overseas to be shipped through Dubai and Djibouti. Le Roux's lieutenant, Nestor Del Rosario, purchased ten Yamaha outboard motors through a shell company in July 2009, shipping them via Hong Kong and Djibouti and then on to Somalia, to accompany ten fishing boats they had bought locally. The equipment for building the factory arrived in Galkayo but hadn't been moved out to the coast. "There were tents for four to five thousand people, a base camp to start construction," Klaussen said. "Generators, drilling equipment, all of it." There were plans for a fish-processing factory, an airstrip, housing, and an onsite mosque for workers—Le Roux even supplied a detailed schematic for constructing a desalination plant and then piping the water inland to Galkayo.

But reality in Somalia tended to defy hypothetical plans concocted abroad. When Klaussen turned his attention to building out the coastal site, he discovered that what looked like a three-hour trip on a map was in fact a seven-hour axle-breaking drive on desert roads. The shoreline property they'd purchased for the fish-processing facility was a wreck, and the structures had to be taken down to the foundation. As soon as they broke ground, they discovered that the whole area sat on a bed of spongy, porous rock. To build a factory and worker housing on top of it—much less an airstrip that wouldn't collapse under the weight of Le Roux's Russian cargo planes—would require feats of engineering difficult even in a developed country. The whole project would cost more, and take longer, than Le Roux had conceived.

Klaussen also discovered that Le Roux's plans for a water pipeline were grandiose at best, madness at worst. "It's not just, okay, we're going to build a pipeline. Who's going to protect that pipeline? It's three hundred kilometers! You've got to have patrols because al-Shabaab wants to fuck you and they are going to come and poison your water. Or steal it. You've got to take all that into consideration." Le Roux might be a genius, Klaussen thought, but he wasn't on the ground, and the previous employees he'd sent to be his eyes and ears had been buffoons.

Even with hundreds of local fighters now in their employ, the security situation remained precarious. Klaussen approved the purchase of a ZU-23 antiaircraft gun, with a range of a mile and a half and bullets with explosive tips, and mounted it on the back of a pickup truck. With al-Shabaab ramping up its attacks outside of Galkayo, the local paramilitary group aligned with Le Roux's operation, Ahlu Sunna Waljama'a, was desperate for more arms to fight them. They arrived at the compound with a formal letter requesting assistance from Klaussen, who emailed Le Roux:

> the situation is that al shabab is 100km away from gaalkaio, we arrested 3 of there group 2days ago and they are now in jail, we are still safe at this moment but serious help is needed asap
>
> Then the sunaa wal jamea mujahidin (the big local tribe who is in control of galmudug and our friends) there requests for help to fight all shabab and destroy them is as fallow.
>
> I got meetings with them every day and any support we give will be purchased by me.
>
> personally we need sniper arms and body armor asap.

"UNDERSTOOD," Le Roux replied. Klaussen wanted $50,000 to feed and equip the men. "APPROVED," Le Roux wrote. "WE WILL SEND THE FUNDS TOMORROW." As for the weapons, he continued:

> THE SITUATION IS WE HAVE A SHIT LOAD OF ARMS ON ORDER, BUT IT IS TAKING TIME (WE HAVE BEEN CAUGHT BY SURPRISE BY THE NEED TO RAMP UP THIS QUICK) . . . WE ARE RAMPING UP WITH PLANES AND CREW BUT IT TAKES TIME.

He also reminded Klaussen that he had offered to send his own security personnel. "WE CAN SEND 500 MEN THERE ON SHORT TERM BASIS WITHIN 72 HOURS NOTICE," he wrote. Where the mercenaries would come from, he didn't say. Le Roux at times seemed to be playing Somalia like a videogame, several levels out of his depth.

Despite the fuckups and delays, Klaussen was proud of what they were building. Against all odds, he felt he'd developed a strong working relationship with Le Roux. His emails asking for more men, or weapons, or resources, tended to come back with one word: "approved." It didn't hurt that, unlike many of Le

Roux's mercenary employees, he knew how to deliver the spread-sheets through which Le Roux preferred to be informed. "That's where I came in quite handy," Klaussen said. "Because with me he could communicate."

The days were hard but rewarding, even fun, as he developed a rapport with the Somalis. He was gratified by how many families the operation was now supporting. When he noticed that a school for girls just outside the perimeter of the compound was housed in a concrete building with no power and a metal roof, he arranged to supply electricity for fans and bottled water for the students. "I thought those kids must be dying in there," he said. "What's it going to cost us? Twenty bottles of water. Fuck that. Le Roux didn't know. I didn't tell him that he paid for it."

At times, the contradictions of life in the compound could be jolting. An accountant Le Roux had sent from the Philippines to oversee the organization's books spent his days posting photos to his Facebook page of himself holding weapons and driving around in the ZU-23 mounted truck. At night, the accountant slept with a teddy bear and wept for home.

When it came to the daily dissonance of Le Roux's Somalia operation, though, the most surreal moment was the sudden appearance—at Klaussen's invitation—of a *New York Times* correspondent. Arriving on a flight back into Galkayo's small airport one afternoon in the spring of 2009, Klaussen noticed a pair of white men, travel-ing with a Somali he knew named Sahal Abdulle. Klaussen struck up a conversation, and one of the men introduced himself as Jeffrey Gettleman, a reporter for the *Times*. Gettleman and a photographer—with Abdulle serving as their Somali translator and fixer—had been traveling around the region for a story on piracy, accompanied by a dozen armed guards. Now their flight out was grounded by mechanical difficulties, and they'd already sent away their driver and security. Klaussen offered to house them for the night in his compound, a mile and a half away. "You got three hundred guards around you, nothing can happen to you," he said. Lacking any bet-ter options, they agreed.

All Abdulle knew of Klaussen was that he and his group were building some kind of fisheries company, employing a large number of local fighters and traveling back and forth to the coast. At the compound, the nature of the operation that had welcomed them was difficult to grasp. "They were this little team in this huge rambling house, in these sarong-like wraps, wearing no shirts, carrying AK-47s, living like outlaws," Gettleman said. ("They didn't look like fishermen," Abdulle said.) "Even though it sounded kind of fantastic, it wasn't totally beyond belief," Gettleman said. "Because there had been a lot of talk about rehabilitating pirates." For years, he knew, the United Nations and other agencies had talked of bringing back the fishing industry, but the idea still inhabited the realm of dreams and policy papers. "It's almost like a white elephant," Gettleman said. "How much energy would it take to freeze fish where it is a hundred degrees?"

A few of Klaussen's employees seemed suspicious of the reporter who had arrived in their midst, but Klaussen was thrilled to have some new faces around. "Of course all the Somalis, they heard it was Americans and thought CIA," he said. "I said, 'No, it's reporters, they're my friends!'" When he offered the journalists guns of their own, they politely declined.

Gettleman marveled at how comfortable Klaussen seemed to feel, operating in what appeared to be an environment entirely hostile to foreign companies. "I've worked all around Somalia and Galkayo is always one of the scariest places," he said. It was also starting to develop a reputation as a place where Westerners were potential targets for lucrative kidnappings. "It had a bad vibe, just nobody was in control. These guys were taking advantage of the lawlessness to say fuck it, we'll get our own guns, we'll go wherever we want. They were like white pirates."

Gettleman was left puzzled by Klaussen's operation, with no way of knowing that he was in the middle of a burgeoning criminal cartel being hunted by the U.S. government. "I got the vibe that he was almost earnest" about the work, he said of Klaussen. "He had respect, and he seemed interested in Somalia and excited to be there. I also thought, if what they were doing was illegitimate, why would they let us stay with them? If they are running a criminal enterprise, why would they invite us in?"

The next morning, the group accepted a ride back to the airport and flew out. When Gettleman won a Pulitzer Prize for his reporting on Somalia three years later, Klaussen sent him a congratulatory note.

Whether Le Roux's intentions for Somalia changed or he was just slowly rolling out a plan he'd had all along, Klaussen wasn't sure. But late in 2009, he felt his boss's priorities shift. The fishing project was burning $50,000 to $100,000 a month, Le Roux said, and it was time for self-sufficiency. Fortunately, he had plans for how to create it. For starters, he'd had Klaussen arrange for a license to import and export prescription drugs in bulk—supplementing the pharmacy recruitment network he'd built for RX Limited—and resell them in Europe or the United States.

But that was just the beginning. The Somalia operation, he announced, would become sustainable by growing drugs. He began shipping in seeds to experiment with: poppies (code name "carrots," as Le Roux established in one email to Klaussen), cannabis ("beans"), and coca ("mustard"). He also hired a Filipino agriculture expert and shipped him to Galkayo, where he converted a room in the compound into a mini-greenhouse for test plantings while Le Roux arranged for a large-scale version to be imported. Le Roux sent obsessively detailed plans about how to set up the operation, including the required pressure for the irrigation systems, initial fertilization quantities, space between planting rows, and water needed per day. "Also there's no soil in Somalia suitable" for growing drugs, Klaussen said. "So we had to basically import loads and loads of soil and fertilize it constantly." No matter, Le Roux was already barreling ahead, forwarding résumés of chemists and agriculturalists that he could hire to ramp up production.

Le Roux then devised still another moneymaking scheme, inspired by the Somali pirates who were now their partners. His plan, Klaussen said, "was to send some special speedboats, military grade, high horsepower. To basically go to the Seychelles, kidnap some rich people, bring them back to Somalia, hold them hostage until they paid ransom, then let them go. Pirate style. Because he loved what the pirates did. For him that was genius. That was fast money, with almost no expense."

As Le Roux's ambitions ballooned, so, too, did his assessment of the weapons it would require to carry them out. In November 2009 Le Roux detailed a list of weapons he said he'd purchased for shipment into the country:

20mm gatling gun 10
at-3 sagger wire guided misile 5
grenades (incendary 500 fragmentation 500) 1000
AKM 5000
PKM 600
DSHKA 300
RPG7 300
GRENADE LAUNCHER TGL-6 40
81MM MORTARS 50
MIXTURE OF DETONATORS 100
C4 EXPLOSIVES 75KG
UNGUIDED INCENDIARY BOMBS 10
ANTI PERSONNEL LAND MINES 200
RPG ROUNDS (HE 1000 THERMOBARIC 1000)
81MM MORTAR ROUNDS (HE 500 WHITESMOKE 500)
7.62X39MM ROUNDS 2MILLION
SAGGER HE WARHEADS 50
SAGGER THERMOBARIC WARHEADS 50
7.62X54MM ROUNDS 1MILLION
12.7X108MM ROUNDS 250 000
40X46MM GRENADES FOR TGL-6 1000
20MM ROUNDS 20 000

DRAGNOV SNIPER RIFLE 10
12MM SHOTGUN RUSSIAN TYPE 10

The arms would be flown in from Ukraine on a Russian Antonov cargo plane, a favorite of international arms dealers.
Klaussen prepared a security force of a hundred men to guard the
plane's unloading. At the last minute, the pilots balked at the size
of the runway and canceled the flight.

To Klaussen, Le Roux's ideas were growing more erratic and
grandiose by the month. Le Roux wanted to make roomfuls of
money in Somalia, he told Klaussen, boxes of cash so voluminous
that they wouldn't be able to store them. He wanted to control his
own country, so he could operate with complete freedom. Ultimately, it wasn't just profits he wanted, but power unfettered by
any government. "He wanted to be the king of his country, that
was his major dream," Klaussen said. "The big man. Sitting on his
fat ass behind a giant desk in his palace."

Klaussen could never understand why Le Roux couldn't just
stick to the plan. "He would have made millions and millions of
dollars every month in Somalia legally," he said. The tuna business
really was there for the taking. And after that there was oil: Decades before, American oil companies had prospected in a more
stable Somalia, believing that it had significant oil reserves to exploit. They'd fled after the overthrow of the country's pro-American
dictator in 1991, and Le Roux claimed to have come into possession
of coordinates indicating where the Americans had drilled. There
could be untold riches under the ground that Southern Ace, with
its protective force, would be uniquely positioned to liberate. Le
Roux purchased a small drilling rig and had it shipped to Somalia.
When Klaussen and his men tried it, they discovered that he'd
bought one insufficiently deep to strike oil.

Klaussen was beginning to realize that Le Roux's appetites were
too great to be satisfied by long-term returns. "He didn't have the
patience," Klaussen said. "It had to happen now. Not next year,
not in six months. No. Now."

Over the course of 2010, Klaussen began spending more and more time overseeing the Somalia business remotely, from Dubai. Le Roux didn't complain, since the operation's banking was conducted in the city, and much of its equipment was either purchased or shipped through it. The strain of his remote posting had ended Klaussen's marriage in the Philippines, and he started seeing a woman in Dubai. The longer he was away from Galkayo, the more his doubts crept in. Navigating between the day-to-day chaos on the ground and Le Roux's capricious demands had become exhausting. One of the compound's cars was hit by an improvised explosive device while Klaussen was away. No one was killed, but several of the guards had ruptured eardrums. When Le Roux insisted they could be treated at local hospitals, Klaussen secretly rearranged the budget to fly them to Djibouti for treatment on The Company's dime.

Worse than the trials of running the operation, for Klaussen, was the feeling that he had begun sliding into a moral purgatory. He had long been acutely aware of, and working alongside, Le Roux's violence and criminality. But the new proposals for Somalia felt different. With Le Roux's cultivation scheme, Klaussen was potentially becoming an international drug producer. The Seychelles tourist-kidnapping plan was even worse: It would cast Klaussen into a role no different than that of violent thugs like Joseph Hunter.

In Dubai, Klaussen finally talked to his girlfriend about his concerns. "She had a basic knowledge of what I was doing, not in detail," he said. "She said, 'Do what you have to do. Follow what your heart says, or what your mind says, in this case.'" She would understand if he wanted to keep working for Le Roux, she told him. "But if I was you, I would walk away from it." That was enough for Klaussen.

He flew back to Galkayo, and a few days later roused the entire compound in the middle of the night, announcing that his mother had a medical emergency. He had to be on the next plane out. There was a U.N. aid flight leaving in the morning, and Klaussen talked the pilot into letting him ride as cargo. "And off I was, I was gone," he said. "When I arrived in Dubai I felt so relieved. But of course then the trouble only started."

After about a week, Klaussen called Le Roux to inform him that he wasn't coming back. "It's getting out of hand," he told his boss. "It's crossing lines that I don't want to cross. I'm done." Le Roux wasn't angry, not at first. "Okay, no problem" is all Klaussen remembered him saying. But with Klaussen's departure, and the Somalian operation now in the hands of the likes of Agent Orange, the wheels started coming off. Money disappeared, and the local security forces' monthly salaries became irregular. Klaussen kept in contact with his former employees, and then suddenly they went dark. An email to his British deputy prompted a reply from a newly created anonymous address. "Hey buddy sorry but I can't talk to you," the deputy wrote. "You gotta understand, I don't want to end up dead."

Then Klaussen got a call from his old friend Chris De Meyer, who was still working for Le Roux in Manila.

"There's a hit on you," De Meyer said.

"A what?"

"Yeah, apparently Le Roux put a hit on you."

"Why?"

"It's about things that happened in Somalia. Joe is on his way to Dubai." "Joe" meant Hunter, which meant that Klaussen was in deep shit.

They'd had a pact, Klaussen remembered: If Le Roux ever asked one of them to kill another, they'd let each other know, and then fake the killing. Hunter, apparently, had decided not to honor it. Klaussen hung up the phone and started making calculations. Hunter would have trouble getting to him at home in Dubai, where he lived in a secure building, in a condo rented from his girlfriend's employer. Instead, he'd likely try to take Klaussen out in the street.

Hunter was a killer, a trained sniper. He wasn't someone to just sit and wait for.

Klaussen looked up the last number he'd had for Le Roux and dialed it. Le Roux picked up.

"It's me," Klaussen said. "What's going on?"

"What do you mean what's going on?"

"Yeah, what's Joe coming to do?"

Le Roux said he didn't know what Klaussen was talking about.

"I know there's a hit on me," Klaussen said. "Give me a reason. Tell me why. If you are going to kill me, tell me why. I want to know if I died for an illusion or for a stupid reason. Or maybe you're mentally ill, I don't know."

Le Roux stopped playing dumb. "I did an investigation," he said. Three hundred thousand dollars had gone missing from the Somalian operation. The remaining employees had pointed to Klaussen. Le Roux cited as proof the condominium that Klaussen was living in, in Dubai.

"Listen, I'll send you all the documents, the financial reports," Klaussen said. "Every dollar is accounted for during the period I was there. So please, I know you're smart enough. I know nobody can cheat you. But check them again. I'm going to call you back in two days. And you tell me again that I took three hundred thousand dollars. If you can show me one dollar that I took from you, send Joe, it's fine. But make sure he's ready. Because I'm going to wait for him." He hung up the phone and emailed Le Roux the records he'd maintained on the project, including a list of serial numbers of all the cash ever spent under his watch.

Then Klaussen looked up the website of the CIA, the first agency that popped into his head, and sent an email to a generic address. In it, he reported that he'd worked for a man named Paul Le Roux, that he had information about large-scale international criminality, and that he was willing to talk. No one replied.

A few days later, Klaussen called Le Roux back, and before he could say anything, Klaussen launched into a prepared speech. "I forgot to say, you call that dog back, because I have a backup of all the information that I know about you: your family in the Netherlands, everything. And it's going to go out, if something happens to me." He'd heard something similar in a movie. He hung up, then called back a few hours later. "Okay, I apologize, I shouldn't have said that. But what did you find out about the money I took?"

"Well, I was going to apologize to you, because you're right, you didn't," Le Roux said. "It doesn't make sense." The dates on the reports Le Roux had received from the guys still in Somalia didn't match the originals that Klaussen had saved. The evidence that Klaussen had stolen the funds, in other words, had been forged. "I told Joe already, called him to come back," Le Roux said. Then the man who had just ordered a hit on Klaussen instead offered him a job, managing the pharmaceutical side of the business, at a salary of $40,000 a month. "Come to Manila and let's talk," he said.

Klaussen declined.

"Listen, you have my word nothing's gonna happen to you," Le Roux said. "You want a job, call me."

Klaussen wasn't naïve enough to trust Le Roux, but he felt hopeful that he had finally escaped the organization. "I walked out at the right time, without breaking too many laws, or serious laws," he said. At least for now he'd managed to wriggle out from under the hit. But he still seethed with a feeling that he'd been betrayed, that after all he'd done and all he'd overlooked, his boss had ordered him dead on an ill-informed whim.

"He lost my respect by ordering a hit on me," Klaussen said. "When I threatened him that I was gonna give him up, I meant it. I meant every single word of that. Apparently he didn't take that seriously enough."

17

The Investigators

2009–2010 . . . More Ufuk *ripples . . . Captain Bruce wants to talk . . .*
Le Roux makes a list . . . Brill goes it alone . . . A source goes quiet

In late August 2009, only a few weeks after returning from meeting with law enforcement in the Philippines, Kent Bailey got a call from a contact at the Australian Federal Police. He'd been exchanging information with the AFP after discovering the Australians had also been investigating Le Roux, who held an Australian passport from his first marriage. Now the Aussies were calling with a significant break. "Kent, have you seen what just happened in the Philippines?" the AFP contact said. The Philippine authorities had interdicted a ship called the *M/V Ufuk* and discovered a cache of weapons on board. A classified cable from the U.S. embassy in Jakarta, where the shipment originated, followed, reporting that the arms had been legally purchased from a company called PT Pindad and authorized by the Indonesian Ministry of Defense. The guns were invoiced for a Philippine company called RWB Arms.

Within hours, Bailey was on the phone with Filipino counterparts he'd met on his trip to Manila. They reported back to him that the ship was licensed to La Plata Trading, and that the guns'

destination was Red White & Blue Arms. The cargo manifest named
Nelson Del Rosario, aka Nestor Del Rosario, and Michael Lontoc,
a well-known competition target shooter, as the recipients. The
names were instantly familiar to Bailey. They were already part of
the intricate map of Le Roux's operation that Kimberly Brill and
Steven Holdren had created in Minneapolis—the website registrations, the shell companies, and the figures connected to them. "All
the pieces started falling together," Bailey said. "Within twenty-
four hours we knew it was Le Roux." The seizure would finally
give them hard evidence that he was more than just an online criminal.

Bailey watched the case develop from afar, in part through Mar
Supnad's stories in the local press. The *Ufuk*'s captain, Bruce Jones,
was telling Supnad he was ready to tell authorities everything
about the syndicate behind the shipment. He'd even surrendered
to the Philippines Bureau of Customs and requested that they place
him into witness protection. Finally, Bailey thought, they might
have the insider they had been seeking.

Working through the Australian agents, he tried to reach Jones,
first to tell him "to shut the fuck up," as Bailey recalled. "We were
like, 'Dude, we'll be lucky if you don't get killed before we get
ahold of you.'" When the Australians finally made contact with
Jones, they were able to meet with him twice to hear what he had.
"A lot of that was confirmation of what we knew, that Le Roux
was behind all this," Bailey said. Jones suggested he might put up
a website with everything he knew. But the Australians got the
impression that Jones wasn't fully cooperating, and he was released back onto the street.

In the meantime, the DEA investigators did manage to engineer
one break. The team put together a presentation laying out why Le
Roux should be added to the U.S. Attorney General's Consolidated Priority Organization Target (CPOT) list, an internal index
of the DOJ's most wanted drug criminals. There were roughly fifty
to sixty CPOT designees at any given time, people considered
members of "the most prolific international drug trafficking and

money laundering organizations" by the DEA, like the Sinaloa cartel head Joaquín "El Chápo" Guzmán. With the *Ufuk* arms case in hand, the team working RX Limited finally had enough to make a case that Le Roux deserved to be among them. He wasn't just a guy peddling pills online, they could now show. He was a new kind of drug kingpin, traveling seamlessly from the world of online pharmacies to that of major arms trafficking. "That was an aha moment," Bailey said. "That was the first time I could put stuff in that frickin' PowerPoint that said, 'What I've been saying? This is the proof.'"

In May 2010, Brill and Holdren flew to Washington, D.C., to present before a Department of Justice review board that votes on CPOT designations. When they finished, the board handed down its decision: Le Roux would be placed on the list. After years of Brill and Holdren trying to explain the power of Le Roux's convoluted, highly technical network, the powers that be finally acknowledged that their hunches about his significance had been right all along.

That night, Holdren told Brill he was leaving the DEA for a job as a criminal investigator at the federal Housing and Urban Development Agency. They'd been working the Le Roux case for nearly three years, and Holdren was looking for a new challenge. In Minneapolis, Brill would have to go it alone.

In her hotel room, Brill allowed herself a few minutes of despair. "It was purely out of exhaustion," she said. "We had gotten this extra focus on the case and raised it to a higher level, and I already knew what that was going to mean. Now there were some additional expectations. And it was kind of an overwhelming feeling that I was going to have to figure these things out, and I wasn't sure I could do it on my own." And then, she said, "I got over it."

The CPOT designation was a calling card that would open doors in other departments and agencies, and bring additional resources. But they still needed that one missing piece to make the case against Le Roux: someone from the inside.

Two months later, Bailey got another call from the Australian authorities, with bad news: the ship captain Jones had been arrested for weapons and drug possession. The Australians tracked him down in jail, where he told them it was all a setup. In a brazen attempt to play both sides, he had met with Dave Smith hoping to recoup the rest of his fee for piloting the boat. "Jones still wanted to get paid, I think he was supposed to get paid fifty grand," Bailey said. So he'd gone to Smith to plead his case. " 'Hey, I delivered the boat, I can't help it if it was seized.' In a court of law in a legitimate deal, he would have been ordered to be paid. But you can't go to a real court."

The two argued, until finally Smith agreed to pay the money. He called someone whom Jones assumed to be Le Roux, then told Jones the money would be placed in a paper bag in his truck, outside the bar. When Jones walked out and retrieved the bag, he found not $50,000 but two ounces of meth and a gun. Moments later, the Philippine police swooped in and arrested him.

Bailey and the Australians discussed their options. If they got Jones out of jail, they feared Smith and Le Roux might "move it to the next level" to silence him. But Jones wanted out, and they decided to hope that their would-be informant wouldn't put himself right back in danger. According to Bailey, he and the Australians decided to spring Jones from jail. (The Australian Federal Police denied having had any role in the release, suggesting instead that Le Roux's organization was responsible.)

For a while, Jones heeded the agents' advice to stay under the radar. By September 2010, it had been a year since the *Ufuk*, with no arrests in the case. Jones decided to venture out, confident, the reporter Mar Supnad said, "that the syndicate was no longer running after him." On the morning of September 21, he drove his wife, Maricel, and young son to the Marquee Mall, in Angeles City, the former site of a U.S. military base two hours north of Manila. They were meeting friends, an American named John Nash and his wife, for lunch.

Jones and Nash knew each other from the expat circles in Subic Bay, where Nash ran a security company. Among other things, his company supplied bouncers for local bars—including one called Blue Rock Resort in Baloy Beach, frequented by Dave Smith—and security for a Sea World–type aquatic animal park called Ocean Adventure. Nash had a reputation as a particular kind of problem solver—"He was known for placing his pistol on the table at the beginning of a negotiation," one acquaintance said—and spoke five Filipino dialects fluently.

At around 2 P.M., the group departed from lunch, Jones and his wife in their gray Mitsubishi Lancer, their toddler in the backseat, with Nash following a few minutes behind. They planned to meet up again at the nearby Mountain Clark Firing Range, where Nash was a regular.

As Jones turned down a narrow residential road, one hundred feet from the entrance to the gun range, a red Honda XRM motorcycle pulled up behind him, carrying two men in helmets riding in tandem. The vehicles approached a speed bump, and the motorcycle zoomed in front, blocking the car's path. The man on the back leaped off, approached the car, pulled out a handgun, and fired into the driver's side window. The gunman then climbed back on the motorcycle, and the men sped off.

Jones was hit multiple times. One bullet passed through his body and struck Maricel in the back. He fell over on top of her, vomiting blood. Maricel froze, terrified, and then opened the door and climbed out. She frantically called Nash, who raced down the road to where Jones's Lancer idled. He pulled Maricel and her son into his car and drove to the hospital. The baby was unhurt, and doctors were able to stabilize Maricel. Jones died slumped across the passenger's seat, his wife's shoes still on the floor next to him.

According to the police report, investigators found four .45-caliber shell casings near the car, but little other evidence. Tandem motorcycle riders are a common style of assassination in the Philippines, not least because helmeted killers can speed off without being identified. Police questioned Nash, who gave his full name as John William Nash, Jr., a forty-nine-year-old American working as a "consultant" in the Subic Bay area. Nash told police that he and his wife had lingered for a minute after lunch, putting some packages in the trunk of their car. He received the call from Maricel and arrived to find "Bruce already bloodied and lying at the front seat of his car." Nash said that Jones had told him previously that he had received death threats and noticed strangers near his home who Jones believed were connected to his "employers" on the *Ufuk*.

Back in England, where Jones had grown up, locals grieved a man they called a "lovable rogue." The captain left behind four children, two in the United Kingdom and two in the Philippines. "He was an amazing chap," an old friend from home told a Bristol newspaper. "Unfortunately, he obviously ended up falling into the wrong circles."

Kent Bailey had never met Jones, and he mourned a different kind of loss. Their best chance at an informant had just slipped away. They'd have to find someone else.

18

The Reporter

2015–2017 . . . On the trail of a killing . . . The bodies pile up . . . A Philippine officer presses the case . . . Corruption at the top . . . An ocean adventure

"When I arrived here, he was already dead," said Roberto Manuel, the Philippine police officer who had been the first at the scene of Bruce Jones's murder. We were standing on a crumbling road outside of Angeles City in December 2015, where Manuel had come upon Jones's blood-soaked car, still running, five years earlier. Occasionally we were interrupted by the audible pop-pop of the gun range a hundred feet down the road, the same one where Jones had been headed after lunch with John Nash. Manuel pulled out some crime scene photos he'd taken on his phone that day. With hand motions, he demonstrated exactly how far from Jones's window the gunman must have been standing when he fired: close enough to ensure accuracy, he said, but not so close as to shatter the window, which was left with four bullet holes. By the time Manuel arrived, John Nash had already left the scene, taking Jones's wife and son to the hospital and leaving Jones to bleed out in the front seat of his car.

Like many dramas surrounding Le Roux, the Jones murder seemed to contain mysteries within other mysteries, unexplained characters who surfaced suddenly, played a role, and then disappeared. I decided to go see Bruce Jones's lawyer, Joe Frank Zuñiga. He had brokered the meeting between Jones and the journalist Mar Supnad, and at the time of Jones's death he reportedly had been negotiating police protection in exchange for Jones telling his story. I wondered if he might recall anything else Jones had said about his dealings with Le Roux. But when I went online to find his address, the first Google result was a headline from a Philippine news site proclaiming that Zuñiga himself had gone missing. According to the article, from July 2012, one morning that June Zuñiga left home for a meeting with "a client" in Subic Bay and hadn't been seen since.

Wondering who else connected to the *M/V Ufuk* had turned up dead, I headed to the Manila office of the National Bureau of Investigation to meet with Peter Lugay, the chief of the NBI special task force investigating the Zuñiga case. The details were relatively sparse, he told me: At 11:45 on the morning of June 20, Zuñiga was seen in the Subic Bay area after a meeting with two men. One of them was Timothy Desmond, CEO of the company that operated Ocean Adventure, the aquatic animal park. Desmond, an American animal behaviorist, had made his name training the killer whale in the movie *Free Willy*. The other man was the head of security for Ocean Adventure: John Nash. Nash and Zuñiga were "close," Lugay told me. "They called each other 'compadre.'" Around the time of the meeting, a witness reported seeing a man near Zuñiga's car being dragged into a white van.

"Unfortunately," Lugay said, "I think we can safely assume that he is dead."

A colleague of Lugay's told me that since taking on the Zuñiga case they had been trying to understand the connections between the disappearances and the *M/V Ufuk*. "Have you encountered the name Herbert Tan Tiu?" he asked me. I hadn't, so he filled me in: Acting on a tip in early October 2010, two months after the Jones murder, the Philippine National Police raided Tiu's house and discovered a cache of Indonesian-made assault rifles they suspected had come from the *M/V Ufuk*.

"What happened to Tiu?" I asked.

"He is also missing," Lugay said.

Next, Lugay's colleague asked me if I'd ever heard of Michael Lontoc. I hadn't. It turned out he was the world-class Philippine target shooter listed as the owner of Red White & Blue Arms. His name had also surfaced publicly in the *Ufuk* case. By now, I could guess the end of Lontoc's story: One afternoon in September 2011, a year after the murder of Bruce Jones, Lontoc had been driving home from a shooting competition in a Manila suburb. As he slowed down at a busy intersection, he received a call on his cellphone. Simultaneously, four men surrounded his pickup truck, firing into it with an Uzi and several handguns. He drove another hundred feet before slamming into a concrete wall, and died on the scene.

Unsurprisingly, with witnesses and informants disappearing, the investigation into the owners of the *Ufuk* fizzled. The Georgian crew members were deported back to their home country. A Philippine court declared that the remaining cases, including one against "Johan" aka "Paul Leraux" and his top deputies, had been "archived." Only one participant, the South African ship captain Lawrence John Burne, was tried and convicted in absentia, after jumping bail.

One former employee of Le Roux's later estimated to me that Le Roux had spent millions making the case go away, funneled through a Filipina lawyer. The source believed he had bought off contacts at the highest level of the government, and paid to have certain friendly officials installed in powerful posts. Another told me that Le Roux had hired a former NBI official to take charge of distributing bribes to law enforcement. He even had a desk at the company's call center, at the BDO building in Makati. Yet another told me that Joe Frank Zuñiga had been part of the syndicate all along—he had actually been in charge of the bribes aimed at keeping the *M/V Ufuk* untouched, and was killed because he kept a piece for himself.

Sitting in the NBI office, I suddenly felt lost in the maze of graft and murders, where every new branch seemed to lead back to Le Roux. Could I even trust the accounts of the agents sitting across from me? I was no longer sure. The only thing I knew for certain was that Le Roux had operated here with a staggering level of impunity. "I don't know how deep this goes," Lugay told me. "We tried to talk to the prosecutor, to set up a meeting about the case, and you know what the prosecutor said? 'Tell your boss I'm not talking to him, because people disappear in this case.'"

By now I was so far down the rabbit hole that there seemed nothing to do but press on, looking for some semblance of logic on the other side. Together with Aurora Almendral, the reporter I'd been working with in Manila, I eventually tracked down one of the Philippine National Police officers who had investigated the Herbert Tan Tiu case in late 2010. The officer had long since been transferred to a small city an hour's flight outside Manila. He would only talk, he said, if Almendral and I came to see him in person. When our flight landed at a single-runway airport nestled in the mountains, a pair of officers picked us up in a black Chevy Blazer and drove us out to the local headquarters, a series of white block buildings spread across a kind of campus. The officer, whom I'll call Inspector R, was now a regional police coordinator here. It was a Sunday, and he greeted us in orange shorts and running shoes, along with what looked to be a bike racing jersey, white and blue with a PNP patch on one arm. On his desk were a series of neatly stacked reports marked "CONFIDENTIAL" and "SECRET."

We sat down across from him, and as he talked he toyed with a pair of cellphones sitting on his desk. In English, he explained that he'd just returned from a special assignment in Mindanao, an island in the south where the Philippine government was fighting a pitched battle against religious extremists loyal to ISIS. These days, he explained, the biggest targets in the Philippines were drug dealers who steered their profits to the militants.

When I started to ask Inspector R about the Tiu case, he immediately cut me off. "You know that what you are looking into, it is very dangerous?" he said. "These are very connected people. You should know that." If we wanted the truth, he said, we would have to keep his name out of it.

I asked him why the case had stalled. "I'll be very straight: It boils down to Paul Le Roux," he said. "He has lots of connections in the government, people that told me I have to slow down, because it could put my family in danger. There were lots of policemen who would not do this case. And there were lots of senior officers who were his friends."

The Tiu case started, he explained, with a tip in October 2010, a few weeks after Bruce Jones was murdered. "There was a Filipino guy who contacted my office, said that there is a Chinese guy who wants to sell guns," he said. A raid on Tiu's apartment produced fourteen automatic weapons stashed around the house and in ceiling tiles—all the exact same kind of Indonesian-made assault rifles that had been discovered during the *Ufuk* incident. Tiu's cellphone was full of photos of weapons, gold bars, and Ferraris, and the officers took him into custody. That, Inspector R said, was when he first crossed paths with Le Roux.

At the station, Tiu was allowed to use his phone to call a lawyer. Then he made a second call and handed the phone to Inspector R. On the other end was a man speaking accented English, who Inspector R later surmised was Paul Le Roux. "I see you have Herbert," he said. "You could be a good friend. What do you want? I'll give you anything you want. You want my Mercedes-Benz? I'll give it to you. You choose."

Inspector R said he declined, telling the man that he planned to file a case against Tiu.

"Okay, I'll send a lawyer," Le Roux said, and hung up.

Clearly, Tiu was tied in to something much larger than a few gun sales. On his phone, the police also found calls back and forth to a number listed as Dave Smith. Inspector R began piecing together the network behind the *Ufuk,* Bruce Jones's murder, and Tiu, all encapsulated in a PowerPoint presentation he later sent me. He contacted the Australian authorities after learning of Le Roux's Australian citizenship; they told him they, and the Americans, were also looking at Le Roux.

Tiu was released on bail and quickly disappeared. A judge let the case drop. Weeks later, a relative of the man who had tipped the police off to Tiu in the first place—whom Inspector R knew only as "Chito"—called to report that Chito, too, had gone missing. Then Inspector R discovered that one of his own officers was under surveillance. Delivery people were showing up at his house with food he'd never ordered, he said, and people in his neighborhood had been offered money for information about him. After the police concluded that both Tiu and the tipster were likely dead, they dropped the case.

But Inspector R kept going. A year and a half after the DEA's Kent Bailey had traveled to Manila and begged the authorities to put Le Roux under surveillance, Inspector R finally did so. He discovered that Le Roux rarely left the two houses he owned in Dasmariñas Village, one of which was running up electric bills five times what could be considered normal. He located an airstrip Le Roux had built in Batangas, along the coast of the South China Sea, where he seemed to be moving cargo in and out on small private planes. He discovered that Le Roux had also purchased a small island off of the eastern shore of the Philippines, facing the Pacific, which Inspector R believed was being used to test explosives. When the target shooter Michael Lontoc was murdered a year later, Inspector R was able to tie it back to Le Roux. "He was a friend of mine," he said of Lontoc. "I used to shoot with him." Lontoc's mother's name was on a warehouse owned by Le Roux, which Inspector R determined was stocked with airplane parts.

Inspector R continued exchanging information with foreign authorities, he said, including the FBI office in Miami and the Australian Federal Police. He gathered tidbits of intelligence from wherever he could get them, including the U.S. Department of Homeland Security, which, according to notes that Inspector R later showed me, was "monitoring the illegal activities of LE ROUX and his cohorts, particularly their involvement in terrorist financing." The Royal Malaysia Police had information that Le Roux was "transporting methamphetamine hydrochloride and its chemical component in different Southeast Asian Transshipment points."

All of it added up to a murderous criminal cartel operating openly in the Philippines. But the memos Inspector R sent to his superiors about Le Roux were answered with silence. Finally, he decided to bypass the chain of command and send a report to the general in charge of the entire Philippine National Police. The general didn't mince words. "I'm not interested," he said. "Make yourself busy with other things."

"That was Le Roux's style," Inspector R told me. "If somebody was investigating him, he would find a way to make sure that they go easy on him. He would just go up the ladder; he knew how the system worked here."

Inspector R's experience reminded me of a story one of Le Roux's most trusted mercenaries once told me. One day in a meeting, he said, Le Roux casually recounted a time when a woman declined to fulfill a certain sexual desire of his. "So he beat her up with a baseball bat," the mercenary told me. "I never saw it. I just heard a story from him and it was confirmed afterwards by the other employees." The woman, he said, turned out to be "the daughter of a senator. It was a big, big, big deal. Of course you can't beat up a senator's daughter, that's not going to happen. In the Philippines you're gone, or you going to a hellhole for the rest of your life. Because that's the kind of people you don't touch."

But in the end, Le Roux turned his grotesque violence to his own advantage, or so the story went. He invited the senator to his office and offered him "two or three million dollars" and a spot on the payroll as compensation "for your baby girl." The senator accepted it all, the mercenary said, "because that was Le Roux, his power in the Philippines. He had . . . not the president, but up the chain. Right hands of the president. Commanders. Generals. He had the Filipino staff working in the U.S. Embassy on the payroll. That's how he knew everything that was going on."

Inspector R had long since left the case by the time we met, but he remained troubled—if not surprised—by the ease with which Le Roux seemed to have bought his way out of any threat. "He's always in my head," Inspector R said. "Paul Le Roux can get away, maybe. Maybe. But God will find a way."

There was one person who I hoped could still shed light on the Jones murder, and on the chain of disappearances that followed: John Nash, the Subic Bay enforcer and former Ocean Adventure security chief who was one of the last people to see both Jones and Zuñiga alive. But Nash, too, proved out of reach—for a different reason.

On a late Friday afternoon in May 2015, Nash had been headed down a narrow beachside road near Baloy Beach, just outside the Blue Rock Resort in Subic Bay. Suddenly, an SUV appeared in front of him, blocking his path. Before he could reverse, another closed in on him from behind. A half dozen agents from the NBI leaped out, weapons in hand, and ordered Nash out of his vehicle. Within moments, they'd hustled him into one of the unmarked SUVs and were on the highway for the drive back to Manila. Suspecting that Nash had sources in the police, the NBI had kept the operation secret—so successfully, in fact, that the next morning the local police announced that Nash had been kidnapped by unknown armed men.

The reason for Nash's arrest was perhaps even more peculiar than its circumstances. When the NBI began pursuing Nash as a person of interest in the Zuñiga case, they checked his American passport with the U.S. embassy. The identity turned out to belong to a long-deceased American named John Nash. The embassy canceled the passport and the NBI made the arrest.

By the time I sat down with Agent Lugay, Nash had been in NBI limbo for more than eighteen months. There hadn't been enough information to charge him with anything other than immigration violations, but since Nash wouldn't say where he was from, the NBI had nowhere to deport him to. They declined to let me see him. Nor did anyone seem to have known Nash by any other name. What's more, Timothy Desmond, the *Free Willy* trainer who had hired Nash to run security, was now himself an international fugitive. In November 2014, after being accused of defrauding an investor behind Ocean Adventure, Desmond, too, had disappeared.

There seemed to be no end to the weirdness. Since I couldn't get in to visit Nash, I decided to go see what I could find out about him in Subic. It was a three-hour trip from Manila, and as Almendral and I descended out of lush mountains with a driver we'd hired for the day, we could see the footprint of the former U.S. naval base. A local reporter suggested we inquire after Nash at the Blue Rock Resort, where Dave Smith had been a regular. Turning up the shore, we passed the pink façade of the Subic Bay Yacht Club, where Oz had embarked on his boat trip with Smith.

The Blue Rock turned out to be a large open-air joint on the beach, with a floating bar just offshore, reached by a hand-pulled ferry. On a weekday afternoon it was populated largely by leathery white guys, scattered at tables or wandering out to the beach with Filipina women who looked half their age, or less. The blenders were humming with tropical drinks. Almendral and I sat at the bar and ordered a round, then I ginned up the nerve to approach a table full of hulking, burned-out men sitting mostly in silence. They turned out to be Australian, and claimed never to have heard of John Nash. A woman who appeared to be the manager would only say, "I haven't seen him around in a couple of years."

We got a similar reaction up the road at Ocean Adventure, where patrons were streaming out at the end of the day's last dolphin show. When we introduced ourselves at the gate, a PR person emerged and proceeded to claim no recollection of Nash or even Desmond, then politely declined to answer any questions.

The roads were empty and unlit as we drove back, winding through the forest in the hills above Subic. Suddenly we turned a corner and there was a policeman standing in the street, waving a baton for us to pull over. After months of hearing about the ties between Le Roux and corrupt police, Almendral and I both wondered if we'd somehow triggered a trap. But there was nothing to do but stop. The officer stood behind our car and motioned for our driver to exit, which she did, walking back into the darkness behind us.

We sat silently, trying to remain calm, and I thought back to the warnings I'd been given about the danger of Le Roux's former network. It seemed appropriately farcical that the threat would finally arrive while I was in pursuit of an interview with a rogue celebrity whale trainer. I'd put not only myself but all three of us in peril, it appeared, chasing a tangent so ludicrous I could barely explain it.

A few minutes later, the driver returned. The cop had been free-lancing; he just wanted a standard bribe of fifty Philippine pesos, about a dollar. She climbed back in and we drove on into the night.

19

The Mercenaries · The Operators

2010–2011 . . . McConnell and Oz looking for exits . . . Dave Smith gets caught . . . A South African hit man . . . RX Limited under pressure . . . McConnell's new duties . . . A mental breakdown

Even after all Lachlan McConnell had seen since he started working for Le Roux in 2008, the assassination of Bruce Jones still shocked him. They weren't close friends, but he'd sailed with Jones, who, like him, seemed like the kind of guy who'd just fallen into a lucrative job with a few moral ambiguities attached. They'd shared the adventure of the *Mou Man Tai* sinking in Indonesia, and McConnell had become friendly with Jones's wife. They didn't deserve that, he thought. But more shocking than the loss was the knowledge of how quickly Le Roux could turn on you, and the ferocity of the revenge he would exact when he did. McConnell had reason to believe he might end up in its crosshairs: His friend and boss Dave Smith had been "borrowing" and spending Le Roux's gold for months, and McConnell had agreed to hold on to some of the proceeds for safekeeping. If someone discovered the stash, he'd have no way to explain it.

The next time he saw Le Roux, McConnell found the nerve to challenge him about Jones's killing. "I said, 'I don't understand why you had that captain killed,'" he recalled later.

"He was going to testify," Le Roux replied.

"His wife and child were in the car," McConnell said.

"I didn't have *them* killed," Le Roux said.

The exchange was enough for McConnell to consider quitting. Many of his gold-shepherding duties in Hong Kong were now handled by a trio of Israelis led by Doron Shulman, who had purchased two houses that were used exclusively for stashing gold. Shulman, a dual Australian-Israeli citizen, was one of a number of Le Roux's employees who had served together in the Duvdevan, the elite division of the Israeli Defense Forces. (The Duvdevan—which means "cherry" in Hebrew—specializes in undercover work in Palestinian communities in the West Bank and Gaza. Most famously, its agents have dressed as Arabs to infiltrate Palestinian militant groups and capture or kill high-value targets.) Le Roux seemed to enjoy the cachet of hiring ex–special forces soldiers, and Shulman and his young compatriots got to see the world on Le Roux's dime.

McConnell, on the other hand, had a family in the Philippines. He didn't need the risks anymore. He could start his own security outfit, with more mainstream clients. But how to quit an organization where the act of quitting was cause for suspicion?

Halfway around the world in Israel, on the pharmaceutical side of Le Roux's business, Moran Oz had also been looking for a way out. Many of the Israelis that he and Alon Berkman had sent to work for Le Roux in Manila had since returned, desperate to get away from what they saw there. "They came back from the Philippines with fear in their eyes," one former Tel Aviv employee said. Levi Kugel, the guitar-playing call center manager Le Roux had sent to deal with Ari Ben-Menashe, told Oz that he'd left the organization in fear after Ben-Menashe had failed to deliver a diplomatic passport for Le Roux. Kugel, afraid the boss might exact vengeance on him, moved to the United States, where he assumed he would be out of reach. Asaf Shoshana, the childhood friend of

Oz's and former Duvdevan soldier who was running Le Roux's timber operations, told Oz that Le Roux had abruptly abandoned the projects. "Paul refused to wire the money, and that was the end," Oz recalled. When local police started looting the equipment at one work site, Shoshana suspected he might be arrested and fled. He said that he called Le Roux and told him that he was done.

"There's no such thing as done," Le Roux replied. "You work for me until I fire you, or something else."

Shoshana told Oz that he feared Le Roux was planning to kill him. Oz persuaded his boss to instead send Shoshana back to Tel Aviv to help run the call center. From there, it was easier to quit. But even Israel began to seem unsafe for anyone who crossed Le Roux. Employees believed that he had connections in the Israeli Mafia through Shai Reuven, and there were stories to back it up. After an employee named Omer Bezalel told Le Roux that he wanted to quit, two men with guns showed up at Bezalel's home with pictures of his relatives in the United States. "Your job is important to Paul," they told him. "You can't leave."

Oz would later claim that he was trapped, working under duress, unable to quit for fear that Le Roux would come after him and his family, which now included two kids. But he was also thriving at the company, making great money—enough to help support his extended family and give to the community. In the year since Oz and Alon Berkman traveled to Kenya in 2009, their responsibilities with RX Limited only increased. Le Roux had expanded his operations in Israel and opened the marketing call center in Maharashtra, India, with 150 employees. "On a day-to-day basis, he didn't seem so scared," said one of Oz's deputies in Israel. "He projected that he was king of the world, making fifty to a hundred grand a month. But of course there is more to the story."

In Manila, Dave Smith appeared unconcerned about Le Roux's vengeance and became increasingly brazen about his stealing. His lack of discretion seemed particularly ill-advised, his fellow merce-naries thought, given that the boss was known to order disloyal employees dead. The fact that Smith himself was the one often ordered to carry out those killings had, perhaps, made him over-confident. But there he was, out on P Burgos Street, the central artery of Manila's red-light district, in a Lamborghini. He'd also bought a carbon-fiber Mercedes, custom-built for racing and shipped in from Germany, a Hummer, and a McLaren. He'd purchased a mansion in a tony suburb of Manila where Le Roux himself owned a house. "He bought the million-dollar place in Alabang, had these exotic cats, and he was going around town splashing money every-where," Patrick Donovan, Smith's former employer and fellow Irishman, said. "I mean, fuck me, you're going to steal money from someone, you stash that shit away. You keep your lifestyle as it is."

"Dave was skimming drugs, he was skimming gold," another employee of Le Roux's, and a friend of Smith's, said. "I remember driving with Dave to see Le Roux, and he would park way down the street. I said, 'Why are you parking this far away?' He said, 'You know Boss wants us to keep a low profile.'" They'd all been warned against flaunting their money in ways that might attract the authorities: no Rolexes, no flashy cars, no drugs. Smith ig-nored all three prohibitions.

In late 2010, Smith began acting even more strangely. He told the friend cryptically that he was getting some accounts in order, almost as if he had a terminal disease. "Then I couldn't get ahold of him," the friend said. "And that wasn't Dave. He would call me ten times a day. His wife couldn't find him. So I emailed Le Roux. I got a response: 'Call me, here's my number.'"

"What's going on?" Le Roux asked nonchalantly when the friend called.

"Have you seen Dave?"

"I sent him to South America a few days ago," Le Roux said. "He's going to be out of contact for a while. You'll report directly to me."

The friend knew something was wrong. Days later he got another call from Le Roux, ordering him to fly to the Philippines and meet at the Mandarin Oriental hotel. When they sat down, Le Roux told him that he had "placed Dave on permanent vacation." "Those are the exact words he used. He was always very careful. I asked him why. Paul said, 'You have to understand, I have partners in Colombia. Dave was stealing from me. If I didn't take care of this, they would take care of me.' Then he said to me: 'You ever try and steal from me, you ever try to get out, and I will liquidate you.'"

There were varying accounts floating around the Le Roux mercenary community of how Smith ultimately met his end. McConnell later heard that he had been snatched, drunk, off of P Burgos Street, thrown into a van, and driven to a remote location. "My understanding was that he was placed in a shallow grave and given a telephone," McConnell said. Le Roux, according to this version, was on the other end of the line. "He says, 'You see what happens?' Then they shot him and buried him." Another version claimed that Mexican cartel hit men had been brought in for the job. Still another had it that Le Roux had him thrown off a boat, much as Moran Oz had been, except with fatal consequences.

The actual facts matched pieces of the rumors, but with one key difference: Le Roux had been present for the job, together with a former South African policeman named Marcus. I tracked down Marcus on LinkedIn, where he listed Southern Ace on his employment profile. When I told him what I'd heard about Dave Smith's murder, he seemed almost relieved to confess the details to me. "I've done some pretty horrible shit with him," he said of Le Roux. "You know, what can I say? I was there, I was involved. My life was pretty fucked up."

Le Roux had first hired Marcus in the summer of 2010, he said, after he responded to an email forwarded by a fellow South African security contractor. The note was from an organization seek-

ing "close-in security or snipers" ready to deploy to Manila or
Somalia. "I was down and out," Marcus told me. He had left the
police force and gone into private security. "Then one or two
things happened and my whole life fell apart. I couldn't find work.
I was financially fucked. So it was a stupid, stupid move to get involved. But fuck, I did." Seven days later he was in Manila, where
he was hired by Le Roux directly—outside of the purview of Smith
and his teams. "It was so secretive, if anything went wrong I was
on my own," Marcus said. "There was no connection between
him and me. Nothing. I eventually had a Filipino guy working
with me, but I was kept in the dark. They hid me in hotels and then
they would send people to go and fetch me."

Marcus's initial job was to surveil employees Le Roux believed
were betraying him. He traveled to Bulawayo, hunting for Le
Roux's cousin Mathew Smith, only to conclude that the cousin
had spotted him and gone into hiding. Then Le Roux ordered him
to look into a real estate agent named Catherine Lee, who he
claimed had stolen money in a failed real estate transaction—
about 50 million pesos, or just under a million dollars. "He wanted
to get some of the money back and find all the details," Marcus
told me. "So first I had to find her. And then I sort of—I almost
had like a relationship with her, trying to get information out of
her. I took her out to dinner a couple of times. We had a whole
fucking thing going."

I asked him if he thought Lee had in fact stolen the money from
Le Roux. "No, no," he said. "The way she was living, I doubted
it. She didn't live the lifestyle of somebody that had a lot of money.
But you know with Paul, once he believed that you stole from him,
it doesn't matter what you say. There's no negotiations."

Before Le Roux could deal with Lee, however, he had a more
pressing matter: Dave Smith *was* stealing from him, and flaunting
it. "He said Dave stole a lot of gold from him and sold it," Marcus
said. "And Dave lived the lifestyle of a very rich guy. I mean, he
had all these girlfriends and houses and cars. It was unbelievable."
Finally, Le Roux decided he'd had enough. One day in December

2010, he told Smith that they needed to bury a stash of gold on his coastal property in Batangas, south of Manila. Le Roux and Marcus picked him up in a truck with a safe in the back and drove him to the property. As Smith started to dig the hole, Marcus walked up behind him, pulled out a 9mm handgun, and shot him in the head.

Smith collapsed but was still alive. Marcus tried to finish the job, but his gun jammed. Smith began screaming as Le Roux and Marcus worked to fix the gun. Then, as if on cue, a group of stray dogs appeared and began running toward them. While Le Roux chased them off, Marcus unjammed the gun and fired several more shots into Smith's head.

Le Roux, seemingly eager to get in on the kill, grabbed an MP5 submachine gun and pumped more rounds into the lifeless body. "That he didn't hit me was a fucking miracle," Marcus said. "But there's so much adrenaline going through at that stage. It was only later when I went back to my hotel and I was thinking about what we did that I thought, 'I can't believe that this guy didn't shoot me.'"

Le Roux had already made plans to dispose of Smith's body offshore. "It's very bad, I know, but some of the stuff was actually funny," Marcus said. "After we did the job, he gave me a fucking roll of Glad Wrap to wrap Dave's body. And I said, 'Are you fucking crazy? You can't do that.'" Instead Marcus took a canvas cover from a nearby boat and wrapped the body up. They loaded it onto a rubber dinghy attached to one of Le Roux's boats and launched them both into the South China Sea. Somewhere five to ten kilometers from shore they stopped and pushed the body overboard. It didn't sink. Le Roux told Marcus to jump in and cut holes in the canvas. "I was too scared," Marcus said. "I just thought if I dive in, the cunt is either going to shoot me or he's going to leave me there." Instead he handed his knife to Le Roux, who jumped overboard to slash the canvas wrapped around his recently murdered employee. In a bit of futile posthumous revenge, Dave Smith still refused to sink. So they removed the motor from the dinghy, tied it to the canvas, and watched the body slowly disappear.

On the return trip to shore Marcus and Le Roux got lost and then trapped on a reef, and after an hour of battling the waves they pulled up on a resort beach several kilometers from Le Roux's property. Before catching a cab back to the truck, they ordered beers at a beachside bar.

Within weeks of this episode in late 2010, Le Roux and Marcus together carried out two more murders: Herbert Tan Tiu, the gun-runner arrested weeks earlier by Inspector R, and Chito, the man who tipped off the authorities to Tiu's gun stash. Each was lured, on separate occasions, to Le Roux's property—"his killing fields," Marcus called it—with promises that he was being relocated to an island for his own safety. Once in the car, Le Roux and Marcus would handcuff their target and interrogate him about helping Smith steal gold. At the property, each man was forced at gunpoint onto a boat. Once out to sea, Chito leaped into the water and Marcus shot him. Tiu was less cooperative, so Le Roux shot him with a taser and Marcus pushed him overboard. As Tiu pleaded for his life, Marcus ended it. This time, they remembered to bring an anchor to weigh down the body.

Le Roux's paranoia over the disloyalty of employees was in full bloom, and he began to see traitors everywhere he looked. Not that there wasn't a kernel of truth in his concern: Filipino employees had always known that some of Le Roux's money was slipping out side doors. That was just part of doing business. While the foreigners he imported from America and Israel blundered around the country, largely naïve about Philippine culture beyond "bar girls" and government bribes, some local hires were quietly finding ways to exploit their boss. "Managing call centers was my job description," one Filipina employee told me. "But he would give me odd jobs, like 'Find me a nightclub to buy.' I looked for so many properties for Paul. I earned money from that, but I didn't think it was stealing. I took commissions, which was only fair." Le Roux, who seemed to be unable or unwilling to distinguish between betrayal and skimming, added her to his hit list. "Paul was looking in the wrong direction," she said. "He should have looked closer."

After Marcus's first three hits, Le Roux ordered him to kill one of the organization's attorneys, a Filipina who had tried and failed to get the cargo ship *M/V Ufuk* returned to him. But he deemed the plan Marcus came up with too elaborate and called off the hit. Marcus left for South Africa, he told me, and never returned.

I asked him if he ever thought about the killings later. "In the beginning I had pretty bad nightmares," he said. "But also for me, coming from my background as a policeman, you shoot people. My mindset was: Don't think of it any other way, it's just a job." Le Roux told him that these people had committed crimes against him. He wasn't the judge, he said, just the man rendering the verdict. "Call it a police mentality if you want. These people, they stole, they robbed, they killed. Only difference is we executed them. I tried to block that shit out of my mind. But yeah, it's something that I don't like to talk about."

One afternoon in January 2011, Lachlan McConnell was summoned to meet Le Roux at one of his favorite Manila spots, the Hard Rock Cafe, in a Makati mall. McConnell knew that Le Roux had recently ordered an audit of his gold stashes, and Dave Smith had been missing for weeks, presumed dead. Le Roux had replaced Smith with Joseph Hunter, who was taking over the security team. If there had been a time to get out, McConnell had already missed it.

He showed up early and ordered a rum and Coke to steel his nerves. When Le Roux arrived, he was carrying a stack of file folders, and motioned McConnell to an empty section of the restaurant. When they sat down, he slid a folder across the table.

"I think you know what this is about," McConnell remembered him saying.

"I kind of do," McConnell said. Le Roux told him he knew about Smith's stealing, and McConnell's part in it.

"So how much gold did he give you?"

Looking down at the folder, McConnell decided it was best to come clean. "First of all, he didn't give me gold," he told Le Roux. "He wanted to take the gold, utilize it, and pay it back. I told Dave to just ask you for the loan. I know you are pretty generous, you would have probably done it."

"I should have kept Dave in a cage," Le Roux said.

McConnell asked if Le Roux was responsible for Smith's disappearance. "Yes, yes," Le Roux said dismissively. "We killed him."

Le Roux demanded banking information for accounts that McConnell had used to stash Smith's money, along with his ATM cards. McConnell would repay every cent, Le Roux told him, deducted from his paycheck. Then he picked up the folder, pulled out pictures of Smith's girlfriends, and asked McConnell if he knew where any of them lived.

Le Roux told McConnell that from that point forward he was going to be assigned to new duties in the United States, opening shell companies for the pharmaceutical side of the business. "I didn't need Dave," he said. "You're lucky I need you."

The reason Le Roux needed McConnell stemmed from a growing set of problems that Oz and Berkman were encountering with RX Limited. In 2011 the online pill business was getting squeezed by the companies handling its credit card payments, known as merchant processors. Afraid that they might be liable for payments on illegal drug sales, the merchant processors began demanding that RX Limited prove it was accredited by a National Association of Boards of Pharmacy program called Verified Internet Pharmacy Practice Site. The VIPPS system, as it was known, had been established to bring some order to the wild west of online drug sales. It was a way to certify which websites were abiding by the DEA's regulations. FedEx, RX Limited's main conduit for shipping pills, began issuing similar demands that RX Limited prove its VIPPS certification.

Catherine Lee's body, discovered in a pile of garbage in February 2012 in Taytay, Rizal, in the Philippines

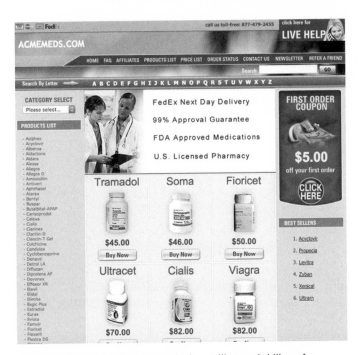

Acmemeds.com, a typical website selling painkillers for Le Roux's RX Limited network

Joseph "Rambo" Hunter being escorted off a plane by Thai authorities in September 2013, following his arrest in Phuket for conspiracy to murder a DEA agent

Five suspects arrested in Thailand in September 2013 for arranging the import of North Korean–made methamphetamine into the United States: (front row) Adrian Valkovic, Kelly Peralta, Philip Shackels, Ye Tiong Tan Lim; (back row) Scott Stammers

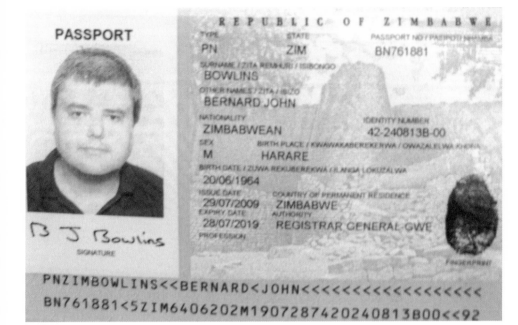

Paul Le Roux's fake Zimbabwean passport, under the alias Bernard John Bowlins

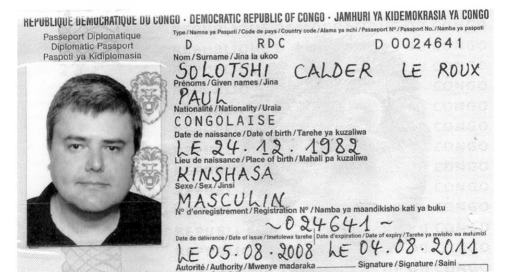

Le Roux's diplomatic passport from the Democratic Republic of the Congo, under the name Paul Solotshi Calder Le Roux

Philippine authorities examining some of the fifty assault weapons that were seized aboard the *M/V Ufuk* in August 2009. Most of the weapons were believed to have already been off-loaded.

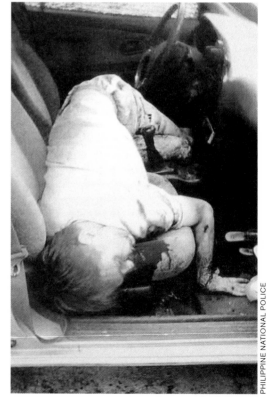

Bruce Jones's body after his murder by tandem motorcycle assassins in Angeles City in September 2010

Le Roux captured by a surveillance camera at Galeão Airport in Rio de Janeiro, date unknown

Immigration photos of Le Roux and his girlfriend, Cindy Cayanan, entering Brazil in 2012

Le Roux and his phone captured on surveillance by the Brazilian federal police

Shai Reuven and Le Roux, captured on surveillance in a mall in Rio in 2012. Reuven was accused of running drug trafficking operations for LeRoux.

Some of the 160 gold bars seized from Le Roux's employees in Hong Kong in May 2012

The wreck of the *JeReVe*, discovered off the coast of Tonga in November 2012

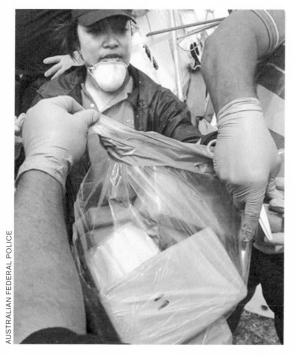

Wrapped bricks of cocaine, totaling two hundred kilograms, that were discovered in the walls of the *JeReVe*. The body of one of its two crewmen was also found onboard.

Scott Stammers and Philip Shackels, two of Le Roux's deputies in his North Korean methamphetamine operation, captured on DEA surveillance in Phuket, Thailand, in 2013

Adam Samia following his arrest in July 2015 in Roxboro, North Carolina, for murder

David Stillwell following his arrest in July 2015 in Roxboro, North Carolina, for murder

Photo from a fake arrest report for Paul Le Roux, generated in Minnesota in 2016. Le Roux was never arrested for cocaine distribution in Minnesota; the report was merely a cover for his arrival there.

The pharmacies themselves had also started getting antsy. The business had become "high risk," one pharmacist in Michigan told Oz. The DEA was watching, and sometimes raiding, pharmacies in the RX Limited network. Others complained that the wholesale pharmacies supplying them were starting to get spooked by the quantities of Ultram, Soma, and Fioricet dispensed by mom-and-pop drugstores.

The brilliant model that Le Roux had created was suddenly under threat from multiple sides. His expansion plans were floundering; the call center in India was mismanaged and dysfunctional. Despite having more than fifty employees per site, they were producing fewer orders than the affiliates that RX Limited had once worked with.

Le Roux sent Doron Shulman, the former member of the Duvdevan who had been working for him in Hong Kong, to negotiate with drugstores directly in the United States. Shulman tried to reassure skittish pharmacists that it was safe to keep filling prescriptions despite the changing laws. If he needed to, Le Roux said, he would open up his own pharmacies around the country. He ordered Jon Wall, the Kentucky supply officer operating under the name Wayne Hatfield, to set up a wholesale pharmacy in Louisville in anticipation of taking over the supply chain.

Oz warned Le Roux that without official accreditation, RX Limited was in danger of losing shipping accounts at its two biggest pharmacies, Schultz Pharmacy and Medicine Mart, both owned by an older pharmacist named Charles Schultz in Wisconsin. "It seems FedEx is going to close Schultz's account in less than thirty days unless they present with a proof that they are VIPPS accredited," Oz wrote in an email. In fact, FedEx was investigating all accounts connected to RX Limited—accounts that were registered in the identity of a Zimbabwean named Robert McGowan.

RX Limited needed a new approach. Le Roux sent Omer Bezalel to the United States to try to stave off disaster. In May 2012, Bezalel set up an entirely fictitious pharmacy, supposedly located at an address in a Florida strip mall, and applied for VIPPS certification. He sent copies of the application to FedEx. In mid-June, the bomb dropped, in the form of an official response letter:

> Pleased be advised that FedEx is terminating ALL services for the above-referenced account number. The termination is effective immediately. FedEx has been informed that you are shipping controlled substances in violation of Federal law.

Like any online retail startup, Le Roux's business had been built on the rise of easy shipping. Without it, the company would collapse. Oz and Berkman hustled to switch shipments to other carriers, but all of them were pressing for proof that nothing illegal was being shipped. RX Limited was going to need new ways to ship drugs, and fast.

This, then, would be McConnell's new job. He knew nothing about the online pharmacy business, but Le Roux deemed him competent enough to find new ways to keep it operating. McConnell, now terrified of crossing Le Roux after he'd narrowly escaped Dave Smith's fate, was in no position to object. He flew to Miami and met with Omer Bezalel, and they quickly opened a new set of companies, using dummy credentials for Robert McGowan. Le Roux also sent a list of U.S. social security numbers that could be used to set up credit cards. He supplied instructions on purchasing burner phones and obtaining new email addresses, in case the DEA was watching. "If you obey these instructions all phone/email communication will be untraceable," he wrote.

Bezalel and McConnell, however, were out of their depth. Their shipping schemes became increasingly extravagant, involving hired couriers who would pick up orders at RX Limited pharmacies and then spread them across FedEx drop-offs to avoid the suspicion of bulk purchases. They instructed the couriers on what size cars they would need—something with a big trunk—and what to do if they encountered the police. They filled out piles of paperwork in the futile hope of somehow scamming their way into VIPPS certification. On August 9, 2011, they laughed in a wiretapped phone call about the absurdity of their own efforts:

MCCONNELL: Wow, this has been a fucked-up couple of weeks, you know?

BEZALEL: We finally got word from the uh, VIPPS Certification . . . they tell us . . . you have seventy-two hours to comply with the list of . . . discrepancies. If you see the list of discrepancies you're gonna say holy shit.

MCCONNELL: Oh really, wow . . .

BEZALEL: Yeah, I'm lookin' at one of the lists and it's unreal. I mean, starting with [laughs] starting with uh, where the hell is this, let's see . . . you've got "you're shipping controlled medications, you are shipping controlled medications to, to states that require you to not ship controlled medications [laughs], website offers"

MCCONNELL: [laughs]

BEZALEL: "ship prescription drugs to states uh, in which it [is] not licensed to do so as indicated by the shipping options available on the order page. Website dispenses prescription drug products without requiring a valid prescription . . .

MCCONNELL: [laughs]

As McConnell traveled back and forth between Manila and Miami over the next few months, the psychological weight of Le Roux's oblique threats began to press down on him. He believed that Le Roux had his family under surveillance, and he spent his time back home racked with anxiety. In Florida, he was now involved in something he'd worked hard to avoid: potentially illegal acts in a country where he knew the consequences could be severe. At one point, he was pulled over by local police, who checked his IDs and let him go. He confided to Bezalel that he thought he was losing his mind.

That October, he finally told Le Roux he was having a mental breakdown and needed time off. Le Roux, incredibly, granted his request. McConnell handed off his responsibilities to Bezalel and bought a ticket back to the Philippines. "I put myself in a hospital under psychological care for two weeks," he said later. The doctors diagnosed him with major depression and severe anxiety, and put him on medication.

For all of McConnell's efforts in Florida, RX Limited's business remained precarious. But it was about to face an even more damaging blow: In December 2011, the DEA announced that Soma had been "scheduled"; it was now a controlled substance under federal law. Pharmacies would need special DEA approval to dispense it. A substantial portion of RX Limited's revenue evaporated overnight.

Le Roux told Oz and Berkman to close the Tel Aviv office. He was downsizing temporarily and moving all customer service to the Philippines. The new initiatives Le Roux had promised at their meeting in Kenya were to be reversed. Their job now was to unwind the operation they had built. Le Roux had already closed down his nascent call center in India and sacked the Israeli he'd sent to run it. Now they laid off workers in Tel Aviv and shipped the computers and office furniture to Manila. There, Le Roux was handing off more responsibilities to his deputies Shai Reuven and Nestor Del Rosario. The transfers that Berkman normally received from Le Roux's accounts in Hong Kong started arriving from new places. Then they became sporadic. Soon the Israeli arm lacked the funds to pay severance owed to laid-off employees.

One afternoon, the former manager of the Indian call center arrived at the office in Tel Aviv and told Oz that the company owed him money. "I'm going to sue for my severance, I got two months' pay coming," he said.

Oz passed the message on to Le Roux. Two days later, the man returned to say that he'd reconsidered. Six men had come to his house and threatened to kill his family while he watched. He handed over a letter stating he was owed nothing.

"You see," Le Roux told Berkman afterward. "I can get to you wherever you are."

A month after McConnell checked out of the hospital, Le Roux summoned him to a meeting at a coffee shop near one of his homes outside Manila. McConnell noticed that Le Roux seemed to have increased his security, with a follow car and a pair of Filipino bodyguards who entered in front of him.

Le Roux had ample reasons for caution: Even as RX Limited struggled, his larger organization had expanded into more and bigger criminal ventures. He was now active in the meth trade, putting him in business—and potentially in conflict—with powerful forces in the Southeast Asian underworld. One Le Roux employee in the Philippines, an Irishman named Philip Shackels, tried to build Le Roux a meth lab in an apartment. Another, Scott Stammers, attempted to arrange meth production in Cambodia with the help of a Cambodian general. Those plans failed, but Le Roux finally hit the meth supply jackpot when a former bartender at Sid's named Kelly Peralta introduced him to a member of a triad organized-crime syndicate in Hong Kong. The contact, a man named Ye Tiong Tan Lim, had access to the highest-quality North Korean–made meth. Le Roux obtained forty-eight kilos, with a promise of much more, and split the load between safe houses in Thailand and the Philippines.

For transportation, he attempted to buy a submarine from the North Koreans to move the drugs. When that fell through, he had his engineers design a small one-man sub for the job. (Le Roux's only legitimate business was a boat-repair shop in Manila.) He attempted to reverse-engineer a Predator drone to create his own for shipping drugs, and built a working prototype in a Philippine warehouse.

Le Roux was also now deep into the international cocaine business. Shackels, after the failed meth lab, redeemed himself by delivering contacts for cocaine suppliers in Peru and Brazil. By 2011,

Le Roux had deals worth tens of millions of dollars in the works. He would use his own boats to pick up loads from the west coast of South America, transport the drugs across the Pacific, and sell them into Asian markets.

Now, meeting with McConnell, Le Roux tried to lure him into the growing narcotics side of the business. He talked about his connections with the cartels and his plans to use unmanned drone submarines and aerial vehicles to transport drugs. "I didn't know if he was full of shit or not," McConnell said, or if "he wanted to make himself bigger than life. Because when you sat down with him he always seemed more of a geek than an international gangster."

Le Roux suggested McConnell return to the company in a new role. He would pay him $100,000 a month, he said, to oversee meth production at a house he owned in a tourist area of Laguna, south of Manila. McConnell delicately indicated to Le Roux that he didn't think the work was for him. Le Roux shrugged, and the meeting ended.

McConnell realized that he'd been given an opening to leave, and now was the time to take it. He went into hiding, moving his family to a separate location, fearing that they would suffer the same fate as Dave Smith. "I lived watching my back," McConnell said. "Because I knew I would be one of the people he would target."

20

The Investigators

*2010–2011 . . . Bailey returns home . . . A U.N. investigation . . .
Looking to flip . . . Zeroing in on Florida . . . The Lachlan McConnell
dilemma . . . The law catches up*

By late 2010, Kent Bailey was back in Minneapolis, having completed his stint at the Special Operations Division in Virginia. At SOD, as he coordinated the international aspects of the Le Roux case, he'd kept Derek Maltz, the special agent in charge of the division, in the loop with quarterly briefings. But as he headed back to Minneapolis to run the local enforcement division, he started to hear grumblings that the case, now four years old, was exhausting his superiors' patience. "I remember Maltz kept telling me, 'You've got to bring this case across the goal line,'" Bailey said. "I joked back, 'I took this case ten yards deep in the end zone, ran it ninety-five yards downfield, and got you a first and goal at the five. Find somebody else to bring it across the goal line.'"

Still, when the assistant special agent in charge of the Minneapolis office suggested that Bailey continue as Kimberly Brill's supervisor, he was elated. Since Steven Holdren's departure, Brill had been handling Le Roux on her own, full-time. That she'd kept it going was a singular feat of investigative prowess. "She never had the support," Bailey said. "She was really kind of going alone. I would call back here and say, 'Hey, you've got to give her an agent, you've got to give her some help.'" Now, returning to Minnesota in January 2011, he could be that help.

The question was: What more could they do? Brill and Holdren had taken out dozens of subpoenas for phone records and search warrants on email addresses, put together complicated foreign legal requests for a half dozen countries, and conducted countless controlled buys. They'd gathered hundreds of thousands of pages of evidence, some of which federal prosecutors had presented in front of a grand jury in 2010 without obtaining an indictment. With the help of agents at the Internal Revenue Service, Brill had built a complex map of Le Roux's bank accounts—the ones he controlled directly, the ones he'd arranged for others to open on his behalf, the ones created with dummy identities.

They also suspected that Le Roux was becoming increasingly murderous. In late 2010, Dave Smith's sister, who lived in California, sent a letter to the U.S. embassy in Manila, explaining that her brother had gone missing in the Philippines. By then, Brill and Bailey knew that Smith was serving as Le Roux's right-hand man and head enforcer—it was Smith, after all, who had set up Bruce Jones in the weapons and drug charges. Bailey in turn had informed his British contacts, who sent out an Interpol notice in search of Smith. "I always believed Le Roux was responsible for Smith disappearing," Bailey said. Given that Smith was likely a U.S. citizen by his previous marriage to a woman in Boston, Le Roux could potentially be charged in an American court with Smith's murder.

But hunches and charts weren't enough to indict. Bailey and Brill decided it was time to start squeezing Le Roux's network. Other than a few isolated pharmacy inspections, they had resisted putting pressure on RX Limited for fear of tipping Le Roux off to the investigation. Now they changed course. "We just had to get somebody on the ground to make some type of seizures," Bailey said. "For about a year of my life I felt like a traveling salesman. I had to go to Detroit three times to get them to open up a case on Le Roux." Everywhere he and Brill went, they'd hear ten reasons why the case wasn't worth pursuing. "How I didn't assault somebody is beyond me," Bailey said. "'Internet? Good luck with that.'"

Slowly he and Brill coaxed other offices into taking on pieces of the case. "I had many conversations with her, saying you've got to let some of this stuff go, you cannot do it all yourself," Bailey said. "You've got to concentrate on the command control at the top. Give this to Detroit, trust they are going to do it. Give this to Newark, trust that they are going to do it. Mobile. Los Angeles. And most of them did exactly that."

For the first time, they were able to obtain active wiretaps—known as Title III, or "T3" wires—on four RX Limited phone numbers. Monitoring them meant even more work for Brill, who alternated between listening in on the conversations and chasing down the leads they generated. Most of what she heard were attempts by low-level operatives in the United States to recruit more pharmacists into the network.

But they hoped that with the right pressure Le Roux himself might slip up and make a call to one of the phones. They focused their attention on Florida, where RX Limited had its only physical locus in the United States, just north of Miami. It was a small rented office, sandwiched between a beauty parlor and a Hertz car rental on a busy avenue in Miami Gardens. There they identified an Israeli named Omer Bezalel who was directing Le Roux's attempts to keep the pharmaceutical business flowing in the States.

Brill organized a surveillance team and set them up at the Miami Gardens address. In addition to Bezalel, they spotted a taller white man operating under the identity of Robert McGowan. Together with Bezalel, he began opening shell companies and bank accounts tied to the address. At first they assumed the man was McGowan himself. McGowan's name had shown up on everything from the

ICANN records for ABSystems to corporate filings in Israel and the United Kingdom, to important RX Limited website registrations. Now perhaps they could finally catch him in the flesh.

The agents decided to have a closer look at McGowan. Working with the local police, they engineered what would seem like a routine traffic stop. When they asked for ID, they expected to see documents with McGowan's name. But instead the man produced a Canadian passport and a Philippine driver's license.

"That's how we identified Lachlan McConnell," Bailey said.

While the DEA's gaze was drawn to Florida, another piece of the Le Roux puzzle was about to emerge from the last place they expected: the headquarters of the United Nations in New York. In July 2011, the U.N. Security Council issued a three-hundred-page document with the dry-as-leaves title "Report of the Monitoring Group on Somalia and Eritrea pursuant to Security Council resolution 1916." In it, a team of investigators outlined the various causes of chaos and instability in the region, from the militant group al-Shabaab to Somali pirates. But Bailey's phone started ringing with people telling him he had to see it. In the back was a five-page section, in an appendix on the growth of foreign private security companies operating in Somalia. It was titled "Case Study: Southern Ace," and the subject was Paul Le Roux.

The U.N. investigators, led by a Frenchman named Aurélien Llorca, noted that Southern Ace had begun operating in the state of Galmudug, in central Somalia, in 2009, "presenting itself [as] 'traders and importers of fisheries products in Hong-Kong.'" The company quickly began recruiting a local militia and arming it with AK-47s, grenade launchers, and truck-mounted antiaircraft guns. They also imported uniforms, flak jackets, and radios from the Philippines. Based on an interview with a Somali military source, Llorca determined that the company was actually owned by one "Paul Calder Le Roux also known as Bernard John Bowlins."

Le Roux's moves in Somalia were mystifying to the U.N. team. The militia Le Roux had backed was entangled in ongoing skirmishes with al-Shabaab, as well as a war between local pastoral nomads and another clan. In November 2010, a battle involving Le Roux's troops raged for several days, "causing allegedly heavy casualties from both sides," the report said. Why Le Roux, operating out of the Philippines, had any interest in a power struggle between two clans in Somalia, the investigators couldn't determine.

They also discovered that Le Roux had begun experimenting with "the cultivation of hallucinogenic plants, including opium, coca, and cannabis" in the Southern Ace compound in Galkayo, importing greenhouses, herbicides, and farming equipment. He had obtained permission to land an Antonov cargo plane at the local airport, and "planned to import by air a large quantity of heavy weapons, including 75 kilograms of C4 explosives, 200 land mines, one million rounds of 7.62 mm ammunition, and five AT-3 'Sagger' anti-tank missiles."

This had all taken place during the height of the Somali sea piracy epidemic. Llorca's team suspected but couldn't prove that Le Roux intended to set up a private security company on the coast, in the hopes of somehow involving himself in the piracy business—either providing protection for shipping companies or funding his own piracy.

Llorca reported that after spending over three million dollars in Somalia, in mid-2010 Le Roux abandoned whatever plans he had in the region. Locals overran the compound and took possession of the weapons, and one of Southern Ace's employees was shot and killed in the ensuing chaos.

The report thrust Le Roux into the news for the first time since his brief appearance in 2007, with a flurry of articles recounting the astonishing facts from the U.N. report and pondering the global reach of a "shadowy South African businessman," as the South African *City Press* described him. "Repeated attempts to contact Le Roux by phone and email proved unsuccessful," the reporter noted.

For Bailey, the U.N. report at least cleared up one mystery he'd pondered since the beginning of the investigation: why Le Roux was placing calls to Somalia from his Philippine cellphone.

Back in the Florida investigation, Brill and Bailey felt like they were closing in on Le Roux's shrinking pharmacy operation. That August, they obtained a T3 wiretap on Omer Bezalel. In one conversation between Bezalel and the man they now knew to be Lachlan McConnell, they could hear that McConnell sounded anxious, distressed over the disappearance of Dave Smith and uneasy about the risks of his new tasks in Florida. "He was kind of going through this mental breakdown," Brill said. "I think he was struggling with a lot of things that he was doing." Bezalel suggested McConnell take a vacation. Bailey decided it was time to bring McConnell in and try to flip him. Finally, they might have the insider they'd been seeking for years, someone who could take the stand in court and point the finger at Le Roux.

But then they overheard something else on the wiretap: McConnell was leaving that same day for Manila, stopping in Los Angeles.

Bailey called the prosecutor, Linda Marks, to discuss whether they should risk intercepting him. Bailey could fly to L.A. and pull him off the plane, warning him that if he didn't talk now, he'd be brought down along with the rest of the organization. But Bailey would be bluffing. While they were 90 percent sure McConnell would turn on Le Roux, they didn't have much evidence of McConnell's own illegal acts to use as leverage. If they were wrong about him, he could alert Le Roux and send him into hiding. "He could call our bluff," Bailey said. "Those are the calculated risks that you take in these cat-and-mouse games." They decided to wait to see if he returned to the United States and wiretap him if he did.

When he showed up in Florida again the next month, they rushed to file for a T3 warrant on McConnell's cellphone. "Kim got up on a wiretap on his phone in six days," Bailey said. "That's so rare it's not even funny."

Brill stayed up all night monitoring the line, waiting for McConnell to make a call. All they needed was for him to admit to some wrongdoing—or to talk to Le Roux directly—and they could swoop in and grab him, hit play, and watch him flip.

And then suddenly, the next morning, he was gone again, abruptly flying back to Manila. "We intercepted him for less than a day and he got on a flight," Bailey said. "All we needed was a couple of days. God almighty. Just a couple days."

Even as Bailey and Brill desperately searched for a direct line to Le Roux, there *were* some members of Le Roux's organization ready to turn him in. Some, in fact, had spent years trying to find a government that would listen. Somehow the connections never quite crossed. First among them was Le Roux's cousin, Mathew Smith. After the firebombing of his house in Bulawayo, Mathew blamed Le Roux, who initially denied any involvement in it. "Had nothing to do with me bud," Le Roux told him in an online chat. "Are you sure it was not someone else u guys owe money to?"

"No buddy," Mathew said. "We owe one person. And that's you. You are my cousin for fucksakes. I worshipped the ground you walked on. Fuck mate, this is bullshit."

But it wasn't until the *M/V Ufuk* incident that Mathew understood how thoroughly Le Roux had played him. When the news broke, Mathew discovered that his father had been listed as an "officer" of La Plata Trading, the company accused of orchestrating the arms shipment. It didn't make sense at first; his father had no recollection of ever signing any paperwork. Then Mathew remembered that when Le Roux had first reconnected with him, back in 2007, he'd offered to pay for Mathew and his father's airline tickets if they sent along their passports. That was all Le Roux needed. In the years Mathew had spent helping to arrange dummies to create companies in Hong Kong, he'd never considered the consequences of his own family member becoming one.

Enraged, Mathew found an email address on the website of the Australian Federal Police. He sent a note saying he had information about an Australian and Zimbabwean citizen, based out of the Philippines, who was dealing in weapons and drugs. In late 2010, an AFP agent responded, and Mathew had several conversations with him. After another six months, the AFP connected him to someone at the CIA. Then things seemed to stall.

Unbeknownst to Mathew, his fellow Zimbabwean Robert McGowan—the real Robert McGowan—was making his own approaches to law enforcement. He had been trying to recover his losses from his dealings with Le Roux after he was left holding the bag on the logging equipment for Le Roux's canceled projects. Then, when the U.N. report on Le Roux's operations in Somalia was picked up in the Zimbabwean press in 2011, McGowan discovered that the company affiliated with it, Southern Ace, was registered to him. Frantic, he called Alon Berkman in Israel, trying to get in touch with Le Roux. Moran Oz remembered the call, and Le Roux's response: "Ignore him."

McGowan then tried another tack, contacting an attorney in the United States who was married to an old friend of his wife's. McGowan asked if he could take legal action against Le Roux, to somehow get his name removed from any companies registered in his identity. He also had evidence that Le Roux had broken into his email. "I need to try and close up everything I have linking me with this guy, including the companies in the USA, Israel & Hong Kong," McGowan wrote to the attorney. "I do not have the resources available to go to each of these countries to shut everything down or to hire lawyers. These people are very dangerous and have already bombed his relative's house here and shot through the bedroom window just missing hitting him. If we take this up with law enforcement in the U.S.A., what sort of protection can we get?"

The lawyer replied that "in the simplest terms you have been the victim of identity theft." The wrinkle, he said, "is that the person who stole your identity is an international gunrunner and drug smuggler." The lawyer said he'd reach out to an acquaintance in the FBI, but couldn't promise anything. Even the U.S. government would be unlikely to guarantee McGowan's safety in Africa.

Nestor Del Rosario, Le Roux's Filipino deputy—the man who'd gone to Iran and orchestrated Le Roux's weapons transactions— also made contact with authorities, approaching the Australian Federal Police under the code name Persian Cat, hinting that he was interested in turning on Le Roux. By the time they passed the contact to the Americans, Del Rosario seemed to have lost his nerve and disappeared.

On November 1, 2011, the U.S. Centers for Disease Control and Prevention formally declared a national prescription painkiller epidemic. "The death toll from overdoses of prescription painkillers has more than tripled in the past decade," the announcement stated. "Overdoses involving prescription painkillers are at epidemic levels and now kill more Americans than heroin and cocaine combined." To Brill, there was never any question that Le Roux's operation was fueling painkiller addictions and overdoses in the United States. She had sought out buyers from RX Limited websites and interviewed them.

Their stories were the ones that would later become familiar as the epidemic mushroomed: A security guard, prescribed Ultram to treat the pain from his shingles, turns to drugsmd.com when his prescription runs out, thinking a doctor is reviewing his order. ("_____ chose Tramadol because he did not want to be on narcotics," Brill's report reads.) An unemployed woman lacking health insurance Googles "tramadol"—the generic name for Ultram—after a bike accident and starts buying from www.tramadolovernight.org. A nurse self-medicates her migraines with pills bought online.

None of RX Limited's biggest three sellers were explicitly included among the drugs that the federal government cited as part of the epidemic. Even as the DEA tried to get a handle on the drugs they did know were abused—like oxycodone (brand name Oxy-Contin) and hydrocodone (Vicodin)—the use of Ultram and Soma had been growing unimpeded, with Le Roux as one of the main engines. "It was like a cancer where the tumor was just multiplying by the day," said John Horton, the founder of LegitScript, the Oregon-based company that monitors illegal online pharmacies. "We knew about those drugs, and the abuse potential. There is no doubt that this guy contributed to the prescription drug epidemic in this country. If you look at how much Soma, tramadol, and Fioricet that guy was selling—it's remarkable."

As long as those three painkillers remained uncontrolled, the legal case against RX Limited would be challenging to make. Not impossible—Le Roux's doctors were prescribing drugs without ever having met their "patients," a potential violation of the federal Food, Drug, and Cosmetic Act. But without controlled substances, the prosecution would be far from a slam dunk. Soma was already considered a controlled drug by some states, and other parts of the DEA had been pushing to get it controlled at the federal level for a decade. But the Food and Drug Administration, whose approval was required, was "dragging their feet," Bailey said. "Big Pharma, you know, they pay. It's like anything else."

In the meantime, the investigators had been hanging their case largely on the idea that Fioricet, containing one controlled ingredient, could be held out as a controlled substance itself. Brill, calling on her legal experience, successfully pushed to obtain a judgment from the DOJ that the full drug qualified as controlled.

Finally, in January 2012, the DEA declared Soma a Schedule IV controlled substance. Behind the scenes, Bailey said, the decision came about because of the investigation into RX Limited and cases like it. The question was whether it had come too late to nail Paul Le Roux.

21

The Pharmacist · The Doctor

2010–2011 . . . Tumpati gets spooked . . . Schultz gets raided

Even for the doctors and pharmacists who believed it was legal, working for RX Limited always had a too-good-to-be-true feeling about it. The money was too good, for too little effort. There were too many patients, with too little vetting. There were too many holes in the system itself, like an "Approve All" button in RX Limited's software that allowed doctors to accept hundreds of patient questionnaires at the same time. Occasionally, their doubt surfaced in emails to company representatives like "Ron Oz," in which they double- and triple-checked that someone was making sure it was all on the right side of the law. And then, all around the country, that doubt turned to fear as the DEA began poking at mom-and-pop pharmacies who had joined the network and doctors who were prescribing for it, hinting that a reckoning was imminent.

For Prabhakara Tumpati, that moment arrived in 2010, when he received a letter from the Pennsylvania Board of Pharmacy, the body that regulates prescription drugs at the state level. The board had taken note of Tumpati's thousands of prescriptions for RX

Limited, and they were considering updating their regulations on how such digital prescriptions could be issued, particularly involving painkillers. It appeared, in other words, as if Pennsylvania might be on the verge of declaring one or all of the network's three biggest sellers—Ultram, Soma, and Fioricet—controlled substances. Tumpati contacted an attorney, who contacted the board, trying to assess whether Tumpati had run afoul of any laws. "The message from the state attorney to our attorney was that it's a good idea, with an abundance of caution, not to continue," Tumpati said.

He'd already grown frustrated with his contact at RX Limited, Aaron Johnson, who seemed uninterested in pushing further in the direction of cutting-edge telemedicine. "I had so many conversations with these people, Aaron Johnson in particular, on how to improve the system," Tumpati said. "I was not trying to make a quick buck. In fact, I was so upset and angry at these people that are paying me only two, three dollars, and I had to fight with them every day trying to increase the rate from two to two fifty to three dollars."

Even if Pennsylvania was changing its laws, Tumpati held a New York medical license. He could have simply uploaded it to the RX Limited system and continued prescribing as a New York doctor. But he decided against it. "I said, 'Well, you know, there are some changes coming up. I don't want to take any risk,'" he said. "I didn't think I *was* taking a risk." So, after earning a million dollars over three years writing online prescriptions for RX Limited, in March 2011 he quit.

That June, Tumpati sent an email to his close friend and colleague in Pennsylvania, Anu Konakanchi, whom he'd signed up to write prescriptions for a commission, warning her that he was getting out. "As you can see, they are specifically trying to target the questionnaire based telemedicine," he wrote, including a link to the proposed state rules. "I am not sure when they will publish the final rule but just wanted to let you know that they are trying to change the rules. It is possible to use existing technology to objectively assess using audio/video consultation but the providers have to implement these technologies. I am telling these guys to change to an audio/video technology but not sure if and when they will improve the system."

Later, he would point out that in sending the email he was acting against his own financial interests, risking losing the commission he got after every prescription Konakanchi wrote. But as it turned out, he didn't. Konakanchi decided to keep filling prescriptions for RX Limited anyway, which meant that even after Tumpati left the organization, he continued racking up his commissions.

Charles Schultz was in too deep—and too stubborn in his belief that the work was legal—to heed the warning signs. By the end of 2011, his two pharmacies had shipped more than 700,000 prescriptions. AlphaNet had wired more than $27 million from various accounts in Hong Kong to Schultz's bank—$3.3 million of which was Schultz's profits from his per-prescription fees. "He thought he'd found a way to sustain his business," Hal Harlowe, his lawyer, said. "He's a decent man who pursued what he thought was a legitimate opportunity but turned a blind eye to the cues that some of the people he was dealing with were, at best, walking along the edge of the law. These folks ran circles around him."

At first there were only small indications of trouble. The number of daily prescriptions had begun declining, from a peak of fifteen hundred a day to eight hundred. The technicians and pharmacists were told to stop shipping drugs to customers in Wisconsin, so they flagged any in-state orders and rejected them in the system. Then, in June 2011, Schultz Pharmacy received a letter from the FedEx legal department. "It has come to our understanding that you are an online pharmacy," it read, "or that pharmaceuticals purchased through online pharmacies are being shipped on your account." If the pharmacy couldn't provide evidence that the system was VIPPS-accredited—officially approved as legitimate by the National Association of Boards of Pharmacy—the account would be terminated. Schultz alerted his contacts at AlphaNet, who proposed switching his pharmacies onto United States Postal Service and UPS accounts until the VIPPS application could be straightened out.

By that point, it was too late. Schultz's fate was already decided by the DEA controlled buys his pharmacies had unwittingly shipped. One afternoon in March 2012, a group of federal agents from the FDA and the IRS arrived at the door of Schultz Pharmacy in Oshkosh bearing a search warrant. They wanted to examine all of Schultz's equipment and records pertaining to the online pharmacy. Schultz immediately admitted his involvement and agreed to cooperate. He had little in the way of information about the larger scheme he'd been a part of—some names and phone numbers, emails back and forth about prescriptions and accounting. He agreed to maintain his relationship with his AlphaNet contacts, and to let the agents record calls to company representatives. Then RX Limited's largest supplier, an eighty-year-old pharmacist in Wisconsin with a heart condition, gave the agents a room to set up in at the pharmacy and served them coffee.

22

The Mercenaries

2012 . . . Hunter's "ninja work" . . . Noimie Edillor creates the
template . . . A new pair of killers . . . The death of Catherine Lee

By early 2011, Dave Smith was dead, and Le Roux promoted Joseph Hunter to reorganize his security teams, at a salary of $12,000 a month. He ordered Hunter to hire a new kill team to tackle the growing list of associates and employees he believed might be stealing from him. They would work with a surveillance group run by a Filipino named Noyt, who would locate and track the targets. Hunter planned to revamp the whole operation, keeping what he liked to call "ninja work"—intimidation and murder—separate from "business," the everyday job of securing Le Roux's operations. Dave Smith, he told Le Roux, had spent more time drinking and womanizing than he had planning missions. Now things would be different.

Hunter rehired his old friend Tim Vamvakias, the former American soldier who had brought him into Le Roux's organization in 2008. He paired up Chris De Meyer, his former finger-breaking partner, with an American of Samoan descent whom everyone in the organization knew only as "Daddy Mac." They'd each earn a $25,000 "sales bonus" for every hit they carried out.

Among their first targets was a woman named Noimie Edillor, a purchasing manager for the organization whom Le Roux had also paid to help move contraband through customs. He now believed she had taken the money and failed to deliver the goods. She also worked part time as a real estate agent, so Le Roux—after assigning Noyt to conduct surveillance on her—suggested that Hunter's kill team pretend to be potential buyers, make an appointment to look at some houses, and then kill her inside an empty one.

On the evening of June 23, 2011, the thirty-one-year-old Edillor told her husband that she was showing a property in a subdivision. He drove her to the entrance and dropped her off. She then climbed into a silver Toyota Innova van with what he assumed were her prospective buyers. When she didn't return or answer her cellphone, her husband went looking for her and found her body lying on the sidewalk in a pool of blood.

When Le Roux, per his usual policy, asked Hunter for proof that the mission had been completed, Hunter emailed him a link to a local news story describing the murder. "There is your fucking proof," Hunter wrote. "Have my guys money tomorrow. They're running around doing your crazy shit and you insult them."

The Philippine police, meanwhile, were baffled by the killing. The file, by the time I got hold of it, offered little beyond the barest details of the murder. But a recent note mentioned that a pair of suspects had been passed along by the DEA: a Samoan known only as "Mac Daddy" and a former soldier in the French Foreign Legion named Chris De Meyer. The murder remained unsolved.

Edillor's killing provided Hunter with the template for the targeting of Catherine Lee, the next name on Le Roux's list. The problem was finding someone to do it. Le Roux had already ordered his South African hit man, Marcus, to conduct surveillance on Lee, but he was unavailable to complete the job. De Meyer and Mac Daddy had gone AWOL after the Edillor murder. So instead Hunter turned to an American named Adam Samia living in Roxboro, North Carolina.

Samia had worked for The Company briefly years before, developing a reputation as the eager beaver of Le Roux's mercenaries. Unlike many of his colleagues, he lacked military experience, and Le Roux's other mercenaries viewed him alternately as a weekend warrior and a dangerous idiot. He'd met Dave Smith more than a decade before through Samia's brother, a police officer in Massachusetts, who had taken a SWAT training course taught by Smith. Samia, who was working construction, had tagged along and played the role of a bad guy in some of the training exercises. Afterward, Smith had encouraged him to start doing executive protection work, and years later brought him into Le Roux's organization. Although Samia had asked Smith for "wet work," he mostly was given humdrum tasks like transporting gold in Africa or guarding a yacht under repair in a Hong Kong shipyard. He hadn't worked a mission for The Company in years.

But Hunter was desperate to keep Le Roux happy. So he emailed Samia, hoping to line him and a partner up for multiple jobs in Manila. "Boss says you are on standby until the other guy is ready and you guys will come here together for Ninja stuff," Hunter wrote. "We want you guys, but are just waiting until you and your partner can get on the same time table."

Finally, in October 2011, Le Roux requested to meet Samia in person in Brazil. Le Roux wired him money to purchase a ticket, only for the would-be international assassin to discover—upon arriving for his departing flight—that he needed a Brazilian visa. "You fucked this up," Hunter replied when Samia emailed to report that he wouldn't be making the trip. "We are not paying for your ticket. You'll be paid to do a job with a result. The key word is 'result.' We do not pay for thinking about it. We do not pay for trying. We do not pay for your time. We pay for the end result."

Despite the fuckup, Hunter still had no other options for the job. Samia identified a partner for the operation, a Roxboro friend named David Stillwell. Stillwell was a former IT contractor with financial problems and a love of guns. Roxboro friends described the pair as well-liked local guys who ran a small gun-paraphernalia company together. They traveled to gun shows to market accessories of their own invention, including a bra that doubled as a holster, called a Bosom Buddy. But aside from a few pictures on Samia's Facebook page showing him brandishing and firing a variety of firearms, they did not otherwise give the impression of being skilled assassins.

In early December, Hunter reported back to Le Roux via email that the hit team's travel dates were set for January. "Adam will be leaving on the 8th and will be here on the 9th and the other guy will leave on the 10th and be here on the 11th. The WU"—Western Union—"of $1,625 goes to Adam Samia Roxboro, North Carolina USA."

In January 2012, Samia and Stillwell arrived in Manila on separate flights, and convened at a hotel above Howzat, a sports bar in Manila's red-light district. Hunter supplied them a dossier for their first hit: a former employee that Le Roux believed had once stolen from him. When Samia and Stillwell failed to locate her at the addresses in the dossier, they concluded she'd gone into hiding. Hunter asked Le Roux for another target. "Need someone we can find now and get done right away," he wrote to Le Roux.

On January 17, Le Roux sent Hunter an email with a new dossier attached: a real estate agent named Catherine Lee.

Samia and Stillwell moved into an apartment as their new base of operations, and in late January Samia emailed Hunter an update mixed with a chipper plea for additional cash:

> Hey Bro we are going to need some OP funds ($3000.00) we both are just about broke we have spent all are money on finding a place to live, the car, phone load, food, taxi's looking for a place to live, Internet, stuff for here an more. I got them to throw a bed an ac so the boss does not have to buy them trying to save were I can!

From Le Roux, Hunter requested the necessary weapons for the job: "1 MP5 SD," a submachine gun with a silencer, along with "1 Rifle Silenced with optics" and "1 .22 or 380 Pistol Silenced."

Le Roux ordered the weapons delivered from the Red White & Blue Arms warehouse. Hunter then set his charges up with more money, along with the weapons and a laptop bag "modified to hold the tool for concealment."

He also gave them detailed instructions on how to carry the murder out. They were to act as real estate buyers looking for property, and arrange to meet Lee in the parking lot of a fast-food restaurant. "Get her into your car and take off so nobody saw you guys together," he told them. "As soon as she gets in the car, drive down the road maybe a quarter mile, about a half kilometer. Turn around and shoot her. It's done. Nobody saw anything. Take a blanket with you and wrap her up."

In early February 2012, Catherine Lee received an email from a Canadian man named Bill Maxwell. Maxwell said that he and his colleague, Tony, were looking to invest in real estate. They had searched online for a broker and found Lee, a well-known agent whose territory ranged throughout the southern part of the Philippines' main island, Luzon. A few years prior, she had served as president of her local chapter of the Real Estate Brokers of the Philippines. Lee was forty-three but looked younger, with a pixie haircut and a welcoming smile. She worked from her home in a house she and her husband had purchased not long before, with the help of a particularly large commission she'd earned. Much of her business came to her over the Internet—enough, at least, that she would be unlikely to think twice about scheduling a meeting with a client by email.

Bill and Tony didn't specify what type of property they were looking for; it could be commercial or residential, a vacation property or a ready-to-build lot, as long as it was a solid investment. For two days, she drove them from property to property, but the men weren't ready to commit. For their third outing, on the morning of February 12, Lee met Bill and Tony on the outdoor patio of a Starbucks in Las Piñas, not far from her house. They were joined by three other real estate brokers she'd enlisted to help with the search.

The Canadians arrived in a silver Toyota Innova van. Bill was around six-foot-one, with a beard and a prominent belly. Tony was clean-shaven and wore a baseball cap. Lee took them to a gated community called Ponderosa, forty miles south of Manila, where they examined a lush lot available for residential development. For lunch they stopped at a nearby spot popular with the locals called Mushroomburger, where they were joined by two property owners Lee knew at around 3:30 P.M.

They then traveled to another piece of land eight miles away, in Cavite. They arrived at 4:30 and wandered around for an hour. When it was time to leave, the three brokers and the property owners departed in one car; Lee joined Bill and Tony in the Innova van.

Sometime in the next few hours, Adam Samia turned and leaned into the backseat, pulled out a .22-caliber handgun, and shot Lee twice in the head at close range. Then he and Stillwell rolled her up in a blanket, and deposited it in a pile of garbage.

Hunter, when he heard how they'd carried it out, was astonished that Samia and Stillwell had botched the killing so thoroughly. "What these guys did, they didn't listen to me," Hunter said later, captured on surveillance tapes. "They went to all these different houses with her, where there was people living in the houses. So every house they went to, people saw them together. They saw their faces. They saw the real estate agent. . . . They did this for like three different days. So like one hundred people saw them."

Le Roux had more targets lined up for the pair, including another former employee and a ship captain he believed had tipped off the authorities to the *M/V Ufuk* weapons shipment. But as Hunter later recounted it, their covers were already blown.

HUNTER: So I got them on the plane. They were Americans, so I got them back to America and then ah, I, I never . . . I didn't give them any more work because they put everyone in danger. I told them, "You know how they would get caught? If the police in the Philippines was smart and not lazy, all they had to do was take the witnesses to the airport and look at each picture of the foreigners and, and then that's, 'Oh, that's the guy!'" Then they have his . . . they have his passport, his photo, right, but the police in the Philippines aren't smart and they don't . . . they're lazy. They don't do nothing. So those guys were lucky. . . . You got to use your brain in this job.

If Samia and Stillwell were troubled by the way the trip had gone, it wasn't evident in their communications. They emailed their expenses to Hunter, who delivered $35,000 apiece plus reimbursements, in cash. They turned over the weapons and the bloody Toyota Innova to Hunter, and Le Roux ordered the van scrubbed down by two Israeli employees in front of his house. Samia informed Hunter that Stillwell was "rolling state side the 29th of FEB, I am heading out the 6th of March, I will drop [off] the car the 5th." They wired their payments home—being careful to split them into increments under $10,000 to avoid getting flagged for money laundering. Then they caught flights back to the United States.

PART III

ENDGAME

23

The Mastermind

2011–2012 . . . Le Roux makes a move

Paul Le Roux always knew that the end would come, or so those close to him would say. The sheer gluttony of his criminal appetite meant he was all but daring law enforcement to take him down. To feed it, his enterprise had grown ferociously, with a logic discernible only to Le Roux. By 2011, he was moving large quantities of methamphetamine across Southeast Asia, using a direct pipeline out of North Korea. He was working on large-scale cocaine deals in South America and testing his own drone designs in the Philippines to help ship the drugs. He was buying and selling weapons around the world—in Sri Lanka, in Indonesia, in Eastern Europe, in Iran—dealing with rogue regimes, warlords, terrorists, and anyone with money.

He was also in the midst of unleashing an orgy of violence in the Philippines, through Hunter and his team of assassins. His hit list now included journalists, random service providers, and former employees, all suspected of betrayals large or trivial. His targets now ranged from Nestor Del Rosario, his once-trusted deputy who had orchestrated the weapons purchases in Iran, to a ship captain

Le Roux suspected of tipping off the authorities to the *M/V Ufuk*. When Le Roux concluded that another employee named Joseph—not Hunter—had conspired with Dave Smith to cheat him, he arranged for a rebel leader to plant a bomb under Joseph's vehicle. The bomb went off; Joseph survived. Le Roux simply moved to the next name on his list.

There were different theories about what eventually spooked Le Roux enough to force him out of the protective cocoon he'd built for himself in the Philippines. Patrick Donovan believed he pulled up stakes because his growing conglomerate had trod on the territory of Chinese cartels that controlled the local drug trade. "Le Roux fell afoul of them when he started fucking bringing drugs on the streets here," Donovan said. "I know there were three people that wanted to kill him. But nobody could get to him, he was such a recluse. Fucker hardly ever came out of anywhere. And when he did it was in the fucking middle of the night or early hours of the morning."

Others said he saw international authorities closing in on him. He had talked for years about how the DEA was on his trail. "The Americans," he would say, "are watching." For half a decade he had been watching the watchers, exploiting the Philippines' rampant corruption to ensure his invulnerabilty to local and international investigations. He had Filipino employees at the U.S. embassy on his payroll, tipping him off to American information requests through FinCEN, the financial crimes enforcement network that Kent Bailey had used to gather intel. Through his paid Philippine law enforcement contacts, Le Roux had heard about Bailey's 2009 visit to Manila. ("We were very careful with what we shared with them," Bailey said of the Philippine authorities. "But it was common knowledge that they would take those requests and try and get money from the people that we were making requests about.") Le Roux had gotten hold of a letter from the FBI's Manila attaché to the Philippine Securities and Exchange Commission, inquiring about his business dealings. From a contact he called "Dragnet," he had purchased documents purporting to be from the CIA about United States operations in the Philippines. (He later sold them to other potential U.S. law enforcement targets, including a local terrorist leader.)

When he couldn't pay for information, he gathered it himself. One former DEA agent told me that Le Roux had tapped into the country's 4G cellphone network to collect his own intelligence. He had even forged a request from the Australian Federal Police and sent it to the Philippine authorities—on what appeared to be actual AFP letterhead—inquiring about investigations into Paul Le Roux.

Le Roux could certainly see that the foreign law-enforcement interest in him was gaining intensity. That, too, had always been a problem he assumed money could solve. In the Philippines, by one employee's estimate, Le Roux was paying upward of $50,000 a month in routine bribes to protect himself. Others talked of judges, police generals, and national politicians that the organization had in its pocket. Le Roux himself would brag that he'd paid a relative of one of the country's highest-ranking officials $1 million in cash, delivered in a bag. There was nowhere that Le Roux's money couldn't reach.

Or so it seemed. In the end, he may have discovered there were limits to whom he could buy off—or, more to the point, whom he could kill. In 2010 a new president, Benigno Aquino, came into office. One of Aquino's top aides, as it happened, had gone to school with Joe Frank Zuñiga, the lawyer for the ship captain Bruce Jones. When Zuñiga disappeared, his wife appealed directly to the aide for help. The local investigation against Le Roux that Inspector R at the Philippine National Police had been discouraged from pursuing suddenly cranked to life. Not long after, Inspector R lucked into a new lead: Le Roux's Filipino head of surveillance, Noyt—whose real name was Ronald Baricuatro— was arrested for stealing a motorcycle. When police searched his backpack they found a shoe box full of papers, seven IDs under different names, a camera, four cellphones, a wig, and two bullets. Under questioning, he told them he'd been hired years before by a man named Dave Smith but now worked directly for Le Roux.

Among his papers were dossiers on Michael Lontoc, the target shooter who had been gunned down in broad daylight, and Nestor Del Rosario. A third file targeted Mar Supnad, the reporter who had interviewed Bruce Jones.

More exposed than he'd ever been, Le Roux needed to find another operating base while the heat in the Philippines dissipated. "He knows the political climate," the former DEA agent said. "Just wait four years: It'll change." Le Roux had nearly endless means at his disposal to escape the attention. He held a fistful of passports, real and fake, including a diplomatic passport that he hoped would provide him criminal immunity. He owned property across Asia, Africa, and Australia. For transportation, he had bought a 115-foot Denison super yacht named the *Texas Star II*, built for maximum speeds of forty knots, fast enough to outrun many coast guards. The yacht, which in a past life had sailed under the name *Thunderball*, was emblematic of Le Roux's transformation from an online pill kingpin to a true mogul of the international drug trade. He was having it serviced in Europe to add night vision capabilities so that the boat could easily spot loads of drugs dropped with a buoy offshore.

For now there remained the practical problem of avoiding the American government's reach. So as he started to feel claustrophobic in late 2011, Le Roux put a safe harbor plan into action. "I got this call from Paul saying, 'I'm going out of the Philippines for a while, maybe a week or a few weeks,'" said Scott Stammers, a security contractor who was working for Le Roux in Thailand at the time. "That was the way Paul was. I wouldn't hear from him for a month and then he'd call me fifty times in a day. He said, 'I pay your salary to be ready.' Then he called and said he was in Brazil."

Paul Calder Le Roux stood on the brink of a future in which he would no longer be just the programmer-made-good with a clever idea for online pharmacies. He was already earning hundreds of millions of dollars online. But as much as money he was chasing a certain status, as a power player in the global underground, a man whose deals—and influence—crossed borders and touched governments. And he nearly had it. "He was cresting," the former DEA agent told me. "He hadn't hit his peak yet. If it had gone six more months, a year, we'd have never got him."

24

The Investigators

2011–2012 . . . Brazil on the case . . . Informants in from the cold . . . Strange liaisons . . . 960 joins the chase

Le Roux was making moves in Brazil. That much Kimberly Brill and Kent Bailey could tell from the wiretaps. After losing track of Lachlan McConnell in Florida, they'd turned their attention to Detroit, where the local DEA office had a wiretap running on Babubhai Patel, the owner of one of RX Limited's larger pharmacies. Patel, unlike most other pharmacy owners, seemed to have direct contact with the organization's operators, people with names like "Ron Oz" and "Allen Berkman." The wiretap captured Patel's calls with Berkman and another Israeli, Doron Shulman—the former member of the Duvdevan—as the company tried to solve its shipping woes. Patel sounded under pressure, citing the riskiness of the operation now that Soma was a controlled substance and the DEA was paying attention.

The investigators also started catching references to Brazil. Dating back to the beginning of the operation, they'd seen calls back and forth between Le Roux's phone and South America. Now they gleaned that he might be be relocating there. The DEA's attaché in São Paulo happened to be an old colleague of Bailey's from Los

Angeles, and when Bailey called he sprang into action, persuading the Brazilian federal police to open their own investigation, complete with extensive surveillance of Le Roux. The Brazilian team would operate in secrecy, and consist of agents pulled from other divisions into a central one called the Sensitive Information Group, known as GISE by its Portuguese initials. They called the investigation, simply, "Operação America."

The GISE agents discovered that back in April 2011 Le Roux had established a company in Brazil, Rainbow Force Technologies. Registered to a local Brazilian woman, it supposedly employed ten people and provided "custom computer programming services." Le Roux had then made a three-week trip to Rio de Janeiro in October 2011. Now Brill drafted an affidavit that would provide the basis for a wiretap, and the Brazilian agents prepared to wrap Le Roux in surveillance from the moment he reentered the country.

On February 16, 2012, he arrived on a flight to Galeão International Airport outside of Rio and stepped up to immigration control. He was traveling with his visibly pregnant Filipina girlfriend, a former employee named Cindy Cayanan, and their young daughter. Le Roux was still married to Lilian Cheung Yuen Pui, the mother of his two older children, who now lived in the Netherlands. But on immigration forms he claimed Cayanan as his wife. Agents tailed them to Avenida Lúcio Costa, a wide boulevard along the beach in an upscale neighborhood southwest of Rio known as Barra da Tijuca. There they were joined by a nanny, in a condo that Le Roux had purchased through an intermediary in a gated community called The Waterways. The GISE agents set up around the complex, and tailed Le Roux on his rare forays out of it.

His support network in the country appeared to be directed by Zion Fadlon, a dark-haired Israeli operating under the name "John Brown." He supplied Le Roux with a pair of cellphones registered to a local Brazilian dummy, which GISE quickly obtained a court order to monitor. The agents also began following Fadlon, who, among other tasks, was seeking office space for Rainbow Force, at Le Roux's direction. He needed a location with access to the highest-speed Internet, and generators so that the power would be guaranteed to stay up twenty-four hours a day. Eventually Fadlon settled on space in a bland twenty-story office building in Rio, and posted a job seeking an IT officer to administer the company's computer systems.

As GISE conveyed to Bailey and Brill everything they were seeing and hearing, the contours of Le Roux's plan began to emerge: He was reconstituting his online pharmacy operation in Brazil, while doubling down on international narcotics and weapons trafficking from his new base. His equipment supplier back in Kentucky, Jon Wall, was now shipping goods directly to the address of the woman on the Rainbow Force registration. The ultimate purpose of those goods—which included satellite phones and "side-scan sonar" used for mapping the sea floor—wasn't hard to imagine.

Over the early months of 2012, Le Roux's employees around the world began showing up on the Rio surveillance. Shai Reuven, the Philippines-based Israeli who now seemed to have a hand in all parts of the business, arrived to talk in person. In surveillance photos the Brazilians took and passed back to the DEA, Le Roux could be seen in a pale-yellow-striped polo and sky-blue shorts, hands on hips, as he chatted with Reuven outside a Pizza Hut in a Rio mall.

It was the kind of direct surveillance of Le Roux that Bailey and Brill had been missing since the investigation began, almost five years before. And they were about to be twice lucky. Some of Le Roux's former employees appeared ready to talk.

It had been more than a year since Robert McGowan, the Zimbabwean whose name was all over Le Roux's companies, had authorized an attorney in the United States to contact the FBI. The request languished, but by early 2012 it finally wound its way to

Kimberly Brill. McGowan was the kind of insider she and Bailey had been seeking for years: a former employee who claimed Le Roux had stolen his identity and was eager to take him down.

Brill and Bailey had been around the informant carousel too many times to be overly optimistic. But in February 2012, Brill called McGowan, with his attorney on the line, to evaluate what he knew. "The SOI [source of information] provided information regarding companies and bank accounts operated by Paul LE ROUX and general information regarding LE ROUX and his operations and some of his associates," Brill wrote in her report of the call. McGowan told her that he'd traveled to Israel, at Le Roux's direction, to meet with Moran Oz and Alon Berkman—whom he could identify—and incorporate Le Roux's call center companies there. He'd done the same in Hong Kong and Florida, he said, ticking off a list of corporate names that matched those Brill had been tracking: Diko, Wilex, and First Globe in Hong Kong; Quality Fountain and Armada Commerce in Florida. Mc-Gowan asserted that he'd never been involved in the pharmaceutical business, and that after the logging project evaporated, Le Roux had simply kept using his name on companies like Southern Ace. McGowan wouldn't be a slam-dunk witness, but he could at least claim firsthand contact with their target.

Then another source came in out of the cold, this one even closer to Le Roux: his cousin Mathew Smith. He had contacted the Australian Federal Police, who after several months referred the whole matter to the CIA office in South Africa. When Brill finally connected with him, the cousin had a dramatic story to tell: After a falling-out in which Le Roux accused him of stealing money, someone had firebombed his house and made an attempt on his life. He suspected it was his cousin.

A few weeks after her phone call with McGowan, Brill flew to Zimbabwe to meet both of them in person. They connected her with a third potential informant, Robson Tandanayi, a local from Bulawayo who had spent years as a paid "dummy," opening companies and transferring assets in Hong Kong, Singapore, and Australia. After years of experiencing Le Roux's network through the digital prism of emails, wiretaps, and Internet traces, Brill was finally talking to the people within it. These were witnesses that Linda Marks, the DOJ attorney, could put in front of a grand jury in Minnesota to finally obtain an indictment against Le Roux. All of them said they were willing to testify about what they knew of Le Roux and his businesses.

The Rio wiretaps were a continuous revelation, a trove of leads and evidence, and a chance, finally, to hear at length from the man himself. "He felt very safe in Brazil," one of the GISE agents said. Safe enough to let down his guard. With Alon Berkman, Le Roux discussed shifting money between accounts in Hong Kong, and establishing new protocols for the call center business in Israel. With Shai Reuven, they heard him trying to arrange new credit card processors for RX Limited. "They'll be on us for money laundering and passport fraud" if the deals weren't made correctly, Le Roux warned. With his wife, Lilian, he arranged for the transport of funds into Brazil through one "Eddie," who GISE agents determined was an Israeli working out of Hong Kong named Yoav Hen. Hen landed in Rio on March 28 to deliver $300,000 in cash.

The surveillance made clear to the American investigators the scope of Le Roux's shift from pharmaceuticals into international weapons and narcotics. In early April, he texted an employee in Hong Kong about a shipment of red phosphorus, a chemical precursor to methamphetamine, bound for Manila by boat. Shepherding the phosphorus, together with a load of computer parts, was Ivan Vaclavic, an Eastern European who—along with Philip Shackels—was one of Le Roux's key lieutenants in the drug trade.

Le Roux alerted Doron Shulman, back in the Philippines, to the impending arrival, instructing him to send a boat out from Subic Bay to off-load the computer equipment and leave the chemicals on board. As with the *Ufuk,* the job was undone by a tip. The Brazilian agents alerted the DEA, who in turn tipped off the local authorities, who detained Vaclavic and the boat.

Back in Rio, the wires lit up, this time with Vaclavic calling Le Roux to report that he was having trouble with the Philippine authorities. He didn't want to say too much; he was being watched by three Coast Guard officers. "I feel like Pablo Escobar," he said. Le Roux told him not to worry, that his men would handle everything "behind the scenes." Over several more calls, Le Roux ordered a safe at one of his properties emptied of 600,000 Philippine pesos, around $15,000. "That should be enough," he said. Not long after, Vaclavic found himself free to go.

The wiretaps also gave the GISE agents an unexpected window into Le Roux's romantic life, which they gathered was unconventional, to say the least. Having left his wife in the Netherlands and traveled to Brazil with his pregnant girlfriend, he'd also arranged for "Eddie" to bring in another Filipina woman, with whom Le Roux stayed at a condo half a block down the beach from the Waterways. At first the agents assumed the second apartment, which Le Roux also owned, was merely a love nest. They dutifully noted his other rendezvous with local women, including the one listed on the Rainbow Force company registration.

But after several weeks of listening to Le Roux's discussions with Zion Fadlon, his local point man, it slowly dawned on them that something more peculiar was going on.

In March, they heard a call from one of the women to Fadlon, informing him that she was having cramps.

"Does that mean you are pregnant?" he asked.

"I'm not pregnant," she replied. "I'm having my period."

"When will you be fertile?"

"Ten days."

When she failed to become pregnant after another series of rendezvous with Le Roux, they heard Fadlon arranging a doctor's appointment to assess her fertility. When Fadlon's calls to another local woman also focused heavily on her fertility cycles, it dawned on the GISE agents what was happening: The young Brazilian women in Le Roux's employ were receiving a monthly salary to conceive his children.

Back in the United States, Brill and Bailey couldn't believe what they were hearing. "That was all on the wire," Bailey said. "It was crazy! 'You are coming into cycle next week?' Like you are breeding two dogs. And she would be saying she wants a big-screen TV, and he was like, 'I'll talk to the boss.'" They soon discovered that Le Roux had already succeeded in his plan, conceiving with a twenty-two-year-old Brazilian. Wiretapped conversations with Fadlon revealed that she'd gotten pregnant on Le Roux's previous trip to Brazil, in October 2011.

On top of it all, Le Roux's girlfriend Cayanan had also given birth in Rio within weeks of their arrival. When Fadlon was heard on the wire making arrangements to officially register Le Roux as the father, the agents finally understood the whole picture: with the babies, Le Roux was attempting to create a novel kind of legal shield. While Brazil maintained an extradition treaty with the United States, the process for extraditing Brazilian citizens was difficult. And it was generally established that the law provided similar protections to parents of Brazilian children. "He didn't come out and say that: 'We're here to have a baby so they won't extradite me,'" Bailey said. "But he was clearly working with this contact in Brazil who was trying to grease the skids." His child with Cayanan—born on Brazilian soil—might give him some protection, but he had to be sure. "The first way wasn't foolproof, so what's another way?" Bailey said. "Impregnate a Brazilian."

Even years later, agents in both GISE and the DEA remained uncertain whether the citizenship gambit would have worked. But at a minimum they knew that his Brazilian connections could tie up the case in the courts for years. If they were going to capture Le

Roux and get him to the United States, they needed to lure him somewhere else—preferably a country from which he could be easily extracted.

Since early 2011, as revelations about the vastness of Le Roux's activities stacked up and he'd made the CPOT list, Brill and Bailey's investigation had finally begun drawing interest from other quarters of the U.S. government. After years of fighting to convince anyone at the DEA that Le Roux was the real deal, they suddenly found themselves fighting off attempts to glom on to the case.

Among those who had started taking an interest in Le Roux were agents in two high-profile sections of the Special Operations Division, where Bailey had once been posted. Known internally as the "nine-five-nine" and "nine-sixty" groups, they were named for the pair of amendments to U.S. drug laws that empowered them. The 959 provision, dating from 1980s efforts to combat cocaine trafficking, made it illegal for anyone to even *attempt* to import narcotics into the United States from anywhere in the world. The 960a provision, established by the 2006 USA PATRIOT Act reauthorization, gave SOD expanded powers to pursue so-called narcoterrorists, drug-trafficking organizations connected to terrorism. The two SOD groups were given wide latitude to conduct investigations and busts outside the United States, and 960 offenses came with twice the penalties of typical drug prosecutions. In the years since the September 11, 2001, attacks, SOD's powers and budgets had vastly expanded under both provisions, fueled by a belief in a growing nexus between America's terrorist enemies and the international drug trade. "They have a big budget, and they do big cases," summed up Bailey.

Much of the two divisions' work was classified, but 960 had conducted some highly public—and at times, controversial—undercover sting operations, in which paid informants played the part of buyers, luring would-be terrorists into drug trafficking, or vice versa. Much of the work involved coordinating with law enforcement counterparts overseas. DEA agents rarely made the actual arrests. In the most famous 960 bust, DEA informants posing as members of the Colombian rebel group FARC helped lure Russian arms trafficker Viktor Bout into a sting operation in Thailand in 2008. But at times 960 seemed to push the boundaries of what qualified as "narcoterrorism," using elaborate fake terrorist plots to reel in small-time drug dealers on the other side of the world.

Le Roux was the real thing, however, a prime 960 target with intersecting weapons and drug operations that spanned the globe. In addition to its resources and international reach, 960 had an advantage over the Minnesota DEA. Brill and Bailey were working with prosecutors from the DOJ's Consumer Protection Division, and after nearly five years, they still didn't have Le Roux under indictment. Cases pursued by 959 and 960 often landed in the powerful and aggressive U.S. Attorney's office in the Southern District of New York, headed by Preet Bharara. The office had extensive experience prosecuting complex international cases—including the conviction of Viktor Bout. Now Derek Maltz, the special agent in charge of SOD, began referring internally to Le Roux as "Viktor Bout on steroids."

At first, the sudden interest at SOD didn't sit well with Bailey and Brill. The 960 group could be condescending, to put it mildly, toward other agents' abilities. To make matters worse, they were horning in on a case they'd once declined. Bailey had worked at SOD, after all, in the Pharmaceutical, Chemical, and Internet division. "Nine-sixty didn't know shit about this case," Bailey said. "When I was back there, I briefed those guys, tried to get them to take the case, to work the guns. Because that was truly outside of Kim's purview. Because 'That's what you guys do and you're good at it.' And they are, like, 'Oooooh, welllllll. That's too hard, we're too busy.' But when you spoon-feed and gift-wrap a frickin' case they sit back and say, 'What took you so long?' "

After Le Roux moved his operations to Brazil, however, Bailey began to see the logic in letting 960 take on the challenge of capturing the man himself. "I'm the one that told Kim, 'Let them do it,' " he said. " 'You can't do all this; this case is too big. They're from SOD, they are not here to take your case. You did all the work. Let them lure him, it's one less thing for us to worry about.' "

Brill came around to the idea, and she and Bailey gave SOD their blessing to run a Le Roux sting. They even offered a suggestion on a place to start: find whoever had talked to U.N. investigators about Le Roux's Somalia operation. "Somebody," Bailey remembered saying, "has got to get this guy to cooperate."

25

The Mole

2012 . . . A call from the DEA . . . Constructing the ruse . . . A deal with the Colombians . . . A sudden request

On a warm evening in February 2012, Felix Klaussen was at a beer hall in Dubai with his fiancée when his phone rang. He glanced down and saw a number he didn't recognize. "I never pick up numbers that I don't know," he said later; but for some reason his curiosity got the better of him, and he answered. On the other end was a friendly American accent.

"Hi, how are you, this is Tom," the man said. "I work for the U.S. government."

It had been a year since Klaussen sent his email to a generic address he'd found on the CIA's website. In the intervening time, he'd managed to put his life as "Jack Anderson," who worked for Paul Le Roux and ran a militia-protected operation in Somalia, behind him. He'd even burned his fake passport in front of his fiancée to prove that there was no going back. After a stint managing a hotel, he'd recently been running his own personal fitness training company. But he was considering swapping careers again. His fiancée was growing uncomfortable with his one-on-one training sessions in the homes of wealthy women who, because of Dubai's strict social codes, found it simpler to exercise in private.

Now, a man claiming to be an agent from the U.S. Drug Enforcement Administration was on the phone, telling Klaussen that his email to the CIA had been passed to the U.S. embassy in South Africa, where the agent had come across it. "I was wondering if you would still be willing to talk," he said.

For a moment, Klaussen wondered if the call might be a setup by Le Roux himself. Could he have intercepted Klaussen's original email? Since he'd persuaded his old boss to cancel the Joseph Hunter hit, and even garnered a kind of apology for accusing him of stealing, Klaussen hadn't felt like he was living under an active threat. "Still, knowing Le Roux, you keep it in your mind," he said. "It's automatic. Because too many people died."

The only contact he'd had with Le Roux in the previous year had been after the U.N. issued its report describing the Somalia operation and its collapse into chaos. Klaussen already knew most of the details, including that one Zimbabwean had been shot dead in a dispute over the equipment, and that his former Somali point man, Liban Mohamed Ahmed, had been briefly jailed as a result. "He was released, but in the meantime the whole business was fucked," Klaussen said. When the organization stopped paying rent, the compound was confiscated and everything they'd shipped in disappeared. Then the U.N. report hit the news. "I sent it to Le Roux. 'What the fuck is this?'" Klaussen said. "He said, 'Fuck them. They can't do anything. It's just a commission. They have no power.'" That was the end of it.

Now the man on the phone, whose full name was Thomas Cindric, was able to convince Klaussen that he did in fact work for the DEA's Special Operations Division, and was investigating Le Roux. In fact, he wasn't just looking for information. He was looking for someone who could help take down the organization from inside.

"Okay," Klaussen said, "how do you see this going?"

"First we'd like to meet and see what you have," Cindric said.

The meeting would have to take place somewhere other than Dubai, so no one could trace Klaussen back to his home. Cindric proposed Cyprus, in a few weeks' time. Klaussen agreed.

On the appointed day, Cindric and another DEA agent named Eric Stouch flew through Dubai and greeted Klaussen at the gate of a Cyprus-bound flight. Once on board, Klaussen took a seat in business class, while the agents who would become his employers trundled back to economy. The DEA had bought his ticket, but Klaussen had arranged for his own upgrade.

Cindric and Stouch booked a hotel conference room in Cyprus, where they all sat down to discuss what Klaussen could offer. "First it was me who had to convince them that I have what it takes," Klaussen said. But this was a moment Klaussen had imagined when he first abandoned the Somalia operation back in 2010. He pulled out an encrypted drive on which he had stored reams of material from his time working with Le Roux. There were emails about arms purchases, copies of Le Roux's IDs—real and fake— financial reports, weapons orders, contact lists. As he walked the agents through the files, he recalled, "They didn't really show excitement. They didn't really show emotion. But it's there. I can feel it. It's in the room." When he finished his presentation, the agents finally let on that they were ecstatic.

But the information Klaussen had wasn't enough. The agents explained that while the case against Le Roux would certainly be bolstered by it, what they really needed was help setting him up. Wherever Le Roux was arrested—be it the Philippines, Brazil, or any of a dozen other countries where he regularly did business— there was the potential that he could buy his way out of jail. Cindric and Stouch needed to somehow get him somewhere that they could control the environment. Le Roux wasn't dumb enough to travel to the United States, so it would have to be somewhere else. They would need not only to entice him into his own capture, but also to create an airtight case against him back in the States. To do that, they'd need Klaussen to go back to work for Le Roux.

When Klaussen said yes, he, Cindric, and Stouch became a kind of subunit within the DEA, a team whose work was largely walled off—even from the likes of Bailey and Brill, who were still doggedly working the case from Minnesota. Together, the three of them outlined a plan to lure Le Roux into the kind of global sting that the Special Operations Division reserved for the world's most dangerous kingpins. Step one involved Klaussen contacting Le Roux to ask for his job back. To do that, he couldn't call empty-handed. He would need to bring his old boss the kind of deal Le Roux couldn't resist.

Every detail had to be perfect. When it was time for Klaussen to make contact with Le Roux in April 2012, the agents flew him to New York to do it, to help establish a U.S. "nexus" for the crime. Sitting on the front steps of the elegant federal courthouse in Lower Manhattan, Klaussen dialed Le Roux's number. He picked up.

"How are you?" Klaussen asked. "You still have that job for me in the U.S.?"

Le Roux was friendly, but told him he had given the job to someone else, months before.

Klaussen said that job or no job, he had something to offer. He had made some interesting contacts in the world of narcotics trafficking, he told him, but lacked his own funds and organization to make anything of them. "They are big people, big deals," he told Le Roux. "Colombians. Hundreds and hundreds of kilos."

Later, Klaussen would marvel that Le Roux never questioned why he had had such a dramatic change of heart, from quitting the organization over its illegal activities and threatening to turn in Le Roux to suddenly approaching him with a Colombian drug deal. "He didn't even ask about it," Klaussen said. "Didn't even bother. He knows what people are capable of when they are really in need of money. Most of his employees are willing to cross the line every time. I was one of the first that stood up and said, 'No, I'm not doing it anymore.' It was a bit of a shock for him, but I'm not sure. I don't think you can shock a guy like that." When he came crawling back, he thought, it merely reaffirmed for Le Roux his outlook on humanity. "See?" he imagined his boss saying to himself. "He is no different than the others."

Le Roux agreed to hire Klaussen back. He would be working at a lower salary, $3,000 a month plus bonuses. "That's how our system works now," Le Roux said.

After the call, Klaussen and his handlers began laying the groundwork for the deal, sending Le Roux a list of contacts that Klaussen would need to meet with, and where. The first stop would be a rendezvous with the Colombians in person. From New York, Klaussen and the agents flew to Panama to meet a paid DEA confidential informant who would be playing the role of "Colombian cartel boss." Unlike Klaussen, he had some experience with undercover stings. He'd been busted by the DEA years before, and began cooperating as part of a plea agreement to keep him out of prison. Now he was doing it for money.

From their meeting in Panama, Klaussen called Le Roux and pressured him to get on the phone with the Colombian.

"I'm here with the guy, he wants to talk to you," Klaussen said.

"Nah, nah, I don't talk to these people," Le Roux said.

"Come on, they came all the way here," Klaussen implored. "Just talk to the freaking guy. He wants to meet you, wants to set up a meeting, set up a deal. These people don't deal with lower-level people like me, they want to talk boss to boss."

Then he handed the phone to the C.I. The imaginary drug boss and the real one conversed for two or three minutes. "Not too much, because of course he doesn't want to give the impression he just talks loosely on the phone. He's supposed to be a professional drug dealer," Klaussen said. "Le Roux didn't like it, but he did it anyway. So I knew he was eating out of my hand."

From there, Klaussen and the agents began working their scheme around the clock. Their motives may have been divergent—Klaussen was out for revenge, the agents for a scalp—but in the intensity of the operation they quickly forged a bond. "Everybody was on full standby 24/7, for six or seven months," Klaussen said. Both Stouch and Cindric had honed their skills as cops on the streets of Baltimore. Stouch, who'd also worked as a detective in Pennsylvania before joining the DEA in 1999, was a triathlete, wiry and fit, with a closely shaved head. "Eric is the quiet but very observant one," Klaussen said. Cindric, who'd started as a DC cop and had a cynical streak, wore his opinions more on his sleeve. "Tom will say what he thinks," Klaussen said. "If it offends you, it offends you." There were endless debates about when and how to push Le Roux, what he would believe, what might make him suspicious. Stouch and Cindric had the benefit of experience with criminal mindsets, while Klaussen knew Le Roux, his methods and his madness. Klaussen admired how thoroughly the agents prepared him, creating a story with enough details to make it believable, but enough flexibility to adjust on the fly. "They always asked me if I was comfortable with it," Klaussen said. "Always. If I said no, it was no. They never pushed me. At any moment if I felt uncomfortable I just had to say the word and it was done."

As the months went on, they methodically laid the trap. If Klaussen told Le Roux he was meeting a contact somewhere—whether Panama or Paris—he and the agents convened there, so that Klaussen could always prove his backstory. "The guy is not stupid," Klaussen said. "You can't just tell him a story. He's going to check it. It has to add up. Everything has to be very, very real." They had photos of the Colombian cocaine, newspapers bought locally as casual proof that he'd been there, emails sent from IP addresses in the right location, airline tickets that matched the trip dates he'd given Le Roux. "For a guy like him, why would he not be capable of hacking into flight manifests?" Klaussen said. "Especially for somebody who is that paranoid."

Klaussen tried to keep Le Roux primed with a flow of information about the deal, anticipating his boss's need to weigh in on the smallest details. "You have to constantly feed his brain with positive information that you are on the right track, that everything is going smoothly," Klaussen said. "With evidence of course, because otherwise he wouldn't believe it. That was the hard part: To keep him out of control. Because he's a control freak, and he's got the brain to do it." The Colombians, Klaussen told Le Roux, were setting up operations in West Africa, centered in Liberia. The cartel, their story went, was interested in making their own meth there. They hoped that Le Roux could provide the precursor chemicals and clean rooms to make the stuff, and maybe even meth cooks to train the Colombians on how to make it themselves. In the meantime, they were also interested in buying some finished product from Le Roux, for distribution in New York. The destination was crucial: to fall under provision 959, the sting needed to make it absolutely clear that the drugs were destined for the United States.

Each detail was perfectly primed to cohere with Le Roux's psychology and worldview. The Colombians were the kind of South American partner Le Roux coveted—he'd once been rumored to have sent Shai Reuven into the country to make contact with one of its biggest cartels, without success. The idea that the Colombians now respected his knowledge appealed perfectly to his ego. "You have to get in his head," Klaussen said. But still, he worried that Le Roux could somehow be several moves beyond them. "With a guy like Le Roux, it's almost impossible. He thinks of a million things in one day. You need a whole team to get around what he's thinking about, what his next move is. He's so unpredictable, it's crazy."

Therein lay the problem: It was difficult to tell whether Le Roux was truly taking the bait or just playing along. For the first month, Klaussen was able to conduct all his business with Le Roux via encrypted email and occasional phone calls. But he and the agents knew that at some point, Klaussen would need to meet the boss in person. Then, in early May, Le Roux sent him a message: "Book a flight to Rio."

The request was typical Le Roux, abrupt enough to feel impulsive, arbitrary enough to feel threatening. Whichever was the case, the urgency of it caught Stouch and Cindric off-guard. There was no time to get the diplomatic visas they would need to travel to Brazil.

The agents offered Klaussen the option of turning down the request. If Le Roux somehow already suspected him, he could be walking into a trap. But they knew as well as Klaussen that nobody ignored the boss's orders and expected to stay employed. If Klaussen failed to show, Le Roux would be instantly suspicious—if he wasn't already.

Klaussen bought the ticket to Rio and booked a cheap hotel, careful to stay within Le Roux's $80-a-night budget. He wouldn't be using the room anyway. The DEA was paying for a nicer one.

26

The Investigators

2012 . . . Big cases, big problems . . . Weighing a tip . . . A scramble for gold . . . New deals in the works . . . Looking for cooks

In the world of law enforcement, there's a saying so commonly recited that it has traveled beyond cliché into the realm of mantra: "Big cases, big problems. Little cases, little problems. No cases, no problems." Kent Bailey loved to deliver it with a pause before the kicker: "I'll take big cases every time." In 2012, he would find ample opportunity to use it.

Now that GISE had Le Roux under surveillance in Rio, and SOD was off working in secret to engineer his capture, the case that had puttered along for almost half a decade began to accelerate. Information that Brill had spent years meticulously corroborating came flooding in, almost as fast as she and Bailey could process it. They could now see up close the kind of control Le Roux exercised over the operation, and how he worked to feed his own insatiable hunger for deals. They'd heard him on the phone, specifying the servers required for the office, arranging a hundred-kilo drug shipment out of Ecuador, and directing the purchase of airline tickets for Ivan Vaclavic to fly to Brazil—all in the same day. The deluge of evidence was almost dizzying. Which leads should they be chasing first? Who among Le Roux's crew was worth taking down?

Those questions were about to become very immediate. On April 17, the wires picked up a cryptic phone call between Le Roux and Doron Shulman, now in Hong Kong operating under the name Justin Collins.

"I wanted to confirm the rates for storage for AN," Shulman said. "Hong Kong for storage ninety per cubic meter."

"Okay, no problem," Le Roux said. "Things have arrived?"

"Yes, they did. I have to talk to the agent not to pay the release fee and confirm."

"Okay, no problem. It's confirmed."

The next day, Le Roux and Shulman spoke again. This time Shulman was calling with a complication:

JUSTIN: AN arrived.

PAUL: OK. Some problem?

JUSTIN: Some of the bags had runny liquid. I do not know if it's because they were pierced and absorbed water, absorbed moisture.

PAUL: Liquid? It should be dust.

JUSTIN: There are two types, but one or two bags are wet. Can it be condensation?

PAUL: Take one of the bags and test with H1, but not the ones that are wet. Get another bag.

JUSTIN: Okay.

PAUL: Then throw away the ones that are leaking so that they do not contaminate the others.

The Brazilian agents now realized what Shulman meant by "AN": ammonium nitrate. They knew enough about it to know that its commercialization in Brazil was tightly controlled by the military, because of its potential as a powerful explosive. Le Roux, it seemed, was shipping it into Hong Kong. They had no idea what the next steps were, nor in whose hands the explosive might eventually end up. They relayed the information back to the DEA.

This left Bailey in a quandary. If the DEA tipped off the Hong Kong authorities about the explosives shipment, there was a chance it could start a cascade of events that would drive Le Roux underground. If they didn't, people could die. Bailey told the office in Brazil to make the call to Hong Kong.

On April 30, officers from the Organized Crime and Triad Bureau in Hong Kong raided a warehouse in Tsuen Wan, north of the city. As expected, they discovered a stash of ammonium nitrate fertilizer. The surprise was in the amount: twenty tons of the stuff, divided into a thousand bags labeled as sodium chloride. Police found Doron Shulman's real name on the warehouse lease, while the fertilizer's shipping documents pointed to a Hong Kong–registered company called Ajax Technology. The cops converged on the company's office on a busy downtown street lined with banks, and took Shulman into custody. When the OCTB searched the office and Shulman's apartment, they found bank records for a dozen other companies with names like GX Port Limited, Cycom, and Southern Ace. They also found sale deeds for two stash houses, five kilograms of pure silver, receipts for tens of millions of dollars in gold bars, and handwritten directions to a meeting in Buenaventura, Colombia, with Luis Caicedo Velandia, aka "Don Lucho"— the head of one of the world's biggest cocaine cartels.

Shulman's lawyer would later argue that, because of his background as a member of the Duvdevan, the elite special forces unit of the Israeli Defense Forces, "he was trained to follow orders without any questions . . . [When told] to look after some valuables in Hong Kong, he did it diligently without any question. Being simple and without experience in finance, he landed himself into deep trouble." In fact the wires showed Shulman to be deeply embedded in significant parts of Le Roux's business, from pharmacy negotiations in the United States to phosphorous shipments in Manila. He had access to the bank accounts of at least ten of Le Roux's companies in Hong Kong, through which more than $200 million had passed in the previous two years. Some of that money had been funneled into gold bars, over three hundred of them, purchased from a Swiss company called Metalor. In 2010, Shulman purchased a pair of houses, in Yuen Long and Sheung Shui, each outfitted with a safe in which to stash Le Roux's gold. Shulman held the only keys to both safes.

Shulman had earned several hundred thousand dollars for this work over the years, and in turn had brought on other former Duvdevan colleagues: Yoav Hen, who appeared on the Brazilian wires using the name "Eddie"; Zion Fadlon's brother Daniel, aka "Gaddafi," due to his Libyan-Jewish heritage; and Omer Gavish, a twenty-six-year-old who filled his Facebook feed with photos from his Hong Kong adventures. Each was paid a few thousand dollars a month to help guard the gold stashes. When they asked questions about the boss, Shulman told them he was a Dutch businessman and they were better off not knowing more.

Now they were about to learn the rest. Shulman's arrest set off a chain of events in Hong Kong that soon bordered on the ridiculous. On May 1, the day after the raid, Shulman's Israeli coworkers began to receive messages directly from Le Roux, captured on the Brazilian wires, telling them to liquidate his gold. The only problem was, the gold was locked in safes inside the two stash houses, and none of them had the keys. First they tried getting into Shulman's apartment, but found it sealed off by the authorities. Le Roux told them to use brute force. They went to a hardware store, bought some metal-cutting tools, and got to work. At the Yuen Long house, they pried a safe out of the wall using a crowbar, and then cut a hole in the back, discovering 161 gold bars, which they placed into duffel bags.

When they arrived at the second house, they were met by another Israeli employee of Le Roux's who had been dispatched from Manila. After a locksmith dismantled the gate, the group set to cutting open the safe inside.

By May 2, the three or possibly four Israelis—in the confusion, the Hong Kong police lost track of a number of Le Roux employees—divvied up the gold bars, worth around $18 million, and climbed into taxis. They drove to Chungking Mansions, a sprawling seventeen-story gray edifice widely regarded as the cheapest immigrant lodging in Hong Kong, and holed up in a dingy room the organization maintained there. The bags were so heavy that they had to drag them through the lobby.

Over the next two days, together with a Filipino named Gordo who had also arrived in the intervening time, they alternated trips to Metalor, selling back the gold where it had originally been purchased. They unloaded eighty-five, then thirty-two, then sixty-four of the bars, depositing over $9.4 million in the bank account of Cycom, the Le Roux–controlled company.

In the days that followed, a herd of bumbling Le Roux operatives converged on Hong Kong in a frenzied attempt either to keep Le Roux's massive store from slipping away, or to get some of it for themselves. Besides Gordo, someone traveling under the name John Miller arrived, collected corporate documents for Cycom, and disappeared. The authorities arrested Ivan Vaclavic trying to enter Hong Kong on May 2. While out on bail, he cruised out of the harbor in a speedboat headed for the Philippines, and then flew on to Rio. There was a mysterious South African referred to only in passing in the court documents, and another Filipino arrested at the airport holding bank-transfer records for $8 million. He, too, jumped bail.

As the Israelis desperately tried to hide the remaining gold, scouting a new house in Yuen Long, the police were on their trail. Officers arrived too late at the two stash houses, finding that both safes had been forced open and emptied, but CCTV footage from one of the houses showed a few men loading heavy bags into a cab. The police located the cab company and then tracked the men to Chungking Mansions. At 2:35 A.M. on May 7, they raided an apartment there, capturing the other Israelis. In their possession were five bags containing 161 gold bars, plus four five-carat diamonds worth $1.5 million and receipts from the previous days' sales.

On the wires in Rio, Le Roux could be heard working the phones trying to get what money he could out of Hong Kong. On May 8, he called Alon Berkman, telling him to transfer as much of the organization's money as possible to bank accounts in Singapore. Next he called his wife in the Netherlands, instructing her to fly to Hong Kong and transfer their money to the Philippines. "Four men are in position," Le Roux told her. "I think it is safe for you to travel to Hong Kong. I suggest you get there early in the morning, around eight in the morning and transfer all the money to Manila."

"You should have told me this before," she said curtly.

"I hope you have liquidity in your money, I told you to keep it that way," Le Roux said. "If you can get into the country, you'll be fine. I'm the target and some of my accounts have already been hijacked. I've already lost a lot of money. Take no extra phone, no credit cards, laptops, just a phone that only has my number from here and the Philippines. Transfer all the money, take it all away."

Two days later, she was arrested trying to enter Hong Kong on her Dutch passport, carrying a slip for a $300,000 bank transfer. She, too, was released, and slipped back out of the country.

If Brill and Bailey were worried about scaring off Le Roux with the Hong Kong tip, the surveillance in Brazil soon dispelled their fears. The GISE agents were shocked at how quickly he got over the losses. "Tens of millions of dollars blocked," one of them marveled later, "and he wasn't bothered after a few minutes." Le Roux could be heard calmly working through the logistics of bigger deals—most of them real, one of them a setup, unbeknownst to him—that would replenish his coffers even as the Hong Kong sei-

zures depleted them. One of the real ones was a large cocaine shipment, set to depart for Asia on a pair of yachts out of Ecuador. A
captain was flying in from South Africa and preparing to travel on
to the Ecuadorian coast to pilot one of the vessels. On one call, Le
Roux and an unidentified contact in Ecuador worked out bribe
money for the Ecuadorian coast guard:

> UNKNOWN: I need to pay thirty thousand U.S. I'll send it to you in the
> afternoon and then you have to pay the Coast Guard and these
> people here.
> PAUL: You cannot do that. There's no way I can send thirty thousand
> by Western Union.
> UNKNOWN: Or a bank account.
> PAUL: Yes, there is no way to send thirty. Not even three thousand.
> They would ask questions, you know?
> UNKNOWN: So let me see . . . maybe I can give you the name of the
> Coast Guard and the names of the guys and you send it to them
> directly.
> PAUL: Yes. yes. No problem, it can be like this.
> UNKNOWN: Right, right. I'll tell him to give you the names for Western
> Union and give you the names of the other people we have to pay,
> and you send the money.
> PAUL: Right. No problem. All right, my friend.

The Ecuador shipment was to be the first of a series of South
American cocaine deals, and Le Roux made arrangements to hire
another South African boat captain, named Kevin Ashby, to purchase boats in South Florida and deliver them south, where they
would be filled with drugs and sent off to markets in Southeast
Asia and Australia. "It's a cyclical thing," he told Ashby. "Buy a
boat, you sail it to Panama, use it in Asia . . . and then go back to
the U.S. and buy another boat."

Le Roux seemed to be taking greater and greater risks, discussing more of his business by phone. In one conversation, he was
heard saying he needed two hundred kilos of methamphetamine a

month. In another, he meticulously arranged the details of getting another $300,000 into Brazil, laundering it through a local currency-exchange business that returned him the equivalent amount of Brazilian reals, delivered in an actual clothing box.

For years, the federal attorneys working with Brill and Bailey had been telling them they were missing the key piece of evidence to indict him, something that would link Le Roux himself to the illegal activities they had so carefully documented. Now here he was, offering those missing links on a wiretapped phone almost daily.

It seemed like the time was right to indict Le Roux. Brill lined up Robert McGowan and Mathew Smith, along with two other Zimbabweans, who were ready to fly to the United States and testify in front of a grand jury about what they knew. The agents from SOD started telling Bailey that, based on what they'd developed with their own informant—Felix Klaussen, whose name remained a secret from Brill and Bailey—the attorneys in the Southern District were ready to indict Le Roux themselves. By the summer of 2012, Bailey was pressuring Linda Marks and her team of prosecutors in the Department of Consumer Protection to get their indictment first, based on what they had. Still, Marks held out for better evidence.

Then, in a call to his wife, Le Roux warned her to stop buying real estate. She should be renting, he said. Buying houses brought attention, and gave the authorities something to seize. When his wife resisted, Le Roux grew frustrated. "Don't you know everything we've been doing is illegal?" he said. "I'm not running a fucking Burger King."

The agent monitoring the wire in Brazil immediately called Brill, who stepped out of a going-away party for a colleague at a Minneapolis restaurant as the agent read her the transcript. "That's the moment we needed," she thought. They finally had enough evidence to indict.

The two sides to the operation, the Minnesota DEA office and the 960 group out of Virginia, were working their investigations independently, coordinating loosely yet each partially in the dark about what the other was doing. But in the late spring of 2012 their paths briefly crossed, when the Brazil wire picked up chatter between Le Roux and his employees about a major deal with a Colombian cartel—the same deal that the 960 group's informant was busy concocting for Le Roux. On the Brazilian wires, Felix Klaussen was referenced only as "Jack," the go-between with the cartel. On May 5, Le Roux had what started out as a coded phone call with Shai Reuven, the highest-level deputy remaining in the Philippines.

"I have another job for you, my friend," Le Roux said on the recording. "I need you to hire us a cook."

"Right," said Reuven.

"Yes, I like Mexican food and I want a cook, you know?"

"Yes."

"There are some guys from Liberia, Liberia right?"

"Yes."

"To our partners. We need to send a cook for them, understand?"

Reuven laughed. "You mean, a real cook, right?"

"No, no, no . . . I'm talking about methamphetamine, man. Are you retarded?"

"What for? For what?"

"For methamphetamine."

"I understand."

"Wake up," Le Roux said. "Jesus Christ. Right?"

"Right."

"See if you can get one and how much he wants to train some guys over there. Right?"

"Understood—no problem."

"I need a list of chemicals he's going to need, you understand, the way he's going to do things, right?"

"I think I can get one in Florida, I'll let you know."

"Send me an email."

The same day, Le Roux told Zion Fadlon, his local helper, that two men would soon be arriving in Rio. One of them, he said, was "some guy called Jack, and he already has accommodations."

27

The Mole

*2012 . . . An encounter in Brazil . . . The Liberian trap is set . . .
Meeting the Colombians . . . An in-flight decision*

Felix Klaussen arrived in Rio for his meeting with Le Roux on May 11, 2012. Without his 960 group handlers to back him up, he'd be forced to trust Brazilian agents he'd never met. After he landed, he checked in with Le Roux by phone. A local DEA liaison drove him to a hotel a few minutes' walk from Le Roux's condo. There, the GISE team that had been monitoring Le Roux arrived to brief him. They were concerned that it wasn't safe for Klaussen to go alone to Le Roux's apartment. Better that he ask for a public meeting, they cautioned. They could have agents stationed in cars outside, with snipers on the roof, and in the condo next door. (They'd cleared out the residents with a cover story that they were investigating a pedophile. "When you say it's a drug dealer, people can get scared," one of the agents said.) But if Klaussen was walking into an assassination, they still wouldn't get there in time. "You have to be careful," one agent told him. "You are dealing with Le Roux, not some street criminal."

I know him better than anyone, Klaussen thought. Demanding his boss meet in public would be as good as announcing he was working for law enforcement. Klaussen saw the choice as simple, binary: He could go to the condo and step into the fictional role he had been crafting for months, or he could get on a plane and return to his old life. Anything in between was a waste of time. He called Stouch and Cindric, who told him that the decision was up to him. "Fuck it," he said. "I'm going in."

A few days later, on May 11, he was standing at the entry to the Waterways Condominiums in Barra de Tijuca. He turned the screw on a wristwatch the DEA had given him, activating its hidden camera. Then he stepped through the doors and took the elevator to the fifth floor. Outside of apartment 505 there were none of the Israeli guards that had once surrounded Le Roux in Manila. His boss opened the door and ushered him inside with minimal pleasantries, looking fatter than Klaussen remembered. From what Klaussen could gather, the only other occupants of the apartment appeared to be one of Le Roux's girlfriends and a baby. Le Roux suggested they talk on the balcony.

He spoke softly, as if to avoid being overheard. "The Americans are watching," he said. "We have to be careful." Klaussen glanced down to the street below them and saw the Brazilian agents' vans—too easily identified, he thought. He tried to parse Le Roux's expression for hints that he knew something more.

They walked through the details of the supposed deal with the Colombians: their planned headquarters in Liberia, their desire to build a clean room as part of their own meth lab, and the suggestion that there could be more business down the road. The Colombians planned to ship the drugs to New York City for sale, Klaussen reminded Le Roux, but they would first need a sample of the meth. Le Roux told Klaussen it would come out of a batch manufactured in North Korea that he had already moved to the Philippines.

Sitting on the balcony across from Le Roux, Klaussen was reminded of how his boss seemed to discuss the most extraordinary aspects of his business in the most casual tones. "He is just so relaxed and so calm, talking about death, about murder, about weapons, about wars," he recalled later. "Like talking about buying some bread or something. The guy's a genius but he is a freaking madman as well."

Klaussen told Le Roux that he was on his way to Panama that evening to finalize the details with the Colombians, and emphasized that Le Roux needed to meet the Colombian cartel head in person, "boss to boss," to put him at ease. Le Roux agreed and told him to make arrangements.

It seemed almost too perfect: Le Roux was signing off on the whole plan—and on tape. As they talked, Klaussen held his arm at what he hoped was a natural angle, but one that could capture Le Roux on the watch camera. He'd trained with his handlers, and knew that he needed only a brief glimpse of Le Roux's face to establish his identity. For the rest, audio would suffice. Suddenly, he noticed Le Roux's eyes focusing downward. Following his gaze, he realized that they were aimed at Klaussen's wrist. The screw on his watch camera concealed a tiny port, and was attached to the watch by a chain. Somehow Klaussen had shaken the screw loose, and now it was left dangling from his arm, like a spider suspended on a thread. Le Roux was staring at it.

"Shitty dive watch," Klaussen said, shaking his head. He grabbed the screw between his fingers and twisted it back in. Le Roux carried on talking.

And then, as abruptly as it had started, the meeting was over and Klaussen was out the door. There was a quick debriefing with the GISE agents. Then Klaussen left for the airport. He'd already given the prosecutors enough to indict Le Roux for planning to traffic methamphetamine to the United States. Now they just needed to spring the trap.

Years later Klaussen would still puzzle over why Le Roux had fallen for it all. They had created an alluring ruse, but Le Roux at the top of his game was equal parts paranoid and calculating. "Maybe I was his kryptonite," Klaussen said. "For some reason he had that unconditional trust in me. Trust is a relative thing when it comes to people like Le Roux." How he had landed in Le Roux's blind spot, he could only speculate. "I'm not even close to his brain capacity," he said. "But I like to care about people. I think that's where we had our biggest differences: He didn't care about anyone." Perhaps he was just desperate, with the DEA closing in on his online operations. Or maybe it was the opposite, as the GISE agents suspected: Le Roux felt safe in Brazil, and just got complacent.

Whatever the explanation, Le Roux wanted too much, too quickly—just as he always had. "He had the security. He had the safety measures—always was able to keep himself out of the picture," Klaussen said. "Even when he was in the picture he was able to get out. It was all very well organized. It was very well protected. It was all laid out to be the most perfect criminal empire ever. But he didn't have the patience."

After the visit to Rio, the fake deal Klaussen was setting up for Le Roux progressed as planned. Le Roux sent Klaussen his bank account number a week later, and the Colombians wired payment for a twenty-four-gram sample of methamphetamine, to be shipped to Liberia and destined for New York. Le Roux ordered the sample sent from Manila out of his North Korean stock, and supplied them with a tracking number. A few weeks later, Klaussen reported back that the Colombians had tested the meth and found that it was clean, nearly 100 percent pure. Le Roux proposed a trade: one hundred kilos of meth in exchange for one hundred kilos of cocaine. The Colombians readily agreed. To Le Roux, it appeared he was the one controlling the direction of the deal.

In midsummer, Le Roux left Brazil and returned to the Philippines. Even with the law enforcement attention he knew was focused there, he told Klaussen, he had unfinished business before finalizing his move to Brazil. In late summer he would be returning to Brazil for good, and he could pass through Liberia on the way, meet the Colombians, and complete the deal.

In the weeks before Le Roux left Rio, GISE caught him on the wire making final arrangements for a real transaction, a shipment of cocaine leaving South America headed for Asian markets. In Florida he'd arranged the purchase of a forty-four-foot luxury sailboat called the *JeReVe*—French for "I dream"—for $105,000. According to its sales listing, its previous owners had sailed it around the Mediterranean and the Caribbean before giving it up. "*JeReVe* is ready to sail and to give a lot of pleasure to its next owner," the ad said. One of Le Roux's captains sailed the *JeReVe* to Panama, where it waited for another skipper to take it south to Ecuador.

Le Roux's calls with an unknown collaborator in Ecuador were conducted in a relatively simple code. "The car looks brand new," his contact told him, to convey that the boat was in place. For Kent Bailey, reviewing the tapes back in the United States, it didn't take decades of law enforcement experience to know that he was listening to a transoceanic drug shipment about to take off. Bailey enlisted in-country DEA agents to meet the boat at its berth in Panama. They arranged a distraction for the crew of the *JeReVe* while they placed a tracking device on the craft, and snapped a photo of the two men Le Roux sent to sail it on its next leg.

In August the boat arrived in Ecuador. Greased by bribe money Le Roux had wired into the country, it cleared Ecuadorian customs on August 20 and sailed out with two crew members: Ivan Vaclavic, who had been detained and then released in both the Philippines and Hong Kong, and another man, unknown to Bailey and the DEA. Now they had a chance to follow a major drug shipment in real time, and hopefully catch whoever received it on the other end. After a brief stop off the coast of Peru, where Le Roux had sourced the cocaine to be loaded on board, the boat began its two-month journey across the ocean.

By that time, the wiretap had gone dark. Le Roux had departed for the Philippines, where the DEA lacked a window into his movements. As the summer months passed into September, Bailey again pressed Linda Marks to speed up her efforts to convene a grand jury and indict Le Roux in Minnesota. But it was too late.

Le Roux's flight to Monrovia, the Liberian capital, touched down on September 25, 2012. Klaussen was already there, having arrived earlier with Stouch and Cindric to set up and rehearse the sting. Le Roux was traveling with his girlfriend, Cindy Cayanan; his right-hand man Shai Reuven was meant to accompany them from Manila, but for some reason plans had changed at the last minute. Klaussen and a driver picked up Le Roux and Cayanan at the airport. "You could see his eyes shining, like he saw potential in that country," Klaussen said. "He liked what he saw. 'We can do good things here.' " At their modest hotel in Monrovia, Klaussen arranged a suite for Le Roux, relishing the irony that his penny-pinching boss was being unwittingly upgraded by the U.S. government. The room adjacent to Le Roux's was staffed around the clock by Stouch, Cindric, and several other DEA agents, monitoring video feeds from cameras next door.

The next morning Klaussen and Le Roux convened at the hotel restaurant for breakfast and planned for their rendezvous with the Colombian that afternoon, at another hotel across the city. Just before he walked in, Klaussen switched on his wristwatch camera.

"Morning," Klaussen said.

"Heyyyy, greetings," Le Roux replied, sounding unusually cheerful. He turned to Cayanan, standing next to him. "Why don't you just hang at another table, okay?" She took a seat out of earshot.

"How was the night?" Klaussen said.

"All good. Not a bad place."

"Well, like I said, probably the best you can get around here. Unfortunately it's raining today, but . . ."

"I think it probably rains the whole year here."

"Yeah it's six, definitely six months. But, what to do?" Klaussen, knowing his boss, lowered his voice and got down to business. "Wrote a few things down," he said. "You know I met with the guy, in Paris, for the Shan thing."

In the hopes of layering other charges on top of the Colombian drug deal, Klaussen had told Le Roux that he had a contact from the Shan State of Myanmar, a semiautonomous region in the heart of Southeast Asia's Golden Triangle. Shan, which for decades had been rife with armed conflict, was a central hub in the region's bountiful opium crop and its production of yaba, the regional form of methamphetamine. Klaussen's source, he told Le Roux, was looking for weapons that could take down helicopters conducting surveillance on behalf of the local authorities. "They gave me the details on the helicopter," he said. "It's the U.S. Black Hawk, and the UH-53, that's bothering them."

Le Roux's reaction revealed just how far his own contacts in the international arms underground now extended. The shoulder-launched missiles they needed could be easily obtained, he said. "Actually it will be cheap, coming directly from the factory," Le Roux said. "The thing is like this: The Russians don't talk on the phone. They are flying to the Philippines to see my guy."

"They are good to go with the Russian thing," Klaussen said. "They are willing to pay more because they have a certain urgency level."

"They have surplus ones being sold from Libya in Lebanon," Le Roux suggested. "Lebanon is the main area where this shit is being moved. They can get used ones there, if they want. But the problem is to transport them."

Le Roux spoke slowly and confidently when hashing out the myriad details of these arms deals: prices, sources, training, shipping arrangements. The South China Sea was a better shipping route than the Bay of Bengal, he noted, avoiding the heavily monitored Strait of Malacca. As to accomplishing the ultimate aim for the weapons, he was happy to offer his advice. "What they need to do is, they need to wait until they are, like, hovering a little close to the ground," he said. "The thing is, they won't fucking expect it. Once the Americans lose some fucking pilots? They won't think twice. You've only got to take one or two down. You don't have to take the whole fleet."

With that, Le Roux was on to other business. "I want to run one thing by you," he said. "I sent a guy to Iran about two years ago.

Everything we want, even the biggest shit, is available in Iran. And there's no questions asked. They will deliver to us anywhere, in any Muslim country, anywhere in the world. Like Indonesia, for example. But we need to fetch up there with a general or some fucking lieutenant from an African country and they front the deal, you know?" Klaussen nodded along. "I'm telling you, my friend, everything you want. Even shit the Russians won't sell us, we can get from them. Fucking seven-meter-long rockets, if you want, the size of this room, you know what I'm saying? They don't give a fuck." At moments, Le Roux almost seemed to be enjoying himself. "Everything is sweet, everything is sweet," he said at one point, a look of satisfaction crossing his face.

Finally the conversation turned to the Colombian cartel boss they were about to meet. "We basically have our talk, I introduce you to him," Klaussen said. "I call him Pepe. Because in Spanish that stands for boss. Just, uh, play a little bit the game, you know. He's very respectful, so I want to be respectful to him as well."

"Yeah."

"You will see. You will like the guy. I don't want to make any comparisons, but he's similar, handling business like you do. Just straightforward, no bullshit."

"Just remind me, what was the trade again?" Le Roux said, closing his eyes and dropping his head. "I forget, there's so many fucking deals." He wanted as much cocaine as the Colombians were willing to give him, but the drug deliveries had to happen offshore. "It's better if a boat never pulls into port," he said. "You know the Americans, they are not on the ground. But they are always looking, you know what I'm saying? Always."

Finally, the meeting wound down as they made arrangements to meet the Colombian at his hotel that afternoon. Before they said goodbye, Le Roux had one more question.

"We need somebody to do a fucking—is there a laundry service here?" Le Roux asked, lifting up a bag of clothes. "These fuckers charge crazy money. It's like two bucks for a shirt and shit here. I'm cheap, dude." For years, Klaussen would be unable to shake the image of Paul Calder Le Roux, a man who presided over a criminal conglomerate worth hundreds of millions of dollars, refusing to pay two dollars to launder his shirt.

That afternoon, Klaussen's driver took him and Le Roux to a nearly empty hotel, where they'd set up to meet the Colombian. When they arrived, Pepe was waiting for them in a room with tile floors and a pair of maroon leather couches, arranged perpendicular to each other. Klaussen gave him a hug. Le Roux shook his hand and settled onto the larger of the two couches, facing Pepe, who sat with the window at his back. Both Klaussen and Pepe were outfitted with watch cameras, but that was overkill: The room itself was wired and the agents were waiting next door.

"I can see why you picked this place," Le Roux said. "Because it's chaotic, it should be easy to move in and out, from what I've seen."

"Very easy," said Pepe.

"Very few people, not too many eyes. It looks like the right place."

"Trust me—what's your name again?"

"Paul."

"Paul, trust me, it's the right place."

The next half an hour was, as far as the law was concerned, largely unnecessary. Le Roux could have been arrested based simply on the meth samples he'd sent, and the conversations he'd had with Klaussen about the shipments bound for New York. But the Southern District prosecutors wanted evidence supporting as many charges as possible: drug dealing, money laundering, arms dealing. So Pepe bounced around details of the drug deals with Le Roux: how and when the meth would be delivered, the possibility of paying in gold or diamonds. With each word, Le Roux seemed to be turning the locks that would keep him in an American prison for decades.

And then the DEA's Colombian informant started freelancing. He abruptly told Le Roux he had a friend who was looking for heavy weapons, something more than machine guns.

"We can do explosives," Le Roux said, at first unfazed. "We can do all kinds of small arms. Whatever you want, we can get it."

"The thing with this guy," Pepe said, "he wants me to deliver it to New York. Do you have a way to deliver it?"

Le Roux let out a long sigh. "That's a tough one," he said. "So why does he want it shipped to New York?"

"He wants the heavy stuff to New York," Pepe said, trying to backtrack. "When he says heavy stuff, I don't know the details."

"Well, I don't know," Klaussen interjected, nervously. "We can see what the details are."

"The problem is always the transportation," Le Roux said, and the conversation moved back to drugs. They had a deal to complete.

"Beautiful, I think that covers everything," Le Roux finally said, when they'd discussed some more logistics.

"We talk tomorrow about the details," Pepe said.

"Beautiful."

"Paul, nice to meet you."

"Good meeting you."

The video from Klaussen's watch camera bounced from floor to wall and back as the men shook hands. He and Le Roux walked to the exit, the sound of flip-flops echoing off the tile floors. "I think the boss is satisfied," Le Roux whispered, as the elevator doors closed.

"He is," Klaussen said. "Like I said, he's a nice guy."

"We're not going to fuck him," Le Roux said as they walked out to the waiting car. "But the weapons is interesting. It doesn't make sense why someone wants it shipped to the fucking U.S."

"Yeah, I dunno," Klaussen said.

"That's asking for trouble."

"That was it," Klaussen said later. "We went back to the hotel." He returned to his room and downloaded the watch video to a USB drive. When a DEA agent came by and knocked, he slid it under the door. Then he sat down and waited.

The end, from Klaussen's perspective at least, was anticlimactic. He was idly staring out the window when he saw a group of officers from the Liberian National Security Agency escorting a handcuffed Le Roux through the hotel's parking lot. They put him in the back of a van and drove off.

Minutes later there was a knock at Klaussen's door. It was Stouch. "It's time to pack your bags, let's go," he said. Everything so far had run exactly according to plan. But now that Le Roux was in custody, it was impossible to predict what would happen next—how soon his operators across the globe might find out, and what they might do. The agents hustled Klaussen out of his hotel and checked him into another one. A few days later, he was on a plane to the United States.

Later, the agents filled him in on the details of what happened back in Monrovia. How, when the local officers had stormed Le Roux's room, the first thing he'd done was slam his laptop lid shut to activate the encryption software, just as he'd always instructed his employees to do. How for a few hours in a local Liberian jail he'd alternated between raging at the police and offering to bribe them. How, when he first saw an American agent, he had railed that they had no jurisdiction to arrest him in Liberia.

None of it worked. The Liberians handed Le Roux over to a group of five DEA agents, including Stouch and Cindric. The agents calmly explained that he had been indicted in New York by a grand jury on charges of conspiracy to import methamphetamine, a violation of sections 959 and 960a of the U.S. federal code. He would be taken by chartered plane to the United States.

"I apologize in advance, but I do not want to get on your plane," Le Roux told them, and then went limp. Dragging his body into a van took several agents, "like trying to move somebody who's dead weight," Stouch later testified.

Once on board and in the air, the agents were exhausted, ready to collapse for the flight home. But suddenly Le Roux wanted to talk. It didn't take any clever interrogation techniques, or indeed any persuasion at all, to flip one of the DEA's most sought-after targets, a man who just hours before had been reveling in his ability to obtain unfathomable amounts of drugs and unlimited supplies of powerful military weapons—a man who had routinely ordered even his closest confidants dead.

As the plane cruised out over the Atlantic, he seemed to have already decided. First he congratulated the agents on catching him. Then he said he wanted to talk. "Just promise me I don't die in jail," he said. "That's all I want." He waived his Miranda rights, signed a consent form to search his laptop and phone, and agreed to start telling them what he knew. "To Paul, everything is a negotiation," a former 960 agent said.

Eleven hours later the plane approached an airport just north of New York City. Paul Calder Le Roux was about to step out of view and into a new life of public service.

28

The Investigators

2012 . . . Le Roux turns on a dime . . . A boat lost at sea . . . Chasing Oz and Berkman . . . The story begins again

A few hours before dawn on a balmy September morning in 2012, Kimberly Brill and Kent Bailey stood on a tarmac in White Plains, New York, awaiting a plane carrying the man they'd been chasing for five years. Beside them was Derek Maltz, the Special Agent in Charge of SOD. Weeks ago, the plan had been different: Maltz had agreed that Brill should travel on the mission to capture Le Roux in Monrovia. But the agents from 960 had pushed back, insisting there was no room for her on the flight. Instead, Brill and Bailey had been invited to meet the plane when it arrived.

It was an ominous sign of things to come, but on this morning, at least, Bailey recalled that Maltz was in a complimentary mood. " 'Kent,' he was telling me, 'I'll never forget the first time you briefed me on this case. You were absolutely right: This guy is the largest international criminal that I've ever dealt with.' " The plane touched down around 3 A.M., and Bailey noted to himself that it seemed large enough to have accommodated not just Brill but a dozen more agents. The investigators from Minnesota caught a

quick glimpse of Le Roux as he lumbered down the stairs, handcuffed and wearing a pair of cut-off sweatpants and a polo shirt.
Then the SOD agents hustled him away, loading him into an SUV
headed for the Metropolitan Correctional Center in Manhattan.

Brill and Bailey had booked rooms in a downtown Brooklyn
Marriott, just across the East River from the MCC and the offices
of the U.S. Attorney for the Southern District. They'd been preparing to join in the initial questioning of Le Roux, who was scheduled for his first formal court appearance later that morning. After
breakfast, they decided to walk over the Brooklyn Bridge, together
with an agent from SOD, to attend the hearing. Partway across,
the agent got a phone call: the hearing was off. Hours before, Le
Roux had met for the first time with a court-appointed attorney
named Jonathan Marvinny, and promptly signed an agreement
stating his intention to cooperate. The deal affirmed what he'd
declared on the plane: he was ready to help. The 960 agents were
hustling him to a hotel room at the same Marriott where Bailey
and Brill were staying, to begin debriefing him.

Bailey turned to Brill. "Well, he's on Team America now," he
said.

There would be no press conference announcing the capture of
one of the most prolific criminals the DEA had ever faced. The
agency had other plans, which now required that no one know Le
Roux was off the street. They'd snatched him out of view of any of
his employees or associates, and now he would start working from
DEA custody as if he were still at large.

It took Bailey and Brill the better part of that day to realize they
were being shut out of Le Roux's case. The U.S. Attorneys in the
Southern District who'd obtained his indictment now had control
of Le Roux, and they didn't intend to relinquish it, no matter who
had first opened the case or how long they'd spent on it. "We
waited all that day, we never talked to him," Bailey said. An agent
from SOD advised Bailey to return home to Minneapolis, but he
demanded that he and Brill receive a briefing on Le Roux's status.

"It probably wasn't until dinnertime, six or seven—I wasn't leaving until we got a briefing," Bailey said. "I think they probably hoped that we would go away."

That evening Bailey sat in a bar with a group supervisor at SOD who told him that Le Roux had offered not just to help catch his associates, but to share information about dealings he'd had with Iran and North Korea. He was now more than a drug and arms dealer, the supervisor said. He was a national security asset.

At the bar, Bailey warned that Le Roux was smart enough to manipulate them, if the agents weren't careful. "Don't get enamored with him," he told the supervisor. "He's a killer. Don't start dancing here because he can sell you a song."

On both sides of the DEA, the ambitions that emerged from a prize like Le Roux had begun to harden into resentment. Bailey believed that the case belonged to Brill—a diversion investigator who had devoted five years of her life to it, clawing and scraping at the evidence to find a way to Le Roux. They'd agreed to let the 960 agents make the arrest, but never expected that 960 would refuse to share the prize with the people who had handed it to them.

Within the 960 group, Bailey's objections were viewed as the grumblings of an agent who hadn't been able to land the case. Minnesota hadn't handed them anything, they believed—they had started with a name in a file and ended with Le Roux in custody. "I'll be honest with you, I don't know if Kent Bailey knows what probable cause is," a former 960 agent told me. "One of his big things was, 'Well, your charge is just too simple. We have a much bigger project going.' What's the old adage: How do you eat an elephant? One bite at a time. Why go after an intergalactic conspiracy? Take a strategic strike. That was our thought."

From my vantage point, hearing about it years later, the intra-agency grappling all seemed a little juvenile, and counterproductive. Lost in the battles over what to do with Le Roux, it seemed to me, was any real accounting for what he'd done, and what he deserved.

One thing was certain: The months and years that Bailey and

Brill had pressed Linda Marks for an indictment that never came were now coming back to haunt them.

"I'm sorry your lawyers suck and mine don't," the SOD group supervisor told Bailey.

A version of that conversation would repeat on a continuous loop over the coming weeks, after Brill and Bailey returned to Minnesota, denied a chance to sit across from their white whale. "Those guys were already saying, 'It's national security, he can't talk to you,'" Bailey said. "My ass it's national security." As the agents back in New York were pumping Le Roux for information, Brill was sitting on a pile of evidence accumulated over years of investigation. "I said, 'Come out and meet with her for a week, she's got all the books,'" Bailey said. "Now he's talking, and they are going and looking up those names, and she already had them. She had lists of targets." The response, he said, was always the same. "'Thanks, nope.' And they went out not knowing. Because they wanted it to be their case."

Everything that followed sprang from that decision, based on the hope that Le Roux would deliver to the U.S. government something worth more than what they had: a multiple murderer, a prodigious global drug and arms trafficker, a solicitor of rogue regimes, and a man who had supplied hundreds of millions of doses of painkillers to its citizens. If he failed to deliver, Team America would be the ones getting played.

While the agents in New York were recalibrating their plans for Le Roux, the yacht *JeReVe* was cruising across the Pacific with two hundred kilos of cocaine and the DEA's tracker on board. Then, on October 5, the tracking signal died. The 960 group thought the two shipmates might have discovered it, while Bailey assumed a more conventional explanation: Its battery had drained, perhaps due to the extra days the boat had spent idling off the coast of Peru. Either way, somewhere north of the Cook Islands in the South Pacific, the DEA lost the boat.

The 960 agents handling Le Roux had him make a call on the boat's satellite phone, hoping to reestablish its location. "My car broke down," the captain told him. "You have to send a car for me." Then Le Roux called the captain's wife, in Thailand, who told him, even more cryptically, that her husband had called her to say he had been "captured by the fish people." The 960 agents suspected he was perhaps being held by pirates.

A massive hunt for the boat was soon under way. The DEA activated a system called the Pacific Transnational Crime Network, and authorities from the Cook Islands and Tonga were on the water, all looking for signs of the *JeReVe*. But a storm was brewing in the region, further reducing the already long odds of finding one forty-four-foot yacht in the vastness of the South Pacific.

On November 5, 2012, a pair of spear fishermen diving in southern Tonga spotted a yacht washed up on a shallow reef. The boat was lying on its side, saltwater lapping against its red hull and broken tiller. A tattered French flag fluttered from a small flagpole at the stern. Its name was written in golden script across the back of the hull: *JeReVe*.

One of the divers climbed onto the clean white deck of the ship, a Sun Odyssey 44, and made a grisly discovery. At the helm was the badly decomposed body of a man, much of it picked away by seagulls. The divers fled the ship, climbed into their own boat, motored to the nearby port of Neiafu, and called the local police.

Bad weather rolled in, and the authorities couldn't return to the *JeReVe* for two days. When they did, a group of Tongan officers examined it. Inside the hull, they took an ax to the interior walls and found a pile of clear garbage bags filled with neatly wrapped brown plastic bricks. Each contained a kilo of cocaine. All told, the boat had been carrying 204 kilos, worth more than $90 million on the street in Australia, where authorities suspected the drugs had been headed. It was the largest drug haul ever confiscated in the South Pacific.

Tongan authorities identified the dead man as a thirty-five-year-old Slovakian named Milan Rindzak. They found several passports on the ship, along with several hundred American dollars, over a thousand dollars' worth of Dominican pesos, and a handful of Polish zloty. At first the local police asserted that there was no foul play in Rindzak's death, but following an autopsy, they amended their assessment to "cause of death inconclusive." He had been dead for days, if not weeks.

No other body was ever located. For months afterward, the Tongan police tried to locate Rindzak's next of kin in Slovakia, but were unable to track down anyone who would claim him. As for Ivan Vaclavic, the man the DEA knew had been on the boat, his fate remained uncertain. An investigation by several Slovakian news outlets would soon reveal that Vaclavic was a cover identity of a man named Maroš Deák, a Slovakian mobster who had disappeared from the country years earlier. (He was rumored to have been fleeing for his life; Deák's brother was later shot dead back home.) In 2011, a man resembling Deák had been stopped in Phuket, Thailand, by local authorities. He was carrying a high-powered Bushmaster rifle that he said he'd bought in the Philippines, and a Thai marine captain's license in Vaclavic's name. Now he seemed to have disappeared with the *JeReVe*.

Bailey, remembering the call that Le Roux had been allowed to make to the boat, theorized that Vaclavic might have killed his fellow passenger, engineered a transfer off the boat, and left it to drift. "He had blunt-force trauma all over his head and body," Bailey said of the dead man. "It could have been caused by the captain or the boat." The former 960 group agent I spoke with was confident about a different theory, albeit one that seemed to me to contain an equal amount of conjecture: Vaclavic, he said, had been captured by pirates at sea. I suggested that if that were so, perhaps the pirates had later set him free. "Yeah, and I'm Santa Claus," he said.

The Tongan authorities, for their part, seemed eager to put the mystery behind them and let the matter drop. They buried the sailor's remains in a local cemetery overlooking the placid blue waters of a harbor called the Port of Refuge.

In Minneapolis, Bailey and Brill still had an ongoing case to confront. Even if they'd lost control of Le Roux himself, they continued to hold out hope of indicting him in Minnesota for his role as one of the biggest black-market painkiller importers in history. And there was the rest of the RX Limited network to dismantle. In October 2012, they flew in Le Roux's cousin, Mathew Smith, along with two other Zimbabweans, to testify in front of a grand jury. Each of them identified photos of Le Roux, to verify that he was on the surveillance tapes and images in Brazil. They described the web of companies, like Wilex and Southern Ace, that they had been sent to Hong Kong and elsewhere to create. Afterward, the investigators took the witnesses to a Vikings-Titans football game.

Brill and Bailey had also coordinated with local DEA offices across the country to round up doctors and pharmacists who'd been some of the largest prescribers and suppliers in the network. Three RX Limited physicians, four affiliate website operators, and a pharmacist, arrested in New York and New Jersey, quickly entered guilty pleas. A housewife in Pennsylvania copped to forging a medical license and authorizing more than fifteen thousand prescriptions. She'd answered an ad for stay-at-home work on Craigslist. Babubhai Patel, the Detroit-area pharmacist captured on the wiretap, was brought in on unrelated charges of massive healthcare fraud.

But these were small targets, not the ones Brill and Bailey were most eager to arrest. They were after bigger fish like Moran Oz, Alon Berkman, and others higher up in the RX Limited chain of command. But arresting Le Roux's lieutenants posed some of the same problems that capturing Le Roux himself had. Moran Oz, Alon Berkman, and Omer Bezalel were living in Israel, whose government might prove resistant to extradition. Most of the crimes they had supposedly committed weren't crimes under Israeli law. Lachlan McConnell and Shai Reuven were both still in Manila, living under a Philippine government that had so far proven less than fully cooperative. To capture these guys, Brill and Bailey needed to lure them somewhere else. And to do that, they needed Le Roux.

The 960 group, however, was focused on putting Le Roux to work in their own sting operations against the likes of Joseph Hunter. They allowed him only enough communication with his RX Limited employees—and enough access to his bank accounts—to keep the network barely alive.

For Felix Klaussen, Le Roux's arrest meant an abrupt and disorienting end to the project that had consumed his life. For nearly a year, he'd spent most of his waking moments thinking about how to convince Le Roux that he was bringing him the deal of a lifetime, constantly vigilant to any slipup that could expose the ruse. Now he spent weeks in a Marriott in Arlington, Virginia, video-chatting with his fiancée, idling while the Justice Department worked through their arrangement with Le Roux and determined whether they needed Klaussen as a witness. He was elated that it had all worked, but unsure how to feel about the deal Le Roux was striking, and where the story might go now that he had exited it.

I came to know a version of the same feeling, years later. I'd never been face-to-face with Le Roux, never tried to sell him a story and risked his wrath. But I could certainly claim a similar obsession with trying to understand him. It had chewed up years of my life as I tried to wrestle the facts to fit a simpler frame, something with a cleaner ending, a story I could hold in my head all at once. In that version of the story, Le Roux's arrest was the close of his saga, justice done. But the maddening contradictions of Le Roux's world were part of what had hooked me in the first place—which is why I knew the story wasn't over yet. This wasn't the end of the game. Just a reshuffling of the teams.

29

The Stings

2012–2013 . . . Back in the game . . . News from the boss . . . The Colombians arrive . . . The perfect hit . . . History repeats

In a typical organized-crime case, authorities work their way up a kind of pyramid, flipping lower-level participants to inform against the lieutenants above them, flipping those lieutenants to inform against bosses, sacrificing small-scale prosecutions in order to pursue the powerful figures at the apex. With Le Roux, the DEA had captured the man who not only sat atop the organization, but the one who had created it, from his own mind, and ran it with ruthless specificity. Le Roux was not just the most powerful force behind The Company—or RX Limited, or any of a dozen names the organization traveled under. He *was* The Company.

The U.S. Department of Justice might have touted that triumph. They might have chosen to prosecute Le Roux to the fullest extent of the law—as they had done with similarly high-profile cases like Viktor Bout's—and then publicly celebrated their almost-certain victory in federal court. But now they decided to invert the pyramid, working their way to the base, cloaked in a blanket of secrecy. Instead of allowing the organization Le Roux had built to quietly disintegrate from neglect, they would use him to hold it together as they pursued the underlings whom he had drawn into it.

In legal circles this was known as "cooperating down," and Le Roux would prove an enthusiastic participant. The speed of his transformation from target to informant was breathtaking. "It was obvious that my situation was a bad situation" was all he would say, with a shrug, when asked later why he'd flipped so easily. Within a day of his arrival in New York, he signed what's known as a proffer agreement. Under the terms of a proffer, Le Roux was free to talk to prosecutors without fear; nothing he told them could be used against him. Whatever he truthfully fessed up to couldn't result in new charges against him. Any lies or omissions, on the other hand, could.

Suddenly the man whom Kimberly Brill and Kent Bailey had worked for years to understand was spilling parts of his story to investigators as fast as they could record them. He was cagey at first about some of the killings he'd ordered—"I'm already at risk of being sentenced to death in the Philippines," he said later in court (perhaps fearing a kind of extrajudicial justice, since the Philippines banned the death penalty in 2006). But eventually he came clean on seven murders. He admitted to bribing officials in the Philippines, China, Laos, Brazil, and all over Africa, to laundering hundreds of millions of dollars, to dealing in massive quantities of methamphetamines and cocaine, to selling explosives to and acquiring weapons from Iran.

The SOD agents who had cornered Le Roux, Eric Stouch and Thomas Cindric, needed more than just names and admissions. To run him as an asset, they'd need to quickly convince his remaining crew that Le Roux was still at large, running his business. "We were trying to maintain the image that he was still free and moving about, specifically in Brazil," Stouch later said. The 960 group also had indicted Shai Reuven in the methamphetamine sting—he'd been scheduled to travel to Liberia with Le Roux but failed to show up—and now the agents left him on the street to help maintain the myth that Le Roux was still free.

To work with Le Roux, the agents needed a judge's approval to pull him out of confinement, after which they would transport him to one of the few locations that now comprised his world: a DEA office near JFK airport, the U.S. Attorney's offices at the federal courthouse in downtown Manhattan, or the airport Hilton. (In one inexplicable security slip, someone allowed Le Roux's record to be publicly available on the Bureau of Prisons website. "Paul Leroux"—without the space—was listed as "Released On: 09/04/2013," perhaps an artifact of the process of moving him in and out of jail.) Once sequestered, Le Roux would spend the day orchestrating a new set of sting operations. He attacked his role with the single-minded devotion that he'd previously shown toward his criminal endeavors.

There was one immediate problem: Le Roux communicated largely using email that passed through his own server, fast-free -email.com, which he had designed to periodically destroy his messages. The agents needed a way to mirror the contents of that email address in another account, so that they could preserve all of Le Roux's communications as evidence. Fortunately, there was one person in the room technically proficient enough to execute such a maneuver. And he seemed happy to be back in the game, even if on the other side. From inside the confines of the Manhattan federal courthouse, Le Roux logged in to his old fast-free-email server in the Philippines and got to work.

From the perspective of his employees scattered around the world, Le Roux had briefly gone dark, but not for long enough to raise alarms. They were used to not seeing him for months at a time. "You could always reach him via email or phone, and that was probably the strangest thing of all when he dropped off for a while," said Tim Vamvakias, who had rejoined the organization when Joseph Hunter took over Le Roux's kill teams. Vamvakias's new job was to run an operation to import tramadol, the generic version of Ultram, directly from Mexican cartels into Texas—foregoing the

RX Limited pharmacies. "The fact that people's daily duties resumed, along with the pay, helped the mystery go unnoticed," he said. "In retrospect it was extreme naïveté on all of our parts."

In December, Hunter suddenly began receiving a flurry of calls and encrypted notes from Le Roux, writing from an old address he rarely used, john@fast-free-email.com. Le Roux told Hunter that he was working on a new project, a big one, that would need him to be at the top of his game. It involved a group he would refer to only as the "South American partners." As a first step, Le Roux wanted Hunter, operating under the names "Jim Riker" and "Ja-Rule," and using his old "rambo@fast-free-email.com" address, to assemble a team of skilled, reliable ex-military men who could handle "specialist jobs." Hunter didn't need him to elaborate.

Hunter sent word to, among others, his old partner Chris De Meyer—who along with "Daddy Mac" had quit the organization after the Edillor murder—that he was seeking new guys. De Meyer declined to rejoin but put the call out to his own network, and soon résumés of prospective new security team members were arriving over the transom.

From Manila to Cape Town, other members and former members of The Company were also hearing from Le Roux, who seemed rejuvenated and ready to launch an array of new ventures. Among the first was Marcus, the South African who had been Le Roux's personal assassin. In early 2013, Le Roux proposed he take on a project in America. "He reopened my email account," Marcus said, "and paid money to my bank account." When Marcus balked at traveling to the States, Le Roux was ready with another idea: Marcus could organize a group of ex-military guys to work in Somalia. Le Roux also suggested that he would retain Marcus again as an assassin, this time to murder Ari Ben-Menashe, the Israeli whom he'd once employed to help procure land and a diplomatic passport in Zimbabwe. (In another strange development the DEA never quite parsed, the real Ben-Menashe reached out to Le Roux, saying he'd heard that Le Roux was in trouble. Ben-Menashe suggested Le Roux take harbor in Israel and work with the Mossad. "I can give you protection," he told Le Roux, according to the former 960 agent. The agents decided to ignore the offer.) Marcus went so far as to send Le Roux the résumés of possible recruits, but then the correspondence abruptly ended. Only years later, Marcus said, "did I realize that this fucking cunt was in jail, trying to set me up to come there."

The phenomenon replicated itself across Le Roux's operations. Scott Stammers, the security contractor who worked for Le Roux in Thailand, heard from him again in late 2012. Stammers was a thirty-four-year-old British citizen born in Hong Kong who somehow retained his English pallor despite years of living in a tropical climate. He had helped coordinate gun- and drug-related operations for Le Roux in the past, and was skilled at sourcing everything from heavy weaponry to methamphetamine precursor chemicals and the cooks to prepare them.

Le Roux wanted Stammers, together with Philip Shackels— a tattooed Irishman who had become central to Le Roux's drug business, forging relationships with South American cartels—to coordinate the logistics for a meth deal. This time it would be for some new associates in Colombia, where he'd previously failed to find the right connection. "He said, 'I won't be in the Philippines for a while, it's gotten too hot there,'" Stammers recalled. "'My partners want to meet you in Thailand.'"

The deal, as Le Roux described it, would be a replay of one he'd done before, with Ye Tiong Tan Lim, who'd previously arranged The Company's acquisition of nearly fifty kilos of meth in 2012. Lim, a balding Chinese man in his fifties with wire-rim glasses, purportedly operated an import-export business but maintained ties to a triad group in Hong Kong. To get to Lim as part of his new DEA duties, Le Roux reached out to Kelly Peralta, a thirty-nine-year-old Filipino who had once worked for him as a manager of his bar in Manila. Peralta's role in The Company had been negligible, at best. Dave Smith had hired him to work at Sid's, Le Roux's bar, after meeting him at the Blue Rock Resort in Subic.

After Sid's closed two years later, Peralta came to Le Roux with an offer: an introduction to Lim, whose triad connections could get Le Roux high-quality meth out of North Korea. Peralta, who spoke English better than Lim, had become the go-between with Le Roux, for which he was paid $25,000.

Now, one year later, Le Roux was back, asking him to make the same arrangement, this time for the South Americans. Peralta agreed to do it. In early January 2013, Lim and Peralta traveled to Thailand to meet the South Americans, who claimed to be senior figures in a Colombian cartel. They were planning to sell the meth in New York, they said. First, they'd need a sample sent to Liberia, so they could test the quality. The whole plan was a modified version of the sting used to ensnare Le Roux himself.

The request was a little unusual, but it didn't faze Lim any more than it had fazed Le Roux. "My boss," Lim said, "only gets [it] from the original source." That source was North Korea.

North Korea's contribution to the international meth trade dated to the mid-1990s, when heavy rains wiped out its thriving poppy crop, opening a lane for lab-made drugs. By 2007, North Korea was producing tons of the stuff per year—"the highest quality product for export" according one U.S. congressional report—which was then smuggled across the border into northeastern China. By 2013 the flow of drugs out of the dictatorship seemed to be lessening; the State Department observed that "state-sponsored drug trafficking may have ceased or been sharply reduced, or . . . the DPRK regime has become more adept at concealing state-sponsored trafficking of illicit drugs."

Lim now made a similar point to the Colombians. "The North Korean government already burned all the labs," he told them, "to show the Americans they aren't selling it anymore." But Lim said he still had access to roughly one ton of ultra-pure North Korean meth. "Only our labs are not closed," he said.

The Colombians asked to visit the labs to verify its origins—if the DEA was going to use Le Roux to get a foothold inside North

Korea's drug production, they would presumably need Lim to give them access. But Lim deflected them, arguing that non–Korean speakers would raise suspicions.

The next month, Lim provided two small meth samples to Peralta, who delivered them to Philip Shackels. Together with Stammers, he shipped the samples via FedEx to Monrovia, hidden inside a photo album. Stammers emailed the tracking number to Le Roux.

The Colombians reported back to Stammers that the two samples had tested at 96 and 98 percent pure, respectively. "I just received the following on the two samples," Stammers then informed Le Roux. "A—Whiter and in smaller granules, B—Clear and bigger shards and harder to break. As per the boys, they are both very good and very strong, but they preferred B." The deal was on.

By March 2013, Joseph Hunter had spent several months collecting and sorting résumés from mercenaries in Poland, Germany, and South Africa. He forwarded his top picks to Le Roux for approval. Together, they settled on three men. None had worked for The Company before. Now they would be unwittingly working for its DEA-constructed mirage.

Dennis Gögel was a twenty-seven-year-old German whose life followed the path of so many of the other contractors who had joined Le Roux over the years. He had been raised by his grandmother in Stadthagen, a small city in northern Germany, after his mother died of asthma and his father abandoned him. He joined the army, he said, "to take control" of his life. He'd served in an elite unit deployed for peacekeeping in Kosovo. On his discharge, in 2010, he'd shifted into private security, first in Afghanistan and then working as an antipiracy specialist on boats threatened by Somali pirates. His Facebook profile consisted largely of photos of him posing with weapons or working shirtless on the decks of ships.

On one of these missions, a fellow contractor told him about a well-paying job involving "a highly specialized security group to protect and secure high-profile clients." He gave Gögel an email address, and Gögel sent off his CV to Joseph Hunter. A few days later, he got an email back. "Got it," Hunter said. "Your definitely in."

Next, Gögel connected Hunter with another former German soldier he'd served with, a high school dropout named Michael Filter, who had also left the service in 2010. With young twin daughters to support, Filter had jumped at the prospect of a job that paid well, for a client that Gögel said "you don't want to know the details about." Filter saw it "as a possibility to do something useful and be able to provide for his girls properly," his sister recalled.

The third team member, Slawomir Soborski, was a Polish ex-policeman. He'd worked for fifteen years in law enforcement, including five spent protecting the Polish president, and would later claim to have provided protection for President George W. Bush and Pope John Paul II. He too had drifted into contract work—including a stint in the French Foreign Legion—but struggled to make ends meet. In February, Soborski received Hunter's job solicitation from a friend in the Foreign Legion and wrote to Hunter directly. "I am convinced that my experience, commitment, and professionalism, confirmed by my references, will lead to the success of your company and mutual satisfaction," he said. His résumé included such qualifications as "sniper," "close-combat specialist," and "parachutist."

With the three recruits, Hunter felt they were ready to get to work for the South Americans. He wrote to Le Roux that Soborski and Gögel in particular were "highly qualified individuals that will get a lot of stuff done for us."

In March, Hunter traveled to Phuket, Thailand, and met Le Roux's South American contacts at one of Le Roux's houses, a stucco ranch with a red terra-cotta roof near the Loch Palm Golf

Club. Gögel, Soborski, and Filter arrived for their first in-person meeting. Hunter had told them to dress like tourists for the trip—"nothing military police looking"—and had wired them expense money for their tickets. Once everyone was present, Hunter, dressed in a Batman T-shirt and cargo shorts, gathered them around the kitchen table. None of them noticed the small video camera mounted inside what looked like an electric junction box in the ceiling, installed by a DEA technician a few days earlier and feeding into a DVD recorder hidden in the panel above it. The DVR in turn was connected to the Internet, transmitting the crew's discussions to a team of local Thai police and DEA agents.

Hunter, projecting the authority of an experienced commander, disclosed the identities of their clients: two men from a Colombian cartel, associates of Hunter's boss, whom he referred to as "Benny." "You're gonna see tons of cocaine," Hunter told them. "You're gonna see millions of dollars. You're gonna see gold."

The team's work, he said, could include surveillance and counter-surveillance of drug shipments, collecting money from people who hadn't paid the Colombians, and carrying cocaine. "There's bonus work," Hunter said. "It's assassinations. So if you are interested in that, you can do it. If you are not interested, you don't have to." A "minor" assassination, he estimated, might earn someone $25,000, with the price escalating "depending on the threat level." Regardless, the three of them would be joining a rarified group. "Once a mission is received, that mission becomes sacred to you," Hunter said. "You will accomplish it to the end at all costs."

For the next hour, Hunter delivered a sermon extolling mercenary life under the boss, pausing only for the occasional "yeah" from his team. "It's just like a military mission," he said. "You see James Bond in the movie and you're saying, 'Oh, I can do that.' Well, you're gonna do it now. Everything you see or you've thought about, you're gonna do. It's real and it's up to you."

Hunter's soliloquy wandered from dramatic recounting of his own exploits to detailed instructions on kidnappings and assassinations. "That one year, we killed nine people," he said. "We hand-grenaded the people's houses. We, ah . . . not kidnapped a guy, but we conned him to come with us. We put him in the ocean, shot at him; he gave us the money back. Ah . . . assassinated people. Ah, what else we did? We smuggled gold. We smuggled weapons.

"You gotta use your head," he continued. "If you gotta kidnap somebody to recover funds, you know how you gotta plan a kidnapping, right? Knock the fucking . . . you knock the guy out in your minivan or your SUV. You already gonna have a place to hide, right? A place to hold him. You just gotta drive there and get to the place, and then once he's inside the building it's no problem. You're gonna handcuff him and all that shit, and then I'm sure he's gonna give you the money, right, or arrange for the money right away. If you have to waterboard him, it's easy, you just put a wet towel on his face and pour water on him about, you know, fifteen to twenty seconds till he talks."

The next day the Colombians arrived at the house. The cartel representatives met individually with each member to make sure that everyone understood the expectations. "You do whatever you have to do," one of the Colombians said. "If we call you and say, 'This fucking guy ain't gonna pay,' that's it. We want you to be magicians. . . . You disappear people."

Hunter's crew moved into villas in Phuket, where Hunter ordered them to stay in shape while awaiting the next assignment. To his younger charges, he appeared introverted, often sullen. But he also sometimes offered the mentorship of a senior officer, a seasoned veteran with a thousand stories and an eye for all the angles. "Hunter and I built a strong bond as he took me under his wing," Gögel later said. "After a short while our relationship expanded, and I began to view Hunter not only as mentor but as a father figure, something I never had before."

The DEA now had two sets of targets on the hook—the North

Korean meth group and Hunter's team—but Cindric and Stouch were careful not reel them in too fast. For Hunter's team, the Colombians first offered up purposefully pedestrian jobs, like conducting surveillance at a distance on a large shipment of drugs in a Thai port. Next, the Colombians dispatched them to Mauritius, an island nation in the Indian Ocean just east of Madagascar, to provide security for a meeting. Here, the two groups of DEA targets would cross paths for the first time. Scott Stammers and Philip Shackels were there, at Le Roux's direction, to negotiate weapons purchases for the Colombians, who said they wanted to buy surface-to-air missiles. Hunter's team was brought for security. The following day, Stammers, Shackels, and the Colombians met with a pair of actual drug dealers, Serbians who were offering to help replace the cocaine lost on the *JeReVe*. The "Serb crew," as Stammers reported to Le Roux, could supply seven hundred to a thousand kilos in South America, for shipment to Australia.

Cindric and Stouch, stationed nearby to monitor the proceedings, watched their already complex operation mushroom into something that required an organizational chart to follow. Besides their faux-Colombian cartel bosses and their five targets—Gögel, Filter, Soborski, Stammers, and Shackels—the April meetings involved ten other criminals who weren't even subjects of their investigation. The chances that someone would find a hole in the sting operation mushroomed with every new mark that showed up.

But as he had in his real business, Le Roux had little problem juggling operations. He would call multiple times a day to check in on their progress, pressing his employees to hurry things up. None of them seemed to find it unusual. Le Roux told Shackels that the organization had suffered huge losses, and that moving the North Korean meth should be his top priority. In mid-May, Stammers and Shackels returned to Thailand to meet with the Colombians about the logistics of the meth shipment.

Shackels, for his part, appeared to be struggling to keep it together. "You seem tense," one of the Colombians said during a meeting.

"Of course, I'm fucking stressed," Shackels said.

At one point, Shackels's hands were shaking so badly he spilled a cup of water on one of the supposed cartel bosses. "What the fuck is wrong with you?" the Colombian said. "You need to stay cool. Just relax."

In meetings with Lim and Peralta, meanwhile, the Colombians set the amounts and price of the shipments, proposing an initial sixty kilos of meth, at $60,000 per. "My friends, can you do the sixty, a little bit, a little more, like one hundred?" Peralta asked. The Colombians agreed, and over the summer months the groups hammered out the details. In emails about the arrangement, they referred to the drugs as "car parts."

Now it was Le Roux, the informant, who had his targets eating out of his hand, just as Felix Klaussen had once duped him. After Mauritius, Hunter proposed to Le Roux that they add Tim Vamvakias to his crew. Now forty-one, Vamvakias had been back in The Company since 2012, stationed at a stash house in Texas. For $7,500 a month, he guarded a large supply of contraband tramadol, the generic version of Ultram, awaiting shipment to buyers on the East Coast.

Hunter thought Vamvakias could be put to better use on the security team. Le Roux agreed to a transfer and a raise to $10,000 a month, as long as Vamvakias was willing to engage in "bonus work."

Stouch and Cindric had planned out the stings so that they intersected just enough with Le Roux's actual business to seem real. And now, after months of slowly establishing that authenticity, the agents began to spring the trap. It was time to begin offering the security team bonus work. Le Roux informed Hunter that he and the Colombians had found a snitch in their organization, a boat captain who had tipped off the DEA and Australian Federal Police to the *JeReVe:*

From: john <john@fast-free-email.com>
To: Jim Riker <mrtiberius2@yahoo.com>
Sent: Thursday, May 30, 2013 12:50 A.M.
Subject: Re:

. . . the situation is our contact in the f b i in ecuador has
been looking into the jereve incident for us, the man who
is responsible has been providing tips to the d e a and a f p,
he is a boat captain that is working for us, he does jobs
for us mainly in the carribean and in africa, he was the one
who handled the jereve for us, and leaked the info to
the u.s agent, him and a particular agent are problems
for us, this is a priority job that will pay allot of money,
i need your suggestion on the best way to handle it, I need
your input on what is needed to fix this issue asap as we
already lost 3 shipments and allot of money, please be advised
he does not know anyone except his handler but he knows
some of our boats, so we need to get this issue resolved
before we loose more money, sis this something your team
can handle? or should i assign it to my south african guys,
the jobs will probably be in africa as the captain is based
there

"My guys will handle it," Hunter replied. "Are you talking
about both the Captain and the agent or just the Captain?"

"Both are a problem, both need to be handled," Le Roux said.
"Informer is 200 000 and 500 000 for the agent." Hunter would
get $100,000 for organizing the hit.

"They will handle both jobs," Hunter said. "They just need
good tools." In a later email to Le Roux, he elaborated on exactly
what tools they would require:

From: Jim Riker <mrtiberius2@yahoo.com>
To: "john@fast-free-email.com" <john@fast-free-email.com>

Hey,

Here is a list of items needed for the job. It includes everything
that they can think of, because they don't exactly know the
plan and how it will be executed, that's why it's so much.
   Two Submachine Guns with silencers (Mac 10, MP5, P90,
MP7,,,something small) Magazines for the Weapons
   Two .22 pistols with Silencers (these are a must)
   Magazines and ammo for these
   One 308 Rifle with Scope and Case for it
   Ammo for it
   Two Level 3A Concealment Vests
   2 GPS's for the evac (one for each guy)
   2 Black Guy Masks (like the ones we have, but all ready in
county)
   2 Two way radios preferably with ear pieces and push to
talk capability
   2 Motorcycles at least 250cc with helmets that have a black
tinted visor
   2 Cars or SUVs with tinted windows
   Stolen License plates for both motorcycles and Cars
   Once they are in place and have a plan additional items
might be required depending on the assesment

At the same time, the Colombians had a new task for the security team—one that for the first time would put them in the sights
of American drug laws. This time the job was in the Bahamas,
keeping watch on a private plane as it was loaded with three hundred kilos of cocaine for delivery to the United States. The team—
now consisting of Gögel, Filter, Soborski, and Vamvakias, with
Hunter coordinating operations from Thailand—arrived in June

for what seemed like a leisurely gig. Soborski posed for photos on the beach, shirtless and holding a drink and a cigar. They scouted out a surveillance location behind a chain-link fence, off a runway at the Nassau airport, and watched through a car window as bags of cocaine were loaded onto a small private plane they were told was headed for New York.

After seeing off the plane, Vamvakias met with the Colombians at a hotel to discuss the upcoming bonus jobs. They had brought along photographs and dossiers on the DEA agent and snitch, as well as information on the location. They wanted the job done in Liberia.

On August 15, 2013, Hunter's team met with the two cartel representatives one last time in Thailand to finalize arrangements for the assassination. Even though they'd worked together for eight months, Hunter had the Colombians searched, took their electronic devices, and insisted that the meeting be held outdoors as an extra precaution against being recorded.

Hunter, Gögel, Vamvakias, and the Colombians—who by this point had paid Hunter a $480,000 down payment for the murders of the DEA agent and snitch—reviewed the assassination plan step by step. (Soborski and Filter had been deemed unready for bonus work; they traveled instead to Estonia to provide security on a staged weapons deal.) The crew studied photos of the intended hits, discussing how to enter and leave Liberia undetected. Gögel and Vamvakias would have both cars and motorcycles at their disposal. Hunter had purchased the "black guy masks" mentioned in his email: latex masks from a Hollywood special effects store, specially designed to conceal the wearer's race. They'd tried them on, Gögel said, and even when they closed their eyes the masks "were blinking with us. . . . Even with real hairs and everything. That's perfect stuff."

Gögel would command the operation—"You run the show," one of the Colombians told him—and suggested they could make the job look like a robbery. "I think we'll probably have to get up close to 'em," Vamvakias noted. "You know what I mean? To make sure it gets done." Among the weapons that Hunter had suggested, they settled on German-made MP7 machine guns, with the power to pierce some bulletproof vests. "That'll guarantee whatever gets in that kill zone goes down," Vamvakias said. The Colombians would then help them get out of the country. "I'm glad you're going to be part of the extraction stuff," Vamvakias told them. "The job's not the headache, it's getting in and out."

On September 24, 2013, everything was in place for both missions. The meth was set to leave the Philippines by container, and Lim and Peralta convened at a hotel in Phuket to await its arrival. "All the main players are now on the ground," Stammers emailed Le Roux, as he, Shackels, and Adrian Valkovic—a member of a local motorcycle club who had signed on as the "deputy ground commander" for the meth shipment, handling security—sat down for a final planning session. "Standing by for meet coordinates and time."

The coordinates never came. Instead, heavily armed commandos from Thailand's Narcotics Suppression Bureau swept in a few hours later and arrested the five men.

Meanwhile Hunter was at Le Roux's nearby Loch Palm villa, awaiting updates on the Liberia assassination job. He was alone and unarmed when a dozen officers from the NSB arrived, led by the deputy police commissioner. They handcuffed him and led him outside, then sat him on the ground by the front door while police officials posed for photos beside him. In images that would soon run in newspapers around the world, Hunter appeared almost expressionless, staring into the cameras with his hands cuffed behind his back. He was dressed in cargo shorts and a T-shirt with a SPRINGFIELD UNATHLETIC DEPT logo and an image of a drooling Homer Simpson asleep on a couch.

Five thousand miles away, Soborski and Filter were picked up

by local authorities at a hotel in Tallinn, the capital of Estonia. The
men were transported to a former Soviet prison; the cops roughed
up Soborski enough that he would later require abdominal surgery.

That same morning, Vamvakias and Gögel stepped off a plane
at Roberts International Airport outside Monrovia ready to assas-
sinate the DEA agent and the snitch. The Colombians were supposed to meet them as they got off the plane, ready with the
weapons, masks, and vehicles. Instead, the Liberian police were
waiting, and the would-be assassins were quickly transferred into
DEA custody and flown back to New York.

It was a year to the day since Paul Le Roux had made the same
trip, with the same result. Two days later, Preet Bharara, the U.S.
Attorney for the Southern District of New York, held a press conference in Manhattan to announce the success of the Hunter operation. "The bone-chilling allegations in today's indictment read
like they were ripped from the pages of a Tom Clancy novel," he
said gravely. "The charges tell a tale of an international band of
mercenary marksmen who enlisted their elite military training to
serve as hired guns for evil ends." Paul Le Roux's name and role
went unmentioned.

30

The Investigators · The Operators · The Pharmacist · The Mercenaries · The Reporter

2013–2015 . . . An audience with Le Roux . . . Oz hears from the boss . . . A rendezvous in Romania . . . A knock at Tumpati's door . . . Under pressure in North Carolina . . . Lachlan McConnell on the run

Kent Bailey and Kimberly Brill were finally granted a chance to sit down with Le Roux—albeit with restrictions—in November 2012. They left their Minneapolis offices at the DEA and flew back to New York. As they sat waiting for Le Roux's arrival in the fifth-floor room of the Manhattan courthouse, Brill was nervous, not knowing what to expect from the man she'd been circling for more than five years. When he was escorted in, Le Roux was polite but guarded at first, seemingly unhappy with the prospect of another quizzing. He'd already begun working on the Joseph Hunter sting operation as part of the 960 team—and now here was a woman from Minnesota with an empty notepad and hours of new questions.

But gradually he seemed to realize that he was talking to the only person who knew as much about his pharmacy operation as he did. Brill had analyzed it from every angle, traced every branch to its endpoint. And she had read his emails, too. For Brill, it soon felt like they were talking as peers. "I don't know that I would call it *fun*," she said. "But it was somebody I could actually talk to who knew what I was talking about the whole time. Where I didn't have to explain." Every question she'd had about RX Limited could now be answered by the man who had created it. They dove deep into the technical aspects of Le Roux's networks: the email servers, the affiliate website back ends, the thousands of Web domains. After a couple hours, Brill had filled the notepad and was writing on its cardboard backing.

Over the course of late 2012 and early 2013, Brill returned to interview Le Roux several more times. She and Bailey had hoped to utilize him as an asset, to help lure Moran Oz, Alon Berkman, and others out of Israel. But the 960 agents who controlled Le Roux had specific targets in their sights, Hunter and the North Korean meth groups, and declined to make him available to help Brill round up her own. Le Roux was permitted to send only occasional communications to the likes of Oz and Berkman, just enough to keep up the charade that he was at large.

After Hunter was busted in the fall of 2013, Bailey and Brill finally got a chance to put Le Roux to work. Brill found him to be an enthusiastic partner in setting up a new ruse. "He had made up his mind that he was going to do as much as he could now that he was in the situation he was in," Brill said. "And information was his currency."

This time Le Roux wouldn't have Colombian partners to dangle in front of the targets. He would have to use cleverness and cajoling to lure Oz and Berkman into a trap. With RX Limited barely functional, first he would have to convince them that he was bringing it back to life.

On orders from Le Roux when he was still a free man, Oz and Berkman had shuttered the Tel Aviv office in 2012. They spent months selling off furniture and equipment. From Brazil, Le Roux had ordered Berkman to transfer as many of his assets as possible out of Hong Kong, where the government was trying to seize them. Oz and Berkman retrenched to Jerusalem—a temporary setback, Le Roux assured them. He was planning a future iteration of the business with new call centers, new pharmacies, new doctors. But his communication became increasingly sporadic. Periodically, Oz wrote to Le Roux to ask about severance payments for former employees in Israel. As the company wound down, Le Roux had wired part of the money, which was owed under Israeli law, and promised that the rest would come later.

And then, in September 2012, Le Roux seemed to disappear entirely. Rumors swirled that he had gone underground because authorities had intercepted one of his boats, carrying arms or drugs. Shai Reuven, who was still running Le Roux's business in Manila, would say only that the boss had gone quiet. The transfers from Hong Kong and the other accounts became increasingly sporadic. "We knew something had happened," Oz said.

In March 2013, Le Roux reappeared with orders for Oz and Berkman to further cut the staff in Israel, and to stop filling orders and paying doctors and pharmacists by the end of the year. The company would relaunch again soon, he now said, with a new office in Eastern Europe and a different model. "Please advice what is the status with the severance payments," Oz wrote back. "You asked me to split it to three, but the people didn't get their second payment and the keep calling me, please let me know what to tell them."

Oz still felt responsible to the Israeli employees who were owed money, some of whom were friends, and none of whom had heard of Paul Le Roux. To them, Oz was the boss. "He was getting phone calls from employees saying, 'You shut down the company, you disappeared, you have to pay us, by law,'" a friend of Oz's said.

In late December, Oz and Berkman stumbled onto an article in the Brazilian newspaper *Folha de S.Paulo* reporting that Le Roux had been arrested. The story, by a reporter who had been tipped off to the Brazilian end of the investigation, was published in Portuguese, but a quick pass through an online translator provided the basic, alarming facts: The DEA had been investigating RX Limited for years and had tracked Le Roux to Brazil, where he was involved in large-scale cocaine trafficking across the Pacific. Worse, the article claimed that the DEA had arrested Le Roux in Liberia and he'd cut a deal, which "led to the arrest of employees in Australia, Hong Kong, Philippines and the United States." The headline was, simply, "The Lord of Crime."

In a panic, Oz left word with Reuven to call him. The next day, the return call came from Le Roux himself. "I heard you guys are getting very excited over this article that appeared in the Brazilian press," he said, laughing.

"Yes, tell me about it," Oz said.

"At the end of the day, the Israelis are the guys that they arrested in Hong Kong," Le Roux said. "Basically, they were grabbed and accused of money laundering."

"Yeah."

"Bottom line, most of that article is actually true, but it's been grossly exaggerated and distorted, okay? There's always surveillance on our operations. That is a matter of fact."

"Mm-hmm."

"And also, that's a big part of the reason why I shut down the old operation, like, when I did, because there's a lot of heat on it."

"Yeah, but everything is okay with you?"

"Everything is okay with me," Le Roux said. "Right now I'm traveling under a different passport. I took some steps—you following what I'm saying?"

"Of course."

"For some reason, the press likes to write about me. I am the lord of crime in this Brazilian newspaper. I run huge militias. You know, they love to write all types of bullshit. Some of it is true, but most of it is grossly exaggerated," he said. "You know, everyone needs to calm the fuck down."

Le Roux told Oz he finally had the rest of the money for the Israeli employees, coming within weeks. And he still planned to start up the company again. "I know you're hurting," he said. "Keep in mind, everyone is fucking hurting right now, you see what I'm saying? But there is light at the end of the tunnel. I have arranged your cash." He just needed to see Oz in person to finalize the transfer. He first proposed they meet in Panama, but Oz declined. When Le Roux suggested Romania, he agreed.

With the benefit of hindsight, it seemed absurd that Oz had fallen for it. Berkman didn't, electing to ignore Le Roux's entreaties and stay in Israel. Was it greed that blinded Oz, or gullibility? His emails made him appear enthusiastic to restart the business with Le Roux, but later he would assert that the only reason he'd gone along with the meeting was in the hopes of getting the employees' severance back. "I didn't go to Romania to get my own salary," he said. In another sense, though, it was a testament to the alternate reality, mythology even, that Le Roux had created around himself. He could have an employee thrown off a boat and shot at, show up in a U.N. report funding a militia in Somalia, get written up in a major newspaper as having been busted for drug running, and an employee would still believe him enough to get on a plane and meet him in a foreign country.

A few weeks later, Oz landed in Bucharest along with a friend he'd invited on the trip. They had an Israeli expat friend in Romania, and the three of them spent two days hanging out and gambling in the local casinos. Oz won a few thousand Euros at his preferred game, roulette.

The meeting with Le Roux was scheduled for the third day, but as the time approached Oz grew nervous. His chief concern was not that Le Roux might be setting him up, but that he might be planning to kill him. He asked the friend from Bucharest to arrange some hired security, "just to make sure that there are no surprises." The friend found a couple of bodyguards he could pay by the hour.

Le Roux had set the meeting for March 13 at the Pullman Hotel, not far from the airport. Oz and his two friends arrived in the morning and met up with the bodyguards, who accompanied Oz to a distant part of the lobby while his friends waited at the entrance. After a half hour, Oz texted them to say that his boss hadn't shown up yet. When the friends checked in a while later, Oz didn't respond.

Worried, they decided to look for him. They found him at another entrance, surrounded by several men and one woman. Oz explained that they were plainclothes police officers, that they'd shown up looking for him and wanted to take him to the station to ask questions. The bodyguards seemed to have slipped away.

The officers asked the friends to accompany them to the station, and the three men climbed into the back of an old unmarked car. Oz seemed terrified that it was another of Le Roux's ruses. "Look, they don't wear police uniforms," Oz said to his friends in Hebrew. "I hope it's not one of his tricks."

He was relieved when they arrived at the Bucharest police station—at least it appeared not to be a Le Roux hit in disguise. His local friend found him a Romanian lawyer, while the other one went to their hotel to retrieve their passports, hoping the whole thing could be cleared up by the evening. After the friend returned, the lawyer told him that Oz had been arrested on behalf of an American agency.

"Go back to Israel, meet Moran's parents, and tell them to get a good lawyer," the attorney told him. "Because they are going to move him to the U.S. for a trial."

Oz spent the next several months in an overcrowded Romanian jail, housed with seven other inmates in a stifling seven-by-ten-foot cell. One of his cellmates had a heart attack and died. Oz's family hired a local lawyer to fight his extradition, but the hearings were all conducted in Romanian, and Oz often had little idea what was happening. His only contact with the American government had been through Kimberly Brill, from the DEA, who briefly showed up to question him after his arrest.

More than anything, he was baffled that the United States had used Le Roux to get to him and not the other way around. He told them about how Le Roux had ordered him thrown off the boat and shot at. He would have helped them, he said, if they'd asked.

Finally, on the last day he could be legally held in Romania, a judge overruled Oz's opposition to extradition, and he was put on a plane to the United States. He landed in Minneapolis and was transported to the Sherburne County Jail, outside the city.

In early 2014, Prabhakara Tumpati was hustling again to keep his head above water. He'd opened three sleep clinics, and two of them were losing money. To help make ends meet, he was picking up call shifts at a hospital near his home in suburban Philadelphia. It had been two years since he had given up prescribing for RX Limited. More recently, his referral fees had stopped coming as well, and his physician contacts still prescribing for it told him it had essentially disappeared.

So Tumpati was doubly surprised to receive a letter from Linda Marks's office at the Consumer Protection Branch of the U.S. Department of Justice, suggesting that his work for the network had been illegal. He engaged a lawyer to respond, but wasn't overly concerned. "I was under the impression that it was more like, 'Help us, we are investigating this guy that has these other things going on,'" he said. After all, he had been the one trying to convince RX Limited that they needed to add video technology so that doctors could see patients virtually. Tumpati's lawyer responded that the doctor didn't believe he had done anything illegal, and that he was willing to come to Washington and sit down with the attorneys.

For a while, that seemed like the end of it. Then, on the morning of March 27, Tumpati had just completed a 7-P.M.-to-6-A.M. shift at the hospital, and was planning to head home and grab a few hours of sleep before heading off to one of his clinics. As he pulled his car into the driveway, he failed to notice a pair of sedans parked near the end of it. He went upstairs to change clothes, and was standing in his thermal underwear when he heard a voice say, "Don't move."

A team of ten officers had arrived, guns drawn, to make the arrest. The agents told Tumpati that they had a warrant and went room to room, grabbing files and computers. Tumpati's wife stood by, calmly praying, and then turned to their four-year-old daughter to comfort her. "She didn't know what was going on or who these people were," Tumpati said.

Once they'd put their guns away, the agents were polite and professional. They agreed to let Tumpati walk to the car without handcuffs, suggesting that he tell his neighbors it had been a case of mistaken identity. They then took him to the local police station, where he was strip-searched and fingerprinted, and transported to a federal processing center in downtown Philadelphia. Only later would he learn that he was to be tried not in Pennsylvania but in Minnesota.

Adam Samia, the trigger man Hunter had brought in to kill Catherine Lee, was—like many of Le Roux's former employees—oblivious to Le Roux's fate. He'd only ever communicated with the boss through Hunter, and after Hunter had accused him of botching the last job in the Philippines, he didn't expect to hear from either of them again. Since 2012 Samia had been back in Roxboro, North Carolina, working on his custom gun holster business with David Stillwell as if the Manila trip had never happened.

Then on November 20, 2013, a former colleague from The Company named John O'Donoghue started a chat with Samia on Facebook.

O'DONOGHUE: you hear bout Tim and Joe?

SAMIA: . . . no what happen

O'DONOGHUE: read this

O'DONOGHUE: http://www.justice.gov/dea/divisions/hq/2013/
hq092713.shtml

SAMIA: Wow . . . holly Shit. . . .

O'DONOGHUE: That is crazy stuff. . . .

SAMIA: very stupid people

SAMIA: they are done. . . . they will never get out

O'DONOGHUE: yeah I would imagine not . . . I can't believe that they are that sloppy.

SAMIA: they got blinded by greed

Almost a year later, in September 2014, when Samia and O'Donoghue chatted again, O'Donoghue had figured out that it was Le Roux who had flipped and was taking people down with him.

SAMIA: Bro. . . . how are you doing . . . anything new . . . I am going crazy need to get back out!!

O'DONOGHUE: Nothing going on. Lachlan indicted by the Feds and will be arrested soon

SAMIA: what for what

O'DONOGHUE: Stuff he did for Le Roux

SAMIA: wtf . . . how many years ago was that from

O'DONOGHUE: Does not matter

SAMIA: did Le Roux get pop too

O'DONOGHUE: got lifted by the Feds in Brazil in 2012 and sang like a canary and set all his guys up

SAMIA: wow

SAMIA: scary shit dude

O'DONOGHUE: So far there have been ten guys who worked for him lifted in diff countries and extradited to US

SAMIA: wow holy shit

SAMIA: that is fucking BS

SAMIA: that's to bad for Lachlan he is a good guy

O'DONOGHUE: He's in a bad way at the moment

SAMIA: have they picked him up yet

O'DONOGHUE: Not yet

SAMIA: wonder if we r going to get brought in to this shit

O'Donoghue: No

O'Donoghue: They were all involved in drugs and taken down by the
DEA

Samia: dumb I would never fuck around with that shit

O'Donoghue: They got greedy and stupid

Three months later, on December 20, 2014, *The New York Times* revealed to the world what O'Donoghue and others on the inside had figured out: Paul Le Roux was in the custody of the DEA, and for the previous year he'd been working to bring down his own organization.

Samia and Stillwell's turn to "get brought into this shit" wouldn't arrive until seven months later, on the morning of July 22, 2015. Stillwell was out picking up some supplies for new holsters at the hardware store. On the way to his office, he was pulled over by a local sheriff and arrested. When the sheriff brought him to the county lockup, he was placed in an interrogation room. Samia was already at the station, having been lured with a question about his gun permits.

Two federal agents stepped into the room with Stillwell and introduced themselves as special agents Eric Stouch and Thomas Cindric from the DEA. "We work for the Special Operations Division out of Virginia," Stouch said, "and we're assigned to work investigations primarily overseas. For several years now we've been conducting an investigation that led us to you." They read Stillwell his rights, and after he declined to ask for a lawyer, began asking questions about his 2012 trip to the Philippines. At first, Stillwell claimed to be shocked by their insinuations, saying he'd only traveled to Manila, his first trip out of the country, to unwind with Samia.

But gradually the agents began to tell him drips of what they knew, and what they claimed Samia had already told them. "David, David," Stouch said. "I understand you're kind of blown away by the circumstances right now. Take a deep breath here, all right? You're a professional. You make holsters, you do it well. We're professionals, we do our jobs well. It's not a coincidence that Adam's in here today, and you're in here. We've come to you for a particular reason, but I think there's some saving grace here with your situation. I don't know, Tom, what do you think?"

"I think there is because . . . I don't think you pulled the trigger," Cindric said.

They told Stillwell they'd been examining his emails, his bank records, his travel receipts. They knew he was there when Lee was killed, Stouch said, "but we don't think you really liked it."

As the minutes passed, Stillwell repeatedly told the agents that he couldn't recall the events in Manila. "No, I get that!" Cindric said. "I get that. My problem is I don't really believe you. And I'll tell you why."

"Okay."

"Because there are significant events of people's lives, and one is watching another man pull out a gun and shoot somebody in the face, twice."

After an hour and a half of back and forth, Stillwell's resistance slowly began to fade, as Cindric patiently ground him down. "Did Adam Samia pull the trigger on that woman?" he finally asked.

"Yes."

"Were you present?"

"Yes."

"Did it happen in the van?"

"It was in a vehicle."

"Who was driving the vehicle?"

"I was driving."

"Were you shocked that he pulled the trigger?"

"Yeah," said Stillwell.

Samia, for his part, would admit only that he had known Hunter. "I've worked with him in the past, yes," he said, "doing security work." The jobs consisted of buying and securing gold in Africa, to be shipped to Hong Kong and Dubai. His 2012 trip to the Philippines had just been for some "advance work," he said. He was "flabbergasted" by the charges. "I've met these people, yes, I've worked with them in the past, but I did nothing, ever, illegal," he went on. "My brother's in law enforcement, all my family is in law enforcement, I've never done nothing wrong."

The agents quickly piled up circumstantial evidence alongside Stillwell's admissions. At Samia's house, they found a camera that contained surveillance photos of Catherine Lee's workplace, along with itineraries from the Philippines trip, and a keychain holding what appeared to be a key to a Toyota Innova van. On a camera of Stillwell's, they found photographs dated February 12, 2012—the day that Catherine Lee was murdered. According to court filings, the photos "appeared to depict, among other things, a white van similar to the one in which (according to witness accounts) Lee was murdered, and a wounded human head." And on a small notebook found in Samia's bedroom, they noticed that he'd written down "Mr. Le Roux, Paul Calder."

"The Fat Man, that's what we called him," Lachlan McConnell said. He was sitting across from me in December 2015 at a Starbucks outside of a mall in Makati City, Manila. A few days earlier, when I'd finally gotten ahold of him, he'd selected this spot for our meeting.

I'd been surprised that I ever heard back from McConnell, having tried without luck to contact him several times before arriving in the country. His name turned up on the website for a security contractor in Manila that listed him on its staff. I had started to assume that the listing was dated—it seemed farfetched that McConnell would be operating out in the open in the Philippines while a fugitive from an indictment in the United States. But one afternoon I decided to drop by the company's office anyway. I left my business card with the receptionist. Later that day, my phone rang. "I'm reluctant to talk on the phone," McConnell said. "There's certain things going on right now, which directly relate to my welfare." He was doing contract work on another Philippine island, but we could meet when he returned. "Literally, there is nothing we can put in writing," he continued. "It will put me in a situation where it will endanger me."

He arrived at the appointed hour, a white guy with thinning hair, in a polo shirt with folded reading glasses hanging from its open collar. "People are still really scared, because there is a strong belief that there are operations still going on," he said. "Money talks in this country. For five thousand pesos"—around $100— "you could have someone taken out." He lit a cigarette, the first of several, and dropped the pack on the table. His own concerns were largely legal: he was facing thirty-five federal criminal counts in the United States, for setting up companies and shipping accounts connected to RX Limited.

For the next hour, McConnell recounted his story, from his hiring by Dave Smith to the gold schemes in Hong Kong and the missions in Zimbabwe, to Smith's murder and Le Roux's threats at the Hard Rock Cafe, to his new duties in Florida and his mental breakdown. He'd always tried to stay on the right side of the law in his work for Le Roux, he said. But somewhere along the way his sense of right and wrong had warped. "Morally I knew it was wrong," he said. "I lost the plot."

McConnell told me that after leaving the organization, he began moving locations with his family, hoping there was no one on his tail. Eventually his paranoia eased, and he started working security again. He stopped hearing from Le Roux, and in 2013, he'd decided to go to the authorities with what he knew. He wrote a letter detailing what he believed to be Le Roux's crimes. Afraid that no agency in the Philippines could be trusted, he arranged for a friend to hand-deliver the letter to the U.S. embassy in Manila, with instructions not to give it to any non-American staff. He never heard back.

I caught up with him as he was trying again to switch sides, this time with a Philippine intelligence agency. McConnell had maintained copies of records about Le Roux's wealth, including his purchases of gold bars and of land that he'd bought in Western Australia. He estimated that there was $16 million in gold left in the Philippines alone, and his plan was to help the agency and other countries confiscate Le Roux's assets. In turn, he believed he would earn their protection against extradition to the United States. "I'm meeting with my handler today," he said. "I'm not asking for money. I think I'm doing the right thing. I want to help, with what little I know, to destroy what Paul Le Roux has left."

He wasn't the only one trying to find Le Roux's stashes. He'd heard talk of South African contractors showing up to ransack Le Roux's houses and dig up backyards. Corrupt Philippine law enforcement agencies, McConnell said, were desperately searching the country for their own share. He likened it to Yamashita's gold, a supposed stash of war loot left behind by General Tomoyuki Yamashita when the Japanese fled the Philippines during World War II. Countless prospectors had lost themselves to an obsession with finding it, wrecking their lives in a vain search for a treasure that was long gone, if it had ever been there at all.

31

The Mastermind

2016 . . . Giving up the fight . . . A shroud of secrecy . . . Le Roux on the stand . . . An Iranian connection

Federal cases often take years to wend their way to a jury, and very few ever make it there. Ninety-five percent end in a guilty plea, largely because most defendants lack the wherewithal to face the power of a federal prosecution—particularly one with the kinds of resources that had been brought to bear on the likes of Paul Le Roux's collaborators. Each member of the North Korean meth group faced multiple charges of conspiring to import drugs to the United States. Hunter, Gögel, and Vamvakias were accused of graver crimes, including conspiracy to murder a federal law enforcement agent and an informant. Soborski and Filter were hit with drug charges related to the Bahamas cocaine shipment for which they'd provided surveillance.

At first, it appeared that Joseph Hunter's case might bring Le Roux into the light. Hunter's court-appointed attorney, a New York criminal defense lawyer named Marlon Kirton, planned an unconventional defense that would use the government's own prized witness against them. In January 2015, he filed a motion asking the judge to dismiss the case against Hunter, alleging that the use of Le Roux as an informant amounted to "outrageous conduct" on the part of the government. In the filing, Kirton appeared to be laying the foundation for a rarely used, and even more rarely successful, defense known as duress. A claim of duress argues, essentially, that a defendant committed a crime because he faced an imminent threat of serious bodily harm or death. A person could be found innocent of a crime, in other words, if someone held a loaded gun to his head and told him to commit it. Hunter, the argument went, had gone along with the assassination plan only because he believed Le Roux would kill him if he refused.

Years before either man was arrested, Hunter claimed, Le Roux had threatened him and his family over a gold deal gone bad. And Hunter was in a unique position to know that Le Roux followed through on his threats. "Mr. _____ literally killed and threatened his associates with the full knowledge of his other associates," Kirton wrote in the motion. (Le Roux's name was still officially sealed, and Kirton was required to blank it out despite the fact that *The New York Times* had revealed it a month earlier.) "How then can law enforcement use this man to engage the same person as part of a reverse sting operation? What choice did Mr. Hunter have? The answer is death."

Hunter's argument was a thin reed, laced with the freakish irony that a man who had carried out hits for Le Roux claimed to be doing so out of fear of Le Roux's hit men. But given the evidence against Hunter, it appeared to be the only reed available.

Federal prosecutors in the Southern District of New York responded that even if Le Roux had threatened Hunter, it had happened long ago. Hunter had ample time to quit the organization and go to the police. Indeed, he himself admitted to having left the organization for a time, returning after his former boss, Dave Smith, was murdered.

Scott Stammers, in the North Korean methamphetamine case, made motions suggesting he might also pursue a duress defense. His lawyer demanded that the prosecution hand over, among other evidence, "all threats made by _____ to Scott Stammers," and "all killings carried out at the directive of _____."

But ultimately both Hunter and Stammers would end up where most federal defendants do. Several weeks after Kirton's filing, before the judge in the case had even ruled on it, Hunter changed his plea to guilty. Six months later, in August 2015, Stammers followed suit. Eventually, all ten defendants across both cases would do the same, pleading guilty and throwing themselves on the mercy of the court.

By the beginning of 2016, I'd been following these cases for two and half years, and Le Roux's name had never so much as been mentioned in an open courtroom. In court, lawyers for the defendants in New York were not only required to redact his name in filings, but to use elaborate hypotheticals to discuss anything related to Le Roux. "Imagine that you have the godfather," one attorney proposed to the judge, in a lengthy back and forth in open court. "A man who is immersed in the most horrific and pronounced crimes you can think of, including murders, and this godfather has his own security team that's involved in helping him carry out murders in organized crime."

At first the fanatical secrecy made sense: Through at least mid-2014, Le Roux was essentially an undercover DEA operative in U.S. custody. By virtue of his cooperation, agents were able to build their elaborate sting operations around the fiction that he was still out in the world; it was essential that his subordinates believe Le Roux was still free, calling the shots. But once the underlings had been arrested, the utility of that fiction evaporated. After his name became international news in December 2014, it was rendered ridiculous. Le Roux might have been able to convince Oz that a 2013 Brazilian newspaper story about him was fake news, but the revelation in *The New York Times* that he was in U.S. custody ended his life as pretend drug boss.

Still, the government guarded facts about Le Roux with the same zealous secrecy, propelled by an internal logic that was itself closed to interrogation. His name might have been public, but Le Roux's case file remained sealed. So, too, did significant portions of the prosecution's cases against Hunter and his team of would-be assassins, the group arrested for trafficking North Korean meth, and the RX Limited defendants indicted in Minnesota.

Even the name of Le Roux's defense attorney was treated like a state secret. In a closed proceeding in August 2013, Le Roux had dispensed with Marvinny, his appointed attorney, and hired a New York criminal lawyer named B. Alan Seidler. ("I was on the case for a while, and now I'm not," was all Marvinny would tell me when I reached him by phone.) Sometime later Le Roux fired Seidler, too, hiring another attorney whose name was sealed. No one I spoke with, including a former federal prosecutor who had worked on sensitive terrorism cases, could find any precedent for sealing an attorney's name when the defendant's name was public. What made the maneuver even more mystifying was that Le Roux's new attorney wasn't appointed by the court. He was being paid by Le Roux—out of what funds was anyone's guess—and could quit the case any time he wished.

Now, as one defendant after another folded and admitted his guilt, any hope I'd had that Le Roux himself might ever be called to testify seemed to be draining away. But there was one defendant whose attorneys thought they had a way to bring Le Roux into the open.

"The government is embarrassed," Robert Richman, one of Moran Oz's attorneys, told me when I traveled to Minneapolis to interview Oz in December 2015. "They don't want to admit that Le Roux is involved." Richman and the other half of Oz's defense team, Joe Friedberg, had started to think their client had the basis for a duress defense. Oz, after all, had been thrown off a boat and shot at by Le Roux's henchman. The only problem was that Linda

Marks, the Department of Justice lawyer prosecuting the case, exhibited no intention of calling Le Roux as a witness much less making him available to Oz's attorneys for a deposition.

At first, their attempts to gain access to Le Roux amounted to legal filings mocking the government's absurd level of secrecy. When they'd asked to speak to Le Roux's attorney, the prosecutor told them that "counsel for Le Roux has requested anonymity because he fears for his safety from 'international associates of Mr. Le Roux,'" Richman and Friedman wrote in a brief. "Given that Mr. Le Roux is more dangerous than any of his associates, one wonders whether the masked attorney has identified himself to his own client. Perhaps even Mr. Le Roux does not know the identity of his attorney, with all meetings conducted in a confessional, perhaps, or with a curtain separating the two, voice disguised." When they'd suggested that they might subpoena Le Roux, Marks had replied that they could do so "only if he is in the United States," and then refused to indicate whether he was. "We feel reasonably confident that Mr. Le Roux is somewhere on planet Earth, but that is only an inference," Richman and Friedman wrote. Wherever he was, they argued that it should be Le Roux who was facing a jury, not underlings like Oz. "The government's use of Mr. Le Roux as an informant is even more egregious here because the government has cut a deal with the principal architect and leader of the alleged criminal enterprise, while prosecuting his employees," they concluded. "It is as if Microsoft was a criminal enterprise, and the government cuts a deal with Bill Gates to take down the entire shipping department."

Mockery aside, the filings were part of a serious legal gambit that Richman and Friedman thought might force the government's hand. The case against Oz was based in part on calls between Le Roux, in U.S. custody, and Oz, in Israel. Digging through the evidence, Richman realized that the U.S. Attorney's Office had recorded them without a warrant. So he filed a motion to have the material suppressed, arguing that U.S. federal law required at least one party consent to a recorded phone call. Richman knew that

Oz certainly hadn't given his permission. Had Le Roux? The government produced statements from DEA agents saying that he had. But Richman and Friedberg argued that if the government wanted to prove Le Roux did so voluntarily, the man himself would need to say it under oath. "Defendant Moran Oz moves for an order requiring the government to produce its favorite informant, Paul Calder Le Roux, to testify at the motion hearing," Richman wrote.

After a few weeks of back and forth, in mid-January 2016 the judge finally handed down a decision: "IT IS HEREBY ORDERED that Defendant Moran Oz's Motion to Produce Government Informant Paul Calder Le Roux for a Motion Hearing is GRANTED."

After years of chasing Le Roux's shadow, at first online and then around the world, here finally was my chance to see him face-to-face, at least in a courtroom. I arrived in Minneapolis on a clear, frigid morning in early March. The hearing was across the river in St. Paul, and I ran into Richman and Friedberg at a café beforehand. They showed me a copy of what appeared to be a fake local arrest record for Le Roux, on cocaine charges, concocted by the Department of Justice as a cover story for his transfer to the Minnesota jail. It was evidence that Le Roux was nearby—and of how far federal prosecutors had gone to keep him under wraps.

There was also some bad news. "Le Roux's lawyer filed an emergency motion to seal the courtroom," Richman told me. In a letter to the court that was itself sealed, the anonymous lawyer argued that Le Roux's family would be put in jeopardy by allowing the media to report on the proceedings. Some of Le Roux's former employees, like Lachlan McConnell, were still at large, and could represent a danger to people close to Le Roux. Later, I got a copy of the letter, which amounted to an unusual prosecution-sanctioned list of accusations against Le Roux's associates. "For example, Chris De Meyer, a former Special Forces French Foreign Legion Sniper, is an un-indicted coconspirator in the Hunter case," the attorney wrote. "De Meyer, known to have access to weapons, is at large and resides approximately 40 minutes from Leroux's ex-wife. De Meyer also participated in murders with and for Hunter. He was a consistent member of Hunter's murder for hire group." He was, the letter asserted, responsible for the murder of Noimie Edillor, shooting her in the head.

The judge allowed the press in the courtroom to hear his decision on the sealing order, and I took a seat in the back of the courtroom, alongside some local reporters and Oz's wife, who had moved from Israel with their two kids. A few minutes later, Oz arrived in jeans and a black jacket, wearing the same dark, trim beard as when I'd met him in 2015. For a man about to share a courtroom with the ex-boss who'd had him shot at and set up, he appeared buoyant. When Richman showed him a printout of Le Roux's fake local arrest record, he laughed aloud.

Linda Marks, the prosecutor, had dark, swept-back hair and was wearing a black suit, sitting with another prosecutor at a table across the courtroom. They'd both flown in from Washington.

The judge opened the hearing by noting the request from Le Roux's attorney to close the courtroom. "Let me turn first to Mr. Oz's counsel," he said. "Do you continue to assert your constitutional rights to have an open hearing, Mr. Richman?"

"Yes, your honor," Richman replied. "I find this procedure somewhat baffling." Le Roux, he pointed out, was a government informant. His name was now public, and court hearings are typically sealed only at the behest of the government, not a witness's private attorney. "This is a matter that has generated great interest," Richman continued. "There are members of the press in the back of the courtroom, as well as Mr. Oz's family." Richman pointed out that Le Roux's identity had been revealed over a year before and "no harm has fallen on the family. And that document also suggests that the government has taken steps to protect the family."

The moment had arrived that could decide whether Le Roux would be forced to publicly answer for his past—from the pharmacy network to the drug-running to the arms shipments to the murders—and for his work on behalf of the U.S. government.

"I am going to deny the request," the judge finally said. "Nothing has been established that would override the strong interest that the defendant has in a public proceeding."

And with that, the hearing began. Linda Marks called Special Agent Eric Stouch, from the DEA Special Operations Division, who entered in a suit, holding a pair of eyeglasses. Stouch testified succinctly to the fact that Le Roux had cooperated voluntarily, that he'd been an eager participant in the sting operation. On cross-examination, Richman—hoping to establish that Le Roux had been so desperate for a deal that he had lied about Oz's role—pressed Stouch on whether Le Roux had ever been promised that he wouldn't be extradited to another country, or that he would avoid facing the death penalty. Stouch admitted that Le Roux had voiced concern about being extradited, but denied that the government had made him any assurances.

Richman then attempted to drive home another point. After the DEA had arrested Le Roux, he asked, wasn't he then allowed to keep operating the same pharmacy network that the United States had sought for years to shut down?

"The Internet pharmacy was still operating, but was winding down," Stouch said.

"And as part of that process of operating the pharmacy, he was continuing to transfer cash to pay salaries and pay doctors and so on, correct?" Richman asked.

"He was transferring cash to pay salaries."

"And that was obviously with the consent of the U.S. government, correct?"

"Yes."

"So during that period of time the U.S. government was operating the Internet pharmacy, correct?"

Linda Marks objected, and it wasn't hard to see why. If the government was going to argue that RX Limited put its customers in danger, they would have to answer for why they had given Le

Roux access to his money so he could keep it operating, just to let them catch lower-level employees.

"Overruled," the judge said.

"No, we were in the process of having him wind it down," Stouch said. "It was still operating and he was paying salaries. Whether the U.S. government was operating the pharmacy, I—we were in the process of shutting it down."

After Stouch, Marks called Travis Ocken, a DEA agent from Minneapolis who had helped Brill in the later stages of the RX Limited case, and had been by Le Roux's side when he communicated with Moran Oz. Ocken also testified to the fact the Le Roux had made the calls voluntarily.

Now it was Richman's turn. "Your honor," he said. "We call Paul Calder Le Roux."

Le Roux entered the courtroom through a side door, escorted by two plainclothes United States marshals. He had a slightly unruly beard that was a darker shade than his silver hair, but otherwise looked surprisingly tropical in a billowy, lemon-yellow T-shirt and orange correctional pants. He was still a fat man—his fake arrest record listed him at six feet, 280 pounds—but he'd lost some weight in his three and a half years in custody.

The marshals unshackled his arms and pointed him to the elevated witness stand. He scanned the courtroom intently as he settled into the chair, as if puzzled by the people who had shown up to see him. For a moment we locked eyes, or at least I thought we did. But his gaze quickly moved on, with an expression of bemused curiosity.

If Le Roux's anonymous lawyer was in attendance, he didn't make his presence known. So, in what amounted to a contorted legal setup, Le Roux—a potential defense witness—was functionally represented by Marks, who offered periodic objections that were indistinguishable from those she might have made for her own witness.

Furthering the role-reversal, Richman adopted an approach not unlike that of a prosecutor questioning a defendant about his crimes. He approached the podium and began by asking Le Roux what his profession was.

Le Roux thought for a moment, then responded in what sounded to my ears like a South African accent, flattened by years abroad—and Le Roux's own efforts to shed it. "Essentially," he said, "I worked as a programmer for many years."

The ostensible purpose of the hearing, to establish whether Le Roux had consented to recordings of his phone calls with Moran Oz, was accomplished in minutes. But Richman was after more, and he pushed Le Roux to admit to a list of the same facts that I had been chasing for years. He confirmed that he had created the encryption software E4M, but denied that he had developed True-Crypt, its famous progeny. He copped to some of his aliases, including Johan Smit, Bernard Bowlins, and John Smith. He admitted having organized the two-hundred-kilo cocaine shipment on the *JeReVe,* out of Ecuador.

It was when Richman began asking about the murders that the casualness of Le Roux's admissions became most dissonant.

"You knew that your legal situation was far worse than just a methamphetamine charge, correct?" Richman asked, probing Le Roux's motives for cooperating.

"In what way?" Le Roux asked. He leaned back in his chair, his arms folded.

"Well, for example, you ordered multiple murders, correct?"

"Yes, that's true."

"And, for example, you ordered the murder of a Filipino customs agent, correct?"

"That's not correct," Le Roux said, leaning into the microphone and furrowing his brow in mild irritation. There, in the skeptical narrowing of his eyes, he displayed the sense of superiority that I heard many of his employees and family members describe.

"What is not correct about it?"

"The individual wasn't a customs agent," Le Roux said. It was a trivial objection: The victim in question, Noimie Edillor, was a part-time real estate agent who also worked for Le Roux, helping him move items through customs.

"So it was a real estate agent, correct?" Richman continued.

"Correct."

"And then there was a second real estate agent, correct?"

"Correct."

"Who was also murdered on your orders, correct?"

"That's true." There was nothing approaching contrition in his manner, nor a hint of any emotion at all. When Le Roux then admitted that he had also ordered the killing of Dave Smith, his tone was as cold and flat as if he had just confirmed what he had been served for breakfast.

Richman walked Le Roux through his decision to cooperate with the U.S. government, fishing for evidence that he'd done so under pressure from the DEA, or in exchange for promises that he would avoid extradition or the death penalty. The greater the benefit that Le Roux expected from the government for his cooperation, the more likely it was that he would lie to help them convict Moran Oz.

"The government has given no assurances in the plea deal," Le Roux replied, sounding well-practiced. "They simply state that they will make it known to the court if I'm truthful and I provide information that's of substantial assistance." He acknowledged that when he'd decided to cooperate on the plane back to the U.S., he'd been formally charged in only the meth deal. The possible sentence was ten years to life, but as Le Roux helpfully pointed out to Richman, the recommended sentence was "only around twelve years."

As Richman tried to maneuver him into admitting that he had cooperated out of fear, Le Roux nimbly deflected him.

Did Le Roux know, Richman asked, that Adam Samia and David Stillwell were being prosecuted in New York for Catherine Lee's murder, and that if he himself had been charged, he could have faced the death penalty?

"I'm not aware of how the laws relate to that case, so I couldn't answer that," Le Roux said.

"You don't know whether you could face the death penalty if you were charged with a murder in the United States?"

"I don't know the law here, so I couldn't answer that," Le Roux said. "If you say so."

When it came to other countries' laws, though, Le Roux displayed a rather detailed knowledge. He admitted that he was vulnerable to criminal charges in the Philippines and Ecuador—the latter "since the cocaine shipment originated there." He'd committed no crimes in Brazil, he said, because it "lacks a conspiracy law." As for his adventures in Somalia, he argued, "Somalia lacks any government, so I am not concerned about whatever actions took place there because they are not crimes."

By this point, Richman had achieved his goal, and the judge seemed to have reached the limit of the latitude he was willing to grant. Richman tried one more gambit. "Isn't it true that you had a reputation for killing people who stole from you?" he asked.

"That is an exaggeration," Le Roux said.

"Nothing further, your honor."

After a brief cross-examination, in which Linda Marks reestablished that Le Roux had agreed to have his phone calls and email monitored, the hearing was over. Two marshals shackled Le Roux and escorted him back through the side door.

Outside the courtroom, Oz's other attorney, Friedberg, seemed almost triumphant, even though the defense team would ultimately lose the motion to throw out the phone and email records. They'd flushed Le Roux out into the open, and if they called him as a witness at Oz's trial, they could easily establish his murderous past through his own admissions. "Certainly, the phone calls will come into evidence, we always knew that," he said. "Getting a look at this guy is worth a lot to us."

The hearing had finally breached the wall of secrecy surrounding Le Roux, or at least a section of it. The same day, a federal judge in New York unsealed a portion of his case file in the Southern District. The docket showed that Le Roux had formally pleaded guilty, after a year of cooperation, at the end of 2013. His final plea deal remained sealed, but the "information" he had signed was now available. There, at last, were the criminal counts that Le Roux was on the hook for: the meth importation plan, computer hacking, and bribery of a foreign official. The information also included crimes that he'd admitted but would never be prosecuted for, including that he had solicited or participated in seven murders. The names were redacted, but it wasn't hard for me to fill them in: Dave Smith, Noimie Edillor, Catherine Lee, Joe Frank Zuñiga, Bruce Jones, Herbert Tan Tiu, and Chito—the man who had tipped off the Philippine police to Tiu's gun stash. Kent Bailey told me that Le Roux denied ordering the daylight assassination of Michael Lontoc, the Philippine target shooter who ran the organization's gun shop in Manila, claiming someone else killed him over a gambling debt.

There was another remarkable fact in Le Roux's unsealed docket, one that held the key to the incredible secrecy surrounding him. Le Roux had confessed to selling technology to the government of Iran, a crime in the United States. Finally I understood why Le Roux had been treated like a national security asset: He was one. Or at least a potential asset. Later, I learned from the former 960 agent that the DEA hadn't been able to turn Le Roux's information about Iran into actionable intelligence. "We were trying to work with the FBI, it just didn't go anywhere," he said. The Obama administration, he said, refused to allow the DEA to send anyone into Iran to pick up the trail of Le Roux's contacts. And they'd missed out on Nestor Del Rosario, who had approached the Australians willing to cooperate before he disappeared. "I don't blame him," the former agent said. "I wish we would have talked to him because he's the one who could really spell out the whole Iranian situation."

Le Roux's North Korean connections, via a Chinese triad group, similarly fizzled. Ye Tiong Tan Lim, the man convicted in the North Korean meth sting, had declined to cooperate, leaving the DEA with no path into the organization. "Lim plays a role of a poor, little old guy," the former 960 agent said. "Lim is legit. He's scared his family would be murdered. And he's probably right. We just never got far with him. We needed him because we didn't understand it. And we would have had to go into Hong Kong. They don't like the Americans."

Le Roux had leveraged his way into a deal with the U.S. government based on a promise that had largely dissolved into vapor, aside from the former employees he'd helped set up. Kent Bailey, for one, believed that the 960 agents had been starstruck by headline-grabbing possibilities and let themselves believe that Le Roux could deliver something bigger than himself. "These are the countries that are in the news, these are hot frickin' items," Bailey said. "His pipe dream was that he was dealing directly with some general in the Iranian army, and Iran was talking about building missiles for nuclear weapons. But people in that world think they are bigger than they are."

32

The Trial

2016–2017 . . . Kent Bailey in the flesh . . . The observer effect . . . McConnell gets pinched . . . RX Limited on trial . . . An outcome foretold

In the spring of 2016, I published a series of articles about Le Roux online, in *The Atavist Magazine,* laying out the still incomplete picture of what I'd learned. The stories, which unfolded at the pace of one article a week between March and May, generated an influx of new sources. Each time a new article went online, I'd hear from people eager to relay their own Le Roux experiences. Some tips came in the form of cryptic emails from anonymous sources offering secrets that went far beyond what I'd reported. A manila envelope arrived at my house containing a foreign government's intelligence report on Le Roux. Someone who claimed to have ties to the U.S. embassy in Manila wrote with information about the status of Lachlan McConnell. A whistleblower at an investment firm in Hong Kong contacted me to provide information on Le Roux's financial records, and Le Roux's relatives emailed with stories of the confident young genius they had known. These I had mostly expected. What I hadn't anticipated were the ways in which I now became a minor participant in the drama myself.

It was, in part, a byproduct of the wall of secrecy the U.S. government had constructed around Le Roux. To the extent that I had pierced it slightly—building on revelations in *The New York Times* and elsewhere—I'd filled a vacuum that the government had created. Defense attorneys who had been denied any information about Le Roux began citing my articles in their court filings, hoping to mitigate the crimes to which their clients had pleaded guilty. Scott Stammers's attorney submitted the articles as evidence that "there was no 'Organization' as alleged by the government, in which Mr. Stammers was a manager. Instead, there was one person, Le Roux, who orchestrated crimes of a massive scale." Philip Shackels's attorney argued that his client lived in fear of Le Roux. "This is corroborated, as we point out in our papers, by reporting by different sources, including the Atavist," he wrote. Joseph Hunter's attorney pointed to the articles as evidence that no statements from Le Roux should be believed on their face. One day at a hearing in the RX Limited case, I puzzled over the familiarity of a photo presented by a defense attorney, only to realize that *I had taken it*, and then had sent it to the lawyer hoping to get his client to verify the location.

Throughout my reporting on Le Roux I had the experience of becoming simultaneously a seeker of information and a source of it. Never before had I chased a story in which so many subjects threw up their hands mid-interview and turned my questions back on me. Could I help them find someone across the world, in the Philippines, or supply a document that a government refused to provide? Could I explain where Le Roux was, and whether he would ever be released from prison? I found myself saying over and over, "Well, I'm not a defense investigator," or, "I'm not a government agent." But now, after some of my reporting was public, I was experiencing a journalistic analog of what in quantum physics is called the observer effect: the inability of a researcher to study a phenomenon without themselves altering it.

My reporting had come full circle in sometimes unsettling ways. I received an email from the ex-girlfriend of a defendant, who contacted me to say that she had a laptop that he'd had given her years before. It had a separate user login, protected by a password she didn't know. She wanted to find out if she had to send it to the police, or if she could just send it to me. After consulting with an attorney, I told her I didn't think that she was required to do anything with it. But given that I couldn't crack it myself, her choices were to contact the U.S. Attorney's office or to keep quiet about it. She chose the former, and I later heard that Thomas Cindric from SOD flew out to her home to retrieve it.

I heard, too, from an accountant in Florida who found my name in a search for Robert McGowan, the Zimbabwean I'd written about. The accountant, who specialized in finding and obtaining lost corporate assets, said he had discovered "unclaimed money related to a former company he registered here in the United States." As the sole director, McGowan would be entitled to reclaim his lost assets. He said the amount was around $50,000. I couldn't locate a journalistic ethics guide that addressed the situation, so I just forwarded the note on to McGowan and left it to him whether to take Le Roux's forgotten money. After all, his name had been listed, without his knowledge, on the incorporation papers. Maybe it was poetic justice.

Before one of my trips to Manila, Joseph Hunter let it be known through an associate that he was concerned about my safety. Be careful, he said. I had trouble processing the idea that the former head of an international kill team was now telling me—out of concern for my welfare—to watch my back. Hunter also relayed a request that I pick up some notebooks and mixed martial arts DVDs he'd left behind in Manila with a friend. Worried that I was being set up, I offered to meet the contact in a public place to look at the items. The contact never showed.

In April 2016, an anonymous tipster emailed to say that Lachlan McConnell had been detained in the Philippines and was facing deportation. For a moment I wondered if it had been my articles that had prompted this, but the truth was much more mundane: Unable to persuade the Philippines to extradite him, the United States had pressured Canadian authorities to cancel his passport. Interpol had issued a "red notice" for McConnell's arrest, and without a valid passport, he was no longer legally allowed to remain in the country. The Philippine police arrested him on immigration charges at his office in Makati, near where he and I had met. A few months later he arrived in Minnesota.

Thunderclouds were gathering over the Minneapolis skyline on the afternoon I walked into Psycho Suzi's Motor Lounge, a tiki bar hugging a bank of the Mississippi just across from downtown. Kent Bailey was already seated at a table out back, overlooking the river. I'd come to town after months of trying to pin him down for an interview, and spent a day waiting for him to break free from a case. "I'm out on the street with my group," he texted me. "We have a search and arrest warrant we need to serve. Of course, we are on doper time." Now he said he had a few hours before an agent's going-away party. One minute after I sat down, the skies opened up, and we hustled inside.

I asked him why he was finally willing to talk now. He was planning to retire in a year, he said. Kimberly Brill was the real brains behind the operation anyway, and he wanted to give her the credit she was too modest to take. "The other thing is, you know what? I ain't hiding anything," he said. "You know what I mean? It is what it is. I think that the story deserves to be put out there." Bailey walked me through the case, from Kimberly Brill and Steven Holdren's first bust of AltGeld, the Chicago pharmacy, to his travels around the world seeking foreign cooperation, to watching the *JeReVe* sail off across the Pacific. "Over the years I've prided myself on working the biggest and best cases," he said. "Le Roux is the *guy*. He's the smartest drug dealer I've ever faced."

Now, though, Bailey seemed concerned that the case against RX Limited's employees was dragging on, with no trial dates in sight. Of the eleven original defendants, three had taken deals and pleaded guilty, including Jon Wall, the Israeli American who'd worked as Le Roux's shipper in Kentucky. In exchange for testifying against Oz and the remaining defendants, prosecutors allowed him to plead guilty to one of his twenty-three counts, carrying a maximum of five years in prison.

Three more RX Limited figures were still at large. Omer Bezalel, the Israeli who'd worked with McConnell in Florida, had, like Oz, been lured to Romania and then extradited to Minnesota. But after he was released on bail to a halfway house, he walked away, presumably returning to Israel, beyond the reach of American authorities. Alon Berkman was in hiding. Shai Reuven, according to beach and nightclub photos he posted on Facebook, seemed to be living unperturbed in the Philippines.

That left five defendants who had refused to take plea deals: Moran Oz and Lachlan McConnell, who were accused of handling operations for the network; Prabhakara Tumpati and another Pennsylvania doctor, Elias Karkalas, who'd written prescriptions for it; and the pharmacist from Detroit, Babubhai Patel, who was already serving a seventeen-year sentence for healthcare fraud. Charles Schultz, like most of the other pharmacists, was indicted in his home state. He pleaded to a single count of conspiracy to distribute controlled substances. "I only have myself to blame," he said in court. A judge fined him $350,000, but declined to impose jail time due to Schultz's failing health. "The prosecution of him was an act of cruelty," his lawyer Hal Harlowe told me. "He was old and infirm. He had gone through his whole life with a good reputation. I think convicting an eighty-two-year-old man to have another notch in their belt was unfortunate."

I asked Bailey why the myriad other people involved in the organization at different levels, from Levi Kugel to Tomer Taggart, escaped indictment. Why prosecute this group, among the many people who'd arguably played serious roles in the business. "There is always going to be somebody who by the grace of God missed it," Bailey said. "It comes down to prosecutorial discretion." The investigators had made their argument, he said, barely containing his bitterness. The prosecutors had chosen the targets. Everyone else was going to skate.

A trial date for Oz and McConnell was finally set for early 2017, almost three years after Paul Le Roux had lured Oz to Romania for the sting, and nearly ten since Kimberly Brill and Steven Holdren had first started poking into RX Limited. They were going to be tried together, alongside the pair of RX Limited doctors from Pennsylvania, Karkalas and Tumpati. Linda Marks's team still refused to make information about Le Roux available, despite the fact that he was the world's most knowledgeable person about RX Limited, and already in U.S. custody. But if the government was doing everything in its power to keep Le Roux out of the trial, the defense attorneys were planning to make him the star of it.

On the morning of February 7, I arrived at the courthouse in St. Paul for the opening day of the trial, in the courtroom of Judge Susan Richard Nelson. The gallery was sparsely populated, no more than a half dozen people, and over the weeks of the trial I would become familiar with my fellow attendees: Oz's wife and a rabbi who came along for support, an occasional local reporter, and, most days, Kimberly Brill from the DEA. The real action was at the attorneys' tables, where each of the four defendants was flanked by a pair of lawyers, and where Linda Marks sat with her team of three prosecutors. (The case of Patel, the Detroit pharmacist, had been severed from the others that morning, and his charges were later dropped.)

"All four of these defendants are charged with conspiring to distribute prescription drugs over the Internet without valid prescriptions," U.S. Attorney Roger Gural said in his opening statement to the jury. "Defendants' Internet operation was not designed to provide medical supervision; it was designed to make money. And some of these defendants made a lot of money." He painted a picture of a conspiracy operating without regard for either the laws of the United States or the safety of customers. "It was quick, just provide a name, a shipping address, what drug you wanted, the quantity you wanted, your credit card information, and a reason for ordering, and a few days later, your drugs would show up at your doorstep.

"You will hear a lot about Paul Le Roux, but he's not on trial here," Gural continued. "This trial is about these four defendants and their conduct, which was to create an international network of website operators, business managers, doctors, and pharmacies that agree to work together to sell massive quantities of prescription drugs to customers in the United States."

Each of the defendants intended to offer a variation on an unconventional defense. They would freely admit to most of the facts as Gural had laid them out. Oz, McConnell, Tumpati, and Karkalas had all clearly participated in RX Limited, in their various capacities. But since they believed that what they were doing was legal, they weren't culpable, even if it turned out that they'd been wrong. "As far as Moran Oz knew, the company and everything he did for the company was completely legal," his attorney, Robert Richman, said in his opening statement. In a different type of criminal trial—for murder, say, or robbery—such a defense would be impossible. Murder is murder, even if you somehow don't know murder is illegal. But the charges brought against Oz and his fellow defendants required what's called mens rea, knowledge on the part of the accused that they are breaking the law.

Oz's and McConnell's attorneys both planned an additional gambit: They would use the duress defense that Hunter had briefly floated before he'd pleaded guilty. Oz and McConnell, the narrative went, had both done Le Roux's bidding because they feared that if they defied him, he would kill them. Oz's defense would hinge on the boat incident in Subic Bay. McConnell's—constructed by the husband-and-wife defense team Marie and Ryan Pacyga—would center on the killing of his friend Dave Smith, and Le Roux's subsequent statement: "I didn't need Dave, you're lucky I need you."

To support their duress defenses, they would do what the prosecution would not: put Joseph Hunter and Paul Le Roux on the stand. "You have heard that RX Limited was owned by Paul Calder Le Roux," Richman told the jury. "What the government neglected to mention to you is that Paul Calder Le Roux is a ruthless, vicious, international criminal. He is a murderer, a drug dealer, and a weapons smuggler. The U.S. government arrested Paul Le Roux in 2012. He is now in federal prison. He should be the one on trial here, but instead he cut a deal with the government to cooperate. The prosecution has hardly even mentioned Paul Le Roux, but we are going to call him to testify in this trial because we want you to know the full story."

On a break the first morning of the trial, Oz and I greeted each other just outside the courtroom. He projected the same warm confidence as he had in our first meeting back in December 2015. "I still can't believe I'm here and he got a deal," he said of Le Roux. He wasn't allowed to work in the United States under the conditions of his bail, so he occupied much of his time studying the Torah. He and his wife had a third child while he'd been awaiting trial. "I'm getting to spend a lot of time with my kids, which I wouldn't get to do in Israel," he said. I asked him if he'd ever considered running, like Bezalel and Berkman had. "No, that's not me, I want to face it because I didn't do anything wrong. I have a family. I have kids. I can't spend my life looking over my shoulder."

From the opening day, the prosecution's case felt muddled, formless. At times they seemed uncertain about what story they were telling. The RX Limited network was a tangled ecosystem of websites, affiliates, doctors, pharmacists, and customer service centers, driven by technology that was not always simple to explain. Each of the defendants represented a different part of that ecosystem, but the story of their guilt always seemed just out of reach.

Marks and her colleagues were sitting on a mountain of evidence, but it quickly became clear that much of it would be useless. Without putting Le Roux on the stand to testify to how it all worked and who did what, they were left to connect fragments of disparate dots themselves. Making matters worse, the prosecutors seemed inexperienced in basic trial procedures. Over and over Judge Nelson sustained defense objections to the prosecution's evidence as third-hand information contained in emails, or asserted by witnesses—at one point stopping to explain to them the basic principle of what constituted hearsay evidence.

If the prosecution was going to convince the jury, it would have to be through its star witnesses, the federal agents who worked on the case. On the second day, Steven Holdren meticulously explained how the RX Limited model worked, and how he and Brill had first uncovered it. But even basic questions about the controlled buys unavoidably devolved into technical arcana.

> HOLDREN: The receipt contained an address, SystemCA.com.
>
> Q: And what, if anything, did you find out about SystemCA.com?
>
> HOLDREN: Conducted a WHOIS search. "WHOIS" is a public database that allows you to identify the owner of a domain name or an IP address. So I conducted a WHOIS search on SystemsCA .com and also Cartadmin.com that was observed during the payment process, and discovered that both names were registered by the domain name registrar ABSystems.
>
> Q: And so that's what led you to requesting records from ICANN on ABSystems?
>
> HOLDREN: Correct.

All of it was fascinating, and certainly would have implicated Paul Le Roux, had he been the one on trial. But he wasn't. He was the man the prosecutors were desperately trying to keep *out* of the courtroom. It was as if the government had decided to proceed with the case they would have tried against Le Roux, instead of the one they were left with, the case against his underlings.

Kimberly Brill testified twice over the course of the prosecution's case. Each was long and grueling: first she was questioned for multiple days by the prosecution, then cross-examined by four separate defense attorneys in turn. On the stand she seemed calm and practiced, if sometimes annoyed at the questions. ("No, I did not record the call," she said at one point, cutting off an elaborate sequence of queries from Robert Richman about an undercover phone buy. "So, you're feeling a little defensive about the fact that you did not record the call, I take it?" he replied. "I don't feel defensive," she said, smiling tightly. "I just knew where you were going.") But her tone sometimes registered the same friendly irritation with her own prosecutors as she displayed to their opponents.

Even in Brill's testimony, Marks and Gural quickly ran headlong into the original challenge that the DEA investigators had faced at the start of the case: The drugs sold by RX Limited weren't listed as controlled. Much of the prosecution hinged on the idea that Fioricet, one of the big three drugs sold by RX Limited, could be classified as a controlled substance. The reality was more complicated: one ingredient in it, butalbital, was indeed a Schedule III controlled substance. But Fioricet, which combined barbituric acid with caffeine and Tylenol, was trapped in a gray area. So gray, in fact, that Brill was forced to admit on the stand that she'd had to consult a lawyer at the DEA to determine Fioricet's status. Gray enough that, as the defense gleefully pointed out, the head of the DEA himself had testified before Congress—right in the middle of the Le Roux investigation in 2011—that Fioricet was "exempted" from the law. Partway through their own prosecution, the government gave up on the argument and dropped the portion of the charges related to controlled drugs.

That still left dozens of charges against the four defendants, just based on the fact that they'd prescribed drugs without a doctor's visit. But prosecutors would still have to show that operators like Oz and McConnell knew that what they were doing was illegal.

The testimony of Jon Wall—Le Roux's former shipping manager from Kentucky, who had taken a plea deal—represented their best hope of doing so. It started off well enough, with Wall describing how he had worked for Le Roux's call centers in the Philippines. He testified that he knew Oz handled money for RX Limited, and that the one time they met in the Philippines, they had played poker. He recounted how, back in the United States, he'd been Le Roux's go-to shipper, buying everything from planes and boats to logging equipment and art. When Le Roux had charged him with recruiting pharmacies in the States, he said, he'd started to believe what he was doing was illegal. The obvious implication was that the other RX Limited employees should have drawn the same conclusion.

On cross-examination by Oz's lawyer Friedberg, however, Wall lost his footing. At first, Friedberg seemed to be goading him into talking as much as possible about Le Roux:

FRIEDBERG: Could you list for the jury the friends you're aware that Mr. Le Roux had?

WALL: When you say "friends," what do you mean?

FRIEDBERG: I don't know if I can do any better than that. Did you know of him to ever have a friend?

WALL: Not really.

FRIEDBERG: Okay. Do you know why?

WALL: I guess people didn't like him very much.

FRIEDBERG: Why?

WALL: He was unpleasant to be around often.

FRIEDBERG: All right. You apparently handled some lawsuits for him, did you not?

WALL: Just one.

FRIEDBERG: How did you do that?

WALL: Uh, it was pretty easy. He bribed the judge.

FRIEDBERG: Did you know he bribed the judge?

WALL: Yes.

FRIEDBERG: How did you know he bribed the judge?

WALL: The attorney told me.

But then, when pressed on how he'd known the prescription drug business was illegal, Wall dropped a bombshell: Le Roux had once told him so, on the phone. Within minutes of making the statement, the defense attorneys had shredded his testimony with the simple observation that he'd never mentioned this phone call in any previous sworn statements. Seemingly overeager to show his worth as a witness, Wall had tripped himself up. The prosecution later had to admit that they had no record of Wall ever making the claim. He had either lied at the time, or he was lying now. Eventually, Judge Nelson ruled that the jury be instructed to discount Wall's testimony entirely.

To incriminate the doctors, the prosecution put forward other former RX Limited physicians and pharmacists, most of whom had taken deals and now testified that they'd always suspected RX Limited was illegal. Among them was Anu Konakanchi, the doctor whom Prabhakara Tumpati had recruited into RX Limited, back when they were so close he had called her "sister."

After two weeks, the prosecution rested, and the defense prepared to present their case. Federal marshals flew Le Roux to Minneapolis, where he waited in preparation for his own turn on the witness stand. Joseph Hunter was transported out of his federal prison cell in Kansas to Oklahoma, where he awaited a final trip to Minnesota. As the prosecution concluded their case, it appeared headed for a showdown with Paul Le Roux at the center.

Still, I couldn't help wondering what I'd just witnessed. Much of the prosecution's case seemed to rely on, as one of Oz's lawyers described it, "an aura of mild criminality." Clearly Oz, McConnell, and the doctors were at times eager and willing participants in various facets of RX Limited's operation. But the evidence meant to convince the jury they'd known they were breaking the law was difficult for me to parse—and I'd been following the cases for years.

There was a brief lull in the trial as the four defense teams each filed what are called Rule 29 motions, asking the judge to dismiss the case. Such motions—a common defense gambit at the midpoint of a trial—argue that the prosecution has failed to prove its case, even in the absence of any defense. Judge Nelson, in assessing them, was required to consider the evidence presented so far in the light most favorable to the prosecution—essentially, to assume that none of it would be disproven. If the defendants' guilt hadn't been proven beyond a reasonable doubt given that assumption, the judge could find them not guilty immediately. Rule 29 motions are largely pro forma exercises. Several lawyers I spoke to had never seen one succeed in a federal trial in their decades-long careers. No one had reason to believe this case would be any different.

Judge Nelson ordered the lawyers to present oral arguments on the motions. Richman stood up to speak first. "Your Honor, in 1987, I became an assistant federal defender in the Boston office and I've been practicing criminal defense since then," he said. "And so it is with a fair number of data points that I say that I have never in my career seen such a complete failure of proof as exists in this case." The flaws in the case were fundamental: The government couldn't prove that email messages they'd relied on were even sent by Oz, much less provide a witness or document showing that he knew the operation was illegal. "It's not even clear exactly what it is that Ron, or Moran Oz, did," Richman said. "We know that he worked for the company. We know that he had something to do with the pharmacies. He participated in closing orders, negotiating prices. Occasionally he would contact a doctor. There is simply no evidence of criminal intent. To the contrary, the evidence is fairly unequivocal that this was a company that was trying to comply with the law."

McConnell's attorneys argued much the same: McConnell had never interacted with doctors or customers, and knew nothing about the drugs they were receiving. "The evidence does not even establish that Mr. McConnell understood the RXL business model among the constellation of other co-occurring Paul Le Roux business ventures," the motion declared.

The government asserted, instead, that the defendants had been "willfully blind" to the illegality of RX Limited, that they'd worked hard to avoid knowing that the business was clearly illegal. "RX Limited was a pill mill, designed to sell addictive prescription drugs," they restated in their response.

On a Monday morning in early March 2017, Judge Nelson called the court to order. "Good morning, everybody," she said. "Rule 29 of the Federal Rules of Criminal Procedure states this court must enter a judgment of acquittal as to any offense for which the evidence is insufficient to sustain a conviction." After a brief review of the law, she turned to the evidence against Oz and McConnell. "Even the most compelling facts presented by the government do not clear the hurdle of reasonable doubt," she concluded. "Therefore, as to Messrs. Oz and McConnell, the Rule 29 motions are granted." They were free to go.

The trial would continue for Tumpati and Karkalas, she ruled, as there was just enough evidence to force the two doctors to put on a defense. But by this point, the outcome of both cases seemed a foregone conclusion. One week later, the jury returned the same verdict for the two doctors: not guilty on all counts.

The results were a disaster for Marks's team. After a decade-long investigation with dozens of targets, they'd failed to obtain a single conviction in federal court beyond the half dozen defendants who had given up and cooperated, most of them in exchange for avoiding jail time. Richman and Friedberg were so outraged by the case that they filed a motion under an obscure law to force the government to pay their legal fees, claiming that the prosecution had been carried out "in bad faith." They ultimately lost, but in a hearing on the motion, Marks's team was forced to admit that their case had "imploded." Judge Nelson excoriated the government once again. "Even 'innocent' mistakes—those that result from inexperience or negligence rather than affirmative misconduct—

carry real and serious consequences when they involve the immense prosecutorial might of the United States," she wrote. "Here, Oz was uprooted from his native country, incarcerated for several months, forced to live in the United States for more than two years while subject to intrusive monitoring, and spent hundreds of thousands of dollars on his legal defense."

The trial's results, examined from one direction, flipped the entire story of Le Roux on its head. The not-guilty verdicts arguably proved that Le Roux had been right all along when he told his employees that the pharmaceutical business was legal. They suggested an alternate history, in which Le Roux had been a legitimate businessman, an Internet billionaire who earned his fortune through cleverness and persistence. He could have been lauded on the covers of business magazines, not hounded across the world by the DEA. If his ambitions hadn't outstripped RX Limited—if he hadn't chosen to leverage his success into a truly criminal empire—he might never have been worth chasing in the first place.

A few months later, I went to see Prabhakara Tumpati, who I'd discovered owned a clinic in southern Brooklyn. He'd expanded his business from sleep medicine into obesity treatment, and his basement office in Bensonhurst was bustling with activity. It was the end of a long workday that for Tumpati had started with a drive from Pennsylvania, and I sat in the waiting area as he walked out his last patient of the day. "It's not easy, right?" he said, gently, of the weight-loss regimen he'd prescribed her. "It takes a little bit of convincing."

Although I'd never spoken to Tumpati during the trial in Minnesota, he'd always struck me as preternaturally cheerful, given the amount of prison time he was facing. Now exonerated and sitting across from me in his office, he was eager to tell me why. He and his family were deeply Christian, he explained, and God had sent prophesies that Tumpati would come out "pure as gold" on the other end of the trial. "This in fact has been the best time of our lives," he said. "Everything about this is a miracle and nobody can believe it. But we can believe it, because it was foretold."

Not that there hadn't been nightmarish aspects to the case, he said. He'd lost weeks of work on the trial, putting a strain on the family's finances. The DEA had confiscated his car and never returned it, even as he continued to make payments on it. But he was adamant that he'd never for a moment doubted that the work he'd done for RX Limited was not only legal, but the future of medicine. It was painful, he said, to watch it be twisted by the government into a crime. "I thought, what am I doing here?" he said. "I'm a churchgoing family guy, never been in trouble, never been on drugs, always paid my taxes. Suddenly you are the next drug lord, and it's all in the mind of one prosecutor who thinks this is not a valid model. Now every single prescription became a drug deal, every cent of money became money laundering, everything that was sent through FedEx became mail fraud."

The prosecutors had offered him a deal at one point, he said: Plead guilty and get ten years in prison. "And they were angry when I didn't take it! Those that didn't have belief in the system, or didn't have the means, or the courage, they took deals. Those that stood and fought it, came out on top. I'm so thankful that I thought of sending a thank-you card to the prosecutor. Really, I'm not telling you this for the story. I'm telling you this because I frankly thought about it. Because we were stronger as a family, we were stronger in our faith than ever before. We were happier, because happiness is internal."

33

The Investigators · The
Reporter · The Mole

*2017 . . . Adding up the winnings . . . Conspiracies abound . . .
Klaussen reaches out . . . A meeting in Hanoi . . . The Mastermind's
fate*

The next time I saw Kent Bailey in Minneapolis, six months after the RX Limited trial, he sounded surprisingly sanguine about the verdict. He was furious at his own prosecutors for their mistakes, but he seemed to have long resigned himself to disappointment, after he and Brill lost the battle over Le Roux with the SOD's 960 group back in 2012. He still believed Moran Oz and the rest of the RX Limited operators deserved to go to prison. "The bottom line is that the reason that Kim started on this case was that we knew that they were causing harm in the United States," he said. "They were using our infrastructure to cause harm to our citizens." Even with the acquittals, dozens of people serving as nodes on the network had faced varying punishments for their involvement in RX Limited: doctors, pharmacists, and operators like Jon Wall who had pleaded guilty in cases from Detroit to Newark to Texas.

Bailey's outlook, in a way, aligned with that of Oz and McConnell's defense attorneys: Le Roux had been the prize, the one man that didn't warrant a deal. "I'm 100 percent convinced that we are right as rain," Bailey said. "And I firmly believe that in New York they let their personal interests cloud their judgment." He'd seen plenty of deals cut in his career, but Le Roux's didn't sit right with him. "He had the most information to give," he admitted. "But you can't forget that he was the shot caller. He does not deserve to get out. He deserves to spend the rest of his life in jail."

Kimberly Brill, true to form, was more diplomatic than her coworker when I asked her how she felt about Le Roux's cooperation. If anything, she noted, the acquittals in Minnesota showed the risks that would have come with taking him to trial. "It could have ended much worse," she said, "as we saw." But she allowed herself a rare moment of disappointment about the way the verdicts had gone. "It's ridiculous," she said. "Because there was a lot of clear evidence of what they were doing. And I don't think that story was conveyed. I don't know if that's a politically correct answer. It was very disheartening."

For years, I tried to convince anyone in the Department of Justice to articulate their motivation for cooperating with Le Roux, and to give me the view from the 960 side of the case. In response, I received a string of variations on "no comment." The DEA's spokesman in Washington told me in several different ways that none of the agents who'd worked on the sting operations would talk. Even former agents who had worked on the case, when I found a number of them, refused my questions and warned me away from digging too far. "You need to be real careful in that you don't want make yourself a witness," one former SOD supervisor told me.

Finally, in early 2018, the DEA allowed me to speak to a former 960 agent who had worked closely on the case. "Look, he's in jail, and is not killing people he would have killed," the former agent said, sitting across from me at a Brooklyn diner one spring evening, a few blocks from the Marriott that out-of-town DEA agents book when in New York for trials. The Iran and North Korean leads might not have born fruit, he said, but the likely conviction of four Americans—including two former U.S. soldiers—who would otherwise still be roaming the world as paid assassins? That was significant. "Do I think it was worth it? Yeah. Should he get fifteen years, should he get thirty years? Probably everybody who was involved in that operation should get a bullet behind the ear. Seriously. They are not good people. They are never going to be productive members of society, ever. So what's justice? I don't know. I did my job, is how I look at it."

The prosecutors who'd worked on the cases refused to speak a public word about Le Roux. A spokesman for the U.S. Attorney's Office for the Southern District repeatedly declined to talk, telling me back in 2015 that "we have no public record information on Le Roux." I got a version of the same answer from the Consumer Protection Branch, where Linda Marks worked. When I introduced myself to Marks one morning outside of a courtroom in Minneapolis, she replied only with a tight smile and a curt "no comment."

The void left by the government's silence was filled, at least in some corners, by wild theories about Le Roux and his exploits. Many of them trickled down to me, and I felt duty bound to at least consider them. I got emails suggesting that Le Roux had been the inventor of bitcoin, and I wasted countless hours trying to determine if there was any connection. (As far as I could tell, there wasn't.) A person close to a former employee of Le Roux's, now in prison, was convinced that Le Roux was part of a larger geopolitical conspiracy—the Clintons, George Soros, et cetera, et cetera—and sent me long explanations of how it all tied together. It didn't. Other people contacted me with implausible stories of how they themselves had crossed paths with Le Roux, how he'd threatened to kill them, or destroyed their business. "You have been fed/led a narrative that has been orchestrated by three-letter alphabet agencies," one of them informed me. When I pressed them for details, they faded away. "There's more to the story," they would tell me, and in some sense, they were right: There were always details, people, connections just out of my reach.

Even my more reliable sources sometimes threw out rumors

they heard, or sent me lists of officials in one country or another who they said had been in Le Roux's pocket. Le Roux, according to one tale, had been planning to carry out a coup in Zimbabwe. (Le Roux himself had heard that one: "There is a lot of strange shit in that country. There was some rumor there I was planning to overthrow the president by force?" he once noted to his cousin Mathew in a 2009 online chat. "These people going to get me killed with stupid shit like that.") A journalist told me he had evidence Le Roux had conspired with a South African security company to move former Libyan leader Muammar Gaddafi's stash of gold out of Libya. He even sent me a document purporting to be notes from the meeting in which it was planned. There was nothing to verify its authenticity. But given what I *had* been able to document, who knew? Le Roux had been involved in so many outrageous, impossible-to-believe acts that it was hard to discount even the most outlandish tales. For a man who had funded his own military protection force in Somalia and pursued drone submarines for shipping meth, nothing was really off the table.

The fate of TrueCrypt, the disk-encryption software that had been built partly on Le Roux's code, only added to the intrigue surrounding him. TrueCrypt had been created by anonymous programmers back in 2004, based largely on Le Roux's first foray into encryption, E4M. Over the next decade, as TrueCrypt became one of the most widely used programs for securing digital secrets, the people behind it remained anonymous. Whether Le Roux had any hand in it, no one seemed to know. At the very least, he had confidence in the software: Former members of Le Roux's organization told me that he had often required them to use TrueCrypt to protect The Company's secrets.

Le Roux's confidence was validated in 2013, when Edward Snowden escaped the United States with a trove of National Security Agency documents, some of which revealed that the NSA had tried and failed to break TrueCrypt. But a year later, the mystery around the software deepened further, when the anonymous devel-

opers behind it suddenly announced on their website that the technology could no longer be trusted. "WARNING: Using TrueCrypt
is not secure as it may contain unfixed security issues," the announcement read. The encryption community flew into a frenzy of
speculation and concern. Had the developers found out that the
NSA had finally compromised the program, and were they alerting
users to that fact without explicitly saying so? (One encryption message board community concluded that the first letters of each word
in the announcement, combined and converted from Latin, spelled
out the warning "Don't use TrueCrypt because it is under the control of the NSA.") Or had they just gotten bored of fixing the
program for free?

The timing of the announcement raised the possibility that Le
Roux's arrest had prompted the TrueCrypt shutdown, either because he himself had been working on the software or because his
disappearance had spooked those who were. "What we did think
was that one of the reasons they shut down was that they might be
under some sort of pressure," Matthew Green, a computer science
professor at the Johns Hopkins Information Security Institute,
who had studied TrueCrypt, told me in 2015. "It's *possible* that
could connect with him being in custody." Le Roux, for his part,
would only admit in his testimony to having created E4M.

Three years later, someone in contact with Le Roux while he
was in custody told me that Le Roux *had* boasted privately of
launching TrueCrypt himself. Le Roux claimed he'd kept his involvement secret and then handed the software off to others, but
had funded TrueCrypt's continued development over the years. Le
Roux also told this source that after his arrest he had taken advantage of the leeway granted by his DEA handlers to operate freely
online, and signaled to TrueCrypt's developers that he was in
prison. Whether they abandoned the software because of Le
Roux's warning or because his funding dried up, the source didn't
know. "It was his baby," this person said. "I still don't understand
why he publicly won't take credit for it."

The most persistent hush-hush story around Le Roux, in my years of reporting, was that he'd once worked for the U.S. government. Rumors swirled that he or Dave Smith, or both, had ties to the CIA, or NSA, or FBI. Lachlan McConnell told me that Le Roux had once claimed to have worked for the NSA as a computer analyst. "I thought, ah, that must be horseshit," McConnell added. But many of the defense attorneys working on Le Roux–related cases also quietly wondered if there was a larger issue behind all the secrecy, something more than just Le Roux's cooperation. "I always assumed that somehow he was maybe a fucking front company for the CIA," said Marcus, Le Roux's South African hit man. "They just did too much shit and got away with it."

I gathered up a scattering of tantalizing clues that Le Roux had deeper American connections. There was his relationship to Ari Ben-Menashe, the former Israeli spy who claimed to have heard from the Zimbabwean government that Le Roux was somehow an American agent. (Ben-Menashe's home in Montreal was fire-bombed in late 2012, much in the manner that Mathew Smith's had been in Bulawayo three years earlier. No one was hurt, and the perpetrators were never caught.) There were cryptic claims by Le Roux to Felix Klaussen about having access to U.S. policy decisions in Somalia. There were his six months in Virginia in the 1990s. And there was just the overall suspicion that, with the number of countries and variety of endeavors Le Roux was involved in, he was bound to have been a useful source to someone, at some point, about something.

After searching fruitlessly for confirmation, I eventually just asked Kent Bailey flat out whether there was any truth to rumors that Le Roux had U.S. intelligence connections. Bailey was in a reasonable position to know—or at least speculate—and I felt he'd been straight with me about everything else. "That's all bullshit," he said. "That was one of the things we thought of, too, and we reached out to see if he was one of their assets. If he is truly working for the CIA, they are never going to admit it. But they would do a better job shielding him, I'm confident."

By late 2017, there was one Le Roux–related case left, one opportunity for me to hear him tell his own story. That October, prosecutors in the Southern District of New York added Joseph Hunter to the indictment for the murder of Catherine Lee, alongside Adam Samia and David Stillwell. Le Roux himself was named as a potential witness in the case, which made sense, given that he'd admitted to ordering the killing. I heard from several sources that Le Roux was still cooperating with SOD, providing new targets for them to chase from his old Rolodex. All of which meant he was still potentially months, if not years, away from sentencing. He remained unlisted in the Bureau of Prisons database that tracks federal detainees.

Unsurprisingly, the former Le Roux employees who had been convicted and sent to prison were mystified that the boss they once feared was now on the other side. One afternoon, I drove out to eastern Pennsylvania to see Scott Stammers, one of the men convicted in the North Korean meth case, at the minimum-security federal prison where he was to be housed for the next fifteen years. The warden had approved the interview on a non-visitation day, and Stammers was waiting for me in a sunny corner of the empty visitation room in his khaki prison jumpsuit. He said that most of what he knew he couldn't afford to tell me. "There's stuff that I can't talk about because of the safety of my family and the possibility of new charges," he said. "I'm not a saint, but I'm not a bloodthirsty monster, shipping drugs around the world."

The most important thing he wanted me to know was that, unlike Le Roux, he had turned down offers to reduce his time in exchange for informing on others. "I can't believe the deal they gave him," he said. "He's a very intelligent man, very calculated. Merciless. He doesn't care. He once told us that we were all monkeys. But I always thought that he wanted to be one of us. He wanted to jump out of helicopters and that's why he surrounded himself with all of us. He didn't care about life, I'll tell you that. In my opinion it meant nothing to him to have someone killed. He demanded loyalty and then he turned into a coward. He couldn't do his own time."

Other convicted Le Roux employees, when they agreed to talk to me, sounded almost wistful about their time working for him. "I always considered it a very unique lifestyle that not anyone could slide into," Tim Vamvakias wrote me via email. "For me personally it felt like a life of Indiana Jones, Jason Bourne, and James Bond all wrapped up in one. You never knew what was coming next." Vamvakias was serving a twenty-year sentence on murder conspiracy charges in Big Spring, a maximum-security facility in Texas. After I succeeded in getting a visit approved, he suddenly wrote and apologized that he could no longer talk to me. "Unfortunately I'm against the wall at the moment due to other factors," he said vaguely. A few months later, in a document the government filed mistakenly and quickly withdrew, I discovered that he had flipped and would testify against Hunter in his murder trial. Vamvakias's name then disappeared from the Bureau of Prisons system.

Vamvakias had suggested I try to find Chris De Meyer, who'd worked closely with Hunter for years. "If you could get ahold of him then I'm sure he could tie up a lot of loose ends," he wrote. "But you'd most definitely have to earn his trust." From what sources told me, De Meyer had quit the organization around 2011 and moved back to Europe. He hadn't been charged in any of the Le Roux–related cases, although his name had surfaced in Le Roux's attorney's letter to the judge in Minneapolis, claiming that De Meyer was a threat to Le Roux's family. He'd shown up in the Noimie Edillor murder case file in the Philippines, which named De Meyer as a suspect, along with "Daddy Mac." The former 960 agent told me that the DEA could never identify Daddy Mac— although they suspected he was an American of Samoan descent— and lacked the jurisdiction to go after De Meyer.

In late 2017 I finally found De Meyer on Facebook, and sent him a message asking if he would talk about his work for Le Roux.

"Must be an error as i know nobody with this name," he responded. "You must have the wrong guy."

I pointed out that he was Facebook friends with people who had worked for Le Roux, and that he'd posted photos of himself in Subic Bay, in the Philippines, all of which seemed like an enormous coincidence. He at first maintained that he'd only once been a bartender in Subic. When I laid out more of what I knew, he finally relented.

"Who exactly did u speak to?" he said. "If u know everything Sir about me . . . well then you know everything. It's a can of worms best kept close."

I told him that I couldn't tell him who I'd talked to. "Some people are afraid you'll kill them," I wrote. "I'm not saying you would, just that's what they are afraid of."

"Sorry sir but I cannot say anymore," he replied. "Please be careful in your enquiries, and no I won't kill you. it's free and well ment from the Hart advise."

After a few more exchanges, though, he couldn't seem to resist. Felix Klaussen, he told me, was the one who snitched on everyone. He "played everything," De Meyer wrote, and "got leroux done."

Then he reiterated that he couldn't tell me anything. "The only thing I ask is not to use stories that are [not] 100 confirmed," he wrote. "Don't listen to druggies and alcoholics with bar stories. They know fuck all. Want the story? Interview Hunter and the boys. If you can reach them. The rest knows fuck all.

"That's all sir I already said too much. I'm in danger just by talking to you," he concluded. "Btw I never killed for le roux or hunter. That's why I'm not in prison."

The email arrived in my inbox on a Thursday morning at the end of March. The correspondent was an obvious pseudonym, "Dirk VanHo." Subject line: "Interesting info on PCL." It appeared at first to be similar to random emails I'd received about Le Roux over the years, but it soon became clear that this one was different. "Hi Evan," it read. "Could you please send me a secure email address as we need to talk I believe! I can say that I am your missing link in the Paul Calder Leroux story. The one with the true answers on the downfall of Leroux."

He was, he said, the man who had lured Le Roux to Liberia.

What motivated him to contact me seemed to be a mix of anger over the Minnesota acquittals and a gap he'd seen in my articles on Le Roux. "Most of your story is correct and accurate and as someone who lived the life and work with PCL I have to say respect!" he wrote. "But to make it complete and perfect you could for sure use my input and evidence."

We switched to encrypted email, and he forwarded me documents to validate his information. He told me he'd run the operation in Somalia, and then unlocked Le Roux for the DEA. Then, at the end of the note, he signed off with his real name.

I'd long suspected that this man was the 960 group informant, based on fragments of information that I'd swept up over the years. But I'd never been able to locate him, or uncover any real proof. So thoroughly had the DEA kept his name out of the public case that I had seen it only twice in all the tens of thousands of pages of documents I had on Le Roux.

I exchanged emails with this man, whom I've referred to as "Felix Klaussen"—the use of a pseudonym was the sole condition I agreed to before he would talk—for several months, as he offered me tantalizing pieces of his story and I tried to coax him into meeting me in person. Since Le Roux's arrest, he said, he had become a kind of professional informant for hire, infiltrating other criminal groups and reporting back to his sponsors. He'd already worked on one other large international drug bust, he said, but now he wondered if he was willing to keep risking his life for cases. He was based in Southeast Asia for the moment, but was reluctant to meet me where he was living. Finally, he told me that he would be traveling in Vietnam that June. If I could be there on the half day when he had nothing planned, he would tell me whatever I wanted to know.

On a broiling afternoon a month later, I stood sweating under a chandelier in the marbled lobby of a hotel just south of Hanoi's Old Quarter. I texted Klaussen that I'd arrived, and a few minutes later he stepped out of the elevator, tall and tan at age forty, still holding on to the swimmer's build of his youth. We found an empty corner where we could order a drink and talk undisturbed. "I've seen so many crazy things, I could write a book myself just about the adventures," he laughed. "It was mental." We talked for the next thirteen hours, shifting from the lobby to the restaurant to Klaussen's room and back as he walked me through his story. We exited the hotel only to stand outside as Klaussen worked his way through a pack of cigarettes.

After it was all over, he told me, he'd found it impossible to return to any kind of normal life. He'd tried going home, but had trouble relating to the people he'd grown up around. "You go back and you see the people you know in a local pub or whatever, and you hear the conversations these people have," he said. "It's so uninteresting—people make such big dramas about nothing, about small, stupid things." That's why he'd returned to the field as an informant, he said. He had discovered that he was good at it, and nothing else could match the feeling of bringing down evil men. (The pay wasn't bad, either. He had been approved for a sizable reward from the U.S. government for his work on the Le Roux case, money that would secure his kids' futures.)

He often ruminated aloud on his own motivations—for joining Le Roux's organization to begin with, and then for devoting his life to destroying it, and him. "Of course at the end of the day I worked for a criminal. So people can call me a criminal as well," he said. "Because I was aware of what he did and still I stayed because I wasn't breaking too many laws. The more and more I found out, the more and more I despised him."

Still, he insisted, Le Roux could have avoided capture and

everything that followed had he just let Klaussen go quietly, instead of ordering him dead. "I'm still angry about it. I will never forgive him that. That he just impulsively ordered a hit on me for no reason. That was his mistake," he said, before harking back to the phone call when he told Le Roux he wouldn't hesitate to turn him in. "I promised him I would take him down, and I did."

As much as Klaussen despised Le Roux, he maintained a respect that drifted into something just short of awe for his boss's pure intellectual brilliance. Le Roux had managed a dozen different operations, alone, in his head. "No matter how bad the guy is, no matter all the people he had killed, all the crimes he committed, no matter how people hate him," Klaussen said, "he's the most versatile criminal in history."

What will the U.S. government do with Paul Le Roux now? In my conversations with everyone from Le Roux's former security team to Philippine federal agents the talk inevitably came back to this question. Nearly everyone marveled at how easily Le Roux had transformed himself into a government asset. Now he seemed poised to literally get away with murder.

"When he didn't see a way out, he just went in backup mode," Klaussen said. "He played it so smart. Outsmarted everybody in the end."

His value as an informant felt, in a way, manufactured: Most of the people that Le Roux had helped the DEA catch had become criminals entirely at his behest. He'd given the U.S. government three people—including former U.S. soldiers gone rogue—who were willing to kill a DEA agent for money, and eight more happy to import drugs into the United States. But balanced against what the DEA knew about Le Roux, it was hard not to think that he had manipulated them into overlooking the gravity of his own crimes. Even the agents involved in flipping him suspected that he hadn't come entirely clean. "I think his definition of what a murder is, and his culpability involved in that murder, is different than what we would determine," the former 960 group agent told me. "For him there's this whole discernment about what he's truly responsible for. I think there's a potential Filipinos got killed, but to Le Roux if he says 'Handle a problem,' and Dave Smith killed some Filipinos, he doesn't feel he had them killed. 'I told them to handle the fucking problem. However they did it is on them.'"

How long Le Roux himself would stay in custody was anybody's guess. His fate will rest in the hands of a federal judge in the Southern District of New York, who will decide his sentence after the cases in which he provided information—including some that may not even yet be public—are resolved. At age forty-six, Le Roux's possible futures range from life in prison to as little as ten years under federal sentencing guidelines. Or the judge could throw the guidelines out the window and give Le Roux time served. He will not be charged for any of the seven murders he admitted to—indeed, the government stipulated in Le Roux's cooperation agreement that they lacked the jurisdiction to prosecute him for the murders anyway—although the judge is allowed to factor them into Le Roux's sentence.

If the case follows the path of other cooperators, a prosecutor from the Department of Justice will someday stand before a judge and argue that Le Roux's cooperation entitles him to the lesser end of the sentence that his charges allow. His one request on the plane back from Liberia was that he not spend his life in prison, and he's likely to see it granted. Having already served five years or more, he might be back out on the street while still in his fifties. But as Le Roux himself noted in his testimony, there are no guarantees. "I think he'll get fifteen," the former 960 agent speculated. "He's got ten more to do."

If and when Le Roux is released, federal authorities could place him in witness protection. They could deport him, setting him adrift to find a new life—or restart his old one. Technically, as part of his plea agreement, Le Roux also agreed to forfeit all the proceeds of his crimes. But officially, as of the RX Limited trial, the

DEA admitted to confiscating only $300,000. The Hong Kong government had clearly gotten much more. In his testimony, Le Roux claimed somewhat laughably that this constituted "the bulk of my assets at the time of arrest," and that his other properties and money "were stolen by unknown parties." I was hard-pressed to find someone from his former organization, or in the U.S. government, who believed him.

Bailey told me that the DEA found one bank account with $8 million in it in Mauritius, which was drained before they could seize it. By whom, they had no idea. "He's betting he's going to do ten years, and he's got millions," Bailey said. "He decided, through self-preservation, that the only way I have a chance to get out of here was to cooperate, give up the information that I can give up, do the guys that I can, hope to get out of jail with a lot of money left. Guarantee that's what he did. He sold a song."

A former employee at an investment firm in Hong Kong, who contacted me after my first series of stories on Le Roux, bolstered the assertion that Le Roux maintained plenty of assets to start again. The firm, the employee said, had helped Le Roux settle portions of his fortune into a trust in the British Virgin Islands, filtered through accounts in Gibraltar and the Netherlands. The trusts listed the children from his marriage to Lilian as beneficiaries. (The former employee also noted that the firm had studiously avoided inquiring as to where the money originated, and ignored red flags like the fact that Le Roux never showed up in person, supplied multiple passports, and added signatories to the accounts that were clearly his own aliases.) I was able to confirm the names of the trusts, but the assets remained hidden from view—and possibly from the reach of the U.S. government, should they even choose to look for them. The former employee said that tens of millions of dollars may have passed through the accounts, which Le Roux accessed as recently as late 2014 or early 2015, well after he was captured by the DEA.

"He's still not done, believe me," Klaussen concluded. "That's the scary part. That guy is going to walk out again, and he is not done with business. The stashes that he has—still has, because I don't know what he gave up. Not everything. And what they seized, it's never going to be everything. He's not that stupid." He paused and said it again. "He's not that stupid that he's going to give up everything. No."

The one man who could shed the most light on Le Roux's plans, Le Roux himself, was still hidden away by the U.S. government. After two years, I was finally able to confirm the identity of Le Roux's attorney, the one who requested that the courtroom in Minnesota be closed. His name was Joseph DiBenedetto. Based in Manhattan, he was known for taking on highly publicized criminal cases, including the defense of John Gotti's brother Peter, once accused in a plot to kill Mafia hit man–turned–government informant Sammy "the Bull" Gravano. DiBenedetto also appeared regularly on Fox News and in other media outlets to discuss legal cases in the headlines. But in this one he'd worked hard to keep his name out of the public eye, for reasons he didn't seem to want to discuss. He never returned any of my phone calls or emails asking him to talk about Le Roux's case and explain why, in this instance, he had chosen to work anonymously.

The Minnesota court did eventually unseal DiBenedetto's 2016 letter. It contained some information on Le Roux's family, reporting that his first wife remained in Europe, where her safety was in jeopardy. Cindy Cayanan, according to the letter, had returned to the Philippines, but soon noticed people following her, and she and their daughter went into hiding. "Based on this information," the letter continued, "Le Roux's handlers are attempting to have Le Roux's family temporarily relocated to the U.S. to ensure their safety." (Later, the former 960 agent told me that the relocation plan was never serious. "To be quite honest with you it was posturing on our part," he said. "He didn't care about them. He was playing a game to try and help them, and help himself. And we just said, 'I'll take care of it, Paul.' ")

Still, the letter raised the possibility that the government might place Le Roux into witness protection if and when he gets out. "I'm sure he's thinking about printing his next passports," Klaussen said. "If the U.S. government helps him disappear, so much the better. For him that's ideal. That's what he wants. For him it's just time to plan the next thing. This time he knows the way they work. They made him smarter, a lot smarter."

Plenty of Le Roux's associates harbored a fear that once he was out, he would seek vengeance against them. But the man who committed the ultimate betrayal against Le Roux, Felix Klaussen, doubted that he would ever bother to come after him. "I'm sure if ever a day comes when he's out and I run into him at an airport or something, he probably smiles at me and shakes my hand," he said. "That's Le Roux."

Others warned that they were ready to exact vengeance in the other direction, for Le Roux's decision to save himself by informing on them while they kept their mouths shut. "I got loads of information. I kept a file, I've got photos, I've got fucking transcripts of emails," Marcus, the South African assassin, told me. Now that Le Roux had sung to the authorities, Marcus was prepared to do the same to his former boss if necessary. "Paul Le Roux must remember one thing: If he ever comes to South Africa, or tries to, I will fucking sort him out."

I often asked people if they thought Le Roux's time in American custody could change him, that he could emerge chastened, maybe even ready to commit his technical brilliance to a positive cause. "I really doubt it," his cousin Mathew Smith said. "He loved what he did and wouldn't give it up. I think it was fun for him, I think he really wanted to be the biggest thing. He wanted the infamy. He told me a few times that when he gets caught, he'll be on CNN."

What Le Roux wanted and why is a subject I puzzled over for years. For some the answer was obvious: money. He was corrupted by it, enamored with it, addicted to the feeling of it flowing toward him, more than he could ever spend. There were naturally those who diagnosed something more fundamental to his nature. "He was a complete sociopath," said the Israeli who had briefly handled the job of procuring women for Le Roux. "You look at the definition of sociopath, inability for empathy and so on. This is him, word for word." My own reporting had revealed him to be, at the least, a monster who never thought twice about ordering the maiming and killing of people around him. There were times when he came off as a sadist who reveled in it.

Some people speculated that his drive was fueled by some submerged pain—his hurt over being adopted, or some other childhood affront for which he was forever exacting revenge on the world. Maybe so. I always suspected that at least a part of the answer dwelled in his life as a programmer. Le Roux had found his place inside code, a universe in which he could bend reality to his will. It seemed to me that he tried to apply the detached logic of software to real life. That's why the DEA schemes must have appealed to him. "Nothing involves emotion for him," the former 960 agent put it to me. "Everything is a calculation." His approach was algorithmic, not moral: Set the program in motion and watch it run.

One afternoon in Tel Aviv, I met a former employee of Le Roux's at a bustling café. I'd had a difficult time persuading him to talk to me at all. He was finally free of Le Roux's organization and had moved on with his life, he said. He hadn't been indicted in any of the cases, despite working for both the pharmaceutical and mercenary sides of Le Roux's business—although he said he planned to wait a few years before traveling to the United States, just in case. After days of deflecting my inquiries, he finally relented and agreed to talk to me anonymously about his time with Le Roux, and to confirm what I had heard from others. We spoke for an hour, and as we stood up to leave, I asked him the question: What did Le Roux want?

"He wanted to be the biggest ever caught," he said. Then he leaned in, pointing at my notebook. "If you publish this story, ultimately you are giving him what he wanted. And by talking to you I guess I am, too. This is what he wanted. This story to be told, in this way."

Epilogue

2017–2018 . . . Justice for Catherine Lee . . . Le Roux spills all . . . Scattered to the winds

On my first trip to the Philippines, in late 2015, I happened to arrive in the middle of a presidential campaign. An outsider candidate named Rodrigo Duterte, the mayor of Davao, a city of 1.5 million people on the volatile southern island of Mindanao, was running on a pledge to institute a massive crackdown on drugs and crime. "All of you who are into drugs, you sons of bitches, I will really kill you," he said in the course of campaigning. If elected, he pledged to kill one hundred thousand drug dealers, dumping so many bodies into Manila Bay that, as he put it, "the fish will grow fat." He was running behind several other candidates at the time, and as with then-candidate Donald Trump in the United States, nobody I talked to seemed to take him seriously. An establishment candidate and close ally of Benigno Aquino, the president at the time, was widely expected to win.

By my last trip to Manila in mid-2017, Duterte had been president for a year, and had wasted no time making good on his promise. Police and unidentified gunmen had killed more than seven thousand suspected drug users, drug dealers, and seemingly random targets in the streets. International human rights groups were shocked by the extrajudicial slaughter, but Duterte was unapologetic. He claimed to hold a list of other names, containing as many as a million people, who were involved in the drug trade in the Philippines. "The human rights people will commit suicide if I finish these all," he said. In fact, he'd taken to bragging that as mayor he'd personally killed a few suspected criminals himself.

Duterte's twisted bravado put me in mind of Le Roux, and how he'd fired a few extra bullets into Dave Smith, almost as if he wanted to claim he had done some of the killing himself. I wondered how much he and his operation contributed to the climate that brought Duterte to power. Not that Le Roux himself ever made a significant public impression in the Philippines, having never been prosecuted for his crimes. But that was precisely the point: The scope of corruption and lawlessness that Le Roux generated and exploited was certainly enough to leave ordinary citizens cynical about their government. I wondered, too, how Le Roux would have fared had he stuck around for the state-sponsored violence of the Duterte regime. One source connected to the Manila underworld told me he'd talked to people in the higher levels of the cartels now active in the country, who said that the killing campaign was targeted only at addicts and low-level dealers, leaving the higher-ups, who knew how to pay for protection, untouched. The drug business, he said, was booming. "They said, 'We're sending in more.' They're stockpiling it," the source told me. "So you killed how many thousands of people? There's no dent in it."

The former 960 agent agreed. "He and Paul would do business together, guarantee you," he said of Duterte. "Paul would have to pay bribes, it would be fine."

When I went back to see Rizaldy Rivera at the National Bureau of Investigation, on one of my last days in Manila, I asked him if there was any chance Le Roux could be extradited, to face the consequences of his crimes here. "Well, if ever there is a move to extradite Paul Le Roux, it will probably come from the NBI," he said. "The problem is, do you think the U.S. government will allow that? They will object to that, because Le Roux is a prize catch."

Rivera had transferred out of the Death Investigation Division and moved downstairs to Environmental Crimes. When Aurora Almendral and I showed up for our lunchtime appointment, we found five guys in the division's office eating pizza and watching daytime talk shows on a small television. While we waited, I noticed a printed-out sign in English, taped to a nearby wall:

DO NOT ACCEPT A BRIBE, FOR A BRIBE BLINDS THOSE WHO SEE AND TWISTS THE WORDS OF THE RIGHTEOUS

When Rivera finally arrived, in a purple button-down and jeans, I wondered if he'd been exiled to a bureau backwater. But he told me he preferred Environmental Crimes to his old gig. "There's so much pressure in the high-profile cases at DID," he said.

Even with the transfer, he'd continued helping the DEA with the Catherine Lee murder case, despite the fact that they hadn't reciprocated with any documents that would help Rivera build an indictment in the Philippines. Together, they'd made progress gathering more evidence against Adam Samia and David Stillwell, the North Carolina men facing trial in New York for Lee's killing.

But he had bigger news to relay. "We recovered the vehicle," he told me.

"You did?"

"Yeah, it is here. It is in my custody."

In February 2017, Le Roux had finally provided the DEA the whereabouts of the Toyota Innova van. It was sitting in a garage, at a house he still owned in the gated suburb of Las Piñas. The authorities, he said, could pick it up from the house's caretaker. Two DEA agents had flown to Manila and driven out to retrieve it. The agents wanted to deliver the van to the U.S. embassy. "But I objected, with due respect," Rivera said. "I said I think the legal chain of custody will be broken." Instead, the van was brought to the NBI for safekeeping.

"Do you want to see it?" he said.

I did. We walked out to a parking lot in the interior of the complex, hemmed in by buildings on all sides. The van looked to be in good shape. Peering inside, Rivera pointed out that the middle seat had been removed, and on the floor under piles of empty water bottles and fast food wrappers was a large, dark stain. "You can plainly see what *appears* to be bloodstains," Rivera said. "But I still don't know if those are really bloodstains. And if they are bloodstains, are they from animals, or human?"

The U.S. authorities had proposed a series of plans to conduct forensic analysis on the van, including sending an FBI team to Manila, or shipping the entire vehicle to Quantico, Virginia. Rivera said the plans, which required the approval of the Ministry of Justice in the Philippines, "never materialized." (Later, U.S. authorities would say that the NBI simply refused to let them have the van.) Since the Philippine authorities lacked the equipment to test potentially five-year-old stains, they wouldn't be able to confirm if what I saw was blood from Catherine Lee.

But there was another way prosecutors might at least put Samia and Stillwell at the scene of the crime. When they searched Samia's house after his arrest, they found what looked to be the key to a Toyota van just like the one now sitting in the NBI parking lot. Rivera told me that DEA agents were returning to Manila with the key to test it out.

A few weeks later, after I was back in the U.S., Rivera sent me a text. The van had started.

The prosecution of Samia, Stillwell, and Hunter for the murder of Catherine Lee would offer the U.S. government another chance to make good on the deal they had cut with Le Roux. The trial was finally set for April 2018 in Manhattan, and the prosecution's filings indicated that unlike in the Minnesota cases, their star witness would be Paul Le Roux himself.

The trial took place inside the white-columned edifice flanking Manhattan's Foley Square, in a courtroom with vaulted ceilings and seating for more than a hundred spectators. The first morning of jury selection, I sat in the gallery a few rows behind the prosecutors' table, where three assistant U.S. attorneys from the Southern District office waited alongside Eric Stouch, from the DEA's 960 group. The three defendants entered under escort by federal marshals: Adam Samia, with his slicked-back hair and self-assured smirk, seemed at times to be almost mocking the proceedings. David Stillwell, who had already confessed to being present at the murder—as the driver—looked shell-shocked. Stillwell's attorney had already signaled in pretrial filings that his defense consisted almost entirely of a procedural question over whether he'd known the job included murder before departing for the Philippines. (The federal murder-conspiracy statute under which the three men were prosecuted required that they knowingly entered into the conspiracy while inside the United States. Simply murdering someone overseas is not, as it happens, illegal in the States.) Joseph Hunter was the most inscrutable of the three. Still an intimidating barrel of a man, he now walked with a cane, and his affect was one of morose resignation. The only question in this trial for him was whether his twenty years in prison would be extended to life.

As U.S. District Judge Ronnie Abrams walked potential jurors through a series of questions to ferret out their biases, the courtroom echoed with the names and places that had once filled the Post-its stuck to my apartment wall. Jury candidates were asked if they were familiar with a cast of characters that spanned the breadth of Le Roux's operation: Tim Vamvakias, Nestor Del Rosario, Shai Reuven, Lachlan McConnell, Mathew Smith, Moran Oz, Bruce Jones, John Nash, and others. They were asked if they were familiar with locations from North Korea to Zambia, Papua New Guinea to the Seychelles, Roxboro, North Carolina, to Taytay, in the Philippines. Catherine Lee's death would be the fulcrum upon which prosecutors would balance Paul Le Roux's story—because it would be Le Roux, not the defendants, who would dominate the trial.

With a twelve-member jury in place, consisting of ten women and two men, Assistant U.S. Attorney Patrick Egan stood up to deliver his opening remarks. "On February 4, 2012, Catherine Lee was riding in the back seat of a van," he began. With her were two men she barely knew: Samia and Stillwell, who had contacted her under the guise of seeking real estate and now intended to murder her. But the story, the prosecutor said, "started long before Catherine Lee got into the van that night."

The narrative that Egan wove together began with Samia, an old friend of Dave Smith's, working alongside Hunter at Echelon, a front group for Le Roux's mercenary teams. For years, Egan said, Samia had been asking Smith and Hunter for "wet work"—assassination missions. In 2011, after Le Roux murdered Smith and elevated Hunter to head the kill teams, Samia's opportunity finally came. He in turn recruited his buddy Stillwell, a weekend warrior type who often falsely told people he'd worked as a military sniper. And the two of them, directed by Hunter, flew to the Philippines for a salary of $10,000 a month plus $25,000 in "bonus money" for each job. "These guys had one purpose: to murder," Egan said. He described the van they'd done it in, and the key found in Samia's house. He told the jurors that they would see video of Hunter—from the DEA's sting operation—describing the murder in detail. "And then you will hear from Paul Le Roux," he concluded. "He will tell you in his own words how his criminal organization worked."

The defense attorneys' openings consisted primarily of reminders to the jury that the government had to prove their allegations beyond a reasonable doubt. "Well, Mr. Egan was pretty dramatic, wasn't he?" Samia's attorney quipped. "His drama is not evidence."

To me their task seemed herculean. Stillwell had confessed and pointed to Samia as the triggerman. Hunter was caught on tape virtually confessing his own role. And with photos of a bloody head recovered from his laptop and the van key from his house, Samia faced a seemingly insurmountable collection of circumstantial evidence. Not to mention that the government planned to present Le Roux as the mastermind who had arranged it all and now could condemn all three men to their fates.

Before we got to that, the prosecutors laid out the gruesome details of Lee's death, the same ones that I had found in the police file three years earlier. She had died immediately, the doctor who conducted the autopsy testified, from two gunshot wounds, one below each eye, that left .22-caliber slugs lodged in her brain.

On day two a juror wrote a note to the judge declaring that she feared for her safety; Judge Abrams replaced her and the trial carried on. I was surprised that she was the only one. The prosecution called a DEA technician in Thailand to establish the validity of the surveillance video of Hunter in Phuket, and then began playing snippets of him describing the murder plan—and how Samia and Stillwell had botched it. An expert in electronic evidence explained how they had recovered files, emails, and photos off of Samia's and Stillwell's digital devices. Then the prosecution began methodically introducing years' worth of emails between Samia and Hunter, Samia and Dave Smith, Hunter and Smith, Hunter and Le Roux.

The main event began midway on the second day, when another prosecutor, Emil Bove, stood and called Le Roux to the stand. He entered from a door behind and to the right of the judge, in a dark blue, short-sleeved prison uniform. He'd maintained his bulk since the hearing two years before, in Minnesota, but his face seemed thinner. His gait was labored as he walked across the courtroom to the witness stand, unshackled but escorted by a U.S. marshal. He pulled out a pair of glasses from a small case in his breast pocket, put them on, and gazed out over the courtroom. If it was infamy he'd been seeking, as his cousin once suggested to me, the smattering of spectators—a few reporters, Thomas Cindric, and several fellow agents from the 960 group—suggested that he hadn't quite found it. I watched him closely and was certain I saw a small smirk pass across his face when his eyes rested on Joseph Hunter, glaring at him from the defendant's table.

Bove quickly established that Le Roux was now forty-five years old, born in Zimbabwe and raised partly in South Africa, and that he had once employed both Hunter and Samia as mercenaries. Then he turned immediately to the matter at hand. "Do you know of a woman named Catherine Lee?" he asked Le Roux.

"Yes, I do," Le Roux said.

"Who was Catherine Lee?"

"Catherine Lee was a real estate broker in the Philippines."

"Sir, where is Catherine Lee today?"

"I had her killed."

"Why?"

"I believed that she was involved in stealing money from me."

"How do you know that Catherine Lee was murdered?"

"I was told she was killed by Joseph Hunter." Le Roux paused to correct himself. "Sorry. What I mean is I was told by Joseph Hunter that she had been killed."

"Did Hunter tell you who participated in the murder?"

"Yes. Joseph Hunter told me that the kill team consisting of Adam Samia and his partner were the ones that killed Catherine Lee."

For the next two days, through his deliberately precise answers, Le Roux recounted many of the same facts that I had spent years prying from the hard-to-find and the reluctant. He claimed that he had made $300 million in his illegal online pharmacy business, employing between one and two thousand people, and then laundered it through gold, diamonds, and timber in Africa and Asia. He detailed how, in 2005, he met Dave Smith, who gave him an entry into the world of mercenaries. At times he seemed to have been overprepared by the prosecutors, mechanically repeating practiced sentences about how his "Echelon mercenaries"—referring to the front company sometimes used to hire Smith's men—were employed solely to "intimidate, shoot, threaten, and/or kill" their targets.

Le Roux offered basic details on almost every one of his ventures. "I set up a front company in Somalia, which pretended to be about a fishing operation, but was actually a front for criminal activity," he said. "My objective in Somalia was to obtain a small territory and set myself up as a warlord using whatever violence was necessary." He'd canceled the project, he said, when he came to believe that the manager was stealing from him.

Le Roux provided his own version of one of the most outlandish stories I'd heard: the planned invasion and coup in the Seychelles. I'd long suspected the story was one of those rumors that spread among mercenaries, embellished each time it was passed along. Le Roux, instead, confirmed its veracity: Dave Smith, Le Roux said, had introduced Le Roux to someone who purported to be related to the current ruler of the country, but wanted him deposed. If Le Roux could provide the force to do it, he'd receive both a safe haven in the Seychelles and a diplomatic passport in return. He had entertained the coup plan seriously enough to send Joseph Hunter to the island nation to investigate it.

"What did he report?" Bove asked Le Roux.

"Hunter reported that approximately thirty mercenaries would be required, thirty Echelon mercenaries," Le Roux said.

"Required for what?"

"To take over the government, basically to defeat any resistance in the Seychelles and take over the government."

In the end, Le Roux said, he'd told Smith the mission wasn't viable in the long term. Sure, Smith's mercenaries could overrun the country. But the current government's allies across the water in Tanzania would inevitably mobilize their much more serious military to come take it back.

Le Roux was dispassionate about the violence he'd ordered. Yes, he had ordered drugs planted on Andrew Hahn, one of the brothers from Zimbabwe who he believed had stolen over a million dollars from him. Yes, he had sent Joseph Hunter and Chris De Meyer to firebomb his cousin Mathew's house. Yes, he had ordered Smith to intimidate Moran Oz, an order Smith had carried out with Hunter and De Meyer by throwing Oz off a boat and shooting at him. On Le Roux's orders, De Meyer had also thrown a hand grenade at a real estate broker's house—not Catherine Lee nor Noimie Edillor but a third one.

"Why did you target this other person?" the prosecutor asked.

"That other person owed me approximately one thousand dollars," he said.

Le Roux did clear up one lingering mystery for me, around John Nash, the man who had been among the last to see both Bruce Jones and his attorney, Joe Frank Zuñiga, alive. Nash, Le Roux testified, had once sold Le Roux fake weapons and cocaine. Le Roux said that he had hired Nash to kill Zuñiga, in exchange for a partial forgiveness of his debt.

When he arrived at the details of the Lee murder, Bove spent hours projecting emails up on the screen. He guided Le Roux through the plans for Samia and Stillwell, who had reported back to him at the time through emails from Hunter.

When the cross-examination began, Le Roux transformed completely, from the helpful witness to the intransigent, reluctant verbal combatant. ("Could you break down that question into smaller parts?" he responded to a two-part question. "It's not precise," he complained about other questions. "I'm not sure what you mean by 'intelligent,'" he said, when asked whether he considered himself such.) Much of his resistance relied on extreme literalism: When shown a copy of his own cooperation agreement, including his signature, he quibbled that he was seeing "only a photocopy of my signature." "I'm not saying I doubt it's the agreement," he said. "I just can't be certain that the text matches the agreement I have." At times he projected the air of a CEO being asked to answer for the actions of a sprawling corporation. "I already testified there were two thousand people who were employed," he said in response to a question about insulating himself from culpability.

"There was no design regarding who I met and who I didn't meet. Anyone was able to come and speak to me at any time. My door was always open."

The defense attempted to portray Le Roux as both a monster and a man who would say anything to get out of prison. Samia's attorney spent the first portion of his cross-examination goading Le Roux to admit that the password to his laptop, when he was arrested in Liberia, had been "HITLER." But establishing that Le Roux lacked remorse was easy enough. "Fair to say that you were planning on murdering anyone that you had determined had double-crossed you?" Hunter's attorney asked.

"That's fair to say, yes," Le Roux said.

Later, Samia's attorney picked up the same line of questioning. "After you killed the first person, did you ever feel bad about it?" he asked.

"I felt bad about the victims, yes."

"It didn't stop you from killing the next one or the next one or the next one, did it?"

Le Roux paused before responding. "It did not." He admitted that at the time he was committing the crimes, he was unconcerned about the consequences in the Philippines. "I didn't care who knew what, whether people knew the crimes were happening or not because I had the police on the payroll," he said. "I was protected."

The bulk of the cross-examination, by three different attorneys, was spent on Le Roux's decision to cooperate. He appeared well-practiced in his answers concerning his agreement with the government. The crimes to which he had pleaded guilty carried a sentence of ten years to life, he said, but he would never be prosecuted for most of what he'd done, from violence to drug dealing. And if he told the truth and provided substantial assistance, they could choose to write his judge a so-called 5K1 letter—named after a clause in federal sentencing guidelines—asking for a reduced sentence. If they did, the judge could venture below the minimum, and even give him time served. But they weren't required to, Le Roux noted again and again. "The government has not made me any promises," he said.

"But you are hoping that when you are sentenced you will receive a sentence of time served, right?" Hunter's attorney asked.

"I'm hoping that when I eventually am sentenced I will receive a decent sentence," was all Le Roux would allow. "I don't know whether I've done enough to warrant a time-served sentence given the horrific nature of my criminal activity," he added, with a tone that sounded more world-weary than contrite. "I'm trying to turn over a new leaf."

"And after any of the murders you were involved in, did you think about turning over a new leaf after any of those?" Adam Samia's attorney asked him.

"I would have to say no," Le Roux said.

Samia's attorney took the time to highlight the glaring contrast between his statements in court and the vigilante justice Le Roux had carried out against the likes of Bruce Jones and Joe Frank Zuñiga.

"So you thought that the punishment for cooperation should be death, right?" he asked.

"Yes."

"Well, do you believe that you should be killed for cooperating?"

"No."

"What makes you different than Mr. Jones?"

"Nothing."

After Le Roux, the prosecution called Tim Vamvakias, the former American soldier who was already serving a twenty-year sentence for his role in the scheme to kill a DEA agent. He recounted much of what he'd told me by email, from his recruitment to Le Roux's hit team by his friend Hunter, whom he called "White Kong" in emails, to the "ninja work" they had both signed on for. The defense attorneys attempted to chip away at his credibility, forcing him to repeat over and over that he was testifying only for the chance of getting his sentence reduced.

Adam Samia was the only defendant to take the stand. When his attorney kicked off his testimony by asking Samia if he had killed Catherine Lee, he leaned into the microphone and said loudly, "Absolutely not." He then spun an implausible story: Rather than surveilling and killing Lee, as the photos on his and Stillwell's phone and laptop seemed to indicate, he had spent the early months of 2012 in the Philippines driving Le Roux's employees back and forth to the airport. The money he'd wired back from the Philippines wasn't payment for the murder but winnings from a mixed martial arts fight.

Ultimately the jury wasn't swayed. After only a few hours of deliberation, they returned with guilty verdicts for all three defendants. The mandatory sentence for their charges is life without parole. Barring a successful appeal, Hunter, Samia, and Stillwell will almost certainly spend their remaining lives in federal prison.

The end of the trial in April 2018 paved the way for Le Roux to be sentenced, although no one seemed to know when that would happen. Buried in the hours of testimony in the Lee murder trial, there was one clue to Le Roux's plans if and when he was released. Le Roux admitted that while in custody in the summer of 2016, he'd broken the jail's rules and contacted an inmate named Mir Islam at another facility in the United States. Le Roux had met Islam in custody the year prior, when they were housed together, and before he'd been transferred to another prison, Islam had told Le Roux he was soon to be released. Le Roux coaxed a paralegal into setting up a series of calls with Islam.

"During these three-way calls, did you make any plans with Mir Islam?" the prosecutor asked Le Roux.

"I discussed opening a call center business," Le Roux said. "I was going to fund it."

The other defendants prosecuted in the Southern District for the drug and murder stings were assigned to federal prisons around the country. **Tim Vamvakias** and **Dennis Gögel,** having pleaded guilty to conspiring to murder a federal agent, received the same sentence Hunter had originally: twenty years apiece. (Vamvakias presumably will receive a reduction in his sentence for cooperating—or even witness protection—but his information has now been purged from the Bureau of Prison's public database.) **Michael Filter** got eight years for surveillance on the cocaine deal, while **Slawomir Soborski** received nine on the same charge. Lengths of sentences in federal drug cases are tied to the amount of drugs in question—even if, as in this case, those drugs were fictitious.

In the North Korean meth case, **Adrian Valkovic,** the "ground commander," was sentenced to more than nine years for offering to provide security for the transaction. **Kelly Peralta,** the middleman on the deal, received a seven-and-a-half-year sentence. **Ye Tiong Tan Lim** went down for eleven and a half years. Large portions of **Philip Shackels's** sentencing hearing were redacted by the government—including almost all of the testimony of his father, a former Irish intelligence officer—for unexplained reasons. Shackels received seven years, with the possibility of a transfer to an Irish prison. **Scott Stammers,** who the government claimed had been a leader in the plan, was sentenced to fifteen years.

In Hong Kong, **Doron Shulman,** who managed Le Roux's gold stores and imported the ammonium nitrate, pleaded guilty to two counts of money laundering and was sentenced to five years in prison. The other Israelis claimed, without success, to have been ignorant of the source of the gold. **Yoav Hen** and **Daniel Fadlon** ultimately pleaded guilty to money laundering and were sentenced to four years in prison. **Omer Gavish** fought the charges but was convicted and received five and a half years. All of them were released early and returned to Israel. Through an intermediary, they declined to speak with me.

In July 2014, the U.S. government finally declared **tramadol—the generic version of Ultram—**a Schedule IV controlled substance. All three of the painkillers favored by Le Roux's networks are now controlled drugs under U.S. law.

In 2013, **UPS** paid $40 million to resolve federal accusations of knowingly shipping drugs for illegal online pharmacies. A year later, after refusing a similar deal, **FedEx** was indicted by a federal grand jury in San Francisco for conspiracy to traffic in controlled substances on behalf of illegal Internet pharmacies. RX Limited was not among the pharmacy networks included, but the former DEA agent in the 960 group told me that Le Roux provided information to the prosecutors in the case. In the middle of a trial that began two years later, when FedEx alleged that DEA agents had failed to inform FedEx representatives that they should stop shipping the drugs, prosecutors suddenly dropped all the charges.

In 2017, **Kent Bailey** retired from the DEA after three decades as an agent. Two weeks later, he started a job as Minnesota state coordinator for the High Intensity Drug Trafficking Area program, facilitating collaboration between law enforcement agencies. **Kimberly Brill** was promoted to Group Supervisor for the Diversion Control Division of the Minneapolis office. **Steven Holdren** is an agent at the federal Department of Housing and Urban Development in Minneapolis.

Eric Stouch remains at the DEA's Special Operations Division. **Thomas Cindric** retired, taking a job with an organization combating ivory poaching. **Derek Maltz** also departed the DEA. Like a number of other ex-SOD agents from the Le Roux case, he entered the private sector, joining PenLink, a "software provider for communications surveillance collection and analysis."

In Brazil, **Zion Fadlon** became the co-owner of the successful Discovery Hostel and Restaurant in Rio. He was never charged with any crimes related to Paul Le Roux. When I traveled there in late 2017, I was unable to locate the women with whom Le Roux had attempted to conceive children.

Jon Wall, after taking a plea deal that could have resulted in up to five years in prison, was sentenced to probation in 2017. As of the trial, he was working as a dispatcher for a concrete company.

Moran Oz returned to Israel, where he ignored requests for additional interviews. **Alon Berkman** remained in hiding, as he had since he was indicted in the United States in 2014. When I reached out to his family in 2016, they claimed to have no way of contacting him. Gone, too, was **Omer Bezalel,** since jumping bail in Minnesota. One source told me he was living openly in Israel, but couldn't put me in touch.

After his acquittal, **Lachlan McConnell** returned to Canada. When I last spoke to him, he declined to disclose his location and said he was considering returning to the Philippines.

Nestor Del Rosario went into hiding. After years of searching for him and hearing speculation that he was likely dead, I finally found a former Le Roux employee who was in touch with him. She passed along a message, but he never responded.

Prabhakara Tumpati lives with his family in Pennsylvania, and runs three successful sleep and obesity treatment clinics across the Northeast. He maintains an interest in pursuing telemedicine. By 2025, the global telemedicine market is expected to reach $80 billion.

After his guilty plea, **Charles Schultz** sold Schultz Pharmacy and shuttered Medicine Mart. He died in 2018 at the age of eighty-six.

Paul Le Roux's girlfriend, **Cindy Cayanan,** was never indicted or arrested by the U.S. government, and appears to run an investment firm out of one of Paul Le Roux's old offices. **Lilian Cheung Yuen Pui** and Le Roux were formally divorced in June 2013. According to the letter from Le Roux's lawyer in 2016, the United States was considering relocating her and her family from their home in Europe, for their safety. I was unable to confirm the existence of his other rumored children in the Philippines.

Le Roux's cousin **Mathew Smith** lives in Bulawayo, where he remains in contact with **Steve and Andrew Hahn,** the latter of whom was eventually released from Philippine custody after two years on false drug charges, trumped up by Le Roux and Dave Smith.

John Nash, as of this writing, remains in the limbo of Philippine immigration custody. In the summer of 2017, Aurora Almendral and I talked our way in to visit him at Bicutan, a wretched open-air detention center housed on a military base in Manila. Nash had been held here for nearly three years without charges, and when he entered the waiting room he seemed nervous and frail. "I wish you'd come earlier," he said. "I read your stories. I follow you on Twitter." He admitted to working for Le Roux, but denied—unconvincingly, to my ear, based on what Le Roux had told authorities—involvement in the deaths of Bruce Jones and Joe Frank Zuñiga.

The **Blue Rock Resort** in Barretto continues to be a hub of intrigue. In April 2013, a man walked up to a table, pulled out a .45, and shot the bar's owner in the back of the head, execution style. The crime has not been solved.

In 2014, the captain who took over for Bruce Jones on the *M/V Ufuk,* **John Burne,** became the only person convicted in the arms-smuggling case. Burne had long since jumped bail and fled the country, but he was sentenced to an eight-year prison term in absentia. In 2016, the *Ufuk* sank under mysterious circumstances in Manila Bay.

Le Roux's super-fast yacht, the *Texas Star II,* after being confiscated by the DEA, was reused in a dramatic operation to capture a prominent Guinea-Bissau drug kingpin off the coast of West Africa. Mechanical problems on board the boat delayed the operation by a month. Afterward, the agency put it up for for sale.

Marcus, Le Roux's hit man, continues to live freely in South Africa. "Fuck, I've already said so much, the last thing I want is people knocking on my door," he said to me after we'd talked for an hour. "I'll never be able to put my fucking feet in America, or they will lock me up, I suppose." He felt he'd paid for the killings in his own way. "I think karma sorted me out for the shit I've done. I got divorced, I lost everything. I had to restart. I rebuilt my life, a good job and everything, and now I'm a bit scared because

I don't know what's going to happen, to be quite honest." He was disappointed, he said, that he'd never get to take the Harley road trip across the southern United States that he had always dreamed about.

After bringing down Le Roux, **Felix Klaussen** moved to Southeast Asia.

In 2014, an international sustainable fisheries organization proposed that **Somalia** redevelop its fishing industry, including small-scale fish processing plants strikingly similar to the one Paul Le Roux had envisioned.

As of this writing, **Paul Calder Le Roux** remains in federal custody in New York City, awaiting sentencing. The last time I saw Le Roux was in the fall of 2018, in a small courtroom on the twelfth floor of a federal courthouse in Manhattan. The hearing—the first in Le Roux's own case that wasn't sealed from the public—had been called to assign him new representation. He'd told the court he was finished with Joseph DiBenedetto and ready to accept free court-appointed counsel instead. I wondered if that meant that he'd run out of easily accessible cash. Or perhaps he saw no need to spend any more of it, given how little lawyering was left to be done on his behalf. The most important factor in his sentencing would be the 5K1 letter from the prosecutors, outlining the assistance he had provided.

His prospective attorney, a local criminal defender assigned to the case named Xavier Donaldson, walked in half an hour late and had yet to be informed of Le Roux's charges, or even his name.

The lead prosecutor, Michael Lockard, stepped up to summarize Le Roux's situation for the judge. "Mr. Le Roux has pleaded guilty in this case, and has assisted law enforcement by, among other things, testifying in a trial," he said. "The court was alerted and we were alerted to some . . . issues between Mr. Le Roux and his attorney." In an aside to Donaldson, he characterized the issues as "a breakdown in attorney-client communications." Le Roux's cooperation with the government was now complete,

Lockard continued, and the last of the defendants he'd testified against, Joseph Hunter, would be sentenced in the new year. The judge could sentence him as soon as the spring.

Sitting only a few feet away from me, Le Roux looked smaller up close, enveloped by his blue jail scrubs. He sat with his shoulders hunched at the defense table, polite and subdued in his answers to the judge's questions. He asked for time to confer with Donaldson before completing the switch. The judge adjourned for two weeks to allow him to do so. "I appreciate it so much, believe me," I heard him say to Donaldson, as he stood up.

Two U.S. marshals moved in to stand guard as he plodded out of the courtroom, glancing periodically over their shoulders to assess possible threats to the U.S. government's once-prized asset. When I looked around the rows of the gallery, though, it was empty except for me.

Acknowledgments

This book required the patience and generosity of hundreds of people. That number includes many sources whom I cannot thank by name, due to the conditions under which they cooperated. I want to express my blanket appreciation to former members of Le Roux's organization, law enforcement agents, attorneys, family members—especially family members, for whom the decision was often wrenching—and many others who provided information. I am more indebted still to those who were willing speak (even partly) on the record, no matter how I view their role in the events or how contentious the conversations. This book is built on their patient and often courageous assistance.

The original series behind this book, in *The Atavist Magazine*, was edited by Katia Bachko, who wrangled it into shape under inhuman deadline pressure. Joel Lovell provided additional editing and essential insights. Sean Cooper worked through the night to copyedit each installment. Thanks to Thomas Rhiel for his design, and Paul Kamuf for his video talents. Seyward Darby, in taking the reins at the magazine, gave me the space to finish this book.

And none of it would have been possible without Jeff Rabb, my business partner—along with Nick Thompson—and the real mastermind behind Atavist and *The Atavist Magazine.*

Any close reader will recognize the crucial role played by Aurora Almendral, an exceptional reporter in her own right, in my research in the Philippines. Without her, the book would be a shadow of its final self. I also benefited from the keen reporting and translation assistance of two other journalists abroad: Daniel Estrin in Israel and Luiza Miguez in Brazil. (Thanks as well to Daniela Pinheiro in Rio.) In the United States, Natalie Lampert and Oliver Conroy provided invaluable research assistance along the way. I was lucky to work with exceptional fact-checkers: Queen Arsem-O'Malley and Riley Blanton on the original *Atavist* series, and Ben Phelan on the book manuscript. All of them saved me from a pile of embarrassing errors, and any that remain in the book are my own.

During my reporting I again and again encountered the generosity of other journalists, in situations when it would have been easy to be cutthroat and competitive. Damon Tabor shared with me the voluminous research he had conducted on Le Roux. Robyn Lee Kriel provided helpful background on Bulawayo and Zimbabwe. Patrick Radden Keefe advised me on how to approach this kind of work. Johnny Dwyer pointed me to details on Dave Smith that he had uncovered for his book on Chucky Taylor and Liberia, *American Warlord.* Thanks as well to the creators of Sqoop (sqoop .com), a service that enabled me to track a maddening number of federal case dockets.

My reporting owes a debt to—and I hope respectfully builds upon—great work done on Le Roux by other journalists. Most importantly, Alan Feuer at *The New York Times* broke critical information—no less than Le Roux's name—and provided me insights on how to chase the rest of the story down. His colleague Ben Weiser did the first reporting on the Joseph Hunter arrest. Julian Rademeyer in South Africa carried out original and dangerous reporting on Le Roux back when no one else was looking. Shay Aspril in Israel was onto CSWW in 2012. Marco Antônio Martins in Brazil uncovered Le Roux's 2012 arrest a year before anyone else. I am grateful to all of them for their work, and their willingness to discuss it with me. Likewise, in the Philippines Mar Supnad, Non Alquitran, and Vic Vizcocho all uncovered important pieces of Le Roux's organization through their reporting. *The Australian*'s Mark Schliebs, in his own series on Le Roux, supplied facts about Le Roux's time in Sydney that I otherwise would not have found. Jefferey Gettleman and Sahal Abdulle generously shared recollections of their time with Felix Klaussen, experiences that were minor footnotes to their courageous work in Somalia. Ronen Bergman provided counsel and assistance in Israel.

I couldn't ask for a better advocate and friend through this process than my agent, David Kuhn, who not only shepherded this book to reality but also provided years of encouragement that gave me the confidence to attempt it. My thanks to the whole Aevitas team, especially Chelsey Heller, Kate Mack, and William LoTurco, for helping make it happen. At Creative Artists Agency, Michelle Kroes and Tiffany Ward have been tireless advocates for *The Atavist Magazine,* as have the management team at Circle of Confusion, and Darren Trattner. I would be lost in LA without Rick Jacobs at Skybound.

I benefited enormously from the input of readers and advisers along the way. Ali Kazemi let me borrow his legal mind countless times to understand my own research. Jon Mooallem not only preserved my sanity with his good humor and wisdom by phone every other week for years, he also helped me access an early draft. Max Linsky was a font of encouragement and thoughtful reflection about this book, and life. Robin Marantz Henig applied her experience and editing acumen to this manuscript with a thoroughness and intensity well beyond what I could have dared ask, improving it many, many times over. This book is also the culmination of years of wonderful editing at magazines that I received from the likes of

Alex Heard, Katrina Heron, Charlie Homans, Tom McNichol, Jeff O'Brien, Jamie Shreeve, Nick Thompson, and Daniel Zalewski.

Andy Ward is an unparalleled editor. I feel extremely fortunate to have had the chance to work with him. He helped shape my thinking on this book from the very beginning, dug into the details at each step, and made every part of it immeasurably better. It was a joy to work with him. The same goes for Chayenne Skeete, Evan Camfield, Barbara Fillon, Melanie DeNardo, Katie Tull, Andrea DeWerd, Tom Perry, Leigh Marchant, Carlos Beltran, Matthew Martin, and everyone else on the Random House team who took this from a jumble of words to a book on the shelf.

My deepest appreciation goes finally to family and friends, too many to name, who supported me in countless ways—from listening to me recount the story's details, to giving me a respite from thinking about them. To my parents and siblings, who have supported me over a lifetime. Lastly to my wife, reader, editor, and anchor, Samantha—and to our girls. I could not have done it without you, and I hope I've made you proud.

Notes

If a subject is quoted by name in the text, those quotes derive either from personal interviews conducted with the subject or a party to the conversation, or from documents and transcripts recounting the statements. Scenes or locations I describe in the first person, I witnessed myself. For all information specifically attributed to a document in the text—e.g., "according to company registration documents"—I viewed and/or possess those documents, unless otherwise noted. There are individuals described in this book who declined to speak on the record, or at all, for reasons personal and professional. Readers should not assume that because I have quoted a subject that that person necessarily spoke to me—often multiple accounts were available from other sources, including the subjects' own recollections in court documents. Neither should a reader assume that if a subject is *not* quoted by name, I did not speak to them. No sources were compensated in any way, directly or indirectly, paid or promised, in the course of my reporting.

Only three names have been altered in this book for anonymity: Felix Klaussen, Patrick Donovan, and Marcus. Klaussen's name I changed for what should now be obvious reasons: He was a high-level confidential informant against a murderous criminal cartel, and is involved in ongoing operations in that capacity. He argued persuasively that revealing his full identity could bring risk to his life. Other than the change of his name, he placed no conditions on my use of our interviews, but I have withheld (not changed) some biographical facts. Patrick Donovan was willing to explain first-hand how corruption in the Philippines operates and to describe his experiences with Paul Le Roux on the condition of anonymity. Because I quoted him often, it became unwieldy not to refer to him by some name rather than a generic honorific. He, too, placed no other conditions on my use of our interviews. And while "Marcus" is the name Le Roux used for his South African hit man, it is not the name that he is known by in his daily life. I used it due to an attribution agreement I made with him before discovering that he was Le Roux's assassin.

No other facts in this book have been changed to protect sources, or for any reason.

In some online correspondence that I quote directly I have corrected minor punctuation, spelling, and syntax issues and cut unrelated asides—all for readability's sake—without altering the meaning or context of the quoted statements. (Some of the interviews I conducted, and conversations I received copies of, involved very casual digital chats that can be confusing if left unadjusted in this fashion.) The chats are otherwise unchanged, and I have elected to avoid correcting other spelling mistakes or including repetitive instances of "[sic]" as long as the language is understandable.

Throughout this book I've tried to be as transparent as possible about my process—indeed, it's the primary reason I appear as a character at all—and to reveal how my reporting came about. But I feel the need to reemphasize here that subjects often provided conflicting accounts of the same events. Memories fade and diverge, driven by time and motive. Given the nature of the events, most subjects did little to document their participation. Indeed, they often actively worked to erase any record of it. Others tried to inflate their role, for reasons clear only to them, or perhaps not even to them. To arrive at this account, I've triangulated subjects' recollections against one another, and against tens of thousands of pages of documentation, wherever possible. At the same time, I'm mindful of the fact that documents also bring risk of bias and misdirection, as they are often the product of government agents looking to justify their work, or of defense attorneys seeking to minimize their clients' crimes. In some cases I've had to judge the reliability of a description of events based on my experiences with the teller, checking and rechecking facts in an attempt to edge as close as possible to the truth of what happened.

There is, of course, one critical witness whose experience I learned about only indirectly: Paul Calder Le Roux. As noted in these pages, outside of his voluminous testimony he has so far remained silent, as have his attorneys, in response to dozens of my requests. What he would say about how I've conveyed his story, I can only infer.

FREQUENTLY CITED CASES AND REPORTS

In notes referencing legal cases, for easier identification I have provided the document number from the case docket (e.g., "Document 990-7," rather than "Defense Sentencing Memorandum") and the overall case citation (e.g., *USA v. Berkman* rather than *USA v. Bezalel,* a subset of the former case). I have dated court filings according to the date on which they were filed. I have dated transcripts of court hearings, including those of both grand jury and trial proceedings, according to the date on which they occurred.

Hong Kong Special Administrative Region (HKSAR) v. Shulman, Doron Zvi, Sentencing Hearing, May 12, 2014, HCCC 297/2013.
Hong Kong Special Administrative Region (HKSAR) v. Yoav Hen and Daniel Fadlon, Sentencing Hearing, June 6, 2013, DCCC 1033 & 1036/2012.
Hong Kong Special Administrative Region (HKSAR) v. Omer Gavish, Verdict, June 24, 2013, DCCC 1033 & 1036/2012 (A).

Hong Kong Special Administrative Region (HKSAR) v. Omer Gavish, Court of Appeal, September 17, 2014, DCCC 1033 & 1036/2012 (A).

Internal Report of the Brazilian Federal Police, Grupo de Investigações Sensíveis (GISE), "Operation America," on surveillance of Paul Calder Le Roux, Processo Criminal 0014974-53.2012.4.02.5101-7, Vara Criminal Federal, 2012.

People of the Philippines v. Lawrence John Burne, Republic of the Philippines Court of Tax Appeals, December 3, 2014, CTA Crim. Case No. O-170.

U.N. Monitoring Group Report, "Report of the Monitoring Group on Somalia and Eritrea Pursuant to Security Council Resolution 1916," United Nations, June 20, 2011.

USA v. Hunter et al., S.D.N.Y, 1:13-cr-00521 (2013–18). Defendants: Joseph Hunter, Timothy Vamvakias, Dennis Gögel, Michael Filter, Slawomir Soborski, Adam Samia, David Stillwell (although Samia and Stillwell were prosecuted for different crimes than Vamvakias, Gögel, Filter, and Soborski, the court used the same case number, as I have done here).

USA v. Stammers et al., S.D.N.Y, 1:13-cr-00579 (2013–16). Defendants: Scott Stammers, Philip Shackels, Ye Tiong Tan Lim, Allan Kelly Reyes Peralta, Adrian Valkovic.

USA v. Berkman et al., D. Minn., 0:13-cr-00273 (2013–18). Defendants: Alon Berkman, Moran Oz, Babubhai Patel, Jonathan Wall, Shai Reuven, Lachlan Scott McConnell, Omer Bezalel, Elias Karkalas, Prabhakara Rao Tumpati, Onochie Aghaegbuna, and Eyad Mahrouq.

USA v. Le Roux et al., S.D.N.Y, 1:12-cr-00489 (2012–18). Defendants: Paul Calder Le Roux, Shai Reuven.

USA v. Charles G. Schultz, E.D. Wis., 1:14-cr-00089 (2012–14).

USA v. Babubhai Patel, E.D. Mich., 2:11-cr-20468 (2011–18).

PROLOGUE

xv **says the South African:** All dialogue and descriptions derive from recordings of the meeting.

xvi **Jack who made the initial connection:** Interview with the man identified in this book as Felix Klaussen. See Chapter 6 notes for further explanation.

xx **walked through the glass doors:** *USA v. Berkman,* Document 990-7, May 22, 2017. The pharmacy was Schultz Pharmacy, one of two owned by Schultz, along with Medicine Mart in Monroe.

xx **700,000 illegal painkiller prescriptions . . . $27 million:** *USA v. Schultz,* Document 22, November 14, 2014.

xx **Inside they discovered:** "Australian Found with 20 Tons of Explosive Materials," *Oriental Daily,* May 4, 2012.

xxi **an Israeli Australian citizen:** *HKSAR v. Shulman.* Also *HKSAR v. Hen, Fadlon.*

xxi **handwritten directions:** Internal Report of the Brazilian Federal Police.

xxi **a pair of spear fishermen:** Interview with Grant O'Fee, former police commissioner of Tonga, conducted by Oliver Conroy. While O'Fee and other authorities weren't definitive on what the divers were up to at the moment of discovery, they cited fishing as the most likely answer.

xxi **Lining the walls:** This and other details derive from both interviews and official police accounts, e.g., "Joint South Pacific law enforcement operation results in huge cocaine haul," Australian Federal Police Media Release, November 16, 2012. See also regional news accounts, e.g., "Decomposed Body, Cocaine Haul Found on Yacht," *ABC News* (Australia), November 15, 2012.

xxi **organized a gathering of cryptography buffs:** Runa A. Sandvik, "That One Time I Threw a CryptoParty with Edward Snowden," *Forbes,* May 27, 2014.

xxi **the agency couldn't break it:** "Inside the NSA's War on Internet Security," *Der Spiegel,* December 28, 2014.

xxii **"The scope of his criminal conduct":** *USA v. Hunter,* Document 591, April 17, 2018.

xxii **just started his shift:** Details on Jimena's discovery derive from an interview with Jeremy Jimena; the Philippine National Police (PNP) case file on the murder of Catherine Christina Lee; and *USA v. Hunter,* Document 580, April 5, 2018.

xxvi **300,000 people:** Philippine Statistics Authority, "Highlights of the Philippine Population 2015 Census of Population."

xxvi **Photos taken at the crime scene:** Philippine National Police (PNP) case file on the murder of Catherine Christina Lee.

xxvii **target-shooting videos on YouTube:** See, for example, youtube.com /watch?v=TOU00HiPuog.

xxvii **below the poverty line:** "Razon: 60% of PNP Men Live Below Poverty Line," *The Philippine Star,* June 3, 2006.

xxviii **5,000 pesos, or around $100:** Human Rights Watch, "Philippines: Death Squad Linked to Hundreds of Killings," May 20, 2014.

xxviii **police technicians were unable to check:** *USA v. Hunter,* Document 574, April 3, 2018, at 71.

xxx **two men were arrested in Roxboro:** "Feds: 2 NC Men Traveled to Philippines in Murder-for-Hire Plot," WRAL, July 22, 2015.

CHAPTER 1

3 **On a hunch:** The details of Brill and Holdren's background and investigation, unless noted otherwise, are drawn from and cross-checked between interviews with Brill, Holdren, and Kent Bailey; trial testimony from Brill and Holdren in *USA v. Berkman;* evidence presented during *USA v. Berkman;* grand jury testimony from Brill, filed under *USA v. Berkman,* Documents 952-1 to 952-7, 2010 and 2012; and interviews with an anonymous Department of Justice official directly familiar with the investigation.

4 **Phentermine is a "controlled substance":** DEA Drug Fact Sheets, dea.gov /druginfo/concerns.shtml.

5 **the DEA had become concerned:** Over the early and mid-2000s, the agency

conducted large pill-mill investigations with names like Operation Baywatch, Operation CyberRx, Operation Lightning Strike, and Operation Control/Alt/Delete. See Michael Leonhart, DEA Administrator, "Warning: The Growing Danger of Prescription Drug Diversion," Statement before the U.S. House of Representatives, April 14, 2011.

7 **Minnesota, Texas, and Illinois:** The three pharmacies in question were, respectively: Ross-West Bank Pharmacy in Minneapolis, El Rancho Pharmacy in Dallas, and La Joya Drug in Chicago.

7 **routine inspections:** It was not unusual for diversion investigators to show up at pharmacies to examine their record-keeping procedures and how well they were securing drugs on site.

7 **hundreds of similar websites:** Nearly all of RX Limited's hundreds of affiliated sites are no longer active online. But snapshots of the sites and information about them—including Acmemeds.com—are available through the Internet Archive's Wayback Machine (web.archive.org) or through the work of watch-dog organizations including LegitScript and the Spamhaus Project.

8 **"Open your own online pharmacy":** RX Limited would also supply affiliates with out-of-the-box templates for their websites.

8 **sending spam email:** At one point, the Spamhaus Project, a nonprofit organization which tracks the largest email spammers on the Internet so that services can block them, would estimate that RX Limited–associated sites were responsible for 25 percent of the spamming sites on their block list. Spamhaus Register of Known Operations, November 2010.

8 **Ultram . . . was developing a reputation for abuse:** See, for example, Max Siegelbaum and Alessandro Accorsi, "Egypt's Wave of Painkiller Addiction," Al Jazeera, November 29, 2013, and Justin Scheck, "Tramadol: The Opioid Crisis for the Rest of the World," *The Wall Street Journal,* October 19, 2016.

8 **the Controlled Substances Act:** 21 U.S. Code § 812.

9 **lack any medical application:** This purely legal categorization is often subject to significant scientific dispute, especially in the case of marijuana, ecstasy, and LSD—all Schedule I drugs that have been shown to have viable medical applications. See, for example, David Nutt et al., "Effects of Schedule I drug laws on neuroscience research and treatment innovation," *Nature Reviews Neuroscience* 14 (2013), at 577–83.

9 **wasn't entirely clear:** This question would later become a central—if confusing—one in the prosecution of RX Limited. The DEA had specifically exempted Fioricet from some of its civil drug regulations (21 C.F.R. § 1308.32). Whether that exemption applied to potentially criminal distribution of Fioricet was a battle that would be fought over years (see *USA v. Berkman,* Document 1045, August 17, 2017).

9 **"Our company is committed":** *USA v. Berkman,* Document 1004, February 8, 2017, at 234.

10 **seventy-two *million* doses:** Interview with Kimberly Brill.

11 **a hotel in Manila:** Interview with Steven Holdren.

12 **Q9 in Canada:** *USA v. Berkman*, Document 1004, February 8, 2017, at 273.

13 **Operation Silent Thunder:** Rene Sanchez, "Meth Production Reaches 'Epidemic' Level on Coast," *The Washington Post*, August 25, 2001.

CHAPTER 2

16 **Charles Schultz was struggling:** Details relating to Schultz and his pharmacies derive primarily from the case file *USA v. Schultz*, particularly the defense and government sentencing reports, as well as interviews with Hal Harlowe, Schultz's attorney. I was unable to obtain an interview with Schultz, who died in 2018, and his family declined to comment on his case.

17 **$3.50 for each one filled:** *USA v. Schultz*, Document 18, November 11, 2014, at 2.

17 **Alphanet's website:** Accessed at web.archive.org/web/20110207170852 /http://alphanet-trading.com.

18 **"put your fees away for a lawyer":** This was the standard script used by RX Limited in its recruitment of pharmacists. From interviews with Moran Oz.

18 **a former DEA agent in Florida:** Interview with Hal Harlowe. I was unable to establish who played the role of the DEA agent.

18 **one technician later said:** From *USA v. Berkman*, Document 952-13, October 16, 2013.

19 **Tumpati was seeking some:** Details relating to Tumpati and his history derive from interviews with Tumpati, an unpublished biographical account provided by Tumpati, and extensive trial testimony, court filings, and evidence from *USA v. Berkman*.

19 **middle of a recession:** While being a doctor is often considered recession-proof employment, there is evidence that the Great Recession of 2008 affected the healthcare services market unexpectedly, as many Americans cut back on doctor's visits and prescription drugs. The research also points to the recession as a reason why patients might turn to unknown online pharmacies for cheaper versions of their medications. See, for example, Karoline Mortensen and Jie Chen, "The Great Recession and Racial and Ethnic Disparities in Health Services Use," *JAMA Internal Medicine*, February 25, 2013.

20 **called Residentscafe.com:** From the Internet Archive, web.archive.org /web/20060421162357/http://www.residentscafe.com:80.

20 **called WikiMD.org:** wikimd.org/wiki/index.php?title=WikiMD.org:About.

22 **a request transmitted across that network on August 27, 2008:** *USA v. Berkman*, Document 5, November 13, 2013, at 13.

22 **at Charles Schultz's Medicine Mart:** *USA v. Berkman*, Document 952-13, October 16, 2013, at 15–18.

22 **down the street from the DEA:** Brill and Holdren used a FedEx Kinkos mailing address for "Sarah Johnson," at 80 South 8th Street, six blocks from the DEA offices.

CHAPTER 3

23 **standing at a podium:** A video of Bharara's press conference was subsequently released by the Southern District of New York.

23 **unsealed an indictment:** *USA v. Hunter,* Document 11, September 30, 2013.

24 **on a golf course:** "Rambo's Lonely Lair," *Bangkok Post,* October 10, 2013.

25 **another dramatic bust:** *USA v. Stammers,* Document 11, November 21, 2013.

25 **Bharara said in a press release:** "5 Extradited, Charged with North Korean Drug Trafficking Conspiracy," DEA Press Release, November 20, 2013.

25 *The Washington Post* **quoted:** The anonymous law enforcement source told *The Post* that the defendants were "part of a sprawling international drug trafficking ring led by a former American soldier, Joseph Manuel Hunter, who has separately been charged with conspiring to murder a Drug Enforcement Administration agent." The characterization seemed designed to squelch further inquiry into the matter: The DEA had caught the "leader," Hunter, and his cohorts. (Sari Horwitz, "5 Extradited in Plot to Import North Korean Meth to U.S.," *The Washington Post,* November 20, 2013.) Later, *Vice News* also made the connection between the cases, citing anonymous DEA sources. (Keegan Hamilton, "North Korean Meth, Motorcycle Gangs, Army Snipers, and a Guy Named Rambo," *Vice News,* March 18, 2014.)

26 **a DEA spokesperson replied:** This in and of itself wasn't necessarily unusual. It was common for the DEA to refuse comment on open cases.

26 **to a** *New York Times* **reporter:** Alan Feuer, "In Real Life, 'Rambo' Ends Up as a Soldier of Misfortune, Behind Bars," *The New York Times,* December 20, 2014.

26 **"Viktor Bout on steroids":** Bout had been the subject of numerous books and magazine articles, and a Nicolas Cage movie was based loosely on his exploits.

27 **a 2008 Federal Communications Commission complaint:** The letter from the FCC was addressed, as it happened, to the same mail drop address that Brill and Holdren had discovered in Florida.

27 **Red White & Blue Arms:** The dealer's website, rwbarms.com, was linked to a registration containing Le Roux's email address.

27 **in a Hong Kong company database:** Many countries offer online databases of all registered corporations, either free or for a fee. In Hong Kong this is known as the Integrated Companies Registry Information System (ICRIS). In the United Kingdom it is known as Companies House. Unless otherwise noted, I obtained information on Le Roux's companies through searches in these databases, or they were provided to me by former members of his organization.

27 **establishing Net Trading LTD:** This was the first document on which I found Le Roux's signature, a jumble of letters piled atop the "R" in "Roux." The address Le Roux gave was an apartment in Rotterdam.

27 **someone named Robson Tandanayi:** Le Roux, as he began registering companies in the names of other people, often returned to the same individuals over

and over again, including Tandanayi, a South African named Edgar Van Tonder, and a Zimbabwean named Robert McGowan.

28 **dozens of Le Roux–connected companies:** For all of these companies, I have obtained corporate filings linking them to Le Roux and his designees.

28 **a defunct software company called SW Professionals:** An archived copy of the site is available at web.archive.org/web/*/swprofessionals.com.

28 **from the prying eyes of law enforcement:** "If you are worried that someone might have access to your documents, emails, sales projections, contracts, tax returns or receipts, romantic letters, or any other private files, then this product is for you," Le Roux had written at the top.

28 **old website for E4M:** To track the registrations on both active and abandoned domains, I used a paid service called DomainTools, which provides full histories of any given website, including who owned it when throughout its history.

28 **whistleblower Edward Snowden:** Runa A. Sandvik, "That One Time I Threw a CryptoParty with Edward Snowden," *Forbes,* May 27, 2014.

29 **terrorist group ISIS:** Rukmini Callimachi, "How ISIS Built the Machinery of Terror Under Europe's Gaze," *The New York Times,* March 29, 2016.

29 **indicted eleven RX Limited employees:** *USA v. Berkman,* Document 5, November 13, 2013.

29 **declined to talk:** "We respectfully decline interview as the case is pending trial," a spokesperson responded to me by email.

CHAPTER 4

32 **one childhood friend:** When I traveled to Israel in 2016 to report on RX Limited and Oz, several friends, including this one, agreed to speak to me but were frightened for their safety if their names were somehow connected to Le Roux.

32 **Oz had just graduated:** Unless otherwise noted, details from Oz's biography and experiences derive from interviews with Oz conducted in Minneapolis and by phone between 2015 and 2017.

33 **online forums like Craigslist:** RX Limited would often post in the "medical/health" section of the sites' job listings. See, for example, *USA v. Berkman,* Document 952-12, April 9, 2013.

33 **Berkman's primary responsibility:** Interviews with Moran Oz. I was unable to locate anyone—including former colleagues and members of his immediate family—who would admit to having seen or heard from Alon Berkman since his indictment became public in 2014. I heard rumors that he had relocated to Thailand or India, while others claimed he was simply waiting out the U.S. charges in hiding in Israel. Whatever the case, I was unable to interview him, and accounts of his role derive from interviews with Oz and others who worked closely with him, along with thousands of pages of evidence in his case, including dozens of emails to and from him.

33 **New hires were supplied:** In addition to Moran Oz, I interviewed a dozen other call center employees, both low-level customer service representatives and call center managers, to understand how the business worked.

33 **one former call center worker:** This particular former employee was an American who took a part-time job at the firm while studying at an Israeli university. "We all thought that we were an outsourcing company for something in the States," he said.

34 **If a state changed its rules:** At one point, Oz maintained a chart listing sixteen states that regulated Ultram, Soma, and Fioricet, RX Limited's primary drugs, at the state level. It included the phone numbers for each state's board of pharmacy. *USA v. Berkman,* Document 948, April 3, 2017, at 17.

34 **Boaz and Tomer Taggart told their employees:** Boaz Taggart did not respond to inquiries when I contacted him while in Israel through a local reporter. Tomer Taggart declined to speak with the reporter about RX Limited, and to meet or speak with me. Details of their involvement were provided to me by Oz and other employees, and confirmed in Israeli corporate records and court documents including, for example, *USA v. Berkman,* Document 1008, February 14, 2017, at 1027.

35 *I'm your boss now:* The original chat transcripts were unavailable, but these lines were reconstructed by Oz in interviews.

36 **the Hard Rock Cafe:** A number of former employees told me that Le Roux favored the Hard Rock in Makati as a meeting place. When I showed a photo to a manager in 2015, he could only offer a faint memory of having seen Le Roux dine there.

36 **to avoid taxes:** *USA v. Berkman,* Document 774, January 17, 2017, at 8–9.

38 **$2 to $3 commission . . . a large map:** *USA v. Berkman,* Document 1005, February 9, 2017, at 63, 156.

CHAPTER 5

39 **government-issue five-by-seven notebooks:** Interview with Steven Holdren.

40 **Cartadmin.com and a second site called SystemsCA.com:** *USA v. Berkman,* Document 1004, February 8, 2017, at 247.

40 **a telephone directory:** Ibid. at 265.

40 **international body called ICANN:** icann.org.

41 **a domain registrar operating in the Philippines called ABSystems:** ABSystems was in fact the *only* registrar operating in the Philippines at the time. See Au Hipol, "IP Views: What's in a Domain Name?," BNU IP Views, May 27, 2008.

41 **ABSystems' own web page:** The site, at yournamemonkey.com, gave the superficial impression of being a typical registrar, like Network Solutions or GoDaddy. It was only when you attempted to actually find and buy a site that there appeared to be no way to do so.

42 **an endless variation of drug-related domain names:** As of 2009, the watchdog group LegitScript would document that RX Limited was connected to thirty-two thousand different pharmaceutical marketing and sales sites, per a database I received from John Horton, the founder and CEO of LegitScript.

42 **subpoena to ICANN:** *USA v. Berkman,* Document 1004, February 8, 2017, at 267.

43 **administrative subpoenas:** For a specific discussion of how Brill and Holdren used administrative subpoenas, see *USA v. Berkman,* Document 1004, February 8, 2017, at 216. For a broader discussion of administrative subpoena use, see, for example, David Kravets, "We Don't Need No Stinking Warrant," *Wired,* August 28, 2012.

43 **paulca@rocketmail.com:** Ibid. at 277–78.

44 **a private, secure email program:** Server73 addresses appeared to be confined to an upper layer of Le Roux's organization, and thus provided a handy way to distinguish between his thousands of employees. Among the addresses investigators located were ron@server73.net, michaelross@server73.net, allen@server73.net, stevelebaron@server73.net, and dimov@server73.net, all of which proved to be aliases for important members of Le Roux's organization. And of course, pleroux@server73.net.

44 **more than twenty separate email accounts:** *USA v. Berkman,* Document 1013, February 22, 2017, at 1917.

44 **under the names Levi Kugel and Alon Berkman:** *USA v. Berkman,* Document 948, April 3, 2017, at 17.

45 **"Please stop sending so many emails":** *USA v. Berkman,* Document 952-16, April 3, 2017.

45 **a July 2007 article:** Jeffrey Young and Kevin Bogardus, "Even John Q. Public Can Hire K Street—if He Has the Cash," *The Hill,* July 3, 2007.

46 **analyst finally unearthed a photo:** Interview with Kent Bailey.

47 **obtained a conviction:** Amy Forliti, "Minn. Online Prescription Drug Seller Faces up to Life in Prison for Scheme," Associated Press, November 14, 2015.

47 **the Consumer Protection Branch:** For a general description of CPB, the only civil division of the Department of Justice that handles civil and criminal prosecutions, see justice.gov/civil/consumer-protection-branch.

47 **file for legal records from foreign governments:** These requests, conducted through what are called Mutual Legal Assistance Treaties, or MLATs, are time-consuming to write and execute. Often they must be drafted by investigators, subjected to legal review by attorneys at the Department of Justice, and translated into a foreign language. Any response must then be translated back into English. In the Le Roux case, investigators had a leg up due to Kimberly Brill's legal background.

47 **FinCEN:** fincen.gov/what-we-do

47 **a program called Fedwire:** For a general description of Fedwire see "Fedwire Funds Services," Board of Governors of the Federal Reserve System, federalreserve.gov/paymentsystems/fedfunds_about.htm.

48 **$250 million a year:** Estimates of Le Roux's RX Limited revenues were difficult if not impossible for investigators to establish accurately, given the volume and variability of bank transfers they were seeing between the United States and Hong Kong, among other locations, and the layers he used to obscure his proceeds. According to Bailey, one IRS estimate for Le Roux's annual revenues was $400 million. Between 2005 and 2010, Kimberly Brill calculated

that Le Roux had sent between $225 million and $275 million into the United States, just to cover wholesale drug costs and commissions, which means his revenues could be multiples of those numbers. (See *USA v. Berkman,* Document 952–1, August 17, 2010, at 30.) Le Roux himself would later estimate his lifetime *profits* at $300 million, a number that investigators and employees alike believed wildly underrepresented his earnings. (*USA v. Hunter,* Document 580, April 5, 2018, at 555.)

48 **roughly the same as Facebook:** In 2007, Facebook's revenues were $153 million. In 2008, they were $272 million. From Facebook Inc., Form S-1, U.S. Securities and Exchange Commission, February 1, 2012.

48 **$50 million in cash:** Interview with Kent Bailey.

CHAPTER 6

49 **had a reputation for looking the other way:** See, for example, United States Department of State Bureau for International Narcotics and Law Enforcement Affairs, "International Narcotics Control Strategy Report: Money Laundering and Financial Crimes," March 2010, at 119; and Clifford Lo and Alex Lo, "Police, Customs Probe Record Pile of Dirty Money," *South China Morning Post,* February 22, 2011.

49 **fifty-year-old Canadian:** Details of McConnell's involvement, unless otherwise noted, derive from interviews with McConnell, filings in *USA v. Berkman,* and other members of Le Roux's organization.

50 **local subsidiary of Metalor:** For further discussions of Metalor's role in the money-laundering scheme, see *HKSAR v. Gavish* and *HKSAR v. Shulman.*

50 **McConnell didn't inquire:** "My job was to move it from the secure locations," he said.

50 **British ex-soldier named Dave Smith:** I was unable to interview Smith, for reasons that will become clear later.

51 **gotten his start . . . provided security:** Lachlan McConnell LinkedIn page.

51 **Smith left the company under acrimonious circumstances:** Interviews with both Lachlan McConnell and the Manila-based security contractor identified hereafter as Patrick Donovan.

51 **hailed from Northern Ireland:** Interview with Patrick Donovan; interview with anonymous former member of Le Roux's organization, now incarcerated.

51 **fighting in the Falklands War:** Interview with Tim Vamvakias.

51 **he surfaced in Liberia:** Details of Smith's work in Liberia derive from Johnny Dwyer, *American Warlord: A True Story* (Vintage, 2016), 105–14. "You really shouldn't be here," Smith once told Chucky Taylor's teenaged American girlfriend. "You shouldn't be mixed up with these people." Smith helped Chucky Taylor build a training facility and firing range for his squad, and declared to new recruits that they would turn them into an elite SWAT team.

52 **a 2004 story on contractors:** Tucker Carlson, "Inside the (Not So) Secret Armies of Operation Iraqi Freedom," *Esquire,* March 2004.

52 **the construction of a shooting range:** *USA v. Berkman,* Document 774, January 17, 2017, at 32.

52 **what he called "dummies":** For a discussion of how Le Roux used "dummies" in his business, see, for example, *USA v. Berkman,* Document 1005, February 9, 2017, at 594.

52 **counted among his dummies:** Both Tandanayi and van Tonder appear repeatedly on publicly available registrations for Le Roux's companies. Tandanayi, I later learned, was a contact Le Roux met through relatives in Bulawayo, Zimbabwe. Van Tonder was an elderly South African whose original connection to Le Roux I could never trace.

54 **So it was with Felix Klaussen:** This is one of two sources to whom I have given pseudonyms. The real person I'm calling Klaussen, over the course of more than thirteen hours of interviews and volumes of encrypted correspondence, argued convincingly that using his real name would present a threat to the safety of himself and those around him. All details of Klaussen's experience come from those interviews, cross-checked against the recollections of other Le Roux employees, unless otherwise noted.

54 **the sailors at Subic Bay:** For simplicity's sake, I use "Subic Bay" or "Subic" to include the general area that encompasses the region surrounding the former base, which includes the geographically distinct towns of Barretto and Olongapo. Descriptions are based on personal visits.

54 **Americans decommissioned the base in 1992:** Bob Drogin, "Americans Bid Farewell to Last Philippine Base," *Los Angeles Times,* November 25, 1992.

55 **served in the French Foreign Legion:** The Legion, a branch of the French Army that accepts volunteers from around the world, is known for its intensive training and hard-bitten soldiers. How long De Meyer actually served is in dispute. Klaussen told me that his former friend lasted only a month, operating under the name Alain Devisère. The press office of the French Foreign Legion declined to confirm or deny De Meyer's enlistment.

55 **an expat-friendly pub:** Sid's was a regular meeting place for Le Roux's employees, none of whom, in my interviews, could recall anything particularly distinguished about it. "This could be a British expat bar anywhere the world over," *Lonely Planet* once described it. "Cross through the doors and enter a world of pints and football." (See *Lonely Planet Philippines* [2006], 103–4.)

56 **the same in Da Nang:** The property purchase, Klaussen said, ultimately fell through.

58 **former U.S. Navy sailor:** The American, who worked for Le Roux for over a year on a wide variety of missions across Africa and Asia, requested anonymity for his own safety. "To be blunt, my biggest concern is the fat man sending some hit squad to end me," he said of Le Roux.

58 **Echelon Associates:** To all outward appearances, Echelon looked to be a legitimate security contractor, offering services such as "risk management" and "executive protection." Job applicants sent résumés, submitted to interviews, and filled out a series of employment forms. Many of Le Roux's mercenaries I

spoke to, however, were also hired directly by Smith or Le Roux himself, and had never heard the name Echelon.

58 **a fake Zimbabwean birth certificate:** I obtained copies of each of Le Roux's fake identities through correspondence with former employees who in some cases had helped Le Roux acquire them.

59 **South African contractor named Marcus:** Although this man lives under another name, "Marcus" is how Le Roux referred to him (see *USA v. Hunter*, Document 580, April 5, 2018, at 399). I initially agreed to grant him anonymity believing he was involved in one particular part of Le Roux's business about which I was seeking information. Later I discovered his role was much greater, and more disturbing. At that point, we had already made an agreement and he declined to allow his name to be used, out of fear of the consequences for him in South Africa.

59 **an Irish ex-soldier named John O'Donoghue:** O'Donoghue was another Irishman who had co-founded Echelon, the security front company, with Dave Smith. From interviews with Tim Vamvakias, as well as *USA v. Hunter*, Documents 576 and 580, April 4 and 5, 2018.

60 **carrying a duffel bag full of American cash:** This incident was described to me by a former contractor and referenced in *USA v. Hunter*, Document 589, April 12, 2018, at 1565.

60 **gold hidden in the tailgate:** Interviews with two contractors who were part of this mission, which involved driving gold into Mozambique and then flying it out on a Russian Antonov cargo plane owned by Le Roux.

60 **supervise logging operations:** Interview with Robert McGowan.

60 **through La Plata Trading . . . the banner of Martenius Trading:** Artifacts of Le Roux's former timber businesses live on in the form of business registrations for companies like La Plata and Martenius, online advertisements for their wood, job listings for roles in the operations, and the LinkedIn profiles of former employees.

CHAPTER 7

61 **a relative from his extended family:** This relative, who was close to Le Roux, asked that their name not be used as a condition for our interview, because they do not share a last name with Le Roux and fear personal repercussions if the connection were to be revealed. Unless otherwise noted, the childhood details here derive from interviews with this relative, Le Roux's cousin Mathew Smith, and his half-sibling Sandi.

61 **born on Christmas Eve, 1972:** I received a copy of Le Roux's real birth certificate from a relative.

61 **a soldier from South Africa:** The relative and Mathew Smith both provided me this version of events.

61 **Other family members recalled instead that Le Roux's father:** Interview with Le Roux's half-sibling Sandi.

62 **154,000 tons of the stuff:** Edwin Mwase, "Shabanie and Mashaba Mines (SMM): It's All About the Money," *The Sunday Mail,* March 22, 2015.

63 **played on a console:** His gaming obsession, according to Mathew Smith, was a space combat game called *Wing Commander.*

64 **later recount to employees:** Le Roux once told a call center manager that he had "made his first million" selling porn as a teenager in South Africa.

65 **one of his early employers:** In addition to my interview with this early employer, I was able to verify Le Roux's early work life through his own extensively documented résumé, which came to light as part of the evidence in *USA v. Berkman.* While it was not submitted at trial, I was able to obtain a copy of it.

65 **spending six months in Virginia Beach:** *USA v. Hunter,* Document 580, April 5, 2018, at 545. Also interview with Mathew Smith.

65 **followed her to Sydney:** Interview with relative. Le Roux's résumé also has him arriving in Australia in 1995.

65 **picked up a variety of contract programming jobs:** Le Roux résumé.

65 **obsessed with his work:** Mark Schliebs, "The Geek, the Guns and the Trail of Bodies," *The Australian,* April 2, 2016. Schliebs was able to locate and interview Le Roux's first wife. "He wanted to see the world and vowed never to be tied down in one spot," Schliebs wrote that Le Roux had told her.

66 **he wrote in November 1995:** Many message boards from the 1990s have been archived and made searchable as part of Google Groups, Google's online message board feature. All quotes here are Le Roux's original writings, and I have confirmed their authenticity by matching their associated email addresses with addresses verified as Le Roux's through other means, such as website registrations and court documents. In this case, Paul Le Roux, "France is a great Country, Australia is a worthless DUMP," alt.religion.kibology, November 5, 1995.

66 **"What kind of a dickhead are you?":** Andrew Murdoch, "Moving to Aus from the US—HELP!," aus.general, November 20, 1995.

66 **a thirty-eight-part post:** Paul Le Roux, "My Nationality, My Views," aus .general, November 12, 1995.

66 **alt.security.scramdisk, alt.security.pgp, and sci.crypt:** These forums, like the Australia-related ones, are archived and searchable on Google Groups.

67 **initially called Caveo:** As late as March 1999, before the software was released, Le Roux was referring to the software as Caveo, per highly technical correspondence with other encryption coders that was forwarded to me.

67 **Le Roux's software allowed:** Details concerning Le Roux's software derive from the release notes on the E4M website, available through the Internet Archive at web.archive.org/web/20010331171326/http://www.e4m.net.

67 **a post to the alt.security.scramdisk board:** Paul Le Roux, "New version of free disk encryption product for NT," alt.security.scramdisk, June 27, 1999.

67 **written "from scratch":** Paul Le Roux, "Public statement by Paul Le Roux," alt.security.scramdisk, June 16, 2004.

67 **a manifesto of sorts:** Image of the E4M.net website available through the Internet Archive at web.archive.org/web/20010331171326/http://www.e4m .net.

68 **Le Roux was helpful and engaging:** See, for example, Le Roux providing friendly technical support at Paul Le Roux, "USB Keyboard does not work with Red Screen," alt.security.scramdisk, January 8, 2002; and Paul Le Roux, "ScramDisk still exist? Attn: Paul Le Roux," alt.security.pgp, January 7, 2002.

68 **"without first telling your wife":** Paul Le Roux, "Drivecrypt PLUS PACK," alt .security.scramdisk, April 6, 2002.

68 **divorced amicably:** Interviews with Le Roux's relatives.

68 **produced no children:** Copy of divorce records from the Family Court of Australia, at Brisbane, December 21, 1999.

68 **a contract programming company called SW Professionals:** The SW Professionals website is archived at web.archive.org/web/20021011100215/http:// www.swprofessionals.com/people.html. Le Roux was also interviewed about his company for a brief story ("Firms Lack On-Demand Computing Strategy," *Africa News,* November 3, 2003), sounding like a by-the-book contract programming entrepreneur.

69 **Hafner wanted to create:** Details from Le Roux's employment with Hafner derive from interviews with Hafner and another SecurStar colleague, Shaun Hollingworth, as well as message board postings in which much of the history of E4M and SecurStar were hashed out publicly.

69 **they'd had a child not long after:** Interview with Le Roux's relative.

69 **Le Roux seemed increasingly bitter:** Paul Le Roux, "Hacker Contest: Break DriveCrypt and Win 50.000 Euro," alt.security.scramdisk, April 13, 2002.

70 **released a powerful free file-encryption program:** "TrueCrypt 1.0 Released," PCReview newsgroups, February 2, 2004.

70 **Hafner suspected:** Details of the dispute between Hafner and the TrueCrypt programmers were captured in multiple message board threads, including "P. Le Roux (author of E4M) accused by W.Hafner (SecurStar)," alt.security .scramdisk, February 3, 2004.

70 **openly soliciting work:** Paul Le Roux, "Paul Le Roux looking for work," alt. security.scramdisk, October 4, 2002.

71 **he went in search of his birth certificate:** Interviews with three Le Roux relatives.

72 **The DEA would come to believe:** Interview with a former DEA agent familiar with the Le Roux case.

72 **Hornbuckle was arrested in South Africa:** "Up for Fraud, Illegal Exports," News24, November 21, 2003.

72 **Le Roux had traveled to Costa Rica:** Le Roux, at the very least, did pursue online gambling in Costa Rica at a later point, sending one of his Israeli deputies, Shai Reuven, to open a gambling venture there. See *USA v. Hunter,* Document 576, April 4, 2018, at 362.

72 **looking for help opening a company:** Paul Le Roux, "FOREIGNER NEEDING YOUR HELP, MAKE A QUICK $500," misc.entrepreneurs, March 2, 2003.

72 **registered the domain names:** Whois history records for RXPayouts.com and BillRx.com, obtained through DomainTools.com.

73 **he incorporated RX Limited in Hong Kong:** According to the Hong Kong Companies Registry, RX Limited was first registered on July 14, 2004.

73 **he moved his family . . . to the Philippines:** Le Roux himself varied on the exact date of his move to the Philippines. At some points he claimed to have done so in 2005 (see *USA v. Hunter,* Document 580, April 5, 2018, at 546). On his résumé, he claimed to have opened his first call center in the Philippines in 2004.

73 **In the incorporation documents:** From Beit Oridan registration documents obtained from Israeli public records, as well as later companies opened by Le Roux: IBS, CSWW, and SCSM.

CHAPTER 8

75 **The Elon Musks . . . of the world:** Elon Musk's history was at times eerily similar to Le Roux's: Raised in South Africa, he, too, had developed an obsession with coding and video games in his adolescence. While Le Roux turned to pornography to make his first money, Musk sold a computer game for his. (See Sean O'Kane, "Play the PC Game Elon Musk Wrote as a Pre-teen," *The Verge,* June 9, 2015.)

75 **They did, tracking me to New Orleans:** "Writer Evan Ratliff Tried to Vanish. Here's What Happened," *Wired,* November 2009.

75 **once occupied both penthouses:** Interview with anonymous call center manager.

76 **before hanging up abruptly:** Later, I was able to persuade this manager, who worked for Le Roux in both Israel and the Philippines, to speak to me anonymously at length over several interviews.

76 **the high-rise offices of Blu:** www.bluenergy.ph.

76 **asked that I keep him anonymous:** In addition to concerns about American authorities, this call center manager, like many who worked for Le Roux, remained worried about power that his former boss still held in the Philippines.

78 **Patrick Donovan, a well-known figure:** Donovan is one of two people whom I have given full pseudonyms. As noted in the text, it was a condition of our interviews, and ultimately I deemed the information he was providing about the Manila underground and corruption worthwhile enough to include. I also worked to check details of what he told me with other sources and documents. In some cases, noted below, that proved impossible.

80 **"That's what your life is worth":** I found plenty of corroborating evidence for this assertion. For example: Human Rights Watch, "Philippines: Death Squad Linked to Hundreds of Killings," May 20, 2014.

80 **bad publicity from a botched job:** I was able to confirm all the details that Donovan gave me about his previous work and arrival in the Philippines, some specifics of which I have withheld here to maintain his anonymity.

81 **availed themselves of Donovan's services:** Donovan's portrayal of himself matches what I heard from others, including one American security contractor who told me that he was known as "the Ray Donovan of the Philippines," after the lead character in the eponymous American TV series—a fixer in charge of bribes and payoffs for rich clients.

81 **At the industry's fringes were "boiler rooms":** For background on the Philippines' prolific boiler room industry, see Sheila Samonte-Pesayco, "PCIJ Report: Filipino Is King of Boiler Rooms," *The Philippine Star,* April 15, 2002; and James Hookway, "Manila Moves to Crack Down on 'Boiler Room' Operations," *The Wall Street Journal,* August 27, 2001.

81 **an Israeli acquaintance:** When I contacted this acquaintance, he at first denied any knowledge of Le Roux, then said, "Maybe I've met him, I'm not going to deny that. I have nothing to say about him." Then he hung up and declined further calls and messages.

82 **"I was escorted in the building":** The details of this meeting derive from Donovan. The only other person present, according to his version, was Le Roux, who has not been forthcoming on his side of the conversation.

83 **at $15,000 a month:** This amount, given to me by Donovan, was later confirmed by Le Roux in *USA v. Hunter,* Document 581, April 9, 2018, at 699.

83 **Smith, by Donovan's account, brought Le Roux Donovan's contacts:** The account of how Smith came to work for Le Roux demonstrates, in many ways, the problem of reporting on Le Roux. The basic outlines of the story that Donovan told me were confirmed in interviews with two other ex-mercenaries who worked under Smith for Le Roux. One, Tim Vamvakias, confirmed that Smith met Le Roux while working for Donovan, and then left to work for Le Roux directly. Vamvakias, however, recalled that rather than telling Le Roux to fuck off, Donovan had in fact done paid work for Le Roux. So too did another former employee of Donovan and Le Roux. When I questioned Donovan about this, he told me that he'd been paid an up-front retainer for Le Roux just to meet with him, but never carried out any work and returned the money. The former U.S. Navy sailor who worked for Le Roux told me as well that he'd heard the story that Smith met Le Roux through Donovan. Lachlan McConnell, on the other hand, said Smith told him only that he and Le Roux had met in a bar. I have included Donovan's story, with caveats, because it is the one that matches most closely the facts I can verify.

CHAPTER 9

85 **a new company called Customer Service Worldwide:** Publicly available registration documents for CSWW include a copy of McGowan's passport.

85 **located on another floor of the same building:** Interview with Shay Aspril, Israeli journalist, as well as his prescient 2011 story about CSWW for the Israeli

magazine *Calcalist:* "An Invitation from Tel Aviv, a Prescription from the Internet, a Drug from America," *Calcalist,* July 28, 2011.

86 **$300,000 a month:** Interview with Moran Oz.

86 **planning an initial public offering:** Interview with an anonymous call center manager who worked in both Israel and the Philippines.

86 **named Asaf Shoshana:** Shoshana declined to speak to me on the record when I contacted him while in Israel in 2016. Details of his participation derive from interviews with Moran Oz, two call center managers who worked alongside Shoshana, and two mercenaries who crossed paths with him in Le Roux's organization. Shoshana's role is also described in *USA v. Berkman,* Document 774, January 17, 2017, at 24.

86 **had Mafia connections in Israel:** Interview with Moran Oz, independently noted by an anonymous call center manager. This fact also appears in the trial testimony of former Le Roux employee Jon Wall. See *USA v. Berkman,* Document 1005, February 9, 2017, at 565. "He has family in Israel that is dangerous, connected to Israeli mafia," Wall stated. Reuven himself did not respond to my inquiries by email, in person at his office, or via social media.

87 **were sent to guard stash houses:** This information will be discussed more thoroughly later in the book.

87 **Levi Kugel:** Kugel did not reply to repeated attempts to contact him at various email addresses and social media accounts. Details of his participation derive from interviews with Moran Oz, interviews with three anonymous call center managers, interviews with Ari Ben-Menashe, and interviews with Kent Bailey at the DEA, which was tracking Kugel as part of its investigation. Kugel's role is also described in documents filed in *USA v. Berkman,* including: Document 811, February 3, 2017, at 5–6; Document 948, March 3, 2017, at 17; Document 774, January 17, 2017, at 13; Document 952-16, March 3, 2017, at 19; Document 952-5, October 16, 2013, at 25; Document 1005, February 9, 2017, at 552.

87 **Ari Ben-Menashe didn't find it terribly surprising:** Details of Ben-Menashe's interactions with Le Roux derive from Ben-Menashe unless otherwise noted. Questions about his reliability are included in the text.

87 **first came to international prominence:** See, for example, *Robert McFarland v. Sheridan Square Press,* August 16, 1996, D.D.C., 95-7201. For a good overview on Ben-Menashe and his history see Brian Hutchinson, "The Unbelievable Life of Ari Ben-Menashe," *National Post,* November 18, 2011.

87 **wrote a book:** Ari Ben-Menashe, *Profits of War* (Sheridan Square, 1992).

88 **Craig Unger once wrote:** Craig Unger, "The Trouble with Ari," *The Village Voice,* July 7, 1992. The investigative journalist Seymour Hersh, who was also burned by Ben-Menashe, once called him "an enigma . . . who has a need to embellish constantly." See Robert Miraldi, *Seymour Hersh: Scoop Artist* (Lincoln, Neb.: Potomac Books, 2013), p. 282.

88 **a bizarre 2002 incident:** See, for example, "Joy as Mugabe Rival Cleared," *The Age,* October 17, 2004; Brian Hutchinson, "The Unbelievable Life of Ari Ben-Menashe," *National Post,* November 18, 2011.

88 **Ben-Menashe said:** I conducted two extensive phone interviews with Ben-Menashe in 2016. When I first reached him, Ben-Menashe wearily informed me that I wasn't the first to inquire about Paul Le Roux. "Joseph Hunter's lawyers came to Montreal to try and get something on him," he said. "I'll give you the same."

88 **hoped to obtain a diplomatic passport:** In addition to Ben-Menashe's account, I confirmed that the diplomatic passport was Le Roux's motivation from a former DEA agent in the SOD 960 group. I confirmed additional details of Ben-Menashe's dealings with Le Roux through an anonymous relative of Le Roux's who attended meetings with Ben-Menashe in Montreal on Le Roux's behalf. See also *USA v. Berkman,* Document 774, January 17, 2017, at 18.

89 **disclosure forms Ben-Menashe filed:** "Supplemental Statements Pursuant to Section 2 of the Foreign Agents Registration Act" by Dickens and Madson Canada, featuring Paul Calder Le Roux, filed November 14, 2007; January 31, 2008; January 31, 2009.

89 **$6 million for their services:** The exact number is difficult to parse from the forms. Ben-Menashe himself told me the number "was more like $12 million." On the forms themselves, though, the number appears to be $6 million. Moran Oz later asserted through his attorneys that Kugel told him that "Kugel transported $6 million to Ben-Menashe in order to get a diplomatic passport for him, and Ben-Menashe stole the $6 million and disappeared." See *USA v. Berkman,* Document 774, January 17, 2017, at 18.

90 **permits in the country:** According to Ben-Menashe, the permits allowed Le Roux's organization to log and export rare kauri trees.

90 **Moran Oz got a call:** The details of Oz and Berkman's trip to Manila were first provided to me by Moran Oz, as well as by court documents in *USA v. Berkman,* including: Document 950, April 3, 2017, at 5–6; Document 774, January 17, 2017, at 10–11; and Document 1045, August 17, 2017, at 5. It was further confirmed in *USA v. Hunter,* Document 580, April 5, 2018, at 401–2.

91 **When Oz arrived at the dock:** I received a firsthand account of the following events from Oz himself, the details of which were later corroborated in interviews with other members of Le Roux's organization, surveillance tapes of Joseph Hunter (*USA v. Hunter,* Document 524-1, March 16, 2018, at 3), and court testimony (*USA v. Hunter,* Document 580, April 5, 2018, at 401-2; and Document 585, April 11, 2018, 1220-21).

CHAPTER 10

97 **millions of drug orders:** Interview with Kimberly Brill.

98 **federal prosecutors . . . needed more:** Interview with Kent Bailey. Linda Marks and the press office of the Consumer Protection Branch declined to comment on the record about the case.

98 **turned up on a list of calls:** Interview with Kent Bailey.

98 **Israeli American named Jon Wall:** Details of Jon Wall's involvement derive

from interviews with Kimberly Brill, Steven Holdren, and Kent Bailey; and court documents in *USA v. Berkman* including: Document 1061, October 3, 2017; Document 416, December 7, 2015; Document 1005, February 9, 2017, at 440–623.

99 **Phalanx Trading:** Kentucky Division of Corporation Business Filings, "Phalanx Trading LLC," established 2009.

99 **computers and servers . . . cars, a yacht, artwork, jewelry . . . drone parts:** *USA v. Berkman*, Document 1005, February 9, 2017, at 96, 169, 177.

99 **a Westwind jet:** Interview with Kent Bailey.

99 **FBI independently flagged:** Ibid.

99 **tried tracking the shipments:** Interviews with Kent Bailey and Steven Holdren.

100 **Bailey approached his boss:** Interview with Kent Bailey. Derek Maltz, now retired from the DEA, declined multiple requests for an interview about the Le Roux case.

101 **a man named Michael Lontoc:** Lontoc was a member of the Philippines Practical Shooting Team, which competes in the World Championships in non-Olympic shooting events. See Joaquin M. Henson, "Pinoy Shooters Gun for Honors," *The Philippine Star*, September 6, 2011.

101 **raided one of Le Roux's call centers:** Per interview with Kent Bailey. I also confirmed details of this raid with an anonymous former call center manager in the Philippines.

101 **world tour would come to include:** Interview with Kent Bailey.

101 **British authorities had arrested:** Details of this incident derive from interviews with Kent Bailey and Kimberly Brill, as well as with an agent from the Australian Federal Police who worked on the Le Roux investigation.

101 **through Robert McGowan:** Interviews with Robert McGowan and Mathew Smith.

102 **a former official at the Department of Justice:** The official, with whom I conducted multiple extended interviews, was intimately familiar with the case. They requested anonymity because they were not authorized to speak in detail about it.

CHAPTER 11

105 **the *Mou Man Tai*:** The boat, which would later become a key element in Le Roux's story, was well-known around Subic, according to an interview with an anonymous friend of Bruce Jones. Other details regarding the *Mou Man Tai* derive from copies of the boat registrations I obtained, and interviews with Lachlan McConnell.

106 **American contractor:** This anonymous American contractor is the same ex-Navy sailor quoted in Chapter 6.

106 **printed $100 trillion notes:** See, for example, Nelson Banya, "Zimbabwe to Launch 100 Trillion Dollar Note," January 16, 2009.

107 **discovered the gold was fake:** Multiple people described variations of these

events to me, in which the Hahns were only partly scammed and stole the rest, or were entirely scammed and stole nothing. The most definitive account I received came from Mathew Smith, but even he seemed unsure of all of the details. The facts that I have confirmed include:

- That over $1 million of Le Roux's money went missing. (One source with knowledge of the situation told me the amount was $1.1 million. Le Roux later claimed that only $800,000 was stolen by the Hahns, but at the time he said that "Steve is short $1.4 or 1.5M.")
- That Le Roux sent mercenaries to Bulawayo and Livingston and Lusaka, Zambia, to investigate the losses, blamed the Hahns for the losses, and demanded that they repay him.
- That Le Roux ordered drugs planted on Andrew Hahn, for which he was imprisoned.
- That Joseph Hunter later shot Steve Hahn in the hand in Bulawayo, on the orders of Dave Smith or Le Roux himself.

My sources for this account include interviews with Mathew Smith, Lachlan McConnell, Tim Vamvakias, an anonymous American security contractor who participated in the hunt for the Hahns, an anonymous family member of Le Roux's who was familiar with it, an investigative account from one of Le Roux's mercenaries, chats between Mathew Smith and Le Roux, and *USA v. Hunter,* Documents 524, 576, 580, 581, 585, 591, 606, March/April 2018. Steven Hahn declined my request for an interview.

108 **moving into a shared house:** Details from interviews with Felix Klaussen. Joseph Hunter declined my requests for an interview, sent directly and through a relative. My communications with Chris De Meyer are described later in the book, but other than admitting he had lived in Subic and once known Klaussen, he declined to speak to me about the facts outlined here.

108 **grown up in extreme poverty:** Details of Hunter's early life, family life, and military service derive, unless noted, from *USA v. Hunter,* Documents 305-1 through 305-7, April 22, 2016.

108 **a friend in his unit was killed:** Ibid. See also the 75th Ranger Regiment page on Facebook, July 30, 2012: "On this date July 30, 1986, Pfc. Michael D. Rudess, assigned to Company A, 1st Battalion, 75th Ranger Regiment as Platoon RTO, died of injuries sustained while conducting a combat live fire training exercise at Dugway Proving Grounds, Utah."

108 **National Defense Service Medal and a Global War on Terrorism Medal:** Service history for Joseph Manuel Hunter, obtained from U.S. Army headquarters on April 15, 2016.

109 **hired and then quickly fired by Blackwater:** Interview with Tim Vamvakias.

111 **Smith came up with an alternative plan:** I heard three different versions of who designed this plan. A former call center manager who was close to Nestor Del Rosario, Le Roux's Filipino lieutenant, told me that Del Rosario had come

up with the plan, in desperation, after Le Roux ordered him to kill Andrew Hahn. Felix Klaussen, on the other hand, claimed that Smith had concocted the plan. Le Roux himself also took credit for it, in *USA v. Hunter,* Document 580, April 5, 2018, at 397–98.

111 **five kilograms of cocaine:** Interview with anonymous former call center manager in the Philippines.

112 **stories of Somali pirates:** See, for example, Jeffrey Gettleman, "Somali Pirates Tell Their Side," *The New York Times,* September 30, 2008; and Arthur Brice, "Somali Piracy Threatens Trade, Boosts Terrorists," CNN.com, October 1, 2008.

112 **scaring off the foreign fishing boats:** In this, Le Roux was right. "During the 1990s, IUU [illegal, unreported, and unregulated] fishing became an initial justification for pirate attacks on foreign fishing vessels," one environmental organization report later concluded. "Piracy became such a risk that distant water fleets (DWF) targeting tuna and tuna-like species dramatically altered their fishing habits and effectively withdrew from Somali waters during the mid-2000s." From Sarah M. Glaser et al., *Securing Somali Fisheries* (One Earth Future Foundation, 2015), xiv, 21.

112 **schools of tuna:** Indian Ocean Tuna Commission, "Examination of the Effects of Piracy on Fleet Operations and Subsequent Catch and Effort Trends," November 12, 2013.

113 **Klaussen found himself in Nairobi:** Most of the details regarding the operation in Somalia derive from interviews with Felix Klaussen. I have confirmed them with dozens of documents and photographs from the project that I personally reviewed, as well as from an independent U.N. investigation into the project (U.N. Monitoring Group Report at 267–72), an interview with the lead investigator on that report, Aurélien Llorca, testimony from *USA v. Hunter* (Documents 576, 580, 581, April 4, 5, 9, 2018), and interviews with two other individuals who witnessed the project in action on the ground.

113 **after a U.S.-backed invasion by Ethiopia:** For a full account see Jeremy Scahill, "Blowback in Somalia," *The Nation,* September 7, 2011.

113 **NGOs limited their presence:** interviews with Aurélien Llorca and a Somali from Galmudug, Sahal Abdulle.

114 **Klaussen tracked the president down:** In addition to Klaussen's account, Sahal Abdulle told me he attended meetings between Klaussen and the president.

114 **the agreement stated:** I obtained a copy of this agreement, with Southern Ace listed at an address in Hong Kong, and signed by one of Le Roux's "dummies," Edgar van Tonder.

114 **Liban Mohamed Ahmed:** U.N. Monitoring Group Report, at 267. When I contacted him, he would say only, "The investigators from the U.N., they got it all wrong," referring to a 2011 U.N. monitoring group report on the incidents involving Le Roux and Klaussen. "I need some recognition that I was innocent, that I was not part of this."

114 **white with fringes of sky blue:** Per photographs of the compound.

115 **transit point for pharmaceuticals:** The drugs were to be obtained—ostensibly to service local communities in Galmudug—through a Somali import-export company that Klaussen and Liban had established together called GalSom Ltd. "We assure that local pharmacies and hospitals get medication and equipment in areas that are dangerous and almost impossible to supply," Klaussen wrote, signing as "Jack Anderson," in an official letter describing the company's pharmaceutical ambitions. In fact Le Roux planned to export the drugs.

115 **corpulent Zimbabwean named Mischeck:** Mischeck did not respond to a request for an interview. Details derive from Klaussen, as well as the U.N. Monitoring Group Report.

115 **notorious Zimbabwean secret police:** Moses Muchemwa, "CIO and Zanu(PF) Members Arrested for Extortion," *The Zimbabwean,* March 17, 2009.

116 **a pair of colleagues:** Neither the Brit nor the Australian responded to my requests for an interview, but I was able to confirm their participation independently through identity documents used in the organization, through Klaussen and two other mercenaries in Le Roux's organization, and through an anonymous agent in the Australian National Police.

116 **feared catching the attention of al-Shabaab:** Whether that fear was entirely warranted is, in hindsight, unclear. Klaussen recalls an increasingly dangerous environment in Galkayo, as does Jeffrey Gettleman. Sahal Abdulle thought that the size of the Southern Ace force seemed like "overkill."

116 **emailed detailed instructions:** All email excerpts derive from copies that I have personally viewed.

117 **prone to conspiracy theories:** Interview with Sahal Abdulle.

118 **aligned with General Mohamed Aidid:** Interview with Klaussen. See also Mark Mazzetti, *The Way of the Knife: The CIA, a Secret Army, and a War at the Ends of the Earth* (New York: Penguin, 2013).

CHAPTER 12

119 **he would flag the order:** This is confirmed in *USA v. Berkman,* Document 900, at March 4, 2017, at 28.

120 **He suggested they find a way:** *USA v. Berkham,* Document 900, March 4, 2017, at 30.

121 **he wrote in one email:** *USA v. Berkman,* Document 1017, March 1, 2017, at 2644.

121 **Anu Konakanchi:** *USA v. Anu Radha Konakanchi,* E.D. Pa., 2:14-cr-00083, Document 1, February 20, 2014.

121 **referred to her as "Akka" . . . Southern Ace:** *USA v. Berkman,* Document 1009, February 15, 2017, at 1242–75, and Document 1010, February 10, 2017, at 1343–35.

121 **eight other physicians:** *USA v. Berkman,* Document 1003, February 7, 2017, at 80.

122 **become a less frequent presence:** *USA v. Berkman,* Document 952-13, October 16, 2013, at 17.

122 **one pharmacist who worked for Schultz said:** *USA v. Berkman,* Document 952-14, October 16, 2013, at 14.

122 **report abnormalities back to Ron Oz:** *USA v. Berkman,* Document 990, May 22, 2017, Exhibits K, Q.

122 **half of all the rogue online pharmacies:** Interview with John Horton of Legit-Script.

123 **one pharmacist said:** *USA v. Berkman,* Document 952-14, October 16, 2013, at 22–23.

CHAPTER 13

124 **Berkman knew something was amiss . . . looking ashen:** Interview with anonymous call center manager who was present at this meeting.

124 **immediately switched locations:** *USA v. Berkman,* Document 950, April 3, 2017, at 6.

124 **his demeanor had changed:** Interviews with anonymous childhood friend of Oz and an anonymous former employee of the Tel Aviv call center.

125 **Le Roux wrote:** *USA v. Berkman,* Document 774, January 17, 2017, at 22.

125 **bring up the boat incident:** Ibid., at 30.

125 **one call center manager said:** This call center manager, who requested anonymity out of fear of retribution from Le Roux, worked for the organization in Israel and the Philippines.

126 **deputy named Nestor Del Rosario:** I spoke to a number of people who were directly familiar with Del Rosario's role, including a Filipino colleague who requested anonymity for fear of Le Roux (I learned Le Roux had once put out a hit on this colleague, as well as on Del Rosario); a call center manager for whom Del Rosario was a mentor and confidant; Felix Klaussen, who was aware of his role; and Kent Bailey and another former DEA agent familiar with Del Rosario's role. His name also appears in court documents in the Philippines, as noted in the text. I was unable to locate Del Rosario, who I was told was in hiding from Le Roux. He did not respond to an interview request through the colleague.

126 **a guy from HR named Ogie:** I was never able to discover Ogie's full name—colleagues believed that Ogie itself was a nickname—and a former DEA agent told me that he died of natural causes. He, along with Del Rosario, were both Filipinos from the straight world who were brought into Le Roux's orbit and ultimately became significant players in his criminal empire.

127 **Le Roux began using email servers:** *USA v. Hunter,* Document 580, April 5, 2018, at 414.

127 **ramped up his use of dummies:** I obtained emails from Le Roux to one of his dummies from early 2009. Corporate filings in Hong Kong and elsewhere also

show Le Roux's name vanishing from listings, replaced by the likes of Robson Tandanayi and Edgar van Tonder.

127 **sell off any Manila properties . . . scout for an island:** This included the two penthouses that Le Roux owned in Salcedo Park Towers in Makati City, per an interview with the anonymous call center manager who was close with Del Rosario.

CHAPTER 14

130 **Thanks to social networking:** Many of the social media examples named here have been taken down over the last several years. All of them were viewed by me and saved as screenshots in my files.

130 **collapsing the ruse:** In one such case, Asaf Shoshana, an Israeli employee, linked to his own fake profile as "Joe Anderson," the profile photo for which was an image of Al Pacino from the movie *Scarface.*

131 **policeman named Marcus:** This is the same Marcus described in Chapter 6.

131 **part of a sting operation:** "I don't know if you are a Fed or what," one military contractor and former American soldier told me when I first contacted him.

133 **article about the mysterious call centers:** Shay Aspril, "An Invitation from Tel Aviv, a Prescription from the Internet, a Drug from America," *Calcalist,* July 28, 2011.

133 **Mathew:** As noted in Chapter 7, I am using "Mathew" to identify him in most cases, in order to avoid confusion with Le Roux's enforcer, Dave Smith, to whom Mathew Smith was not related.

136 **transcripts of chats:** All quotes derive directly from these chats.

138 **an article written by him for some travel magazine:** The relative could remember only that the article concerned the Alps, began with a train ride, and was written under a pseudonym. I was never able to locate it.

138 **on behalf of mysterious "Brazilians":** While Le Roux did conduct drug transactions with Brazilians, according to a former employee familiar with them, I never encountered any evidence that his money laundering was done on behalf of anyone but himself.

142 **"I had to kill my father":** The actual role of Le Roux's biological father, Darroll Hornbuckle, in his business was a mystery I was never able to solve to my satisfaction. DEA agents and Le Roux's relatives confirmed that Hornbuckle was indeed Le Roux's relation, but were all unclear on to what extent he'd reentered Le Roux's life. Hornbuckle was certainly involved in the online prescription pill business. His name appears connected to both Le Roux's websites and others, including one that was later prosecuted in Louisiana called ecaremd.com (Hornbuckle, however, was not accused in the case). Several employees told me—without realizing that Hornbuckle was Le Roux's father—that Hornbuckle had been one of the company's affiliates, that he and Le Roux had fallen out, and that Le Roux had cut him out of the business and taken his customers. So it remains entirely plausible that Le Roux had—as he intimated—threatened to kill his own father.

143 **"for one particular event"**: Donovan did not recall the nature of the event, and no longer had access to the supposed plans. But my own research indicated that if such plans were made, the event in question was likely held on Seychelles Independence Day, each June 29, which involves an annual celebration at Unity Stadium on the main island. See, for example, Betymie Bonnelame, " 'We Are One Nation,' President of Seychelles Says on Independence Day," *Seychelles News Agency*, June 29, 2017.

143 **he remembered as the Maldives**: Later, Le Roux himself would admit sending Hunter to the Seychelles to assess the feasibility of the plan: *USA v. Hunter,* Document 576, April 4, 2018, at 354–57.

CHAPTER 15

145 **received a tip**: Interview with Mar Supnad. As noted in Chapter 14, Patrick Donovan claimed to have initiated the tip. Le Roux himself believed that the tip was called in by a ship captain, whom Le Roux later added to his hit list. Another former employee of Le Roux's told me that in fact the authorities had been aware of the shipment from the beginning, and the "tip" was simply a cover for their decision to seize the ship when they failed to receive the full amount of an agreed-upon bribe.

145 ***M/V Captain Ufuk* . . . Lawrence John Burne**: *People of the Philippines v. Burne.*

145 **twenty large unmarked wooden crates**: Details of the *M/V Ufuk* confiscation derive from interviews with Mar Supnad, interviews with National Bureau of Investigation agents, Philippine court documents, and local news reports of the incident.

145 **remainders of a much larger shipment**: A former Le Roux employee involved in the shipment later confirmed to me that the majority of the arms were offloaded before the ship was raided.

146 **traced back to Dave Smith**: Text of Senate Resolution P.S. Res. No. 1327, Fourteenth Congress of the Republic of the Philippines, "Directing the Appropriate Committee to Investigate . . . the Gun Smuggling Incident in Mariveles, Bataan." I later confirmed the facts of this story with a copy of the boat's registration.

147 **Jones had already been working**: Interview with a friend of Jones's from Subic, interview with Lachlan McConnell, interview with former American Navy sailor and security contractor.

147 **stopping in Ghana**: Mar T. Supnad, "British Captain of Arms Ship Seeks Gov't Protection," *Manila Bulletin,* August 26, 2009.

147 **along with Joseph Hunter**: *USA v. Hunter,* Document 305-1, April 22, 2016, at 9.

147 **His wife was pregnant**: Interview with Mar Supnad, confirmed by an anonymous former employee of Le Roux's involved in the shipment.

147 **another mercenary, Chris De Meyer**: In *USA v. Hunter* (Document 305-1, April 22, 2016, at 9), Hunter refers to "a friend" who came on the mission. I

later confirmed with an anonymous former employee of Le Roux's that the friend was De Meyer.

148 **published his story:** Mar T. Supnad, "British Captain of Arms Ship Seeks Gov't Protection," *Manila Bulletin,* August 26, 2009.

148 **charged thirty-seven people:** Edu Punay, "37 Charged over Gun Smuggling," *The Philippine Star,* September 5, 2009. See also *People of the Philippines v. Burne.*

CHAPTER 16

150 **Hong Kong and then Mexico:** Interview with Kent Bailey. The DEA received notice that Le Roux—now flagged around the world—had flown from Hong Kong to Rotterdam to Mexico. Bailey frantically called the DEA's office in Mexico City. "We've got to get the Federales on him," he said. Given the power of the Mexican drug cartels, the DEA trusted only a few vetted units in the Mexican federal police. They leaned on one to find Le Roux and follow him. But not long after the Mexican agents picked up Le Roux's trail, they were pulled off the case when one of their commanders was shot in an unrelated drug bust. "Rightfully so, but it hurt us," Bailey said. Le Roux was gone again. "Never did figure out what he was doing in Mexico." My own speculation is that the timing of this trip matches up with Ari Ben-Menashe's recollection of Le Roux showing up in person for a meeting in Mexico while Ben-Menashe was vacationing there.

150 **Also found among the accused:** *People of the Philippines v. Burne.* That "Michael Archangel" and "Michael Vaughn" are aliases for Shai Reuven derives from an interview with Mathew Smith and copies of forged documents. The use of "Michael Ross" derives from interviews with Lachlan McConnell and court documents including *USA v. Berkman,* Document 5, November 13, 2013, at 1.

151 **cocktail of arrogance and incompetence:** On one mission, he had arrived at the airport in Johannesburg traveling under a fake passport for "Michael Vaughn," only to discover he'd failed to get a visa in his fake name.

151 **a fishing vessel called the *King Yue I*:** Information about Le Roux's involvement with the *King Yue* haul comes from an interview with a former employee directly familiar with the transactions, as well as Peter Lugay of the Philippine National Police. There were numerous accounts of the ship's dumped cocaine in the Philippine press: for example, Cecille Suerte Felipe, "P165-million Cocaine Seized in Samar," *The Philippine Star,* July 2, 2010. Other details derive from the Guam legislature's commendation of the U.S. Coast Guard captain who pursued the vessel ("Relative to Recognizing and Commending Lt. Commander Matthew Salas and the Crew of the United States Coast Guard Cutter Sequoia for Their Efforts in Preventing the Illegal Trafficking of One Metric Ton of Cocaine," I Mina'trent A Na Lihesla Turan Guahan 2010 (Second) Regular Session, Resolution No. 414-30) and a DEA recognition of the cutter ("U.S. Coast Guard Cutter Recognized by the Drug Enforcement Administration," June 8, 2010).

152 **an airstrip constructed . . . an island to facilitate shipments:** Interview with Inspector R of the Philippine National Police.

152 **sent to Colombia:** Interview with an anonymous call center manager, confirmed in *USA v. Hunter,* Document 587, April 12, 2018, at 1314.

152 **another Israeli was rumored:** Interview with Felix Klaussen.

152 **Del Rosario was ordered to fly to Tehran:** Interview with a former DEA agent in the Special Operations Division 960 group who worked on the Le Roux case. I always found this aspect of Le Roux's business the hardest to believe: that he'd sent people like Del Rosario, cold, into places like Iran, and they'd come back with contacts with whom Le Roux could buy and sell weapons or drugs. I put the question to the former DEA agent, who was a party to extensive Le Roux debriefings.

"He wasn't like a guy with Iranian contacts," I said. "It was just 'Nestor, go into Iran and find some people'? I mean, that's a very enterprising person."

"Correct," the former DEA agent told me. "He's a true entrepreneur. And the reason [Le Roux] sent them, he said, is that the Filipinos are very nonthreatening people. They'll talk to them. That was his thought. And he was right."

152 **an explosives formula he had perfected . . . missile-guidance . . . more than twenty engineers . . . underground mining:** *USA v. Hunter,* Document 580, April 5, 2018, at 424, 572, 694, 697.

153 **several through Craigslist:** Interview with a former DEA agent in the SOD 960 group.

153 **If you had an idea:** The former employee who told me this had worked on drug deals for Le Roux and had direct knowledge of Le Roux's wider narcotics operations.

153 **stashed them for Le Roux:** Joseph Hunter later claimed in conversations recorded on surveillance tape that he and Chris De Meyer had helped Smith bury the gold under the hot tub. See *USA v. Hunter,* Document 411-5, July 31, 2017, at 12.

154 **McConnell reluctantly agreed:** *USA v. Berkman,* Document 774, January 17, 2017, at 41–43.

155 **Le Roux was wiring millions:** Copies of wire transfers and correspondence with Le Roux discussing them.

155 **Nestor Del Rosario . . . purchased ten Yamaha outboard motors:** Copy of the commercial invoice.

156 **ZU-23 antiaircraft gun:** Interview with Felix Klaussen, confirmed with photos and video of the truck from employee Facebook pages. Range from "ZU-23 23MM Antiaircraft Gun," Federation of American Scientists, April 27, 2000.

156 **Ahlu Sunna Waljama'a:** Interview with Felix Klaussen. Also U.N. Monitoring Group Report, 267–72.

158 **An accountant:** The employee did not respond to requests for an interview.

158 **had been traveling around the region:** Details of Gettleman's time in Galkayo

derive from an interview with Gettleman; an interview with his local fixer, Sahal Abdulle, who was present for the trip; and interviews with Felix Klaussen.

160 **won a Pulitzer Prize:** Gettleman won the 2012 prize in international reporting.

162 **They'd fled after the overthrow:** See, for example, Mark Fineman, "The Oil Factor in Somalia," *Los Angeles Times,* January 18, 1993; and Michelle Nichols and Louis Charbonneau, "Western Oil Exploration in Somalia May Spark Conflict," Reuters, July 17, 2013.

CHAPTER 17

167 **exchanging information with the AFP:** Interview with Kent Bailey, confirmed with an agent of the AFP whom I interviewed under the official stipulation that his name not be used.

167 **A classified cable:** "GOI CLAIMS MIX-UP IN SMALL ARMS SEIZED IN THE PHILIPPINES," September 2, 2009, obtained through WikiLeaks.

168 **surrendered to the Philippines Bureau of Customs:** Copy of an internal presentation obtained from a Philippine National Police inspector.

168 **Consolidated Priority Organization Target (CPOT) list:** For general discussion of the CPOT list see, for example, U.S. Department of Justice Organized Crime Drug Enforcement Task Forces, "FY 2016 Interagency Crime and Drug Enforcement Congressional Submission," 5–7.

170 **two ounces of meth and a gun:** In addition to my interview with Bailey, information on this arrest also surfaced in Andrew Drummond, "British Captain Seeking Protection Arms Deals in Philippines," *London Evening Standard,* September 22, 2010.

170 **On the morning of September 21:** Details of the day derive from the Philippine National Police case file on the murder of Bruce Jones; photos obtained from the case file; my own visit to the murder scene; and an interview with Roberto Manuel, a PNP officer who arrived first on the scene.

171 **one acquaintance said:** This source, a longtime Subic Bay resident who knew both Nash and Jones, requested anonymity out of fear of retribution from Nash or his associates.

172 **a "lovable rogue":** "Maverick Bristol Sailor Was Gunned Down in Philippines," *Bristol Post,* September 23, 2010.

CHAPTER 18

174 **Zuñiga himself had gone missing:** Carlos Santamaria, "Where Is Lawyer Joe Frank Zuñiga?" *Rappler,* July 5, 2012; also Edu Punay, "De Lima Orders Intensified Search for Missing Lawyer," *The Philippine Star,* July 5, 2012.

174 **training the killer whale:** Timothy Desmond, "The Killer Whale Who Kills," *International Herald Tribune,* March 8, 2010.

174 **raided Tiu's house:** I later discovered that details of the raid had emerged in the local Philippine press: for example, Non Alquitran, "Chinese Trader

Faces Gun Raps over Seized Galil Rifles," *The Philippine Star,* October 9, 2010.

175 **Lontoc had been driving:** This and other details are from the Philippine National Police case file on the murder of Michael Lontoc.

175 **deported back to their home country:** Interview with Mar Supnad.

175 **the remaining cases . . . tried and convicted in absentia:** *People of The Philippines v. Burne.*

175 **Joe Frank Zuñiga had been part of the syndicate:** According to this version, Zuñiga had been the conduit for law enforcement bribes before the *Ufuk,* but this time had attempted to play both sides, keeping half the bribe money. I heard no other reference to Zuñiga working for the organization from law enforcement or former employees.

177 **The Tiu case started:** Details in this account derive primarily from Inspector R, obviously, but I have cross-checked them with official PNP reports supplied to me, as well as with a scattering of local press; testimony from *USA v. Hunter,* Document 580, April 5, 2018, at 520; and copies of correspondence between Inspector R and the Australian Federal Police.

178 **knew only as "Chito":** Having seen various spellings of the nickname in Philippine reports and U.S. court documents, I've elected to use the one given to me by Inspector R.

178 **an airstrip Le Roux had built:** PNP surveillance photos of the airstrip.

179 **The general didn't mince words:** When I contacted him by phone while in the Philippines, the general declined an interview.

180 **announced that Nash had been kidnapped:** "Police Says American 'Abducted' in Olongapo," *Subic Bay News,* May 4, 2014.

181 **immigration violations:** John Nash official charge sheet, Philippine National Bureau of Investigation, May 6, 2014.

181 **Desmond, too, had disappeared:** "Judge Orders Arrest of Ocean Adventure Exec," *Subic Bay News,* November 6, 2014.

CHAPTER 19

184 **Doron Shulman, who had purchased two houses:** Information on Shulman derives from *HKSAR v. Shulman.*

184 **specializes in undercover work:** See also, for example, "Duvdevan Unit," IDF official description, idf.il/en/minisites/duvdevan-unit/; Yaniv Kubovich, "PTSD Plagues the Israeli Special Forces That Inspired Fauda," *Haaretz,* April 22, 2018; "Profiling Israel's Elite Undercover Unit Duvdevan," *Middle East Monitor,* October 12, 2015. For a comprehensive look at Israeli military units and assassinations, see Ronen Bergman, *Rise and Kill First* (Random House, 2018).

184 **looking for a way out:** Interviews with Moran Oz and a childhood friend. "Friends in the neighborhood said Moran wants to get out of the company, but he can't," the friend told me he heard at the time. "I understood he was mixed up with some criminal, but nobody knew who."

184 **one former Tel Aviv employee said:** I later learned that this former call center employee, whom I interviewed in a bar in 2016 after he requested anonymity, had himself once been threatened by Le Roux's henchmen.

184 **Kugel . . . assumed he would be out of reach:** Interview with Moran Oz; also *USA v. Berkman,* Document 774, January 17, 2017, at 18.

185 **Le Roux had abruptly abandoned the projects:** Interview with Moran Oz; confirmed by an interview with an anonymous former Le Roux mercenary who worked with Shoshana.

185 **to help run the call center:** Interview with Moran Oz; also *USA v. Berkman,* Document 774, January 17, 2017, at 25.

185 **Israel began to seem unsafe:** Ibid., at 25–29.

186 **in a Lamborghini:** Interviews with Lachlan McConnell, Patrick Donovan.

187 **confess the details to me:** Those details matched those presented in court, including *USA v. Hunter,* Document 580, April 5, 2018, at 399–400, 408, 518–22; and Document 581, April 9, 2018, at 725–35.

187 **an organization seeking "close-in security or snipers":** From a copy of the original recruitment email.

190 **one Filipina employee told me:** This former employee requested anonymity after having already been subject to threats against her life by Le Roux's organization.

191 **one afternoon in January 2011:** *USA v. Berkman,* Document 774, January 17, 2017, at 42–44.

191 **He showed up early:** Details of this meeting derive from interviews with Lachlan McConnell and *USA v. Berkman,* Document 774, January 17, 2017, at 42–44.

192 **business was getting squeezed:** Interviews with Kimberly Brill and Steven Holdren from the DEA, interviews with Moran Oz and Lachlan McConnell from Le Roux's organization, as well as documents from *USA v. Berkman,* e.g., Document 35 at 7–8.

193 **one pharmacist in Michigan told Oz:** *USA v. Berkman,* Document 707, December 13, 2017, at 12.

193 **starting to get spooked:** *USA v. Berkman,* Document 37, October 9, 2013, at 11.

193 **three call centers in India:** Interviews with Moran Oz, Eliel Benaroch, and an anonymous call center manager who worked at the Indian facilities.

193 **Le Roux sent Doron Shulman . . . ordered Jon Wall:** Interview with Kimberly Brill; also *USA v. Berkman,* Document 952-3, October 9, 2012, at 21, 34–35.

193 **open up his own pharmacies:** *USA v. Berkman,* Document 952-16, April 3, 2017, at 6.

193 **Oz wrote in an email:** *USA v. Berkman,* Document 990-13, May 22, 2017, at Exhibit R.

193 **set up an entirely fictitious pharmacy:** Ibid. at Exhibit Y.

194 **official response letter:** Ibid.

194 **He flew to Miami:** *USA v. Berkman,* Document 774, January 17, 2017, at 46.

194 **Le Roux also sent a list:** *USA v. Berkman,* Document 990-13, May 22, 2017, at Exhibit R.

194 **to avoid the suspicion of bulk purchases:** *USA v. Berkman,* Document 879, February 26, 2017, at 7.

195 **they laughed in a wiretapped phone call:** *USA v. Berkman,* Document 35, October 9, 2014, at 9.

195 **began to press down on him:** Interview with Lachlan McConnell.

196 **The doctors diagnosed him:** *USA v. Berkman,* Document 774, January 17, 2017, at 46–47.

196 **it was now a controlled substance:** "Placement of Carisoprodol into Schedule IV," 76 Fed. Reg. 77330, December 12, 2011.

196 **Le Roux told Oz and Berkman:** Interview with Moran Oz. See also *USA v. Berkman,* Document 990-2, May 22, 2017, at Exhibit BB.

196 **the former manager of the Indian call center arrived:** *USA v. Berkman,* Document 774, January 17, 2017, at 24.

197 **Le Roux told Berkman:** Interviews with Moran Oz.

197 **Le Roux summoned him to a meeting:** Interviews with Lachlan McConnell.

197 **meth lab in an apartment:** *USA v. Hunter,* Document 580, April 5, 2018, at 532.

197 **a former bartender . . . introduced him:** Ibid. at 533; also *USA v. Stammers,* Document 170, April 4, 2016, at 8.

197 **split the load between safe houses:** *USA v. Stammers,* Document 168, April 4, 2016, at 7.

197 **buy a submarine . . . built a working prototype:** *USA v. Hunter,* Document 580, April 5, 2018, at 536.

197 **a boat-repair shop in Manila:** Ibid. at 539.

197 **deep into the international cocaine business:** Ibid.; also, an anonymous former Le Roux employee involved in the deals.

CHAPTER 20

200 **dozens of subpoenas . . . search warrants on email addressess:** Overall the investigation included "nearly 30 email search warrants (which alone amassed 785,000 documents)" per *USA v. Berkman,* Document 948, April 3, 2017, at 19–20.

200 **presented in front of a grand jury in 2010:** *USA v. Berkman,* Document 952-1, August 17, 2010, at 1–57.

200 **With the help of agents at the Internal Revenue Service:** *USA v. Berkman,* Document 952-11, November 14, 2012, at 4–6.

200 **sent out an Interpol notice:** Philippine National Police internal document, "Special Report Surrounding the Death of Michael Lontoc."

200 **Smith was likely a U.S. citizen:** "To my understanding, he was a U.S. citizen," Bailey told me, but he remained frustrated that he was never able to

confirm it. Another former DEA agent, from the SOD 960 group, acknowledged Smith's likely American citizenship as well. Patrick Donovan, who once employed Smith, told me definitively that he had seen Smith's American passport, but was unable to locate a copy.

200 **for fear of tipping Le Roux off:** Interview with Kent Bailey. Kimberly Brill did not recall being concerned about tipping Le Roux off, since he was so insulated from the American portion of his business, but acknowledged that Bailey may have experienced this concern more firsthand, as he was dealing with many of the international aspects of the investigation.

201 **obtain active wiretaps:** Interview with Kimberly Brill. See also *USA v. Berkman,* Oz complaint, Document 39, October 10, 2013, at 8.

201 **known as Title III:** As opposed to subpoenas, which would give the investigators information on the numbers called and received by a certain phone number, T3 wiretaps allow them to listen in real time to conversations. The name derives from Title III of the Omnibus Crime Control and Safe Streets Act, as amended by the Electronic Communications Privacy Act of 1986.

201 **a small rented office:** *USA v. Berkman,* Document 952-3, October 9, 2012, at 39.

201 **Israeli named Omer Bezalel:** *USA v. Berkman,* Omer Bezalel complaint, Document 37, October 9, 2013.

201 **a taller white man operating under the identity of Robert McGowan:** Details of the surveillance derive from interviews with Kent Bailey and Kimberly Brill, as well as Brill's grand jury testimony (in *USA v. Berkman,* Document 952-3, October 9, 2012, at 38–40) and the criminal complaint against McConnell (*USA v. Berkman,* Lachlan McConnell complaint, Document 35, October 9, 2013).

202 **three-hundred-page document:** U.N. Monitoring Group Report at 267–72.

202 **a Frenchman named Aurélien Llorca:** Interview with Llorca. The named author of the report, Matt Bryden, confirmed that Llorca was the lead investigator on the report.

202 **the South African *City Press* described:** Julian Rademeyer, "SA Businessman Linked to Somali Militia, Drug Trade," *City Press,* August 28, 2011, page 10.

204 **In one conversation:** Interviews with Kimberly Brill and Kent Bailey.

204 **Bailey called the prosecutor:** These details derive from interviews with Kent Bailey. Linda Marks declined to comment.

205 **Brill stayed up all night monitoring the line:** Interview with Kimberly Brill.

205 **his father had been listed:** *People of the Philippines v. Burne.*

206 **an AFP agent responded:** Interviews with Mathew Smith and Kent Bailey. The AFP declined to comment on this aspect of the investigation.

206 **was registered to him:** Southern Ace Ltd. shareholders report, U.K., ICC Shareholder Reports, October 11, 2013.

206 **he called Alon Berkman:** Interview with Moran Oz.

206 **contacting an attorney:** Details of McGowan's conversations with the attor-

ney derive from email correspondence obtained from McGowan, interviews with Kimberly Brill, and a copy of Brill's interview with McGowan found in *USA v. Berkman,* Document 990-7, May 22, 2017, at Exhibit V.

207 **Nestor Del Rosario . . . also made contact with authorities:** Interviews with Kent Bailey and a former DEA agent with the SOD 960 group.

207 **formally declared a national . . . epidemic:** "Prescription Painkiller Overdoses at Epidemic Levels," CDC news release, November 1, 2011.

207 **She had sought out buyers:** Details from Brill's interviews with buyers derive from her reports, contained in *USA v. Berkman,* Document 991-2, May 22, 2017, at Exhibit O.

208 **potential violation of the federal Food, Drug, and Cosmetic Act:** See, for example, *USA v. Berkman,* Document 5, November 13, 2013, at 6.

208 **a judgment from the DOJ:** D. Linden Barber, Associate Chief Counsel, DEA, "Internet Dispensing of Non-controlled Drugs and Exempted Prescription Drug Products," March 26, 2010, contained in *USA v. Berkman,* Document 952-17, April 3, 2017, at Exhibit 6Q.

208 **DEA declared Soma a Schedule IV controlled substance:** "Placement of Carisoprodol into Schedule IV," 76 Fed. Reg. 77330, December 12, 2011.

CHAPTER 21

209 **a letter from the Pennsylvania Board of Pharmacy:** Interview with Prabhakara Tumpati.

210 **who seemed uninterested:** *USA v. Berkman,* Document 952-6, November 12, 2013, at 37–38.

210 **after earning a million dollars:** Ibid. at 35.

210 **he quit:** *USA v. Berkman,* Document 1003, February 7, 2017, at 133.

210 **sent an email to his close friend:** Copy of personal correspondence obtained from Tumpati.

211 **more than 700,000 prescriptions . . . $3.3 million amounted to:** *USA v. Schultz,* Government sentencing report, Document 22, November 14, 2014.

211 **number of daily prescriptions . . . flagged any in-state orders:** *USA v. Berkman,* Document 952-14, October 16, 2013, at 9–10.

211 **a letter from the FedEx legal department . . . switching his pharmacies:** Among many other court documents, see *USA v. Berkman,* Document 722, December 20, 2016, at 6.

212 **arrived at the door of Schultz Pharmacy:** Interview with Hal Harlowe. The agents also raided Medicine Mart; see *USA v. Berkman,* Document 990-7, May 22, 2017, at Exhibit G.

212 **let the agents record calls . . . served them coffee:** Interview with Hal Harlowe.

CHAPTER 22

213 **Le Roux promoted Joseph Hunter:** *USA v. Hunter,* Document 230, December 9, 2015, at 19–20.

213 **at a salary of $12,000 a month:** *USA v. Hunter,* Document 580, April 5, 2018, at 410; also Document 585, April 11, 2018, at 1187.

213 **a Filipino named Noyt:** *USA v. Hunter,* Document 576, April 4, 2018, at 371; also Document 580, April 5, 2018, at 426.

213 **Now things would be different:** Document 580, April 5, 2018, at 405.

213 **rehired his old friend Tim Vamvakias:** Ibid. at 412–13. Also, interview with Vamvakias.

213 **Chris De Meyer . . . "sales bonus":** *USA v. Hunter,* Document 580, April 5, 2018, at 407, 410–13.

214 **taken the money and failed to deliver the goods:** What exactly Edillor was responsible for letting through, I couldn't establish. In surveillance tapes, Hunter was captured describing the incident this way: "She was a customs agent. I guess that they had some kind of business with him, with her when they get stuff through customs, right? But she didn't . . . They paid her and she didn't do it" (*USA v. Hunter,* Document 115-1, January 30, 2015, at 7). Le Roux described Edillor as "somebody who handles purchasing products, issuing invoices, issuing checks, and also assisting me and getting items through customs" (*USA v. Hunter,* Document 580, April 5, 2018, at 407, 425–26).

214 **after assigning Noyt to conduct surveillance on her:** *USA v. Hunter,* Document 580, April 5, 2018, at 426.

214 **Edillor told her husband:** Philippine National Police case file on the Noimie Edillor killing.

214 **emailed him a link:** *USA v. Hunter,* Document 580, April 5, 2018, at 432.

214 **a local news story:** Non Alquitran, "Customs Broker Found Dead," *The Philippine Star,* February 15, 2012.

215 **he lacked military experience:** Interview with Tim Vamvakias; see also *USA v. Hunter,* Document 585, April 11, 2018, at 1176.

215 **He'd met Dave Smith . . . training course . . . executive protection work:** *USA v. Hunter,* Document 589, April 16, 2018, at 1546–48. Also Document 408-1, July 31, 2017, at 6–7.

215 **asked Smith for "wet work":** *USA v. Hunter,* Document 580, April 5, 2018, at 407. Also Document 585, April 11, 2018, at 1178.

215 **guarding a yacht:** Interviews with an anonymous former U.S. Navy sailor and contractor for Le Roux.

215 **needed a Brazilian visa . . . Hunter replied:** *USA v. Hunter,* Document 256, March 6, 2016, at 3. Also: Document 580, April 5, 2018, at 447, 451.

215 **Roxboro friends described the pair:** "Neighbor Speaks After Roxboro Men Arrested in Murder-for-Hire Plot," WRAL Raleigh, July 23, 2015.

216 **a bra that doubled as a holster:** Petula Dvorak, "Just a Weekend with the Hubby in Suburbia at the Death Bazaar," *The Washington Post,* June 8, 2015; Danielle Battaglia, "2 N.C. Men Accused in International Killing for Hire," Greensboro *News & Record,* July 23, 2015.

216 **Hunter reported back to Le Roux:** Details from Samia and Stillwell's time in

the Philippines derive from dozens of court documents and days of testimony in court—including presentation of specific emails, travel records, and records of financial transactions. For a broad overview with most details contained here: *USA v. Hunter,* Document 253, February 24, 2016; for many of the specifics, see the testimony in Document 580, April 5, 2018.

217 **she had served as president:** Real Estate Brokers of the Philippines newsletter, June 2015.

217 **with a pixie haircut:** Bestmaro Real Estate listings, at Bahay.ph, bahay.ph /agent/best_maro_realty/real_estate.html.

217 **she and her husband had purchased:** Interview with Rizaldy Rivera.

217 **Bill and Tony didn't specify:** Details of Lee's last days derive from the Philippine National Police case file on Catherine Lee; NBI internal presentation by Rizaldy Rivera, "The Catherine Lee Murder Case"; and interviews with Rivera.

218 **Hunter said later:** *USA v. Hunter,* Document 115-1, January 30, 2015, at 1–29.

218 **Le Roux had more targets:** *USA v. Hunter,* Document 580, April 5, 2018, at 484–87.

219 **They turned over the weapons:** Hunter, according to court testimony (ibid., at 515), then attempted to have the barrel on the gun replaced at the Mountain Clark Firing Range—the same gun club outside of which Bruce Jones had once been gunned down. When the owner declined to do so, Le Roux had the gun returned to his warehouse and back into regular rotation with his henchmen.

CHAPTER 23

223 **moving large quantities of methamphetamine:** Among other sources, *USA v. Stammers,* Document 168, April 4, 2016, at 7.

223 **dealing with rogue regimes . . . terrorists:** *USA v. Hunter,* Document 576, April 4, 2018, at 358.

223 **His targets now ranged from Nestor Del Rosario:** Philippine National Police case file on Ronald Baricuatro y Lopez, originally dated February 3, 2012. See also *USA v. Hunter,* Document 580, April 5, 2018, at 425.

224 **arranged for a rebel leader:** *USA v. Hunter,* Document 580, April 5, 2018, at 408–9.

224 **He had talked for years:** Interview with Mathew Smith.

224 **"The Americans . . . are watching":** Interview with Felix Klaussen.

224 **employees at the U.S. Embassy:** *USA v. Berkman,* Document 774, January 17, 2017, at 52.

224 **tipping him off to American information requests through FinCEN:** Specifically, Le Roux received information about what's called an "Egmont request," the Egmont Group being a collection of "financial disclosure unit" agencies of which the U.S. FinCEN bureau is a member. Interview with a former DEA agent in SOD 960 group.

224 **his paid Philippine law enforcement contacts:** Interview with a former DEA agent in the SOD 960 group.

224 **he had purchased documents . . . He later sold those documents:** *USA v. Hunter,* Document 581, April 9, 2018, at 742–43, 744–45.

225 **tapped into the country's 4G cellphone network:** Interview with a former DEA agent in the SOD 960 group.

225 **forged a request from the Australian Federal Police:** Interview with an anonymous AFP agent who investigated Le Roux.

225 **upward of $50,000 a month:** Interview with Marcus, Le Roux's South African hit man.

225 **Le Roux himself would brag:** *USA v. Hunter,* Document 581, April 9, 2018, at 743.

225 **had gone to school with Joe Frank Zuñiga:** Interviews with Inspector R, a former DEA agent in the SOD 960 group, and Felix Klaussen.

225 **whose real name:** *USA v. Hunter,* Document 576, April 4, 2018, at 372.

225 **searched his backpack:** Philippine National Police case file on Ronald Baricuatro y Lopez, originally dated February 3, 2012; also copy of an internal presentation obtained from a Philippine National Police inspector.

226 **Le Roux needed to find another operating base:** "He had to bail," as Felix Klaussen put it to me. "Because now he kicked somebody in the nuts that he couldn't buy off."

226 **a diplomatic passport:** Copy of Le Roux passport from DRC, in the name of Paul Solotshi Calder Le Roux, born 1982 in Kinshasa.

226 **115-foot Denison super yacht:** Interviews with Felix Klaussen and a former DEA agent in the SOD 960 group. I also obtained images of the yacht.

226 **sailed under the name** *Thunderball:* Malcolm Wood, "The Ghost of Yards Past: Denison Yachts," *Superyacht Times,* August 18, 2017.

CHAPTER 24

228 **had a wiretap running:** The local office had been investigating Patel already in a separate healthcare fraud case, obviating the need for Brill and Bailey to obtain their own. See *USA v. Berkman,* Document 707, December 13, 2016, at 12. Also *USA v. Patel,* Document 674, December 7, 2012.

228 **another Israeli, Doron Shulman:** *USA v. Berkman,* Document 952–3, October 9, 2012, at 19–20.

229 **Brazilian team would operate in secrecy:** Interviews with an anonymous member of the GISE team that investigated Le Roux and Marco Antônio Martins, a Brazilian journalist who reported on the operation.

229 **"Operação America":** Internal Report of the Brazilian Federal Police.

229 **Rainbow Force Technologies:** Company registration, Rainbow Force Tecnologia em Software LTDA, *Dun & Bradstreet Worldbase,* October 1, 2015.

229 **Brill drafted an affidavit:** Interviews with Kent Bailey.

229 **arrived on a flight to Galeão airport . . . traveling with:** Details of Le Roux's

dealings while in Brazil, unless otherwise noted, derive from the extensive Internal Report of the Brazilian Federal Police, an interview with an anonymous GISE agent who worked on the investigation, and interviews with Kent Bailey and Kimberly Brill.

229 **still married to Lilian Cheung Yuen Pui:** Official divorce records, Federal Circuit Court of Australia, June 24, 2013.

229 **a dark-haired Israeli:** Zion Fadlon Facebook page.

230 **now shipping goods directly:** *USA v. Berkman,* Document 952–3, October 9, 2012, at 26–27.

231 **Brill called McGowan:** Details from this call can be found in *USA v. Berkman,* Document 990 at Exhibit V, May 22, 2017.

231 **another source came in out of the cold:** Interviews with Mathew Smith, Kent Bailey, and Kimberly Brill.

231 **a third potential informant, Robson Tandanayi:** Interviews with Tandanayi and Kimberly Brill.

235 **two high-profile sections:** "FY 2015 Performance Budget Congressional Submission," U.S. Department of Justice DEA, at 9. The group created under this provision at SOD is also known as the Bilateral Investigations Unit or Bilateral Case Group. For a discussion of the purpose and origins of the 959 and 960 groups, see "The History of the Special Operations Division," DEA Museum Lecture Series, April 22, 2015.

235 **The 959 provision:** 21 U.S. Code § 959.

235 **the 960a provision:** H.R. 3199—USA PATRIOT Improvement and Reauthorization Act of 2005, 109th Congress, March 9, 2006. See also Andrea Villa, "Combatting Narcoterrorism," *University of Miami National Security & Armed Conflict Law Review,* vol. 6 (2015–16), at 148–49.

235 **a growing nexus:** "Combating Transnational Organized Crime," Drug Enforcement Administration Special Operations Division, May 29, 2014.

236 **seemed to push the boundaries:** See, for example, Ginger Thompson, "Trafficking in Terror," *The New Yorker,* December 14, 2015; and Trevor Aaronson and Murtaza Hussain, "Merchant of Doubt," *The Intercept,* November 30, 2016.

236 **including the conviction of Viktor Bout:** "International Arms Dealer Viktor Bout Convicted in New York of Terrorism Crimes," Department of Justice news release, November 2, 2011.

CHAPTER 25

238 **Felix Klaussen was at a beer hall:** Unless otherwise noted, details of the interactions between Klaussen and the DEA were provided in extensive interviews with Klaussen, checked against an interview with a former DEA agent in the Special Operations Division 960 group who worked on the Le Roux case and documents including court files, photographs, videos, and the Internal Report of the Brazilian Federal Police on "Operation America."

241 **make contact with Le Roux:** *USA v. Le Roux,* Document 9, September 26, 2012, at 2–3.

243 **worked as a detective:** *Carl v. Good et al.,* M.D. Pa., CV-05-0353, Document 34, November 20, 2007, at 2.

243 **a triathlete:** Yudhijit Bhattacharjee, "The Sting: An American Drugs Bust in West Africa," *The Guardian,* March 17, 2015.

244 **rumored to have sent Shai Reuven:** Interview with a former DEA agent in the Special Operations Division 960. Also *USA v. Hunter,* Document 587, April 12, 2018, at 1314.

CHAPTER 26

246 **traveled beyond cliché:** A Google search of "Big cases, big problems," turns up hundreds of articles and books, which variously claim it to be an adage coined by a wide variety of law enforcement entities.

247 **now in Hong Kong:** *HKSAR v. Shulman,* Sentencing Hearing, May 12, 2014, HCCC 297/2013.

248 **officers . . . raided a warehouse:** "Australian Found with 20 Tons of Explosive Materials," *Oriental Daily,* May 4, 2012.

248 **handwritten directions:** The notes also included cryptic references to a mysterious Le Roux employee known as "Mr. Big": ("Big's contacts father one of the biggest suppliers and exporters sho not cross with them. $25 million on his head") and to drug delivery ("Depends what we are going to use yachts or cargo ship. Lots of air patrols, not easy to pick up is specially made submarines. . . . Submarines can take up to 2 tons").

248 **"Don Lucho":** Caicedo Velandia was reportedly arrested in June 2010 and extradited to the United States, and began working with the DEA to dismantle his and other Colombian operations, which would date the note found in Hong Kong to before mid-2010. See, for example, Robert Beckhusen, "Brutal Drug Lord 'El Loco' Had a Secret Boss," *Wired,* January 8, 2013; and Elyssa Pachico, "Colombia's 'Madman': Security Boss or Top Drug Lord?," *Insight-Crime,* January 7, 2013.

248 **Shulman's lawyer would later argue:** *HKSAR v. Shulman.*

249 **More than $200 million:** *HKSAR v. Hen, Fadlon.*

249 **earned several hundred thousand dollars:** *HKSAR v. Gavish.*

249 **using the name "Eddie":** Internal Report of the Brazilian Federal Police.

249 **aka "Gaddafi":** *USA v. Hunter,* Document 581, April 9, 2018, at 752.

249 **who filled his Facebook feed:** Omer Gavish Facebook page.

249 **Shulman told them:** *HKSAR v. Gavish.*

249 **a chain of events:** Unless otherwise noted, the details of these events derive from the accounts provided in court in the cases of: *HKSAR v. Shulman; HKSAR v. Hen, Fadlon; HKSAR v. Gavish; HKSAR v. Gavish,* Court of Appeal, September 17, 2014, DCCC 1033 & 1036/2012.

250 **They drove to Chungking Mansions:** When I visited Chungking in the sum-

mer of 2017, a manager described the room rented by Le Roux's people as "not as nice as a hostel," and a place "only criminals would stay."

250 **he cruised out of the harbor in a speedboat:** Anonymous former member of Le Roux's organization.

251 **On the wires in Rio:** Internal Report of the Brazilian Federal Police.

252 **named Kevin Ashby:** Internal Report of the Brazilian Federal Police. It was unclear if Ashby ever took the job. He died in 2015 of natural causes in Thailand.

253 **"I'm not running a fucking Burger King":** This specific transcript was not included in the Brazilian intelligence reports I obtained, but three different sources recited it to me independently, including both Brill and Bailey. While Bailey remembered Le Roux as having said McDonald's initially, Brill was far more certain that it was Burger King.

CHAPTER 27

256 **Better that he ask for a public meeting:** Interviews with Klaussen and an anonymous GISE agent.

257 **on May 11:** *USA v. Le Roux,* Document 9, September 26, 2012, at 3.

257 **their own meth lab:** Ibid. at 2.

258 **a quick debriefing:** Interview with an anonymous GISE agent.

259 **wired payment for a twenty-four-gram sample . . . one hundred kilos of cocaine:** *USA v. Le Roux,* Document 9, September 26, 2012, at 3, 4.

260 **a forty-four-foot luxury sailboat:** Archived copy of *JeReVe* sales listings at theyachtmarket.com and boattrader.com.

260 **cleared Ecuadorian customs:** "Vital Connection," *Platypus Magazine* (Australian Federal Police), June–December 2014, pp. 15–18.

260 **Ivan Vaclavic:** As noted later in the text, there is a great deal of confusion about Vaclavic's fate. But both Bailey and the former SOD agent confirmed to me that he was on the boat, as did another anonymous former member of Le Roux's organization who was familiar with the shipment.

260 **off the coast of Peru:** Interview with Kent Bailey.

261 **a contact from the Shan state:** In an interview, the former DEA agent in the SOD 960 group told me that the agents had contacts inside the Shan state who had agreed to backstop their story, were Le Roux to try to investigate its authenticity. He never did.

262 **the region's bountiful opium crop:** See, for example, "Getting Higher," *The Economist,* April 12, 2014.

264 **the Southern District prosecutors wanted:** Interview with a former DEA agent in the SOD 960 group.

266 **offering to bribe them:** *USA v. Berkman,* Document 497, March 2, 2016, at 16, 55.

266 **five DEA agents:** Ibid. at 15.

266 **violation of sections 959 and 960a:** *USA v. Le Roux,* S.D.N.Y, 1:12-cr-00489, Document 13, December 15, 2014, at 2.

267 **Stouch later testified:** *USA v. Berkman,* Document 497, March 2, 2016, at 10.

267 **suddenly Le Roux wanted to talk:** Interview with a former DEA agent in the SOD 960 group.

267 **seemed to have already decided:** *USA v. Berkman,* Document 497, March 2, 2016, at 10.

CHAPTER 28

268 **in White Plains, New York:** *USA v. Berkman,* Document 497, March 2, 2016, at 9.

268 **Beside them was Derek Maltz:** Interview with Kent Bailey.

269 **loading him into an SUV:** Interview with Kimberly Brill.

269 **the agent got a phone call:** Interview with Kent Bailey.

269 **Le Roux had met:** *USA v. Berkman,* "Declaration of Paul Calder Le Roux," December 21, 2015. This document does not appear to have been included in the case file; I received it through correspondence with a party to the case.

271 **the tracking signal died:** Details on the lost ship and the call to it, unless otherwise noted, derive from interviews with Kent Bailey, the former SOD agent, and an anonymous former member of Le Roux's organization with direct knowledge of the journey and those on board, as well as from the Australian Federal Police, including "Vital Connection," *Platypus Magazine* (Australian Federal Police), June–December 2014, pp. 15–18.

272 **spear fishermen:** Interview with Grant O'Fee, former police commissioner of Tonga.

272 **At the helm:** "Joint South Pacific Law Enforcement Operation Results in Huge Cocaine Haul," Australian Federal Police Media Release, November 16, 2012. See also regional news accounts, e.g. "Decomposed Body, Cocaine Haul Found on Yacht," *ABC News* (Australia), November 15, 2012.

272 **neatly wrapped brown plastic bricks:** *JeReVe* photos, released by the Australian Federal Police.

272 **identified the dead man:** "Body on Tonga Drugs Yacht Identified as a Slovak National Milan Rindzak," *The Australian,* November 27, 2012; also Michael Field, "Body Found on Tonga Drugs Yacht Identified," *Stuff* (New Zealand), November 27, 2012.

273 **several Slovakian news outlets:** Rasťo Striško, "Slovák na jachte s kokaínom. Bol to Maroš Deák, tvrdí zdroj," Noviny.sk, May 27, 2013; "Zlom v kauze kokaínovej jachty: Skonal na lodi brat zavraždeného Deáka?," Topky.sk, March 6, 2013. Some of these accounts asserted that the body on the boat might have been Vaclavic/Deák, but later accounts established that it was Rindzak.

273 **a man resembling Deák:** "Phuket Expat Nabbed at Checkpoint with High-Powered Rifle," *Phuket Wan,* November 12, 2011.

273 **buried the sailor's remains:** "Unclaimed Remains on Drugs Yacht to Be Buried in Vava'u," *Matangi Tonga,* January 22, 2013.

274 **in front of a grand jury:** *USA v. Berkman,* Document 952-3, October 9, 2012, at 23–25.

274 **Three RX Limited physicians:** See *USA v. Riccio,* S.D.N.Y., 0:12-cr-00868, Document 2, November 20, 2012.

274 **A housewife in Pennsylvania:** *USA v. Berkman,* Document 900, March 3, 2017, at 2.

274 **Babubhai Patel . . . was brought in:** *USA v. Patel,* E.D. Mich., 2:11-cr-20468, Document 634, December 7, 2012.

274 **weren't crimes under Israeli law:** *USA v. Berkman,* Document 948, April 3, 2017, at 22. While Israel does maintain an extradition treaty with the United States, the process can be slow, particularly for Israeli citizens and in cases where the alleged crime is not necessarily a crime under Israeli law. The Department of Justice claimed that mail and wire fraud, charged in the indictment, were extraditable offenses from Israel (see *USA v. Berkman,* Document 989, May 22, 2017, at 39).

CHAPTER 29

277 **all he would say:** *USA v. Berkman,* Document 497, March 2, 2016, at 56.

277 **a "proffer agreement":** *USA v. Berkman,* "Declaration of Paul Calder Le Roux," December 21, 2015.

277 **he said later in court:** *USA v. Hunter,* Document 581, April 9, 2018, at 771.

277 **the Philippines banned the death penalty:** See, for example, Felipe Villamor, "Philippines Moves Closer to Reinstating Death Penalty," *The New York Times,* March 1, 2017.

277 **he came clean on seven murders:** *USA v. Hunter,* Document 580, April 5, 2018.

277 **Stouch later said:** *USA v. Berkman,* Document 497, March 2, 2016, at 11.

277 **also had indicted Shai Reuven:** *USA v. Le Roux,* Document 17, August 9, 2017.

277 **failed to show up:** Interview with a former DEA agent in the SOD 960 group.

278 **locations that now comprised his world:** Ibid., and see also *USA v. Berkman,* Document 497, March 2, 2016, at 46.

278 **Le Roux's record:** To this date, the mysterious record remains. I could find no one in the Justice Department able to explain the slipup.

278 **periodically destroy his messages:** *USA v. Berkman,* Document 497, March 2, 2016, at 11–13.

278 **logged in:** *USA v. Hunter,* Document 580, April 5, 2018, at 416.

278 **run an operation to import tramadol:** *USA v. Hunter,* Document 585, April 11, 2018, at 1183–89.

279 **Hunter suddenly began receiving:** *USA v. Hunter,* Document 305–1, April 22, 2016, at 10.

279 **"Jim Riker" and "JaRule":** *USA v. Hunter,* Document 580, April 5, 2018, at 419.

279 **"specialist jobs":** *USA v. Hunter,* Document 115, January 30, 2015, at 3.

279 **Hunter sent word to . . . had quit the organization:** *USA v. Hunter,* Document 580, April 5, 2018, at 412. According to emails later revealed at trial, De Meyer had told Hunter that his mother was sick. Tim Vamvakias would testify to another account of why De Meyer quit: "I know Chris and his partner committed a bonus job. They committed a murder and I know that Chris, once they finished, I know that Chris made several excuses but he actually took his money and went out to Australia. I know him and another guy was supposed to be out partying in Australia after all this, spending their money." See also *USA v. Hunter,* Document 585, April 11, 2018, at 1199.

279 **De Meyer . . . put the call out:** While De Meyer is not referenced by name in many of the court documents, surveillance transcripts of Hunter meeting with potential recruits mention him, as a "mutual friend" or "Chris."

279 **Le Roux proposed:** Interviews with Marcus, as well as copies of three emails from Le Roux.

280 **Scott Stammers:** Details of Stammers's involvement, unless otherwise noted, derive from an interview with Stammers, as well as court documents including *USA v. Stammers,* Documents 11 (July 31, 2013), 79 (August 27, 2015), 133 (February 23, 2016), 136 (March 4, 2016), 163 (March 23, 2016), 168 (March 31, 2016), 177 (April 26, 2016).

280 **a tattooed Irishman:** Surveillance photos of Stammers and Shackels.

280 **with Ye Tiong Tan Lim:** Unless otherwise noted, details of Lim's involvement derive from court documents including *USA v. Stammers,* Documents 11 (July 31, 2013), 119 (January 11, 2016), 125 (February 22, 2016).

280 **a balding Chinese-Filipino man:** Sari Horwitz, "5 Extradited in Plot to Import North Korean Meth to U.S.," *The Washington Post,* November 20, 2013.

280 **Kelly Peralta:** Unless otherwise noted, details of Peralta's involvement derive from court documents including *USA v. Stammers,* Documents 11 (July 31, 2013), 167 (March 28, 2016), 169 (April 4, 2016), 170 (April 4, 2016).

281 **North Korea's contribution:** See, for example, Raphael F. Perl, "Drug Trafficking and North Korea: Issues for U.S. Policy," Congressional Research Service, January 25, 2007; "International Narcotics Control Strategy Report," U.S. Department of State, March 2013.

282 **Joseph Hunter had spent several months:** Unless otherwise noted, details of Hunter's involvement derive from court documents including *USA v. Hunter,* Documents 23 (September 30, 2013), 104 (January 12, 2015), 115 (January 30, 2015), 138 (March 13, 2015), 206 (October 3, 2015), 230 (December 9, 2015), 305 (April 22, 2016), 570–591 (April 2–17, 2018).

282 **Dennis Gögel:** Unless otherwise noted, details of Gögel's involvement derive from court documents including *USA v. Hunter,* Documents 11 (September 30, 2013), 189 (August 27, 2015), 198 (September 17, 2015), 308 (May 5, 2016).

282 **His Facebook profile:** Archived copy of Gögel's Facebook page.

283 **Michael Filter:** Unless otherwise noted, details of Filter's involvement derive

from court documents including *USA v. Hunter,* Documents 23 (September 30, 2013), 187 (August 21, 2015), 190 (September 2, 2015), 204 (September 23, 2015).

283 **Slawomir Soborski:** Unless otherwise noted, details of Soborski's involvement derive from court documents including *USA v. Hunter,* Documents 23 (September 30, 2013), 136 (March 13, 2015), 210 (October 8, 2015), 223 (November 5, 2015), 348 (September 6, 2016).

283 **Polish ex-policeman:** "Były polski policjant zabijał na zlecenie? 'Niczym się nie wyróżniał,'" TVN24, October 1, 2013.

284 **installed by a DEA technician:** *USA v. Hunter,* Document 574, April 3, 2018, at 108–16.

284 **transmitting the crew's discussions:** For a full transcript of the surveillance, see *USA v. Hunter,* Document 115, January 30, 2105.

286 **Cindric and Stouch stationed nearby:** Interview with a former DEA agent in the SOD 960 group.

287 **that they add Tim Vamvakias:** Unless otherwise noted, details of Vamvakias's involvement derive from court documents including *USA v. Hunter,* Documents 23 (September 30, 2013), 161 (July 11, 2015), 171 (July 27, 2015), 181 (August 12, 2015), 184 (August 13, 2015), 585 (April 11, 2018).

290 **a Hollywood special effects store:** SPFX Masks, spfxmasks.com.

291 **heavily armed commandos:** "American Drug Gang Arrested," *Pattaya Daily News,* November 20, 2013.

291 **cargo shorts and a T-shirt:** Photos of Hunter arrest.

291 **picked up by local authorities:** In addition to court documents, see also "One German, One Polish Ex-Military Arrested in Estonia at US Request," Baltic News Service, September 28, 2013.

292 **Two days later:** A video of Bharara's press conference was subsequently released by the Southern District of New York.

CHAPTER 30

293 **sit down with Le Roux:** Interview with Kimberly Brill.

293 **gradually he seemed to realize:** Interview with Kent Bailey.

294 **shuttered the Tel Aviv office:** Interview with Moran Oz.

295 **Oz wrote back:** *USA v. Berkman,* Document 402, November 23, 2015, at 5.

295 **an article in the Brazilian newspaper *Folha de S.Paulo*:** Marco Antônio Martins, "O senhor do crime," *Folha de S.Paulo,* December 26, 2013.

296 **the return call:** *USA v. Berkman,* Document 990, May 22, 2017, at Exhibit GG.

297 **along with a friend:** Details of this trip derive from interviews with Oz and the friend, along with court documents in *USA v. Berkman.*

297 **at the Pullman Hotel:** *USA v. Berkman,* Document 802, February 1, 2017, at 49.

298 **spent the next several months:** *USA v. Berkman,* Document 950, April 3, 2017, at 2.

298 **who briefly showed up:** Interviews with Moran Oz and Kimberly Brill.

299 **transported to the Sherburne County Jail:** *USA v. Berkman,* Document 950, April 3, 2017, at 2.

299 **Prabhakara Tumpati was hustling:** Details of the subsequent events, unless otherwise noted, derive from interviews with Tumpati and an unpublished biographical account provided by Tumpati.

300 **only ever communicated:** *USA v. Hunter,* Document 580, April 5, 2018, at 594.

300 **started a chat with Samia:** Ibid. at 6, as well as *USA v. Hunter,* Document 587, April 12, 2018, at 1459.

301 **Samia and O'Donoghue chatted again:** *USA v. Hunter,* Document 256, March 6, 2016, at 7.

301 **"Stuff he did for Le Roux":** The name is redacted in available court documents, but in context clearly refers to Le Roux.

302 *The New York Times* **revealed:** Alan Feuer, "In Real Life, 'Rambo' Ends Up as a Soldier of Misfortune, Behind Bars," *The New York Times,* December 20, 2014.

302 **he was pulled over:** *USA v. Hunter,* Document 351, September 16, 2016, at 3.

302 **Two federal agents stepped into the room:** *USA v. Hunter,* Document 408-1, July 31, 2017.

303 **Stillwell's resistance slowly began to fade:** Later, Stillwell would recant his own admissions, with his lawyers arguing that he'd never properly waived his Miranda rights. The court rejected the argument. See *USA v. Hunter,* Document 344, August 19, 2016, at 1.

304 **At Samia's house, they found:** *USA v. Hunter,* Document 606, June 27, 2018, at 33–35; also Document 576, April 4, 2018, at 169–73.

304 **According to court filings:** *USA v. Hunter,* Document 260, March 11, 2016, at 1.

304 **Lachlan McConnell said:** When I first interviewed McConnell in December 2015, we spoke on the condition that he not be identified by name. After his trial concluded in 2017, he granted permission to place his statements on the record.

304 **website for a security contractor:** Archived copy of osi.com.ph.

305 **arranged for a friend to hand-deliver the letter:** *USA v. Berkman,* Document 774, January 17, 2017, at 52.

306 **Yamashita's gold:** There are countless news articles on the realities and unrealities of Yamashita's treasure. See, for example, Seth Mydans, "In Wilds of Manila, a Hunt for Lost Treasure," *The New York Times,* March 5, 1988.

CHAPTER 31

307 **Ninety-five percent end in a guilty plea:** "Plea and Charge Bargaining: Research Summary" at 1, Bureau of Justice Assistance, January 24, 2011.

307 **planned an unconventional defense:** *USA v. Hunter,* Document 104, January 12, 2015.

308 Federal prosecutors in the Southern District . . . responded: *USA v. Hunter,* Document 115, January 30, 2015.

308 made motions suggesting: *USA v. Stammers,* Document 65, April 17, 2015, at 7.

309 changed his plea to guilty: *USA v. Hunter,* Document 138, March 13, 2015, at 2.

309 Stammers followed suit: *USA v. Stammers,* Docket report, August 27, 2015.

309 one attorney proposed: *USA v. Stammers,* Document 79, August 27, 2015, at 9.

310 hired a New York criminal lawyer: *USA v. Le Roux,* S.D.N.Y., 1:12-cr-00489, Document 12, December 15, 2014, at 1.

311 legal filings mocking the government's absurd level of secrecy: *USA v. Berkman,* Document 363, November 3, 2015.

311 Richman and Friedman wrote: *USA v. Berkman,* Document 370, November 3, 2015, at 1.

312 "Motion Hearing is GRANTED": *USA v. Berkman,* Document 450, January 15, 2016.

312 a fake local arrest record: Sherburne County Sheriff's Office Arrest Report Paul Calder Leroux, February 29, 2016.

312 the anonymous lawyer argued: *USA v. Berkman,* Document 489, February 29, 2016.

313 The judge opened the hearing: Unless otherwise noted, all details from the hearing derive from my personal attendance, as well as *USA v. Berkman,* Document 497, March 2, 2016.

319 formally pleaded guilty: *USA v. Le Roux,* Document 3, February 5, 2014. (The document itself is dated December 30, 2013.)

319 the "information" he had signed: *USA v. Le Roux,* Document 13, December 15, 2014.

CHAPTER 32

321 a series of articles: "The Mastermind," *The Atavist Magazine,* March–May 2016.

322 Scott Stammers's attorney submitted: *USA v. Stammers,* Document 177, April 26, 2016, at 4.

322 Philip Shackels's attorney argued: *USA v. Stammers,* Document 192, June 15, 2016, at 29.

322 Joseph Hunter's attorney pointed to the articles: *USA v. Hunter,* Document 503, March 6, 2018, at 5.

322 I received an email: The subject requested anonymity out of a fear for her family if she were to be pulled into the case.

324 Interpol had issued . . . a few months later: *USA v. Berkman,* Document 667, November 23, 2016, at 17.

325 allowed him to plead: *USA v. Berkman,* Document 416, December 7, 2016.

325 **Bezalel . . . walked away:** *USA v. Berkman,* Document 292, 272, March 16, 2015, at 1.

325 **already serving a seventeen-year sentence:** "Pharmacist/Pharmacy Owner Sentenced to 17 Years for Health Care Fraud, Drug Offenses," U.S. Attorney's Office Eastern District of Michigan news release, February 1, 2013.

325 **A judge fined him $350,000:** "Pharmacist Sentenced in Internet Pharmacy Case," U.S. Department of Justice news release, March 14, 2014.

326 **Roger Gural said in his opening statement:** Unless otherwise noted, all details from the trials derive from my personal attendance and from trial transcripts, including *USA v. Berkman,* Documents 1002–1016, February 6–March 10, 2017.

327 **To support their duress defenses:** *USA v. Berkman,* Document 371, November 3, 2015.

330 **the head of the DEA himself:** "Statement for the Record of Michele M. Leonhart Administrator Drug Enforcement Administration," Subcommittee on Commerce, Manufacturing and Trade, United States House of Representatives, April 14, 2011.

332 **one of Oz's lawyers described it:** *USA v. Berkman,* Document 875, February 26, 2017, at 2.

334 **the motion declared:** *USA v. Berkman,* Document 901, March 4, 2017, at 4.

CHAPTER 33

338 **one former SOD supervisor told me:** Another said that he had signed an exclusive movie deal for the rights to his version of the Le Roux story, and therefore could not discuss the case.

339 **As far as I could tell, there wasn't:** Among many other issues, no former member of Le Roux's organization, or investigator who tracked him, ever mentioned him even using cryptocurrencies, much less inventing the most prominent one.

340 **he once noted to his cousin:** Personal chats between Paul Le Roux and Mathew Smith.

341 **suddenly announced on their website:** Announcement at truecrypt.sourceforge.net.

341 **a frenzy of speculation:** See for example Dan Goodin, "Bombshell TrueCrypt Advisory: Backdoor? Hack? Hoax? None of the Above?" *Ars Technica,* May 29, 2014.

341 **One encryption message board community:** Graham Cluley, "Did TrueCrypt's Developers Embed a Hidden Latin Message for Us All?" grahamcluley.com /truecrypt-hidden-message/, June 16, 2014.

342 **Ben-Menashe's home in Montreal was firebombed:** Brian Hutchinson and Graeme Hamilton, "Montreal Home of Self-Described Israeli Spy 'Gutted' in Alleged Firebombing," *National Post,* December 3, 2012.

343 **added Joseph Hunter:** "Manhattan U.S. Attorney Announces Charges Against Former U.S. Soldier for Conspiring to Kidnap and Murder as Part of

a Murder-for-Hire Scheme Overseas," Department of Justice news release, October 16, 2017.

343 **a potential witness in the case:** *USA v. Hunter,* Document 445, October 13, 2017.

344 **wrote me via email:** Using the federal prison system for electronic communication, called CorrLinks.

344 **filed mistakenly and quickly withdrew:** Vamvakias was described in the document as "CW-1," but was easily identified by its details. *USA v. Hunter,* Document 515, March 14, 2018.

349 **life in prison to as little as ten years:** *USA v. Hunter,* Document 581, April 9, 2018, at 777; see also Document 580, April 5, 2018, at 576–77.

349 **lacked the jurisdiction:** *USA v. Hunter,* Document 580, April 5, 2018, at 586.

349 **stand before a judge:** The formal process of requesting leniency for a cooperator, called a "5K Letter," is a motion filed under section 5K1.1 of the U.S. Sentencing Guidelines. For a discussion of the practice see Shana Knizhnik, "Failed Snitches and Sentencing Stitches: Substantial Assistance and the Cooperator's Dilemma," *New York University Law Review,* vol. 90 (November 2015), 1722.

349 **agreed to forfeit:** *USA v. Le Roux,* Document 13, December 15, 2014, at 6.

350 **confiscating only $300,000 . . . Le Roux claimed:** *USA v. Berkman,* Document 497, 83, March 2, 2016, at 43.

351 **the defense of John Gotti's brother Peter:** Joseph DiBenedetto, "Loose Lips Sink Ships, but Should John Gotti Jr. Have Testified in Order to Avoid Another Hung Jury?," *The Huffington Post,* March 18, 2010.

351 **DiBenedetto's 2016 letter:** *USA v. Berkman,* Document 489, February 29, 2016.

EPILOGUE

355 **he said in the course of campaigning . . . killed more than seven thousand suspected drug users:** Six months later, the number had grown to twelve thousand. "Duterte's 'Drug War' Claims 12,000+ Lives," Human Rights Watch report, January 18, 2018.

356 **"The human rights people will commit suicide":** Felipe Villamor and Richard C. Paddock, "Philippine Mayor Accused of Drug Links by Duterte Is Killed by Police," *The New York Times,* October 28, 2016.

357 **provided the DEA:** *USA v. Hunter,* Document 580, April 5, 2018, at 541.

358 **the NBI simply refused:** *USA v. Hunter,* Document 576, April 4, 2018, at 305.

359 **The trial took place:** Unless otherwise noted, details of the trial derive from my own personal attendance and trial transcripts at *USA v. Hunter,* Documents 570 through 591, April 2–17, 2018.

359 **a cast of characters:** *USA v. Hunter,* "Questions for Jurors," Document 569-1, April 24, 2018, at 4.

367 **an inmate named Mir Islam:** Islam, a hacker known by the handle Joshthe-God, had pleaded guilty of multiple cyber-crimes, including "doxing" (exposing personal information of other people, including celebrities such as Kim Kardashian) and "swatting" (a form of harassment that involves calling in hoax emergencies in order to engineer a heavily armed police response against a target). See, for example, Brian Krebs, "Serial Swatter, Stalker and Doxer Mir Islam Gets Just 1 Year in Jail," krebsonsecurity.com, July 11, 2016.

367 **The other defendants:** Unless otherwise noted, information about an individual's current whereabouts derives from interviews with that person. All information is current as of September 2018.

368 **twenty years apiece:** "Former U.S. Soldier Sentenced in Manhattan Federal Court to 20 Years in Prison," S.D.N.Y. news release, July 16, 2015; "Former German Soldier Sentenced in Manhattan Federal Court to 20 Years in Prison," S.D.N.Y. news release, September 25, 2015.

368 **Michael Filter got eight years:** *USA v. Hunter,* Document 204, September 23, 2016.

368 **Slawomir Soborski received nine:** *USA v. Hunter,* Document 352, September 22, 2016.

368 **Adrian Valkovic . . . sentenced to more than nine years:** *USA v. Stammers,* Document 124, January 22, 2016.

368 **Kelly Peralta . . . received:** *USA v. Stammers,* Document 176, April 14, 2016.

368 **Lim went down:** *USA v. Stammers,* Document 200, October 11, 2016.

368 **redacted by the government:** *USA v. Stammers,* Document 192, June 15, 2016.

368 **Shackels received seven years:** *USA v. Stammers,* Document 181, May 11, 2016.

368 **Scott Stammers . . . was sentenced to fifteen years:** *USA v. Stammers,* Document 195, June 3, 2016, at 12.

368 **Doron Shulman . . . was sentenced to five years:** *HKSAR v. Shulman.*

368 **Yoav Hen and Daniel Fadlon ultimately pleaded guilty:** *HKSAR v. Hen, Fadlon.*

368 **Omer Gavish . . . received five and a half years:** *HKSAR v. Gavish.*

368 **U.S. government finally declared tramadol:** "Schedules of Controlled Substances: Placement of Tramadol into Schedule IV," 21 CFR Part 1308, 79 Fed. Reg. 37623, July 2, 2014.

369 **UPS paid $40 million:** "UPS to Forfeit $40 Million over Illegal Online Pharmacy Shipments," Reuters, March 29, 2013.

369 **prosecutors suddenly dropped all the charges:** Sudhin Thanawala, "Prosecutors Drop Drug Trafficking Case Against FedEx," Associated Press, June 18, 2016.

369 **Kimberly Brill was promoted:** Interview with DEA public information officer.

369 **Thomas Cindric retired:** Interview with DEA public information officer.

369 **Derek Maltz also departed:** Interview with Derek Maltz; LinkedIn page for Maltz; penlink.com.

369 **Zion Fadlon became the co-owner:** Personal visit to the hostel. Jay Forte, "Exploring Rio While Staying at Discovery Hostel in Glória," *The Rio Times,* July 14, 2015.

369 **He was never charged:** Interview with an anonymous GISE agent.

369 **Jon Wall . . . was sentenced to probation . . . working as a dispatcher:** *USA v. Berkman,* Document 1075 (October 12, 2017); Document 1062 (October 3, 2017).

370 **the global telemedicine market:** Accuray Research, "Global Telemedicine Market Analysis & Trends Report 2017," Research and Markets, February 23, 2017.

370 **Charles Schultz sold Schultz Pharmacy:** Interview with Hal Harlowe.

370 **appears to run an investment firm:** Archived copy of the company's website.

370 **formally divorced:** Official divorce records, Federal Circuit Court of Australia, June 24, 2013.

370 **released from Philippine custody:** Interview with Mathew Smith.

371 **shot the bar's owner in the back of the head:** Tim Elliott, "Man Shot over Private Life, Colleague Claims," *The Sydney Morning Herald,* April 8, 2013.

371 **only person convicted:** *Republic of the Philippines v. Burne.*

371 **the *Ufuk* sank:** Argyll Cyrus B. Geducos, "Mysterious Sinking of Cargo Ship Attracts Crowds at Manila Bay," *Manila Bulletin,* July 18, 2016.

371 **was reused in a dramatic operation:** Interviews with Felix Klaussen and a former DEA agent in the SOD 960 group. The operation in question, for which the boat was renamed the *Al Saheli,* was described in detail in David Lewis and Richard Valdmanis, "How U.S. Drug Sting Targeted West African Military Chiefs," Reuters, July 24, 2013.

371 **"they will lock me up":** To the contrary, I couldn't find anyone at the DEA enthusiastic about pursuing Marcus, or other figures still at large from Le Roux's organization—including those already under indictment. In Marcus's case, since he seems to have never killed any Americans or planned any murders with Americans, and wasn't involved in the drug trade, it appears the U.S. government would likely not have jurisdiction to prosecute him even if he landed in their lap.

372 **sustainable fisheries organizations proposed:** Sarah M. Glaser et al., *Securing Somali Fisheries,* One Earth Future Foundation, 2015.

Index

ABOUT THE AUTHOR

EVAN RATLIFF is an award-winning journalist and the co-founder and former editor-in-chief of *The Atavist Magazine*. As a longtime contributor to *Wired, The New Yorker, National Geographic, Outside,* and other magazines, he has reported from around the globe on transnational crime, science and technology, the environment, terrorism, and corruption. He is a two-time finalist for the National Magazine Awards, and his writing has been selected for numerous *Best American* collections. His 2009 *Wired* story "Vanish," about his attempt to disappear and the public's effort to find him, was selected by the magazine as one of the twenty best stories in its history. He also cohosts the acclaimed *Longform* podcast and was a founding editor of *Pop-Up Magazine,* a live journalism event that tours the United States. He is the co-author of *Safe: The Race to Protect Ourselves in a Newly Dangerous World,* about innovation and counterterrorism, and the editor of the collection *Love and Ruin: Tales of Obsession, Danger, and Heartbreak.*

cazart.net
Twitter: @ev_rat